THE CONCEPT OF JACKSONIAN
DEMOCRACY

THE CONCEPT
OF JACKSONIAN
DEMOCRACY

NEW YORK AS A TEST CASE

BY LEE BENSON

PRINCETON, NEW JERSEY
PRINCETON UNIVERSITY PRESS
1961

Publication of this book
has been aided by the Ford Foundation program
to support publication,
through university presses, of works in the humanities
and social sciences

✧

Printed in the United States of America

Third Printing, 1967

TO PAUL WALLACE GATES
TEACHER AND FRIEND

PREFACE

I N AN EARLIER, more leisurely age, this book might have been called *Some Aspects of the Transformation of American Society from the Aristocratic Liberal Republic of the Late-Eighteenth Century to the Populistic Egalitarian Democracy of the Mid-Nineteenth Century, with Special Reference to New-York State.* Considerations other than contemporary taste, however, have led me to call it *The Concept of Jacksonian Democracy: New York as a Test Case.* For, although the book examines the impact of egalitarian ideas upon New York politics from 1816 to 1844, I conceive it to be essentially an essay on the clarification of historical concepts.

Like other students of men in society, historians develop concepts, or ways of looking at their subject matter to make it intellectually manageable. But it seems safe to say that historians have not as a group tended to view analytically and study systematically the problems inherent in the construction and use of their concepts. What combination of phenomena are designated by a particular concept? How are the phenomena related to one another? Can indices be developed that will help researchers to observe the presence or absence of such phenomena? How? Inadequate study of these and related conceptual problems has, I believe, hampered the efforts of American historians to resolve the substantive controversies that have long engaged their attention.

No attempt is made in this book to deal with all the problems that historians encounter when they use concepts. On the contrary, in order to suggest the need for sustained, systematic work on general conceptual problems, I try to answer two specific questions: what empirical phenomena can logically be designated by the concept Jacksonian Democracy? Does that concept help us to understand the course of American history after 1815?

Searching for tentative answers to those two questions, I have concentrated upon one state. Single cases do not verify general conclusions, of course. But to verify general conclusions eventually, it is necessary to begin somewhere. And in my opinion, particularly because questions related to Jacksonian Democracy require the study of mass behavior, they are better essayed by increasing the precision of research than by widening its geographic scope.

I believe that the approach adopted in this book will add to its representative character. Although it may be argued that New York during the Jacksonian period was so heterogeneous that it must be considered unique, few specialists would deny that it contained many towns, wards, and counties that more or less resembled towns, wards, and counties in other northern states. Since my data have been collected on the local as well as the state level, generalizations based upon them probably do not apply uniquely to New York. At any rate, although it is not claimed that this book provides general answers to questions about the meaning and utility of the concept of Jacksonian Democracy, it is hoped that the book provides new material for a reconsideration of the concept.

It is a pleasure to acknowledge that the manuscript benefited from critical readings by my wife, Eugenia Singleton Benson, by Daniel Aaron, David M. Ellis, Richard Hofstadter, James C. Malin, Charles G. Sellers, Jr., Harold Syrett, and George R. Taylor, and from the stimulating company of Fellows at the Center for Advanced Study in the Behavioral Sciences, 1958 to 1959. I am also grateful for the resources made available to me by the Director of the Center, Ralph W. Tyler, and by its other administrative officers, Preston S. Cutler and Jane A. Kielsmeier. My thanks go also to Mary Hurt who typed several drafts of the manuscript with unfailing patience and good humor, and to the many staff members of the Columbia University Library, New-York Historical Society, New York Public Library, and New York State Library, who gave me the benefit of their expert knowledge and cheerful assistance.

I am indebted to many people, but particularly to Dr. Leland C. DeVinney and the other officers of the Rockefeller Foundation who recommended generous support of an exploratory study designed to adapt to historiography procedures developed in other disciplines. The study has been carried out at the Bureau of Applied Social Research, Columbia University. The present book is one of a series of publications reporting upon the results.

Columbia University
January 1960

CONTENTS

CONTENTS

THE CONCEPT OF JACKSONIAN
DEMOCRACY

. . . If I let myself believe in anything on insufficient evidence there may be no great harm done by the mere belief; it may be true after all, or I may never have occasion to exhibit it in outward acts. But I cannot help doing this great wrong towards man, that I make myself credulous. The danger to society is not merely that it should believe wrong things, though that is great enough; but that it should become credulous.
—WILLIAM E. K. CLIFFORD, *Lectures and Essays* (1886), 345.

He who would do good to another must do it in Minute Particulars:
General Good is the plea of the scoundrel, hypocrite & flatterer,
For Art and Science cannot exist but in minutely organized Particulars . . .
—WILLIAM BLAKE, in GEOFFREY KEYNES, ed., *The Complete Writings of William Blake* (1957), 687.

CHAPTER I

FROM POPULISM TO EGALITARIANISM

"AFTER living a dozen years in New York," wrote Oliver Wolcott, a veteran of early nineteenth century political wars, "I don't pretend to comprehend their politics. It is a labyrinth of wheels within wheels, and it is understood only by the managers." Variations on this theme by skilled readers of political signs, as well as the actual course of events, suggest that the "managers" were almost equally baffled when they contemplated that "vast deep," that "most unfathomable of subjects, the politics of the State of New York."[1]

Despite the complexity of its politics, New York is a good place to begin a systematic study of the concept of Jacksonian Democracy. As we shall see, after 1815 some of the nation's most significant political movements either originated or developed most fully in New York. Its decennial censuses from 1825 to 1875, and other printed sources (for example, almanacs, gazetteers, registers), supply much of the raw data needed to study political behavior systematically. New York then had the largest population of any state in the Union. In 1840, for example, it was only one of 30 states or territories, but generalizations about its politics represent generalizations about the politics of 17 per cent of the American white population.

Considerations other than size of population make New York a good state for testing generalizations about American history. Although it cannot be regarded as the United States in microcosm, New York can reasonably be regarded as the North (that is, free states) in microcosm.[2] We find in New York, during the period covered by this book, an extraordinary range of social relationships, processes, and phenomena. It contained some of the oldest settled areas in the country and some just emerging from the frontier stage; it contained the largest, most dynamic city in the country, as well as sparsely settled communities which had remained relatively static for many decades. Except for slave plantations and coal mines, its econ-

[1] As quoted in De Alva S. Alexander, *Political History of the State of New York* (New York, 1906), 1: III; Herbert D. A. Donovan, *The Barnburners* (New York, 1925), 3.

[2] Support for this argument is found in David M. Ellis, "New York and Middle Atlantic Regionalism," *New York History*, 35: 3-13 (January 1954); Frederick Jackson Turner, *The United States: 1830-1850* (New York, 1950 printing), 92-143.

[3]

omy included every form of economic activity significant in the United States. Moreover, its boundaries, stretching from the Atlantic Coast to the Great Lakes, encompassed almost every religious, ethnic, and social group to be found anywhere in the North; and they tended to live in distinct geographic areas, which helps us to identify their political behavior.

A. The Decade of Confusion, 1816-1826

The decade after 1816 stands out as a period of great confusion, even in a state where confusion is the political norm. Unfortunately, because we lack intensive, cumulative studies, we can now offer little more than impressionistic generalizations about New York politics during these years. I assume, however, that political parties were nonexistent—if we define political parties as competing organizations which are relatively stable and which "put forward candidates for office, advocate particular courses of governmental action, and, if their candidates win, create enough of a sense of joint responsibility among various officials to aid them in the fulfillment of a group responsibility for the direction of government."[3]

Admittedly, this assumption contradicts the traditional view that the original Jeffersonian "Republican Party" continued to dominate politics in New York after the War of 1812, particularly after the Federalists gave up the organizational ghost in 1820. If the assumption is valid, those who claimed the name Republican held such different principles, sought such different objectives, and were grouped together so loosely in so many different and antagonistic factions that to think of them as constituting a political party is to confuse names with things. Some continuity existed in New York politics after 1816, of course, and some distinct patterns can be found. But I maintain that the literature assumes *certain* continuities and patterns whose existence has not been demonstrated. Intensive research may show that they were actually nonexistent.

1. Where Did the Federalists Go?

To my knowledge, no one has yet retraced the political paths followed by ex-Federalists after 1820. And yet the literature tends to assume a straight line of descent from Jefferson's Republican Party to Martin Van Buren's Republican faction to Andrew Jackson's "Democratic Party." It also assumes that the overwhelming majority

[3] V. O. Key, Jr., *Southern Politics in State and Nation* (New York, 1949), 298-311.

of Federalists aligned themselves with De Witt Clinton's Republican faction. Then, under the successive disguises of Clintonian Republicans, National Republicans, and Whigs, ex-Federalists continued their aristocratic battle against the democratic and egalitarian aspirations of "the people."[4]

Unfortunately, this delightfully simple historical pattern of continuing struggle between Hamiltonians and Jeffersonians breaks down at too many critical points. Even before 1819, when the Republican Party in New York formally split, the available evidence suggests that there were factions within factions, as well as "wheels within wheels." After the split, the Van Buren and Clinton factions worked equally hard to attract Federalists and to advertise their unshakeable devotion to the Republican Party and to Republican principles. Significantly, one influential group of Federalists opposed Clinton so fervently that they sounded a requiem for their party in 1820 and publicly proclaimed their "high-minded" resolution "to unite ourselves unequivocally, and without reserve to the great republican party of the state and union."[5]

How many erstwhile Hamiltonian "aristocrats" followed the lead of their "high-minded" brethren into the Van Buren ranks and re-entered the political lists, washed of ancient sins and marching under "Jeffersonian democratic" banners? Lack of evidence prevents a firm

[4] The study probably most responsible for fixing this assumption in the literature is Dixon Ryan Fox, *The Decline of Aristocracy In The Politics of New York* (New York, 1919), *passim*. Though this famous dissertation contains many illuminating insights (some of which have not yet been fully exploited), it is important to recognize that it was written at a very early stage of Professor Fox's life-long researches in New York history. Critically analyzed, it presented only flimsy evidence to bolster the assumption of Federalist-Whig, Republican-Democratic continuity, and its dominant assumptions were based on Charles Beard's economic determinist interpretation of American political history. The material presented in this chapter, I believe, supports the belief that a careful study will fail to validate Fox's assumptions. In fact, Fox himself substantially altered his views two decades later in a brilliant series of lectures which have been relatively neglected by historians. Compare *ibid., passim*, with his *Yankees and Yorkers* (New York, 1940), 1-26, and *passim*. For example, discussing early New York politics in the later work, Fox wrote a passage which contrasts sharply with the views presented in his dissertation: ". . . The party lines were not closely drawn between rich and poor. So assured were the aristocrats of their social place and so various their backgrounds that they did not move together as one interest; families faced each other as Capulets and Montagues." *Ibid.*, 19-20.

[5] Jabez D. Hammond, *History of Political Parties in the State of New-York* (Cooperstown, N.Y., 1846, 4th ed.), 1: 527-531; Robert V. Remini, "The Early Political Career of Martin Van Buren, 1782-1828" (Columbia University, Ph.D., 1951), 246-248, 261-262, 283-286. For a sympathetic account of the metamorphosis of "high-minded," anti-Clintonian Federalists, see Robert W. July, *The Essential New Yorker: Gulian Crommelin Verplanck* (Durham, N.C., 1951), 29-71.

answer to that question; but it cannot be said that the available evidence supports the view that party battles continued in New York between Jeffersonian "populists" and Hamiltonian "aristocrats" during the 1820's. Since Alexander Hamilton was dead, speculations as to what he would have done in those years can only be speculations. It is worth noting, however, that his sons headed the procession of "high-minded" Federalists into the Van Buren camp, and that their baggage train included the *New York Evening Post*, the newspaper Hamilton founded to advance the cause and doctrines of Federalism.[6]

As the *Evening Post* eventually became an influential "radical" organ of the Van Buren Republicans, so James A. Hamilton became an influential figure in the Van Buren-Jackson alliance. In fact, Andrew Jackson found the son of Alexander Hamilton so impressive that knowledgeable observers believed him to have "the ears of Jackson more than any other individual" when his first Cabinet was formed in 1829.[7] One Federalist sprig does not form a Republican branch, of course. But James A. Hamilton's example does suggest the present dangers of making firm statements about the political development of ex-Federalists and their physical or spiritual descendants. Numerous other individual examples can be cited; perhaps the most revealing is the conversion to the Jackson Party of James Fenimore Cooper, the antidemocratic, antileveling scion of a great Federalist landed magnate.[8] And, according to the classic historian of early New York politics, "such eminent federalists as Chancellor Jones, Thomas J. Oakley, and many others, early declared in his [Jackson's] favor."[9]

6 Hammond, *op.cit.*, 1: 528-529.

7 See the letter of William Coleman to James A. Hamilton, February 19, 1829, in James A. Hamilton, *Reminiscences* (New York, 1869), 94. For the intimate political relations between Van Buren and Hamilton, and the latter's influence upon Jackson, see the letters and memoranda in *ibid.*, 62-285.

8 For a perceptive discussion of Cooper's "close attachment to the Democratic party in the Jacksonian years," see Marvin Meyers, *The Jacksonian Persuasion: Politics and Belief* (Stanford, Cal., 1957), 42-75. Meyers notes that "Cooper never felt himself a traitor to his class, or a rebel, or even a critic in any fundamental way; on the contrary, it seemed to him natural that the children of Federalist diehards should be 'almost always decided democrats.'" *Ibid.*, 43. In my opinion, Meyers' adherence to the Jacksonian Democracy concept prevented him from seeing the full significance of Cooper's position. See also the earlier treatment of Cooper in Fox, *Yankees and Yorkers*, 200-205.

9 Hammond, *op.cit.*, 2: 255. That Jackson had great attraction for leading Federalists is perhaps most spectacularly demonstrated by the case of the "Old Patroon." Stephen Van Rensselaer, than whom there was no more aristocratic Federalist, wanted to vote for Jackson in 1824-1825 when the presidential election was thrown into the House of Representatives. He "favored Jackson until the

2. Political Liberalism in the 1821 Constitutional Convention

Closely examined, the major political developments of the early 1820's provide little support for the traditional historical account of continuing party battles between Jeffersonian "liberals" and Hamiltonian "conservatives." As a working definition, early nineteenth century political liberalism and political conservatism, respectively, are defined as belief in and disbelief in universal suffrage, popular election of government officials, and popular nomination of candidates by delegated party conventions "fresh from the people." *Implementation* of those beliefs is taken to signify the difference between eighteenth and early nineteenth century political liberalism. If we use those criteria, the historical record suggests that the Van Buren Republicans had to be dragged, kicking and screaming, into the politically liberal nineteenth century.

Ever since Dixon Ryan Fox published his pioneering study of the decline of aristocracy in New York politics, the Constitutional Convention of 1821 has been viewed as recording the final victory of political liberalism in the state. If we use the criteria suggested above, however, the date must be advanced from 1821 to 1826, when universal male suffrage was passed. When this is done, it becomes easier to estimate whether the Van Burenites' conversion to political liberalism owed more to expediency than to conviction.

In 1821, it is true, Van Buren led the dominant group which triumphed over the small band of diehards wedded to the eighteenth century concept of freehold suffrage. But those spokesmen for the *ancien régime* were anachronisms—echoes of the past who represented no influential body of opinion.[10] The convention debates show that the real battle was fought not over extension of the suffrage but over universal male suffrage; in 1821 the champions of political liberalism lost that battle. And in the light of subsequent developments, it is

time that he thought Adams would be the eventual winner." Confiding his views to a kinsman on January 22, 1825, he said "I feel inclined for 'Old Hickory' myself." William B. Fink, "Stephen Van Rensselaer And the House Election Of 1825," *New York History*, 32: 323-330 (July 1951).

[10] Hammond, 2: 15-49; Fox, *Decline of Aristocracy in New York*, 229-269; Remini, *op.cit.*, 301-307. Hammond divided the convention delegates into three groups: one set of "extremists" wanted to retain the freehold suffrage qualifications; a second set wanted white manhood suffrage; the third set "may be called conservatives, who were for abolishing the freehold qualification, but, at the same time, were for placing some restrictions on the right of voting." Van Buren was "among the most prominent men of the conservative corps." *Op.cit.*, 2:48-49.

worth noting that even those liberal "democrats" were outraged by the idea that free Negroes should continue to enjoy the same rights as free white men. On this issue, therefore, they joined the conservative majority led by Van Buren and supported its efforts to write a property restriction clause into the Constitution that limited suffrage to a small fraction of the Negro population.

Far from leading the liberal movement for political equality, Van Buren led the conservative opposition to universal suffrage and popular election of officials. He used his formidable talents to defend the "stake in society" theory of suffrage, that is, property owners, not people, should vote. As he repeatedly insisted, his proposals for suffrage extension simply granted to owners of "personal property" and to "householders" the right that freeholders already enjoyed. Addressing himself to the diehards opposed to suffrage extension, he stoutly denied any intention "of introducing into the most sacred sanctuary of the constitution, a mob or rabble, violent and disorganizing as were the Jacobins of France; and furious and visionary as the radicals of England are sometimes represented."[11]

Having easily beaten down the spokesmen for the Right, Van Buren also succeeded in beating down the "radical" democrats of the Left who demanded universal suffrage. Whatever other gentlemen might think proper, he sarcastically observed, he would not go so far as to confer this "precious privilege" indiscriminately "upon every one, black or white, who would be kind enough to condescend to accept it."[12] To check "the dangerous and alarming tendency" developing in the convention, he cited some of "the many evils which would flow from a wholly unrestricted suffrage." Chief among them would be the enlarged electorate in New York City, for "the character of the increased number of voters would be such as would render their elections rather a curse than a blessing." With universal suffrage in operation, the increased number of legislative seats proposed by the convention would not go to the "hardy sons" of western and northern New York, but "would be surrendered to the very worst population of the old counties and cities."[13] Paying homage to the "stake in society" theory of representative government, Van Buren

---

[11] L. H. Clarke, *A Report of the Debates And Proceedings of The Convention of the State of New York . . . 1821* (New York, 1821), 129-135.

[12] *Ibid.*, 142.

[13] *Ibid.*, 181-182. The quotation below is from p. 182. It is perhaps instructive to note that two leaders of the movement for universal suffrage in the 1821 Convention, Peter R. Livingston and Erastus Root, wound up in the Whig Party as opponents of Van Buren.

[8]

warned that once universal suffrage was enacted, "the door would have been entirely closed against retreat, whatever might be our after conviction, founded on experience, as to the evil tendency of this extended suffrage. The just equilibrium between the right of those who have, and those who have not, an interest in the government, could, when once surrendered, never be regained, except by the sword."

When the Convention of 1821 finally adjourned, the Van Buren faction could claim victory on all major fronts; universal suffrage had been defeated, some long overdue reforms in government organization had been achieved, and the governor had been given the power to appoint local justices of the peace. These officials exercised considerable influence in their constituencies and, according to a recent sympathetic biographer, Van Buren's "real object" in blocking their popular election was to bring the appointing power to Albany. Once lodged at Albany, that power would be placed "under the care of his organization." Confident that his faction would win the next election, Van Buren also believed that, by gaining control of the justices of peace, "the Bucktails [Van Buren Republicans] would secure an iron grip on the political life of the entire state, right down to the smallest hamlet."[14] But, as Bobbie Burns has noted, things do not always work out according to plan.

3. Populistic Democracy Arrives and Conquers in the mid-1820's

The "Bucktails," emboldened perhaps by sweeping success at the polls in 1822, decided to resist the growing demands in New York for the popular election of president and for an end to nominations by congressional and legislative caucuses. The political explosion that followed further fragmented the Republican Party and thoroughly upset political alignments in New York.

Briefly stated, to guarantee their power to cast the state's votes for William H. Crawford in 1824, the Bucktails used control of the state senate to block passage of a law restoring the people's right to choose presidential electors.[15] Moreover, to pay off old scores, they expelled DeWitt Clinton from the Canal Board—an expulsion legally arbitrary and politically inept. Seizing upon the current American antagonism to the European "Holy Alliance,"

14 Remini, 309-312.
15 *Ibid.*, 384-413, 435-447; Hammond, 2: 139-180; Fox, *Decline of Aristocracy in New York*, 286-297.

"the anti-caucus, anti-Crawford, anti-Van Buren" factions promptly tagged their opponents with the nickname, "Albany Regency."[16]

During the 1824 state and national campaigns, all possible changes were rung upon the Albany Regency theme, and a new era began. Anti-Regency politicians whipped up popular frenzy against the "Royal Cabinet," "the cabal," and "the junto," which had conspired against the "people's rights." From Montauk Point to the Niagara frontier, the "monstrous usurpation" of power by "King Caucus" was denounced and "People's Candidates"—headed by Clinton—were nominated to oppose the Regency at the first delegated party convention in New York history. "Huzza for the people!!!" was the battle cry against the "unholy Alliance," and men marching to the polls were urged to remember that "the present controversy is the PEOPLE against a purse proud overbearing ARISTOCRACY."[17] Populistic democracy had arrived in New York.

Not only did populistic democracy arrive in 1824, but the "People's Party" and DeWitt Clinton conquered so decisively that political liberalism soon disappeared as a live issue in New York. Private convictions notwithstanding, all "practical politicians" thereafter loudly proclaimed devotion to "equal political rights for all." After the fall of the Regency in 1824, the shape of the future was plain—so plain, in fact, that politicians of all faiths felt compelled to adopt the same strategic doctrine, although their tactics continued to differ. They and their party represented "the people," their opponents represented the "aristocracy."

Political conservatism ended, not with a bang in 1824, but with a whimper in 1826. By then, the Van Burenites had publicly come to appreciate the virtues of populism. With their support, the constitutional amendments that Clinton recommended in 1824 were passed. In effect, those amendments established universal suffrage (except for Negroes), and subjected presidents, as well as justices of the peace, to popular election. Moreover, copying their opponents' tac-

---

[16] See the *Ulster Plebeian* (Kingston, N.Y.) from January 14 through November 1824. For typical sentiments, see the issues of April 21, p. 2, and September 15, p. 1. "Albany Regency" had become a common term of abuse by September.

[17] *Ibid.*, September 29, 1824, p. 2; October 13, 20, 1824, p. 1; November 17, 24, 1824, p. 1; December 1, 1824, p. 2; Harriet A. Weed, ed., *Autobiography of Thurlow Weed* (Boston, 1883), 1: 102-121; C. H. Rammelkamp, "The Campaign of 1824 in New York," in American Historical Association, *Annual Report . . . 1904* (Washington, 1905), 177-201. For convenience, the *Memoir of Thurlow Weed*, edited by his grandson, Thurlow Weed Barnes, published in 1884, will be cited here as the second volume of Weed's *Autobiography*.

tics, the Van Burenites abandoned caucus nominations in favor of delegated political conventions "fresh from the people."[18]

Although two distinct sets of candidates competed for popular support in 1826, two distinct parties had not yet developed. At any rate, I cannot discern significant principle or policy differences between the contending factions. Local issues and interests, personal loyalties and antagonisms, political alliances and animosities produced by the 1824 campaign, different attitudes toward the national administration of John Quincy Adams, maneuvers preparatory to the 1828 presidential campaign—all combined to produce factional rather than party politics. Perhaps the kaleidoscopic, factional character of New York politics in the mid-1820's is suggested by these observations: Van Buren was secretly trying to form an alliance with DeWitt Clinton, his longtime foe; although Clinton was all-out for General Jackson, most of Clinton's supporters apparently favored the Adams administration; Van Buren had definitely decided to oppose Adams, but remained publicly "non-committal" toward Jackson and other potential candidates.[19]

Given the lack of conflict over principle or policy, it is not surprising that the 1826 campaign lacked popular excitement. Since the outcome was very close, both on the state and county levels, many voters who had been swept away by the 1824 Clintonian tidal wave must have found their way back to Van Buren political moorings. Significantly, the voting returns show no distinct regional patterns. Most counties divided only narrowly in their support for the competing Van Buren and Clintonian Republican factions, and even gimlet-eyed observers would have had difficulty in detecting that the completion of the Erie Canal in 1825 had had any impact upon voting behavior in 1826.[20] But the New York electorate did not remain becalmed for long.

B. The Egalitarian Impulse, Antimasonic Style

If 1824 was the year when the movement for political equality reached its climax, 1827 was the year when political equality became the weapon of the movement for social and economic equality.

[18] Hammond, 2: 181-233; Willis F. Johnson and Ray B. Smith, *Political and Governmental History of the State of New York* (Syracuse, N.Y., 1922), 2: 67-81; Remini, 491-492, 502-503.

[19] Hammond, 2: 208-236; Fox, *Decline of Aristocracy in New York*, 302-317; Alexander, *op.cit.*, 1: 344-357; Remini, 492-553.

[20] The party percentages were calculated from the official state canvass printed in the *Albany Argus* (s.w.), December 16, 1826, p. 2.

The People's Party had established the proposition that, in the eyes of the law, all white men were politically equal. Broadly conceived, the mission of the Antimasonic Party was to establish the proposition that in America all white men must be regarded as *socially* equal and, so far as the law was concerned, must be allowed equal economic opportunities. "Free, and *therefore* equal" conveys the essence of that Antimasonic "blessed spirit" which radiated from western New York and eventually shaped the permanent character and style of American politics.

1. Transportation Revolution and a Rising Level of Aspiration

That attempts to trace the complex, subtle relationships between economic and social phenomena frequently result in intellectual disaster cannot be denied. Yet I cannot suppress the belief that a strong causal relationship existed between what George R. Taylor calls the Transportation Revolution and the egalitarian movements that lead me to call the years from 1825 to 1850 the Age of Egalitarianism.[21]

Long before 1815, H. St. John de Crèvecoeur thought he detected something different about this "new man," the American. What made him different was a spirit of independence and resourcefulness unknown to the Old World. By 1815, a shrewd contemporary observer (Hezekiah Niles of *Niles' Review*) was emphasizing, as the distinguishing feature of the American national character, "the almost universal ambition to get forward."[22] Such claims need not be taken literally to accept the proposition that the general level of aspiration was higher in the United States than elsewhere in the early nineteenth century world. Before 1815, however, the relatively underdeveloped economy sharply limited the ability of most men to *realize* the national ambition "to get forward."

Static is not the word for the American economy between 1790 and 1815, but it had not yet attained the dynamism that later became its most striking characteristic. True, the land was rich and the people were ready and willing. Or, to use Walt W. Rostow's

---

[21] George Rogers Taylor, *The Transportation Revolution: 1815-1860* (New York, 1951), 3-152. In my opinion, Taylor's concept, the transportation revolution, is an extremely important contribution to a better understanding of all phases of American history during the 1815-1860 period. For a brilliant interpretation of what he calls the "Communications Revolution," see James C. Malin, *The Contriving Brain and The Skillful Hand In The United States* (Lawrence, Kansas, 1955), 1-231.

[22] As quoted in Taylor, *op.cit.*, 4.

happy phrase and illuminating concept, the United States possessed the natural resources and most of the social and cultural characteristics required to launch it on the "take-off stage" of economic growth.[23] To some extent, political factors held back the take-off, but another set of factors held it back even more. A country of continental proportions, the United States required revolutionary changes in transportation and communication before it could realize its potential. For a variety of reasons, the requisite changes occurred soon after the end of the War of 1812.

Athough the Erie Canal did not initiate the transportation revolution, its phenomenal success, even before its completion in 1825, served to galvanize the American economy. Inspired by the Erie, men all over the country now saw opportunities where before they had seen obstacles. Put another way, the spirit of enterprise flourished before enterprise itself felt the invigorating effects of the great boom in canals, turnpikes, steamboats, and railroads.[24]

In short, my hypothesis holds that the boom in transportation and the dynamic expansion of the economy acted as powerful stimulants to movements inspired by the egalitarian ideals of the Declaration of Independence. I do not contend that one-to-one relationships existed between the revolution in transportation and the rise in egalitarianism. But it is suggestive, at least, that William H. Seward observed their reciprocal relationships—and acted upon his observations.

From the time that Seward appeared on the political scene in 1824, the reciprocal relationships among internal improvements, social equality (broadly conceived), and free public education formed the dominant theme in his speeches, writings, and actions. Speaking on "Education and Internal Improvement" shortly after he became governor in 1839, he summarized eloquently the political philosophy and working principles around which he had built his career: "Much

---

[23] The reference here is to Rostow's "take-off" concept. I find that concept useful, but have a number of reservations, particularly in respect to American economic growth. For one thing, Rostow tends to give disproportionate emphasis to industrial developments and to slight the impetus given to growth by rapid expansion and extension of commercial agriculture. In my opinion, the impact of the transportation revolution on agriculture was at first as important as its impact upon industry, and a complex interaction of economic, political, social, and cultural factors produced the "take-off" stage in the United States during the *1830*'s. The concept is discussed in Walt W. Rostow, "The Take-Off into Self-Sustained Growth," *Economic Journal*, 66: 25-48 (March 1956), and *The Process of Economic Growth* (New York, 1956), *passim*.

[24] Taylor, 32-36.

as mankind cherish the love of liberty, it is not the only object of desire. Give them freedom, and they will demand improvement as the natural means of gratifying their rational desires. In this country the people are free in their political, social, and religious action, yet from one boundary to the other they are excited with the desire of improvement, and they will not be disappointed or delayed in their efforts. It is the object of republican institutions to encourage and stimulate improvement of the physical condition of the country, and to promote the moral and intellectual advancement of its citizens; to discourage military ambition, and shun the causes which produce stagnation of enterprise and promote personal faction, that engross the passions of the people, and arrest the progress of improvement.

"If the theory of our constitution was fully expounded by its founders, its most complete security is to be effected by *the highest attainable equality in the social conditions of our citizens* [italics added]. Power will always unite with the *few* or the many, according to the extension or limitation of knowledge. *The highest attainable equality is to be accomplished by education and internal improvement as they distribute among the whole community the advantages of knowledge and wealth* [italics added]."[25]

2. Transportation Revolution and Antimasonry

In 1839 Seward made liberty the precursor of the national "desire of improvement"; a decade earlier he had helped to launch the Antimasonic movement, whose goal was "the highest attainable equality in the social conditions of our citizens" and whose development owed much to the transportation revolution. Other factors contributed to the movement, of course. Chief among them perhaps were the great religious revivals which gave western New York its name, "The Burned-Over District" (that is, fired by religious and moral passions). And yet, as the historian of that district has suggested, it seems reasonable to think that subtle, causal relationships existed among the building of internal improvements, the dynamic economic expansion evident in New York by 1825, and the religious revivals, Antimasonic crusade, and benevolent movements that followed.[26] For example, as will be discussed below, it seems significant that the leaders of the movement to crush "the Monster Institution"

[25] George E. Baker, ed., *The Works of William H. Seward* (New York, 1853), 3: 213.

[26] Those relationships are traced in an excellent intellectual history, Whitney R. Cross, *The Burned-Over District* (Ithaca, N.Y., 1950), 55-137.

of Freemasonry also led the movements for "internal improvements" and "free enterprise."

Some surface facts of the Antimasonic story have been recited many times, but I believe we have a long way to go before penetrating to the core of what John B. McMaster has called "the most remarkable" political party in American history.[27] If we ignore the events leading up to it, let us say the story began in September 1826, just 50 years after the signing of the Declaration of Independence. The setting was the thriving village of Batavia, Genesee County, western New York; the plot initially centered around the fate of William Morgan, a "renegade" from the Masonic Order who had written a book purporting to reveal its secrets.

Word of Morgan's decision to violate his Masonic oaths leaked out and set in motion a series of mysterious persecutions which culminated in his kidnapping and subsequent disappearance. Though the details have never been fully established, Morgan most probably "was tied in a weighted cable, rowed to the center of the Niagara River at its junction with Lake Ontario, and dropped overboard. In any case, it cannot be proved that he was ever seen again."[28]

Morgan was never seen again, but David Miller, the Batavia printer who published his revelations, had not been silenced. Having suffered from Masonic wrath, Miller struck back at his "persecutors" by publishing a lengthy account of the events which led up to the abduction and probable murder of Morgan. Filled with lurid speculations and impassioned rhetoric, it called upon the public to demand vindication of the majesty of the laws and punishment of the Masonic criminals.

[27] John B. McMaster, *History of the People Of The United States* (New York, 1900), 109-120. The standard account is Charles McCarthy, *The Antimasonic Party*, in American Historical Association *Annual Report, 1902* (Washington, 1903), 1: 367-574. An excellent doctoral dissertation, this broad-ranging study is now more than fifty years old. A series of intensive state and local monographs is badly needed if a new synthesis is to be attempted. Like McCarthy's study, a recent dissertation examined the Antimasonic movement on a national scale. But it provides an illuminating survey of its rhetoric rather than its politics. (Leslie Griffen, "The Antimasonic Persuasion," Cornell University, Ph.D., 1951.)

For suggestive although somewhat conflicting interpretations of the movement in New York and Vermont, see Cross, *op.cit.*, 113-125; and David M. Ludlum, *Social Ferment in Vermont: 1791-1850* (New York, 1939), 86-133. An early history of Antimasonry in New York, written by one of its leaders, is found in Hammond, *History of Political Parties*, 2: 369-403. Thurlow Weed's extremely detailed recollections of the movement are valuable, but must be treated with even more than the normal caution required by such documents. See Weed, ed., *Autobiography*, 1: 210-354.

[28] Cross, 114-115.

Whatever the reasons for the fervent response to Miller's call, it touched off indignation meetings throughout western New York and led to a series of trials and official and unofficial investigations over the next few years. An injury to one member of society, Antimasons stressed, was an injury to all—and duty as well as interest required men to act. "Every member of the civil compact is mutually interested in protecting the rights of individuals. If one citizen is wronged with impunity, the rights of all are liable to invasion. One murder, unavenged, emboldens the perpetrator to multiply his atrocities. It is no less our interest than our duty, therefore, to aid, by the use of all proper means, in vindicating the majesty of the laws."[29]

Working to vindicate the majesty of the laws, Antimasons let imagination take wing. Numerous "free presses" (that is, free from Masonic control) were soon accusing the Masonic Order of almost every evil practice known to or imagined by man. Seceding Masons, eager to clear themselves of the stigma of their former associations, as well as ex-Masons now genuinely convinced that the Order's existence threatened "republican institutions," publicly testified to the truth of the accusations against it.

Masons who remained loyal insisted that the Order was being blamed unfairly for the criminal activities of a few irresponsibles. Turning upon their accusers, they charged that self-seeking men, animated by base motives of envy and personal aggrandizement, had whipped up bigotry and fanaticism against Masonry. As one Antimasonic leader later put it, "By mutual crimination and recrimination the excitement was stimulated to the highest pitch of violence almost ever witnessed in the country, entering into all the religious, political and social relations of society." The excitement mounted until it spilled over into politics. According to Thurlow Weed, another Antimasonic leader whose later recollections seem in this instance to be trustworthy and whose experience makes him an expert observer, creation of the Antimasonic Party had this result:

"The feeling of Masons, exasperated by the existence of a political organization which made war upon the institution of Freemasonry, became intensely so by the renunciation of Masonry by ministers, elders, and deacons of the Presbyterian, Methodist, and Baptist churches. The conflict therefore became more embittered

[29] Antimasonic Broadside, October 1827, in the Cornell University Collection of Regional History. All Antimasonic broadsides cited are from the Cornell collection.

and relentless personally, politically, socially, and ecclesiastically, than any other I have ever known in our country. Thousands of Masons, innocent of any wrong, and intending to remain neutral, were drawn into the conflict, when all were denounced who adhered to the institution. On the other hand, the Anti-Masons maintained that the abduction and murder of Morgan resulted legitimately from the obligations and teachings of the Order."[30]

3. Republicanism, Egalitarianism, and Secret Societies

As time passed and Morgan's disappearance remained a mystery, the original issue underwent a series of transformations. The question of the fate of one man became the question of whether there existed a secret society powerful enough both to establish a system of private justice and to thwart attempts to punish the executioners. Frustration seems to have contributed largely to this transformation. Local citizens' committees failed to get county and state organs of government to take what they regarded as appropriate action in connection with Morgan's kidnapping. And official resistance to the growing demands for punishment of his "murderers" encouraged the conviction that a gigantic conspiracy existed and extended over the entire state.[31] Once the conspiracy cry arose, the question became: Is *any* secret society compatible with republican institutions?

The impassioned attack upon secret societies had many facets, but attention here focuses upon the charge that secret societies *necessarily* endangered the principles of equal rights and equal privileges. Opponents viewed the mysterious events surrounding the Morgan affair as proof that Freemasonry gave its "infatuated votaries" grossly unfair advantages in the great American race for wealth, power, and prestige. A secret society so powerful, its opponents charged, that it could get away with murder and boast that it pos-

---

[30] The first quotation is from Hammond, 2: 375; the second, from Weed, ed., *Autobiography*, 1: 302-303.

[31] A typical expression of the conspiracy theme is found in a broadside urging support for the Monroe County "Anti-Masonick Ticket: Considerations of imperious duty impel us to the course we have adopted. The masonic fraternity have outraged humanity, and violated all law. The nature of their offence is so complicated—the offenders so numerous—and their evasions have been so manifold—that justice has only been enabled to pursue her course with tardy and faultering [*sic*] steps. In a dark day of the investigation, we supplicated the legislature to quicken her pace, and strengthen her arm, but it was a MASONIC LEGISLATURE, and we were coldly repulsed! We now appeal to the SOVEREIGN PEOPLE. Let *their* verdict be awarded upon the merits of this question." Monroe County Antimasonic Broadside, October 1827.

sessed "power in all places where power was desirable,"[32] could obviously advance its members' interests in many unscrupulous and devious ways. At a time when the transportation revolution was raising the level of aspiration to unprecedented heights, "equal opportunity for all" was the perfect battle cry. Thus the Antimasons depicted themselves as leading a crusade against the Monster Institution which created "odious aristocracies by its obligations to support the interests of its members; in preference to others of equal qualifications."[33]

Appeals designed to satisfy the increasingly widespread and deeply felt demand for equal opportunity in all phases of American life were, I believe, the most powerful weapons in the Antimasonic arsenal of argument. "Every man's observation and experience will furnish instances of Masonic interference with almost all the transactions of life. They exercise an embarrassing, pernicious, and persevering influence upon our social political and business intercourse. The 'sign' and the 'grip' perform their sworn cabalistic office at times and in places innumerable."[34] What was the "real" object of the Masonic Order, as distinct from its professed, praiseworthy purposes? "The real object of the institution, is, to procure UNFAIR ADVANTAGES to its members."[35] Since its secret operations and binding oaths gave the Order the power which its officers boasted about,

[32] Griffen, "Antimasonic Persuasion," 35-39. The quotation below, from a Masonic Address delivered in 1825, is an excellent example of the Masonic oratory which aroused suspicion and resentment. This particular quotation came to be widely used by Antimasons as "proof" of their accusations against the Order. "What is masonry now? It is powerful. It comprises men of rank, wealth, office, and talent, in power and out of power; and that in almost every place where power is of any importance, and it comprises among other classes of the community, to the lowest, in large numbers, active men, united together, and capable of being directed by the efforts of others, so as to have the force of concert throughout the civilized world.

"They are distributed too, with the means of keeping secret, and the means of co-operating, in the desk—in the legislative hall—on the bench—in every gathering of business—in every party of pleasure—in every enterprise of government—in every domestic circle—in peace and in war—among enemies and friends—in one place as well as in another." (*Albany Evening Journal*, November 12, 1830, p. 2.) All citations in this chapter are to the semiweekly edition of the paper.

[33] "Declaration of Seceding Masons," July 4, 1828, quoted in Griffen, 211. The frenetic rhetoric employed by the Antimasonic orators had them inveighing against "this SERPENT—this MONSTER . . . the mysterious Order of Free Masonry." *Ibid.*, 377. But the "Monster" theme was not confined to wild-eyed orators; it runs through Weed's editorials. For a typical example, see *Albany Evening Journal*, December 21, 1830, p. 2.

[34] Monroe County Antimasonic Broadside, October 1827.

[35] *Address* of the Antimasonic State Convention, February 1831, in the *Albany Evening Journal*, February 25, 1831, p. 2.

Masonry "destroys all principles of equality, by bestowing favors on its own members to the exclusion of others equally meritorious and deserving."[36] By using its influence unfairly to advance the social, political, and economic interests of the few, the Order operated to thwart the legitimate aspirations of the many. Therefore, be it "Resolved, That it is the peculiar aim of Anti-Masonry to restore equal rights, equal laws, and equal privileges to all men, by rendering ineligible to office, the adherents of the blood-stained order. . . ."[37]

To understand the political history of Antimasonry, we must recognize that it designed its appeals to win support from men brought up in the Republican faith. Whereas the would-be "Kings and High Priests" of Masonry engaged in foul, unrepublican conspiracies to secure unequal privileges for themselves, "Anti-Masonry goes for the 'fair thing between man and man'—our fathers called this a Republican principle."[38] In essence the Antimasonic argument can be stated in this syllogism: Equal opportunity was the hallmark of a republican country. Freemasonry destroyed equal opportunity by secretly using its great powers to favor the interests of its members. Freemasonry, therefore, could not be permitted to exist in the republican United States.

Perhaps the best summary of the Antimasonic view of the struggle to preserve and enlarge the promise of American life is in the "Address Of The Minority Of The Members Of The [New York] Legislature Of 1831":

"On the one side is an aristocratic nobility, composed of men bound together by the most terrific oaths, which conflict with the administration of justice, with private rights, and with the public security; a privileged order, claiming and securing to its members unequal advantages over their fellow-citizens, veiling its proceedings from scrutiny by pledges of secrecy, collecting funds to unknown amounts and for unknown purposes, and operating through our extended country at any time and on any subject, with all the efficacy of perfect organization, controlled and directed by unseen and unknown hands.

"On the other side, a portion of your fellow-citizens ask for equal rights and equal privileges among the freemen of this country. They say it is in vain that this equality of rights and privileges is secured

[36] Quoted in Griffen, 211.

[37] Antimasonic Convention, Oswego County, in *Albany Evening Journal*, October 10, 1832, p. 2.

[38] Antimasonic Convention, Livingston County, in *ibid.*, September 28, 1832, p. 1.

in theory by our constitution and laws, if by a combination to subvert it, it is in fact no longer enjoyed. They point you to masonic oaths, and to the effects of those dreadful obligations upon our elections, upon witnesses in courts of justice, and upon jurors. They show you one of your citizens murdered under their influence, and the offenders escaping with impunity. They exhibit to you the power of your courts defied, and the administration of justice defeated, through the instrumentality of those obligations. And they ask you whether our country can any longer be described as a land 'where no man is so powerful as to be above the law, and no one so humble as to be beneath its protection.' They say to you that no man can tell who will be the next victim of masonic vengeance, or of masonic perjury. And they call on you to put an end to these enormities, and prevent their recurrence, by destroying their source; and for that purpose to use the *only* effective weapon in your power; a weapon yet preserved to you, your own free and independent ballots."[39]

As noted earlier, many questions relating to the emergence and impact of the Antimasonic movement have yet to be investigated. But at present, these assertions seem reasonable: The movement extended egalitarian doctrines to embrace all aspects of American life, invested the egalitarian impulse with a religious intensity, drastically changed the style and substance of American politics, and thereby accelerated the dynamic pace of American economic growth. The People's Party won the battle for political equality in New York, but it was the Antimasonic Party that gave full expression to the egalitarian impulse.

[39] Conveniently reprinted in Baker, ed., *Seward's Works*, 3: 348-349. The *Address* was drafted by Seward.

CHAPTER II

ANTIMASONRY GOES POLITICAL

POPULAR indignation erupted shortly after Morgan disappeared but failed to influence the 1826 election. Aside from coming late in the year, demands for "justice" seem at first to have been nonpolitical and bipartisan. Moreover, the highest state positions were the ones at issue, and Antimasons had not yet extended their charges of dereliction of duty beyond local officials. But as frustration spread and deepened among the moralistic, Bible-oriented Yankees who had swarmed into western New York, indignation began to transform itself into political action. If corruption existed in high places, and if an "infidel" secret society controlled the entire apparatus of government, then republican institutions were endangered and *the people* must act.[1] "Let the friends of good order and civil law rise in their strength, and drive back to the dark regions from which it sprang this *'Beast with seven heads and ten horns.'* . . . Repulsed at all points, we will appeal for redress to the ballot-boxes!"[2]

A. Spontaneous Combustion Fires a New Party

Early in 1827, prior to the town elections, village committees began to pass resolutions declaring "Freemasons unfit for any office of confidence." By the end of the year, to an unprecedented extent in the United States, popular conventions had nominated candidates and the Antimasons had elected town and county officers all over western New York. According to their earliest historian, "The result astonished all—even the anti-masons themselves—and opened the eyes of politicians to the growing power of this new party." Since statewide contests were not held, it is difficult to measure the fluctuations in voting patterns. But a large proportion of the region's voters must have abandoned old political ties, for fifteen Antimasons were elected to the State Assembly.[3] A new political party was taking shape.

1 Jabez D. Hammond, *History of Political Parties in the State of New York*, 2: 371-381; Whitney R. Cross, *The Burned-Over District*, 115-116; Leslie Griffen, "The Antimasonic Persuasion," 235-246.

2 Monroe County Antimasonic Broadside, October 1827.

3 Hammond, 2: 381-384; Harriet A. Weed, ed., *Autobiography of Thurlow Weed*, 1: 242-243, 299-302; Charles McCarthy, *The Antimasonic Party*, in American Historical Association, *Annual Report, 1902*, 1: 371-374; Cross, 115-116.

Unless present appearances are deceiving, the new party was largely spontaneous in origin; it was a populistic reaction to the efforts of the Clintonian and Van Buren factions to steer clear of the issues growing out of Morgan's disappearance. Masons ranked high in both factions. And with the 1828 presidential election approaching, cautious politicians hesitated to call upon the unpredictable Antimasonic genie. Since they found no outlet in existing organizations, "in defiance of the counsels of political leaders," and with "utter disregard of all previous political designations and distinctions," men joined together to put down "this abhorred conspiracy" against republican institutions and Christian morality. And, since the new party united old opponents who shared only a common antagonism to Freemasonry, it logically restricted itself to a single plank: destruction of the "Monster Institution" by the electoral process. Said one of its leaders, Antimasonry's "first and principal purpose was to aid in the execution of the laws by the ballot box; to strengthen the arm of justice by the elective franchise."[4]

Though the Antimasons obviously drew inspiration from the 1824 populistic campaign—as enemy of the people, the Monster Institution of Freemasonry substituted marvelously for the "Albany Regency"—they developed and exploited an extraordinarily significant innovation in American political strategy. Pushing democratic ideology to its Rousseauan logical limits, they argued that no restrictions could be placed upon the will of the people. Rousseau made the "general will" the standard of morality, but he had doubts about how best to ascertain it. The Antimasons had no such doubts. If the people were supreme, if their will must prevail over every standard and every institution, then the electoral process could properly be used to "reform" *all aspects* of American society. The Antimasons acted on these premises and gave the widest latitude to the claim that in a free country "public opinion . . . must properly govern everything, which is properly subject to governmental power."[5]

But what aspects of society were properly subject to governmental power? Who made that decision? And how was the decision made known and implemented? "Under a republican government, inasmuch as the people are the depositories of their own liberties, and are charged with the responsibility of preserving the purity of their

4 Hammond, 2: 378.

5 *Address* of the Antimasonic State Convention, February 1829, quoted in Griffen, "Antimasonic Persuasion," 201.

institutions, and transmitting them unimpaired to their posterity, they are the proper judges of the evils which should be driven from among them, *and the expediency and propriety of the means to be adapted for that purpose* [italics added]; and since no man claims their suffrages as a matter of right, the ballot boxes afford a remedy peculiarly adapted to the removal *of all evils which may be beyond the reach of the judicial, executive, or legislative departments of government* [italics added]."[6]

Phrased in the rhetoric of populistic democracy, here was ideological justification for what Chancellor Kent in 1821 had called the constant tendency of "the majority to tyrannize over the minority,"[7] and what Tocqueville a decade later stigmatized as the "TYRANNY OF THE MAJORITY" in America.[8]

Evil was defined by the majority, and whatever it defined as evil must be eradicated. "Public opinion is against masonry—thus it should be given up for the sake of democracy."[9] The same ultra-populistic doctrine in harsher accents: "The people, the democracy of this country, have passed sentence of extermination against Free Masonry. From their judgment there is no appeal, and against their will it is folly to contend."[10]

Suppose Masons denied that their Order was evil, refused to bow down to the momentary passions of a self-proclaimed majority, and argued that it could only be punished for violating a law of the land. Since the Antimasons proclaimed their devotion to majority rule and to the majesty of the law, how could they demonstrate that they represented the will of the people and that they would not use illegal means to reform society? "Voting is the only decisive means by which public opinion can be directly ascertained upon the subject [of masonry]. . . ."[11] Moreover, by expressing their disapproval of masonry at the polls, "the people" could bring about the Order's destruction.

6 Antimasonic Convention, Newburgh, N.Y., October 1830, in *Albany Evening Journal*, October 22, 1830, p. 1.

7 As quoted in Dixon Ryan Fox, *The Decline of Aristocracy in The Politics of New York*, 254.

8 Alexis De Tocqueville, *Democracy In America* (New York, 1945, the Phillips Bradley edition), 1: 258-262.

9 This was Antimasonry, Vermont style. The quotation is from the Woodstock *Vermont Courier*, in David M. Ludlum, *Social Ferment in Vermont: 1791-1850* (New York, 1939), 98.

10 *Address* of the New York "Young Men's Anti-Masonic State Convention," in *Albany Evening Journal*," September 28, 1830, p. 3.

11 *Address* of the National Antimasonic Convention, September 1831, in *ibid.*, October 14, 1831, p. 1.

In 1830, anticipating—more accurately, helping to create the basis for—Tocqueville's observations on the "Power Exercised by the Majority in America upon Opinion," the Antimasonic "Young Men" pointed to previous successes and observed: "No man in our country long adheres to any principles which exclude him from popular favor. Here the people are emphatically sovereign: on their will depends the existence of all political men. This will is indicated through the medium of the ballot-boxes. And in these depositories of public opinion must Free-masonry meet her doom. Such we believe to be the surest and least exceptionable method of abating this great moral and political nuisance. . . ."[12]

To explore the historical implications of the doctrine that public opinion *should* reach everywhere and *must* conquer all is a tempting digression. The point here, however, is that the emergence of the Antimasonic Party caused all aspects of American life to become grist to the political mills. Whatever impurities existed in America —more precisely, whatever impurities the majority *thought* existed —could now be quickly removed by that perfect sifting machine, the electoral process.

1. Masonry, the Albany Regency, and the Jackson Party

In its early phase the Antimasonic movement directed its egalitarian fury almost entirely against the Monster Institution. Given the movement's social composition, however, the enemies of the people soon came to include the Albany Regency and the "Jackson Party." Contrary to assumptions underlying the concept of Jacksonian Democracy, Antimasonry represented an impassioned, leveling attack by members of the "lower classes" against the village and urban "aristocracy." "It has been a reproach to our [Antimasonic] cause that it takes first among the lower classes. They are not wise who believe this and fail to examine its character; for in this country the lower class are at the head of all. The PEOPLE are sovereign."[13]

---

[12] Compare *Albany Evening Journal*, September 28, 1830, p. 3 with Tocqueville, *op.cit.*, 1: 263-265. Though Tocqueville made no references to Antimasonry, in major respects his conclusions read as though they were summaries of Antimasonic doctrines. This is only one of many examples which might be given of why Tocqueville's commentary must be used with the greatest caution "as a key to the immediate subject of the work, Jacksonian America." For a different assessment, see Marvin Meyers, *The Jacksonian Persuasion*, 24-41.

[13] *New York Whig*, August 7, 1832, p. 1; its editor was Henry Dana Ward, a leading figure in the Antimasonic movement. See also Cross, 116-117, 121-124; Ludlum, *op.cit.*, 97-100; Griffen, "Antimasonic Persuasion," 266-267. "While the Anti-Masonic

Not only the unfairness of privilege but the arrogance of pride fanned resentment among men who burned with unfulfilled aspirations in the Age of Egalitarianism. Admittance to Masonic lodges apparently represented a distinction "successful" Americans acquired to signify their passage to a higher social status. Even before the transportation revolution and economic expansion stimulated ambition and accelerated the related processes of class mobility and class differentiation, nonmembers resented the prestige associated with membership in the Masonic elite group. "Twenty years ago [about 1810], I had many reasons for despising masonry. I had observed that the *newly initiated* among my neighbors soon became somewhat haughty in their manner, and treated me with a kind of scowl, a sneer, that bordered on contempt."[14]

Rochester village served as the organizational center of political Antimasonry in its early stages, but, according to Whitney Cross, the most recent and perceptive student of the movement, its strongest support came from the poorer farmers and rural residents of western New York. "The rural folk were more sensitive [than the urban] to the appeal of an ism. Egalitarian democracy was either more strongly rooted or more easily nourished by clever propaganda there. The evangelistic churches, which took up Antimasonry strongly, held more complete sway generally in country than in city. Probably lodges had prevailed only in the larger towns, and in so far as Masonry did represent a harbor of social or political privilege the farmer or resident of a smaller hamlet was the object of discrimination. Perhaps the movement may justly be described as an early evidence of rural jealousy toward urban superiority, or at least toward the controlling middle class of the larger villages and county towns. Clearly and strongly, it had an agrarian cast in that it aligned

---

sentiment was strong among the farmers, it was weak in the villages, especially among the wealthy and influential classes." Weed, ed., *Autobiography*, 1: 301.

[14] Letter signed "Anti-Cable Tow," in *Albany Evening Journal*, November 9, 1830, p. 3. The social climate in which Antimasonry flourished is indicated by this 1829 attack upon the "back country aristocracy" of rural New England: "Village Aristocracy—In almost every village of much importance, there is among certain persons who would be considered, or fancy themselves actually to be above others, a spirit of pride, or what is called aristocracy, which is one of the greatest evils—we should be pardoned for calling it one of the greatest curses—that can afflict society. . . . For the spirit of aristocracy, could it have its way, would end in nothing short of despotism. There is much of it in our New England villages. . . . It is, virtually, treason against Republicanism—against our government; and we should not care if it were made punishable by law." Quoted in Ludlum, 97.

leaseholders and renters against the resident agents of absentee land-lords."[15]

Other considerations aside, it was almost inevitable that a move-ment directed against the resident agents of absentee landlords would attack the Regency—the Jacksonian Democracy concept to the con-trary. Not only did the Regency fail to act as the instrument of the "common man" in western New York, but it had long been af-filiated with landlord interests[16] and resisted antirent movements which arose sporadically in the state. By 1827, moreover, the Regency program had crystallized around the state rights doctrine, opposi-tion to the national and nationalizing administration of John Quincy Adams, and open support for the presidential aspirations of Andrew Jackson. Jackson was both a high and a steadfast Mason, as were many Van Burenites. In contrast, Adams publicly affirmed that he never had and never would belong to the Order, and volunteered to expose the secrets of Phi Beta Kappa as his contribution to the move-ment for social equality and an open society.[17] Obviously, Antima-sonry presented great opportunities to New York politicians who supported the Adams administration on the national level and opposed the Regency on the state level.

Political Antimasonry may have been largely spontaneous in ori-gin, but its age of innocence was short-lived. In 1828, as Thurlow

[15] Cross, 116-117. Accepting the essential validity of the Jacksonian Democracy concept, he went on to say: "Thus a set of nonpolitical considerations served for many years to keep in the anti-Democratic column votes which on grounds of interest alone might well have joined the Jacksonians against the merchants and millers of the canal towns." Actually, Cross had noted on those pages that the New York Jack-sonians were "affiliated with landlord interests." Thus, apart from other considera-tions (as will be shown below), it was logical for the poorer farmers to be anti-Jack-sonian. Like Bray Hammond and other historians, Cross failed to appreciate the significance of his own findings because he could not break out of the limits set by the Jacksonian Democracy concept. (See Chapter XV below.)

[16] Ibid., 116; Paul D. Evans, The Holland Land Company (Buffalo, N.Y., 1924), 334-426; John T. Horton, et al., History of Northwestern New York (New York, 1947), 1: 88-94. In my opinion, the Jacksonian Democracy concept has served to obscure the close ties between the Jackson Party and many of the state's largest landed proprietors. The political leaders who led the attack upon the Holland Land Company and the Pulteney and Hornby Estates in western New York were Antimasons and then Whigs. For example, a Wayne County Antimasonic broadside, dated November 1830, linked the "Jacksonian Masonic Republican" Party with the "oppressors" of the region's debtor-farmers and presented the Antimasonic candi-dates as fighting "to relieve the settlers." It began: "No Oppression! Justice to the Old Settlers! Ananias Wells and Seth Eddy, opposed to the Aristocratic measures of the Agents of the Pulteney and Hornby Estates."

[17] Hammond, 2: 382-384, 388-394; Weed, ed., op.cit., 1: 302-303; McCarthy, 376-393.

Weed, Francis Granger, and other pro-Adams, anti-Regency leaders took over and steered the movement along a clearly defined partisan course, new political alignments began to take shape. Irrespective of previous political affiliations, a large proportion of the loyal Masons felt it necessary to support the Jackson Party, now under attack by the Antimasons. Similarly, as the Jackson Party and Masonry became more closely identified, the Antimasons who previously had been evenly divided in political sentiment now became zealous supporters of Adams.[18]

Aside from its intrinsic interest, the political conflict between Masons and Antimasons illustrates how "reference group theory" might help us to understand the process of party crystallization in the late 1820's and early 1830's; this theory might also advance our understanding of American history in general. The concept of the negative reference group, as defined by Robert Merton, "is a general concept designed to earmark that pattern of hostile relations between groups or collectivities in which the actions, attitudes and values of one are *dependent* upon the actions, attitudes and values of the other to which it stands in opposition."[19]

Under Van Buren's skillful supervision and control, the Jackson Party in New York constituted a tightly-knit, well-drilled political faction. But "the friends of Adams" are best described as a loose, heterogeneous political coalition. Composed of Antimasons and nonmasons, as well as some Masons whose political sentiments took precedence over fraternal obligations, its common denominator was antagonism to Jackson, or to his friends in New York, or to both. As might be expected, the bases of opposition to the Jackson Party, as well as the programs of the disparate elements in the Adams coalition, differed widely. Consequently, Weed's efforts to achieve closer working relations among all "anti-Jackson, anti-Regency" men achieved only limited success. In 1828, despite the obvious disadvantages of independent action, the Antimasonic Party resisted the

18 Weed, *op.cit.*, 1: 302-303. Weed's recollections are supported by the material in Hammond, 2: 381-391. Moreover, the *Address* of the "Republican State Convention" in 1834 conceded that a great number of "republicans" had gone over to the Antimasons, particularly in western New York. *Albany Argus* (s.w.), September 16, 1834, pp. 1-2. (All citations in this chapter are to the semiweekly edition of the paper.)

19 Robert K. Merton, *Social Theory and Social Structure* (Glencoe, Ill., 1957, rev. ed.), 300-301. Reference group theory, in my opinion, has great potential application to American history. For an illuminating discussion of its development, see *ibid.*, 225-386.

[27]

overtures of the "friends of Adams," insisted upon maintaining its distinct identity, and nominated a separate ticket for state offices.[20]

2. Cross-Currents in the 1828 Campaign

The cross-currents that buffeted New York politics during the 1828 campaign are suggested by the existence of two tickets for the presidency and three for state offices. Significantly, both national and all three state tickets claimed to represent the "Republican electors" of New York. No convincing evidence exists that the Van Buren faction should be regarded as the lineal descendant of the Jeffersonian Republican Party and its opponents as Federalists in disguise.[21]

The gubernatorial candidate of the Adams Republican faction— Adams, it will be recalled, had been elected as a good Republican— was Smith Thompson. For many years an important Bucktail leader, he had been so close to Van Buren that one of the "Little Magician's" sons was named Smith Thompson Van Buren.[22] And the Adams candidate for lieutenant governor, Francis Granger, is acccurately described as a "born Republican." His father had been named post-master-general by Thomas Jefferson himself. He had held that office for thirteen years while the Republicans ruled the Washington roost and while young Granger "was studying at Yale and fighting Federalism."[23] Solomon Southwick rounded out the all-Republican roster of gubernatorial candidates; he had been a "most zealous" adherent of that political faith prior to his visitation by the "Blessed Spirit" of Antimasonry.[24]

Weed and most other Antimasonic leaders supported Adams in 1828. The great majority of Antimasons probably voted for him,[25] but the Antimasonic "Party" officially adopted a neutral position in the presidential election. Still a one-issue movement in 1828, it re-solved "wholly to disregard the two great political parties that at

[20] Glyndon G. Van Deusen, *Thurlow Weed: Wizard of the Lobby* (Boston, 1947), 46-48; McCarthy, 377-381; Weed, *op.cit.*, 1: 303-307.

[21] *Address* of the "Republican State Convention," in *Albany Argus*, September 23, 1828, p. 2.

[22] Robert V. Remini, "The Early Political Career of Martin Van Buren, 1782-1828," 214, 222-223, 254.

[23] De Alva S. Alexander, *Political History of the State of New York*, 1: 361-362.

[24] Hammond, 1: 190-191.

[25] Weed, 1: 301-309. Weed's claim that the Antimasons became supporters of Adams is borne out by an analysis of the county percentages. With few exceptions, the vote for Adams was almost identical with the combined vote of the gubernatorial candi-dates opposed to Van Buren.

this time distract this state and the union." Furthermore, the process of identifying Masonry with the Jackson Party had not been long underway, and the Regency tried desperately to keep the Antimasonic issue out of the 1828 campaign. To quote the later analysis of a contemporary observer: "As yet, neither of the great political parties in the state seemed willing to come to an *open* [italics added] quarrel with the anti-masons: indeed, they both showed some evidence of a desire to caress, conciliate and use them for their purposes. Antimasonry all this time aimed to stand independent of and in opposition to both."[26] Antimasonic independence placed Weed, Granger, and other leaders in an awkward position. While working zealously for Adams, they led, without being able to control, a political party officially resolved to defeat the gubernatorial candidate of the Adams faction.

Although it would be convenient to treat the "friends of Adams" as the National Republican Party, no such party existed in 1828— at least in New York. (In fact, contemporary newspaper accounts suggest that no such party existed in the country at large.) Its imaginary existence has given rise to serious misconceptions concerning New York politics. They not only failed to constitute either a new political party or the old Federalist Party in disguise, but the pro-Adams, anti-Jackson men were organized so loosely that they lacked even a distinctive name in 1828. Thus their nominating convention was referred to as the Administration Convention (that is, favorable to the Adams administration), and during the campaign their newspapers praised "the friends of the Administration."

Perhaps the Adams faction is best described in the opening words of its convention's proceedings: "At a convention of Republican Delegates from the several counties of the State of New York, friendly to the National Administration. . . ."[27] Apparently, no formal attempt was made to establish a National Republican Party in New York until December 1830, and even then it seems to have succeeded only in a number of eastern counties.[28] Nevertheless, although no

26 Hammond, 2: 386-392. The quotations above are from pp. 387 and 391, respectively.

27 *New York Commercial Advertiser*, July 26, p. 2; October 9, 30, 31, 1828, p. 2; *New York American*, July 23, 26, 28, August 7, September 24, October 27, 30, 31, 1828, p. 2. The Convention proceedings are found in *ibid.*, August 7, pp. 1-2.

28 *Working Man's Advocate*, December 18, 1830, p. 1. The "National Republicans" were so loosely organized that they never made an independent nomination for a statewide office after 1828; either explicitly or implicitly, they endorsed the Antimasonic tickets. The impression that the Antimasonic movement was absorbed by the

such party existed in 1828, the title suggests the real difference between the Republican factions.[29]

Whatever principles and policies the Jackson Party may have adopted in other states—and the 1828 campaign displayed American political flexibility and eclecticism at their best, or worst—it was emphatically a "state rights" party in New York. As its *Address* to the voters made clear, it wanted the election to turn on the issue of state rights.

Of course, the *Address* indulged in the wild exaggerations typical of American political campaigns. The election in 1828 was not between two Republican factions; as in 1800, the battle was between "the Democracy and the Aristocracy of the country," a description so fanciful as to be more than usually absurd. But, after a long arraignment of the administration as derelict to true republicanism, it came to the real difference between the friends of Jackson and the friends of Adams. The 1828 election represented a "mighty political conflict, which like its memorable predecessor in 1800, tests the spirit, the strength and the wisdom of our happy constitution. *The great question of power between the states and the federal government is again to be decided* [italics added]. . . ." Ironically, in view of Jackson's later exercise of presidential power, the *Address* denounced Adams for resurrecting another "federalist" doctrine, the principle of "absolute Executive authority." Thus if Jackson were defeated, "the war upon popular rights and state sovereignty would be combined."[30]

Though the Jackson and Adams "parties" differed sharply on the "state sovereignty" doctrine, the national, state, and local contests actually turned on a wide variety of issues, more or less unrelated to each other. It seems accurate to say that the 1828 election in New York consisted of a set of separate campaigns coinciding

---

National Republican Party reverses the actual course of events. As a matter of fact, many "friends of Adams" hastily jumped on board the Jackson bandwagon after the 1828 election returns convinced them of the error of their ways. See Frederick W. Seward, ed., *William H. Seward: An Autobiography* (New York, 1891), 1: 70-75; Hammond, 2: 393. Like the other autobiographies, memoirs, and reminiscences of this period, the two cited here use the term National Republicans as though it were current in 1828.

[29] "National Republican," as the title for *one faction* of the Jacksonian opposition, began to appear in correspondence in the latter part of 1830 and the beginning of 1831. It received what one scholar calls "the final stamp of approval as the party's official title" in the February 22, 1831 issue of the *National Intelligencer*. (Samuel R. Gammon, *The Presidential Campaign of 1832*, Baltimore, 1922, 160-162.)

[30] The *Address* was printed in the *Albany Argus*, September 30, 1828, p. 2.

in time; misconceptions are bound to arise if we regard the antagonists in New York as representing political parties in the modern
sense (see the definition on p. 4). Yet one significant generalization appears tenable: in 1828 none of the "reforms" that historians
have come to associate with the Age of Egalitarianism received much
attention *on any level* from any faction. State rights, national policies, Antimasonry, the candidates' characters, qualifications, and
lack of them—all were disputed. But abolition of imprisonment for
debt, free public education, and "free enterprise" attracted little
attention. "Reform" was not yet on the New York political agenda.[31]

Analysis of the 1828 election statistics reveals several interesting
results. Comparison of the state and county party percentages for
president and governor makes it seem reasonably certain that the
great majority of Antimasons voted for Adams. And, instead of
showing that Jackson enjoyed "great popularity," the returns show
that he barely squeaked through to victory with 51 per cent of the
votes; the Jackson gubernatorial candidate had slightly less, 49.5
per cent. Though he failed to receive a majority, Van Buren became
governor because Thompson and Southwick divided the votes cast
in opposition to him.[32]

When we compare the county percentages, it is clear that a great
many men who had been political associates were now political antagonists. Numerous counties which were evenly divided in 1826
went strongly for one ticket or another in 1828. For example, in
1826 the Van Buren faction received 48.0 per cent of the vote in
Genesee County (scene of the Morgan kidnapping); two years later
it received 29.6 per cent. On the other hand, in Ulster County (an
eastern county where Masonry was strong) its vote for governor
rose from 45.8 to 63.3 per cent.

The opposite trends in Genesee and Ulster counties illustrate that
distinct regional patterns in the state's voting behavior emerged in

31 This generalization derives from a study of the articles, editorials, county *Addresses,* etc. printed during the campaign in the *Albany Argus, New York American,*
and *New York Commercial Advertiser.* More systematic analysis of a wider range
of sources, however, may reveal that the generalization requires modification in respect to some areas within the state.

32 The official canvass of the votes for presidential electors is found in Edwin Williams, *New-York Annual Register . . . 1830* (New York, 1830), 71. Unfortunately,
the canvass was by congressional districts; some districts included several counties.
However, an unofficial compilation of the county returns for 1828 is found in the
Albany Argus, November 23, 1832, p. 3. The figures for the counties within a congressional district tally with those given in the official canvass. The 1828 gubernatorial
official canvass is printed in the *Argus,* December 16, 1828, p. 2.

1827 and 1828. Firmly based west of Cayuga Bridge, the Antimasons barely managed to carve out footholds in counties to the east. In a number of northern, central, and eastern counties, the Adams faction received the highest percentage of any ticket. The Jackson Party received considerable support throughout the state, except in western New York, but its largest majorities tended to cluster in the river counties from Manhattan to Albany.

Unless we view the 1828 campaign in perspective, we are likely to misinterpret the relative strengths of the Antimasonic and Adams state tickets. That Southwick (Antimason) had 12.1 per cent, compared to Thompson's 38.5 per cent, might suggest that the friends of Adams were by far the most powerful element in the anti-Regency, anti-Jackson coalition. But in 1828 the Antimasonic political organization was still rudimentary, still concentrated in western New York, and still entangled with the other two factions. Thus one of its most prominent leaders, Granger, was the Adams faction's candidate for lieutenant governor; another, Weed, directed the Adams campaign in the western part of the state. It seems reasonable to infer, therefore, that the vote for Thompson and Granger actually was cast by a variety of anti-Regency, anti-Jackson groups. Certainly it cannot be regarded as an accurate indicator of the so-called National Republican strength in New York.

B. The Anti-Regency Coalition, 1829-1830

Held together solely by the political exigencies of the 1828 campaign, the friends of Adams Republican faction promptly fell apart once the election demonstrated that it no longer had a national or state administration to serve as a rallying point. The Antimasons' response to the election was very different. Having made an impressive debut in state politics and elected a number of senators and assemblymen to the legislature, they promptly went to work to tighten their political machinery and spread their crusade.

In February 1829 the Antimasons met at Albany and formally resolved to disavow all connection with any other political party and to nominate full tickets at subsequent elections. Moreover, they raised their level of aspiration. They adopted a resolution calling for a *national* Antimasonic convention.[33] By the time the 1829 convention opened, the crusade had already been carried to other states. Weed's *Anti-Masonic Enquirer* (established in Rochester in 1828)

[33] Hammond, 2: 392-393; McCarthy, 384-386.

had attained considerable circulation in Ohio, Pennsylvania, and Vermont. By the time the convention adjourned the movement was on its way toward transformation from an amorphous emotional crusade to an organized political party. After February 1829 it dominated the "anti-Regency, anti-Jackson Party" in New York and largely determined its ideology, character, policies, and style.

1. The Working Men's Party and Antimasonry

Although Antimasonry underwent a structural change at the Albany convention, it remained essentially a one-issue movement. Exposure and destruction of the "beast with seven heads and ten horns," the "hydra-headed monster" of Masonry, continued to furnish the main themes of its orators and to sum up its main objectives.[34] Late in 1829, however, something new was added to the New York political scene and Antimasonry underwent further transformation.

A thorough study of the short-lived "Working Men's Party" of New York City is not available. But it seems fairly clear that the immediate origins of the party can be traced to factional conflicts within Tammany Hall. Sensing that reform was "in the air," some dissident Tammany leaders attempted to gain political power by crystallizing the inchoate sentiment for reform, translating it into a specific program and nominating candidates pledged to that program.[35]

To the astonishment of contemporary observers, the assembly ticket, nominated by the Working Men late in October, received

[34] According to the account in Hammond, *History of Political Parties*, the Antimasons officially confined themselves to their "own peculiar principles" until the Utica Convention of August 1830. "Here, for the *first time*, in an anti-masonic convention, were opinions avowed upon important political measures. These opinions, now avowed, were in general accordance with those opposed to the dominant party; and were, doubtless, made public with a view to obtain the support of those who, though disagreeing with them upon the subject of free masonry, still otherwise held to the same common political principles." *Ibid.*, 2: 396.

[35] My conclusions largely derive from the material presented in an unusually good Master's Essay: Samuel Savetsky, "The New York Working Men's Party" (Columbia University, M.A., 1948). This essay corrects misconceptions found in earlier accounts. It contains a collective biography of the party's leaders and an analysis of voting statistics by wards, which support its conclusion that the Working Men's Party arose largely because of a factional dispute in Tammany.

Though limited in usefulness because it uncritically accepts the view that the party was primarily a spontaneous, working class reform movement, some useful material is also found in Philip S. Foner, *History of the Labor Movement in the United States* (New York, 1947), 121-142. For a thoughtful survey, see Edward Pessen, "The Workingmen's Movement of the Jacksonian Era," *Mississippi Valley Historical Review*, 43: 428-443 (December 1956).

over 6,000 votes early in November 1829—a figure not much below the Tammany total. Under the circumstances, the relatively large Working Men's vote appeared to demonstrate that New Yorkers were ripe for a social reform party, or at least would respond favorably to a party that pledged itself to social reform.[36]

Belief led to action. "Working Men's parties" quickly formed in Albany, Troy, Utica and other cities and villages. When we consider the composition of these parties and the circumstances of their creation, however, we need not take literally the title Working Men. That proletarian banner waved over merchants, lawyers, physicians, bank directors, clerks, cashiers and speculators, as well as some farmers, mechanics, and working men whose calloused hands made their credentials more bona fide. In his classic history of early New York politics, Jabez Hammond, himself a onetime Working Men candidate and leader, offered a convincing interpretation of the sudden appearance and growth of the party: "Adhering masons and other men who could not or would not join the anti-masonic party, but who were opposed to the Albany Regency and the Jackson Party, seeing no prospect of resuscitating [sic] the national republican party, flocked to the standard of the working men. . . . This party, if it deserves the name of a political party, was too disjointed, and composed of materials too heterogeneous to continue long in existence. The intelligent men who joined it were many of them zealous [Henry] Clay men, and mingled with it for the purpose of preventing those who would not act with the anti-masons from acting with the Jackson party."[37]

Hammond's stress on the transient, heterogeneous character of the Working Men's Party seems justified when we consider its history in New York City. Within eight months after the November 1829 election, which had demonstrated its potential appeal, the party split into three factions.[38] And yet, except for the plank on religion, the three factions agreed essentially on the following platform:

---

[36] Savetsky, "Working Men's Party," 14-23.

[37] Hammond, 2: 330-331. In 1830 Hammond had been a candidate of the "Farmers, Mechanics, and Workingmen's Party" in Albany County. That the name does not truly reflect the party's character may be gathered from the fact that Stephen Van Rensselaer, Jr. presided over a "Workingmen's" meeting which endorsed Hammond. *Albany Evening Journal*, November 3, 1830, p. 3. Reports of other "Workingmen's" meetings and conventions during the campaign support Hammond's later analysis of the movement. See *ibid.*, August through November 1830.

[38] Savetsky, *op.cit.*, 24-44.

Equal Universal Education
Abolition of Imprisonment for Debt
Abolition of All Licensed Monopolies
Entire Revision or Abolition of the Present Militia System
A Less Expensive Law System
Equal Taxation on Property
An Effective Lien Law for Laborers On Buildings
A District System of Elections
No Legislation on Religion[39]

Though it expressed a common set of demands, that platform specifically belonged to the "Advocate faction," that is, the faction supported by and centered around the *Working Man's Advocate*.

Unlike a large majority of the Working Men in the city and state, in 1830 the *Advocate*'s followers refused to support the Antimasonic gubernatorial ticket; instead it nominated independent candidates. The last plank in its platform, "No Legislation on Religion," held considerable political significance. By 1830, in addition to embracing most of the "Workey" reforms and nominating a prominent "Workey" for lieutenant governor, the Antimasons had become firmly identified with the movement to abolish Sunday mail deliveries and other "Sabbath-breaking" practices. Thus, as will be discussed in greater detail below, the *Advocate* denounced the coalition of Antimasons, Working Men, and "zealous Clay men" as the "Church and State Party"—a denunciation that illuminates both the quasi-religious character of the Antimasonic crusade and the anticlerical character of its opposition.[40]

As the quotation from Hammond suggests, the informal coalition of Antimasons and self-styled Working Men constituted in some respects a marriage of convenience. Although the Antimasonic Party dominated the union, the Workeys and Clay men who supported its ticket had some semblance of organization in a number of localities. On their own these two factions were unable to offer effective opposi-

---

[39] *Working Man's Advocate*, October 29, 1830, p. 3.

[40] *Ibid.*, October 30, 1830, pp. 1, 3; November 6, 1830, p. 3; November 13, 1830, p. 2. After the election, the paper stressed the religious issue as the basis for its failure to join the coalition. The coalition's success would have been disastrous "inasmuch as it would have been proof positive that one of the most important of our measures —'No legislation on religion'—or, in other words, *perfect freedom* of conscience was becoming unpopular." *Ibid.*, November 13, 1830, p. 3. My impression is that the *Advocate's* subsequent return to the Jackson Party stemmed largely from its anticlerical position.

tion to the Albany Regency.[41] But the advantages of coalition were not wholly one-sided.

As has been true of other American third parties which have attained rapid growth, by 1830 Antimasonry's success threatened to deprive it of a reason to exist. Two sets of statistics measure the decline of the Masonic Order in New York and the rise of the movement dedicated to its extermination. In its 1825 heyday the Order counted about 480 lodges and 20,000 members in the state; by 1828 Antimasonry had been so effective that only 130 lodges remained; by 1830, 77; and by 1835 the Order had shrunk to 49 lodges with less than 3,000 members. On the other side of the popularity seesaw, the New York Antimasons began in 1827 with 9 "free presses" and increased them to 23 by 1828, 32 by 1829, and 46 by 1830.[42]

Even before the compilation of such statistics, the Masonic Order's debility manifested itself in many ways and places. On the Fourth of July, 1830, for example, the Antimasons of Cayuga County, led by William H. Seward, staged a mock Masonic celebration. According to Seward, its enthusiastic reception left "little room to doubt that the popular sentiment of the county was revolutionized."[43] Beating a near-dead "monster," however, is not an activity calculated to sustain political enthusiasm. For the Antimasons to continue to attack the Albany Regency and the Jackson Party, the 46 free presses as well as the rest of the Antimasonic apparatus needed other issues.

Using the term figuratively, we can say that organizations, like individuals, have an instinct for self-preservation. Numerous examples support the view that leaders' reluctance to terminate organizations whose goal has been achieved is a law of American voluntary associations.[44] More specifically, Antimasonic leaders felt disinclined, simply because they had nearly driven the Monster Institution back to the dark regions from which it sprang, to allow the movement to fade away. And yet it would be passing beyond skepticism into cynicism to overemphasize the ambitions of politicians like Weed, Granger, and Seward, in accounting for the further transformation of the Antimasonic Party.

[41] Hammond, 2: 330-331, 393-397; Weed, *op.cit.*, 1: 366-369; Seward, *op.cit.*, 1: 78-80; McCarthy, 393-398.

[42] Griffen, "Antimasonic Persuasion," 233, 779.

[43] Seward, *op.cit.*, 1: 77-78; *Albany Evening Journal*, November 23, 1832, p. 2.

[44] See the chapter, "Preserving Organizational Goals," in David L. Sills, *The Volunteer Way* (Glencoe, Ill., 1957), 62-77.

Having originated as a near fanatical crusade for social equality, dedicated to the proposition that the ballot box was the proper instrument of social reform, Antimasonry, logically enough, responded positively to the issues brought into prominence by the Working Men. Moreover, once the original Antimasonic fury was partially sated, it is not surprising that men banded together politically should add other issues to their program. Further, to gain control of the state in order to *uncover and uproot all Masons in high places,* Antimasonry had to win support from men opposed to the Albany Regency on grounds other than its identification with the hated Order. Thus when Weed established the *Albany Evening Journal* in March 1830, while pledging it "to the cause, the whole cause, and nothing but the cause of Antimasonry," he apparently saw no contradiction in promising also to advocate "zealously on all occasions, domestic manufactures, internal improvement, the abolishment of imprisonment for debt; repeal of our militia system; *and all other measures calculated to promote the general interest and welfare of the people* [italics added]."[45]

2. Antimasonry Adds Demands for Equal Legislation

Closely examined, the demand for the "Abolition of All Licensed Monopolies" represented a logical extension of the egalitarian impulse which originally moved the Antimasons to action. In effect, they posed the following questions: In a free society, why should not all men have equal legal access to the opportunities opened up by a rapidly expanding economy? For example, why should bank charters be available only to members of the Albany Regency or to their friends and supporters? Was it not a denial of equal rights and privileges for the Regency to use control of the legislature to strengthen its political machine by rewarding supporters with highly-prized charters and punishing opponents by denying them charters?

Some time was to pass before the egalitarian impulse became translated into specific demands for "free banking," "free railroad," and "general incorporation" laws that removed political obstacles to rapid economic growth. But the process gained considerable momentum in 1830 when the Antimasons expanded their program and denounced the Regency for failing to secure "the rights of citizens

---

[45] *Albany Evening Journal*, March 22, 1830; Weed, *op.cit.*, 1:360-364; McCarthy, 393-394; Glyndon G. Van Deusen, *Thurlow Weed*, 54-57.

by equal legislation" and to enforce "the demands of equal justice."[46]

Once we recognize that the Antimasons and the Working Men both proclaimed an egalitarian ideology, we can recognize that the coalition between them in 1830 was a natural marriage of conviction as well as of convenience. Weed and other anti-Regency politicians gave nature a helping hand, of course. But the "logic of history" dictated the Antimasonic-Working Men coalition, since it united the movement for equal legislation with that for equal justice. Taken over by the Antimasons, the equal legislation doctrine embraced all existing Working Men's measures (except the church-state plank) and was capable of indefinite future extension.[47]

To stress doctrinal similarities is not to overlook the political value of the 1830 union. Other considerations aside, the political facts of life dictated the coalition of Antimasons, Working Men, and Clay men who agreed, in Weed's words, that the state should take all "measures calculated to promote the general interest and welfare of the people." To achieve "equal justice," as defined by Antimasons, or "equal legislation," as defined by Working Men, or positive state action, as defined by Clay's supporters, required the overthrow of the Albany Regency. For, contrary to an assumption basic to the Jacksonian Democracy concept, the Jackson Party resolutely resisted social reform in New York.

3. The Jackson Party and Social Reform

Except for the illusions that the Jacksonian Democracy concept has fostered, it seems unlikely that historians would have come to associate the Jackson Party with the democratic, egalitarian, and social reform movements of 1825 to 1850. After all, the Working Men's Party in New York City originated as a revolt against the

[46] "Resolved, That the present administration of this state, has proved itself entirely incompetent to all the following great and leading objects of government: the preservation of the lands and property of the state; the enforcing of the demands of equal justice; the securing of the rights of citizens by equal legislation; the improving of the moral condition of the people by necessary alteration in our jurisprudence; and the elevating of the character, increasing the wealth, and developing the resources of the state, by means of internal improvement." Resolution adopted at the Antimasonic state convention in August 1830. See its proceedings, *Albany Evening Journal*, August 20, 1830, p. 2.

[47] According to the *Working Man's Advocate*, "Universal Education" was the most important objective of the reformers. "We may pass the wisest laws in the world: we can secure *no* rights to our children unless we secure to them an entrance into the Temple of Knowledge." (November 6, 1830, p. 2.) Also see Savetsky, "Working Man's Party," 63; and the interesting discussion in Edward Pessen, "The Social Philosophies of Early American Leaders of Labor" (Columbia University, Ph.D., 1954), 284-308.

conservative, corrupt rule of Tammany Hall, the local agency of the Jackson Party.[48] And since the Van Buren Regency firmly controlled all branches of government in New York—thanks in large measure to the majorities provided by Tammany Hall—to attack the system of "licensed monopolies" was inevitably to attack the Regency.

Far from opposing the charter system that resulted in "licensed monopolies," the Regency not only supervised its operations but defended its validity. Far from responding favorably to the reform movements taking political shape in 1829 to 1830, the resolutions and *Address* of the Regency's "Republican State Convention" in 1830 ignored demands for abolition of licensed monopolies, abolition of imprisonment for debt, and establishment of a system of equal education for all. As I read the convention proceedings, they reveal that the Jackson Party in New York was out of sympathy with the social and humanitarian reforms, egalitarian doctrines, and "free enterprise" ideology which have been treated as integral components of Jacksonian Democracy. Far from championing or sympathizing with "radical" Working Men, Jacksonian leaders denounced them for advocating doctrines that "strike at the very root of established morals and good order of society." One resolution directed against dissidents who challenged the rule of the Tammany Sachems and the Albany Regency helps to dissolve the rhetorical fog and reveals much of the inner spirit of the Jackson Party. It affirmed "that our adherence to regular nominations is the polar star of our political security. . . ."[49]

During the 1830 campaign the Van Buren Republicans continued to attack the Antimasons and Working Men for having injected class divisions into politics. For example, the *Albany Argus* printed lengthy reports of "great Republican" meetings that deplored "the division of our community into classes,"[50] and lengthy articles that excoriated the factions that displayed themselves "as Anti-masons, as Working-men, as Agrarians, as Fanny Wright men, and in short anything but sound, discreet and honest citizens." Unlike good Republicans, these factions "all agree in making it their cardinal principle, and it is almost the only principle which either of them distinctly avow, to divide society into classes according to their professions, occupations, or associations, and to array the bitter, persecut-

[48] Savetsky, 14-23, 107-109.
[49] See the *Address* and resolutions in *Albany Argus*, September 14, 1830.
[50] *Ibid.*, October 22, 1830, p. 2.

ing, and proscriptive feeling, the violent and unyielding prejudices, the deep and enduring hostility of each class against the other, and particularly against every individual who will not join either."[51]

If we discard preconceptions about the liberal, reform, or radical character of the Jackson Party in New York, we can see from its 1830 campaign record in that state that its fundamental principle was "the just right of the States"—the principle on which Jackson based his famous veto of the Maysville Road Bill. (Jackson vetoed the bill on the ground that the congressional appropriation for building the road lacked constitutionality since it was a local rather than a national project.) The Jacksonians made customary obeisances to "economy in government," but advocacy of state rights was the only positive note which they struck. This claim is easily established. Speaking with authority as the recognized organ of the New York Jacksonians, the *Argus*, in a postelection editorial hailing the "Republican" victory as "A Signal Triumph for the National Administration," emphasized its faction's reliance upon the state rights doctrine.

4. The Dividing Line in Politics—State Rights

In reply to the *National Intelligencer*'s assertions that the New York outcome did not really indicate support for the Jackson administration, the *Argus* accurately noted that "the [Maysville] Veto, and the dictum of the appropriation of the national funds for local improvements, were particularly and elaborately discussed. The opposition to, and support of, the Administration, was considered as the 'dividing line'—nearly the whole argument of the [state convention's] Address . . . was directed to that position—it was strongly urged throughout—and at the conclusion, the appeal was repeated and enforced. . . ." Moreover, the *Argus* continued, in all the county and district addresses to the electorate, the strong argument urged "was the 'principles and policy' of the National Administration. . . ."[52]

It may be a moot point whether Jackson's veto of the Maysville Road should really be attributed to Martin Van Buren, but the "strict construction" doctrine of the veto fitted the latter's conception of a "sound republican" creed. More significantly, it fitted Van Buren's conception of sound political strategy for New York Re-

51 *Ibid.*, October 26, 1830, p. 3.
52 *Ibid.*, November 23, 1830, p. 3.

publicans. In 1825, as a United States senator, he had fought the plan of the Adams administration to have the federal government play a broad, positive role in respect to internal improvements, and had proposed a constitutional amendment to prevent federally sponsored public works. Federal interference could logically be expected to find wide and strong opposition in New York, he was convinced, because "there is no state in the Union that has so much interest in it as ours; growing out of our past expenditures [on the Erie Canal] & liability to future contributions for like works in other states."[53]

Hailed by Van Buren as sound political strategy in 1825, the defense of state rights formed the doctrinal core of his faction's *Address* in 1830. As the *Argus* later claimed, that *Address* made Jackson's veto of the Maysville Bill the central issue of the campaign. Emphasizing that New York had paid for its own canals, the *Address* argued that it would be an "unequal and unjust" policy for the federal government to use "our money to build internal improvements in other states." Like the Antimasons and the Working Men, the Jacksonians proclaimed their opposition to "unequal and unjust" legislation. But to the Jacksonians such legislation meant federally sponsored public works which benefited other states. If we recognize that the Maysville Road controversy firmly fixed "the just right of states" as the central dogma of Jackson's party, we can more easily understand New York politics after 1830.

All-out support for the national administration on the Maysville veto transformed the Van Buren Republican faction into a political party in the modern sense. Unlike 1826 and 1828, when only tenuous connections existed among local, state, and national issues, the Regency in 1830 deliberately drew them together and shifted the focus of interest from state to national politics.

Analysis of the *Argus'* triumphant editorial suggests the reasoning that produced the shift. The Republican victory, it claimed, represented a mandate for "the measures and principles of the National Administration." But the result was "not by any means as favorable to Gen. Jackson and the Administration, as it will be when that question comes in a more direct shape before the people, that is, when the question shall be simply upon an electoral ticket for or against Gen. Jackson."[54]

Regency strategy treated the 1830 election as a referendum on

[53] As quoted in Remini, "Van Buren," 515.
[54] *Argus*, November 23, 1830, p. 3.

Jackson and national policies; Antimasonic strategy concentrated upon state issues. The latter's *Address* to the people emphasized the evils of Masonry, the failings of the Regency administration, and the need for social reforms and positive government actions to improve the general welfare.[55] But in the eastern counties, where Antimasonry had not taken hold, "Clay men" fought Jacksonians on their own grounds. Ignoring the Masonic question, they denounced the state rights doctrine and praised Henry Clay's "American System."[56] In other words, the anti-Regency coalition did not constitute an integrated political party in 1830. It was composed of divergent groups who agreed on some issues, disagreed on others, and supported the same candidates in order to defeat a common political enemy. But the allied groups maintained their distinct identities. Although only two tickets were nominated, the two-party system had not yet been restored.

That New York voting behavior still remained in flux in 1830 is apparent from the election returns.[57] As usual, fluctuations in voting behavior cannot be calculated from the state totals. Compared to Van Buren's 49.5 per cent in 1828, the Regency gubernatorial candidate's vote increased slightly, to 51.2 per cent. Unity of the opposition on a single ticket prevents direct measurement of Antimasonic strength. But the conclusion seems reasonable that it had absorbed almost all the "friends of Adams" in western New York and constituted the dominant force in central counties such as Madison, Tompkins, and Cortland.

On the county level, the percentage changes from 1828 demonstrate that many voters were still in the process of switching political affiliations. Analysis of the returns supports the *Evening Journal's* postelection charge that from ten to fifteen thousand Clay Masons in eastern and northern New York had voted the ticket of their longtime foes, the Albany Regency, to defeat the Antimasonic candidates. As "evidence" was produced which purported to show that the hated Order had officially commanded its members to support the Regency, the *Evening Journal* reverted to the traditional theme which it had soft-pedalled during the campaign. It challenged the

[55] *Albany Evening Journal*, August 20, 1830, p. 2.

[56] See the reports of Working Men and National Republican county conventions and meetings in *ibid.* all during the campaign.

[57] The party percentages for 1830 are calculated from the statistics in Edwin Williams, *New-York Annual Register . . . 1832*, 46-57.

Argus' interpretation of the election as a victory for state rights and Jacksonism, and claimed that nothing but Masonic power had prevented the Regency's defeat. "The dark and dangerous influence of this overgrown, secret order, is now made manifest to the whole people. Its influence has polluted the elective franchise, and surreptitiously changed the political destinies of the state. It is now apparent to the world that no man who refuses allegiance to this privileged Order, is secure in his electoral rights."[58]

Such outbursts may have served as an emotional release for Weed and other disappointed Antimasonic leaders, but they failed to contribute to the delicate task of uniting the anti-Regency, anti-Jackson groups in New York. The conjecture seems reasonable that by 1830 undiluted Antimasonry had reached the point of diminishing returns; a positive program probably had more chance to defeat the tightly-organized Regency machine. At any rate, the Antimasons increasingly shifted emphasis to the reform measures brought into prominence by their Working Men allies, and to other state and national issues.[59]

C. Antimasonry Converts to Social Reform

One example illustrates the generalization that the Regency's opponents constituted the main driving force behind the New York reform movements of the 1830's. Abolition of imprisonment for debt was not a new issue when the Working Men's rebellion against Tammany drew attention to it in 1829. And, since the Van Buren faction controlled the legislature almost continuously after 1821, it could have been enacted at almost any time the Regency so desired. It is revealing, therefore, that imprisonment for debt was not abolished in New York until 1831.

Attention here is focused on the symbolic rather than practical significance of the reform. Positions taken on it serve as indicators of fundamental attitudes and values—more precisely, perhaps, as indicators of the extent to which politicians and parties translated profession into practice.

[58] *Albany Evening Journal,* November 9, p. 1; Nov. 12, p. 2; November 16, pp. 2, 3; November 23, p. 2; November 26, p. 1; November 30, p. 1; December 3, p. 1; December 7, p. 2; December 17, p. 2. The quotation is from the editorial of November 12, p. 2. All issues cited are for 1830.

[59] Hammond, 2: 397-398; McCarthy, 406-411. Compare the resolutions and *Address* adopted at the August 1830 Antimasonic convention with the *Address* issued by its legislative representatives in April 1831. *Albany Evening Journal,* August 20, 1830, p. 2; April 29, 1831, p. 2.

1. Abolition of Imprisonment for Debt

According to an article which appeared in the *Evening Journal* during the 1830 compaign, the Antimasons in the assembly had forced through a bill abolishing imprisonment for debt, only to have a Regency agent "strangle" it in the senate.[60] Not necessarily the most trustworthy form of evidence, this campaign charge gains credence from the positions subsequently taken by the influential *Albany Evening Journal* and *Albany Argus*. The recognized organs of the Antimasonic and Jackson parties, respectively, their editorials reflected and shaped party policy.

During the 1831 legislative session, the *Evening Journal* was enthusiastic and uncompromising in its support for the bill to abolish imprisonment for debt, the *Argus* was remarkably unenthusiastic and equivocal. In fact, the *Argus'* editorials appear to justify the *Journal*'s charge that powerful Regency leaders were resorting to complicated maneuvers to prevent passage of "this most important measure." It was an Antimason who wrote the bill that finally passed on the last day of the legislative session, if the scholarly editor of Millard Fillmore's papers credits him correctly with being its "principal author."[61] (Fillmore was then a young Antimasonic assemblyman on his way to higher things.) Consistent with their editorial positions during the legislative proceedings, the *Journal* hailed the bill as a great victory for reform, the *Argus* belittled it: "Whether this bill, which changes so materially the mode of enforcing the collection of debts, will prove as salutary in practice, as its friends have anticipated, or whether, by the intricacy and extent of its enactments, it will lead to greater oppression of the debtor and to increased litigation, as its opponents have predicted, time will show."[62]

Recollections of elder statesmen—more accurately, perhaps, recollections of men who in their old age write books depicting themselves as young statesmen—are notoriously unreliable. Convincing evidence, however, supports the claim in Seward's *Autobiography* that Antimasons unitedly supported the bill to abolish imprisonment for debt, while Jacksonians divided on it and yielded only to "the rising

---

[60] *Ibid.*, November 2, 1830, p. 1.

[61] Frank H. Severance, ed., "Millard Fillmore Papers," Buffalo Historical Society *Publications* (Buffalo, N.Y., 1907), 10: 53-54.

[62] See, for example, *Albany Evening Journal*, March 15, 25; April 5, 8, 22, 29, 1831, p. 1; *Albany Argus*, March 22, April 29, 1831, p. 2. The quotation above is from the last issue cited.

tide of popular feeling."[63] The addresses to the people, issued at the close of the 1831 legislature by its "Minority" (Antimasonic) and "Republican" (Jacksonian) members, provide such evidence. By tradition, legislative addresses pointed with pride to their signers' accomplishments, viewed with alarm their opponents' activities, and exhorted voters to reward their party for good deeds and punish the opposition for bad ones. Although legislative addresses did not necessarily indicate the views of all or even of a majority of the members of a party or a faction, they did show what parties or factions stood for.

The Republican legislators issued a long *Address*. Approximately half of it sang the praises of Jackson's policies and Jackson's virtues. Much of the remainder denounced the "motley array of disappointed politicians and ancient federalists, who have rallied around the standard of anti-masonry." It also found space for the claim that Fortune only smiled upon her favorite children, the Americans, when sound Jeffersonian and Jacksonian Republicans had tenure of office: "The seasons of prosperity for the nation, have been those in which the republican party has had the ascendancy. The reign of federalism has been uniformly attended by disorder and confusion, and by those impending evils, which always follow a departure from the doctrines of republicanism." But the *Address* maintained eloquent silence about reform measures enacted by the 1831 legislature, and ignored the opportunity to congratulate its party upon having abolished imprisonment for debt.[64]

In illuminating contrast to the Jacksonian *Address*, the Antimasonic *Address*, written by Seward, proudly recited the bill's legislative history. It credited its party with passage of the bill, blamed the Regency party for "secret and insidious" opposition, and attacked Edwin Croswell for having led the opposition. Editor of the *Argus*, Croswell was a high-ranking member of the Regency and the state printer who had benefited handsomely from the legal notices required by the old debtor laws. According to the Antimasonic *Address*: "The strong force of public sentiment carried the bill through the assembly, in defiance of the secret and insidious opposition of the

---

[63] Seward, *op.cit.*, 1: 191-192. See also the account in Weed, *op.cit.*, 1: 379-380. The chairman of the committee which drafted the original bill was Silas M. Stillwell, elected on the Tammany ticket in 1830. But he later abandoned that party and was the Whig candidate for lieutenant-governor in 1834. *Ibid.*, 1: 404.

[64] *Albany Argus*, April 26, 1831, p. 2.

leaders of the [Regency] party. In the senate, attempts to defeat it were made by those legislative manoeuvres which are so conveniently adapted to the purposes of men desirous of avoiding the responsibility of a direct outrage upon public opinion. Amendments were proposed by that body, utterly inconsistent with the whole frame of the bill, calculated to perplex and render them impracticable. . . .

"During the arduous struggles to obtain this law, opposition was constantly encountered, from the immediate political friends of the state printer, who left no means untried to defeat any and every bill, which in its results would encroach on his enormous income. Such, fellow-citizens, is the lamentable condition of your government, that no public measure, however important to your welfare, or however strongly demanded by your wishes or your interests, can be accomplished, if it in any way lessens the perquisites of a set of men who have come to consider public offices as their private property."[65]

The argument from silence is frequently misleading. Yet the nature of the documents analyzed—partisan addresses designed to claim all possible credit for legislative accomplishments—makes the Jacksonians' silence significant. Together with the other evidence presently available, it lends credibility to Seward's claim that the Antimasons unitedly supported the bill that abolished imprisonment for debt and forced its passage "in defiance of the secret and insidious opposition" of powerful Regency leaders.

[65] *Albany Evening Journal*, April 29, 1831, p. 2.

CHAPTER III

"BANK WAR" AND RESTORATION OF
THE TWO-PARTY SYSTEM

HE JACKSON PARTY in New York was vulnerable to attack on an issue of much greater significance in American history than imprisonment for debt. That issue had long been agitated, but questions about the proper relationships among the state, banks, and the expanding economy were just beginning to find a prominent place on the political agenda. Logically enough, the Antimasons enthusiastically pressed those questions upon the Jackson Party.

A. Van Buren Republicans and State-Licensed Monopolies

Abolition of licensed monopolies, it will be recalled, was a key Working Men's demand. To contemporaries, the most noxious and harmful of these monopolies were probably the banks chartered by the State of New York. Created in 1829 under Van Buren's sponsorship, the Safety Fund System contributed significantly to the stability and strength of the banks. But it did not alter their monopolistic character. (The significance and provisions of the Safety Fund System will be discussed in the next chapter.) In fact, by improving banking conditions, the law establishing the Safety Fund greatly increased the value of charters. Moreover, its provisions permitted men to acquire bank stocks by paying in only a small fraction of the authorized capital, and produced quick profits for the Regency's friends. Thus the Safety Fund did more than strengthen the banks: it increased the Regency's political capital. Contemporary and would-be entrepreneurs knew that the Regency controlled the government apparatus that granted charters and distributed stock;[1] they also knew that it was dedicated to the principle of rewarding friends and punishing enemies.

During the 1830 campaign the Antimasons did not directly challenge the Safety Fund System; however, they did accuse the Regency

[1] *Albany Evening Journal,* October 1, 1830, p. 3; March 11, 1831, p. 1; April 12, 1831, p. 2; May 3, 1831, p. 2; Jabez D. Hammond, *History of Political Parties in the State of New York,* 2: 297-302, 429-430, 447-449; Harriet A. Weed, ed., *Autobiography of Thurlow Weed,* 1: 382-383; Bray Hammond, *Banks and Politics in America* (Princeton, N.J., 1957), 354-356, 391-393, 556-560.

of proposing supplementary legislation which would have relieved certain banks from taxation and imposed a direct tax upon the people. The *Evening Journal* keyed its attacks to this accusation and excoriated the "gigantic political Bank scheme [the Safety Fund], projected by Mr. Van Buren," as a "monster" institution.[2] (Antimasons tended not to believe in venial sins. Familiar through long practice with the vocabulary of abuse that was normal to sectarian religious disputes, they depicted their opponents as guilty of cardinal crimes, banded together in "monster institutions.")

As applications for bank charters poured in during the 1831 legislative session, Antimasons found numerous opportunities to identify the Jackson Party with "licensed monopolies." Summarizing their position at the legislative session's closing, their minority *Address* charged, "While measures to promote the public interest have either been neglected, or when pressed on the attention of the majority, have been shuffled off and evaded; plans for the aggrandizement of their political friends, and for the advantages of banks, and of applicants for bank charters, have been pursued with remarkable industry, care, and vigilance."[3] The Antimasonic charges may well have been true. But true or not, they made "good politics" for a faction which dedicated itself to equal rights and equal privileges and which worked to unite all opponents of the Regency and Jackson administrations.

Viewed from the perspective of a tough-minded political operator like Thurlow Weed, the Antimasons' strategic problem was to shift targets and thereby gain new recruits, while holding on to old adherents. We can easily recognize this fact of political life, but we must also recognize that reform movements develop a momentum and logic of their own. That the egalitarian impulse initially directed against the "privileged Masonic order" should have found another outlet in the campaign against "licensed monopolies" is not surprising. In both cases, the principle, the rhetoric, and the essential objective were the same. Just as Freemasonry had been accused of securing unfair advantages for its "votaries," in 1831 the Albany Regency was accused of abusing its political power to stack the economic deck in favor of privileged entrepreneurs. "We are constrained to believe that the political organization which controls this state is

2 *Albany Evening Journal*, October 1, 1831, p. 1.
3 *Ibid.*, April 29, 1831, p. 2.

combined with a moneyed aristocracy, existing in the city of Albany, which owns the Mechanics' and Farmers' bank. We find the officers and large stockholders of that institution, and their immediate connections, the most prominent leaders in the dominant party, and influencing every executive and legislative measure. We find them embarking with the highest officers in the state, in speculations where the power of government, or the influence of its officers, can be brought to aid their projects of aggrandizement. We find them owning banks in the interior, and establishing associations with those institutions in every part of the state.

"It is believed to be owing to their influence, that you have witnessed the astonishing spectacle of a bank commissioner, selected to preside over one branch of the legislature. Their identity of interest with the canal commissioners, with the canal board, with the comptroller, and with a majority of the bank commissioners, enables them to exercise a most dangerous influence over all the moneyed institutions in the state, and particularly by their power of distributing the enormous revenues collected from the canals, and the surplus of those revenues now amounting to a million and a half dollars. This identity of interests causes a combination of political influence, which bids defiance to all legislative control."[4]

As noted above, although it originated much earlier, the antimonopoly movement first attracted considerable attention in 1829 when the Working Men were organized in New York and elsewhere. Jacksonians did not serve as leaders of the movement but as its targets. Moreover, inauguration of the Safety Fund System and increasing attacks upon bank monopolies represented a direct cause-effect sequence. One major event in the sequence was the 1830 coalition of Antimasons and Working Men; another was the adoption in 1831 of New York legislative resolutions opposing recharter of the Bank of the United States. (Since the Bank's charter expired in 1836, it could not operate thereafter, unless Congress passed appropriate legislation.)

1. The Regency Diverts Attention from State to Federal Monopolies

Antimasons chose to attribute the resolutions against the Bank primarily to the Regency's money-grabbing desire to free the state banks under its control from indirect regulation by the federal in-

4 *Ibid.*, April 29, 1831, p. 2.

stitution.[5] But passage of the resolutions also offered the Regency the political advantage of diverting hostility from the "monied *monopolies*" in New York to the "monied *monopoly*" in Philadelphia.[6] The Regency-controlled legislature had chartered and continued to charter state banks. Since the New York Jacksonians lacked responsibility for the federal "monopoly," when Antimasons attacked homegrown monsters they found it politically expedient to divert attention to distant evils.

Additional light is thrown on the history of the Bank War when we note that the *Working Man's Advocate*, although opposed to the Antimasons, took a very dim view of the legislative resolutions which opposed recharter of the Bank of the United States: ". . . We are by no means prepared to say that it were wise, in gradually suppressing the Banking Monopoly, to begin with the U.S. Bank. It is not at all clear to us, that the tender mercies of the Local Bankers are one particle more to be trusted than those of Mr. McDuffie's favorites [officers of United States Bank]. Thus, while our legislature madly persists in granting charter after charter to private companies, as they have done this very session [1831], we take little interest in how the U.S. Bank question is settled."[7]

After the legislature passed the resolutions which opposed recharter of the Bank, the *Advocate* renewed the attack: "Destroy the U.S. Bank, and let it be replaced by no National Bank whatever, and what would be the consequences? Why that the Wall street brokers would live in clover; and the Southern or Western Merchant would have to pay 2, 3, or 4 per cent to have the local notes of his State exchanged for those of our's."

To shift attention from the New York "licensed *monopolies*" to

---

[5] *Ibid.*, March 11, 1831, p. 1; April 15, 1831, p. 2. "The Albany Mechanics' and Farmers' Bank is the monied organ of the Albany Regency. Under the Safety Fund System, their power is almost without bounds. The Bank of the United States stands in the way of this gigantic political Engine. They are anxious to remove this salutary, but troublesome check upon their operations." *Ibid.*, April 15, 1831, p. 2.

[6] *Albany Argus*, March 12, 1831, p. 1; April 15, 1831, p. 2; April 22, 1831, pp. 1, 2. Before the Regency began its campaign in 1830 against the United States Bank, the antimonopoly movement was almost exclusively concerned with institutions created by state or local charters. In the 1831 legislative debates, for example, the charge was made that no evidence had been presented of popular support for the resolution opposing the Bank's recharter. The resolution's objective was not to express, but "to create a public opinion" against the Bank. See the remarks of Dudley Selden as quoted in *ibid.*, April 19, 1831, p. 1. See also J. Hammond, 2: 349-352, 406-407; B. Hammond, *Banks and Politics*, 369-386.

[7] *Working Man's Advocate*, April 2, 1831, p. 1. The quotation below is from *ibid.*, May 7, 1831, p. 1.

the Philadelphia "licensed *monopoly*" clearly called for delicate handling. But it offered the Regency great political possibilities. And it
is worth emphasizing that expediency joined with principle. The
campaign against the federal Bank could consistently derive from
the state rights doctrine upon which the Van Burenites had built
their party and Jackson had based his Maysville Road veto.

As the Antimasons logically extended the campaign against social inequality to include economic inequality, the Jacksonians logically extended the state rights doctrine to attack a national bank as
well as a national system of internal improvements. But to fight recharter of the United States Bank on the ground that it violated
the "just right of states," or was corruptly administered, or was
injurious to New York interests, did not constitute the campaign for
free enterprise which some historians have seen in the Bank War.
Such a campaign would have required a radical change in the Safety
Fund System, a radical change which the Regency then viewed
with alarm. As the next chapter will indicate, it was not until
their political stock depreciated sharply during the Panic of 1837
that Van Buren and company came to appreciate free enterprise.

Despite passage of anti-United States Bank resolutions in the
1831 and 1832 legislatures, the Regency apparently did not find
atmospheric conditions right for battle on the issue until Jackson's
veto message of July 1832 "burst like a thunderclap over the nation."[8] Analysis of the *Address* issued by the "Republican Delegates"
after their return from the Baltimore national convention of May
1832 supports that conclusion.

2. The Jacksonian Counterattack: a New Monster in Philadelphia

The Baltimore convention of May 1832 nominated Van Buren for
vice-president, unanimously chose Jackson to succeed himself, but
failed to agree on an *Address* to the electorate. The convention ad-
justed itself to prevailing conditions—that is, the political climate
varied considerably in different latitudes—and advised the state
delegations to "make such a report or address to their constituents
as they might think proper." Published in the *Argus* less than three
weeks before Jackson's message was released,[9] the New York *Address*
emphatically reported that the state rights doctrine continued to

[8] The phrase accurately describing the impact of Jackson's veto message is from
Arthur M. Schlesinger, Jr., *The Age of Jackson* (Boston, 1946 printing), 90. For a
different treatment of the Bank issue than is presented here, see *ibid.*, 74-114.
[9] *Albany Argus*, June 26, 1832, pp. 1-2.

serve as the dividing line between parties, as it had since "the earliest stage of our constitutional history." Republicans had ever been the doctrine's staunch defenders, Federalists, under whatever name they disguised themselves, ever its relentless opponents.

The United States Bank issue, judging from the limited space and prominence given it, ranked low on the *Address'* scale of political significance. The *Address* opposed the Bank's recharter, but briefly and moderately. Jackson's policy on the "Indian Question" received approximately equal space and prominence, for example. But Jackson's 1830 veto of the Maysville Road Bill inspired lengthy eloquence. "Although there is no act which has more strongly excited the hostility of the opposition than this, none has furnished to the true friends of the Constitution more grateful and convincing evidence of the *restoration* [italics added] of the government to its original principles on an important branch of internal policy." Praise for the vice-presidential nominee sounded the same note: "The principles by which Mr. Van Buren has been governed in his legislative course are derived from the doctrine of a strict construction of the constitution."

Jackson vetoed the bill for Bank recharter on July 10, 1832. A skillful document painstakingly drafted, the message immediately transformed the nature of the campaign and hopelessly outdated the earlier *Address* of the "Republican Delegates." After July 10, the "war" to rescue the American people from the federal bank overshadowed all other issues.[10]

Apart from their unequal intrinsic significance, attacks upon a "Monster Bank" had greater political potential than attacks upon a Maysville Road. As Antimasonry had previously demonstrated, to track down and slay monsters was politically rewarding. It might be conjectured that something in the national character makes Americans more responsive to attacks upon "evil," personified in the shape of malignant creatures or institutions, than to attacks upon "error," in the form of abstract principles. At any rate, after Jackson dragged the Monster Bank to the center of the political arena, the Regency

---

10 This generalization is based primarily upon a comparison of the relative emphasis given to the Bank issue by the *Argus* before and after the veto message. "For no other document within our recollection, has the demand been so great as for the Veto Message of President Jackson. The People have literally taken the matter *into their hands*—The remark applies to every part of our state.—Thousand and tens of thousands have been printed in pamphlet form and in extra newspapers." *Ibid.*, September 7, 1832, p. 1.

leaders could update the People's Party slogan, "Remember the Aristocrats at the Polls." Once they had been the targets of that slogan; now they rallied "The Democracy, Against the Aristocracy and the Bank."[11] Between 1824 and 1832, populist rhetoric had come full circle in New York.

As the Regency's slogan suggests, the impact of the veto message owed much to its demagogic style. To characterize the message as demagogic is to state a fact, not impute a value judgment.[12] Arthur Schlesinger, Jr., one of Jackson's most admiring biographers, has hailed it as "brilliantly successful" in diverting attention from its "basic contradictions by its passages of resounding and demagogic language."[13]

But an even higher tribute to the demagogic qualities of the veto comes from Thurlow Weed, a politician whose extraordinary gifts and long experience in that art lend greater weight to his judgments. In his *Autobiography*, Weed claimed that, as part of his plan to play down the Bank issue, the *Evening Journal* had carefully neglected to print Daniel Webster's reply to the veto message. When pro-Bank men called upon him in 1832 to insist that he print Webster's reply, he offered this justification of his tactics of salutary neglect: "I urged that the issue was a dangerous and damaging one, and that the greater the efforts in favor of the bank the greater would be our losses among the 'rank and file.' Judge Spencer asked if I did not consider Mr. Webster's argument against the veto unanswerable? I replied that as far as justice and reason were concerned, yes; but that as a popular question, two sentences in the veto message would carry ten electors against the bank for every one that Mr. Webster's arguments and eloquence secured in favor of it. These sentences, when I was called on to point them out, were, first, that our government 'was endangered by the circumstance that a large amount of the stock of the United States Bank was owned in Europe'; and second, that the bank was a contrivance 'to make the rich richer and the poor poorer.' "[14]

---

[11] *Ibid.*, October 2, 1832, pp. 1, 4. This was the *Argus'* title for the *Address* adopted at the Republican state convention in September. During the campaign, the Democracy was increasingly used as another name for Republicans.

[12] Hammond, *Banks and Politics*, 405; John W. Burgess, *The Middle Period* (New York, 1901), 202-209.

[13] Schlesinger, *op.cit.*, 90-91. To avoid misunderstanding, I think it best to state explicitly that I do not share the view that Jackson was primarily responsible for the Bank War. On the contrary, I believe he served primarily as an instrument of other men. At present, however, that belief is only impressionistic.

[14] Weed, *op.cit.*, 1: 372-373.

Weed did not quote with literal accuracy, and his recollections may show the wisdom of hindsight rather than contemporary sagacity. No matter. The point is that the veto message transformed the character of the 1832 campaign in general and the strategy, tactics, and rhetoric of the New York Jacksonians in particular. But to see the war against the Monster Bank as a new departure in American history is, in my opinion, to see discontinuity where there is direct continuity. *Seen in historical context, the Jacksonian "Bank War" becomes a brilliant political counterattack—not a bold offensive on behalf of free enterprise.*

Long before the veto message of July 10, the Jacksonians, like their opponents, had followed contemporary custom and stigmatized opponents as "federalists" and "aristocrats." Particularly after the 1824 campaign so smashingly demonstrated its potentialities, all factions made denunciation of "aristocrats" a ritual feature of New York politics, almost as standardized and devoid of content as tributes to revolutionary heroes in Fourth of July orations. To quote the newspaper of the independent Working Men's faction on the 1830 campaign: "Aristocracy is so unpopular here, that aristocrats will not be called by their own proper names. They steal other people's. Now they are Regular Republicans; then again Working Men."[15]

During that same campaign Weed had effectively satirized the Jackson Party's claim to a monopoly upon Republicanism by printing an unpaid "advertisement" for the "Grand Political Restorative, or ALBANY REGENCY PATENT REPUBLICAN PANACEA." He took the liberty of "signing" their names and attached glowing testimonials from "high minded and honorable gentlemen [who] from our infancy up to 1820, were afflicted with the grievous leprosy of Federalism." All other remedies failing, we tried "the incomparable Regency patent Republican Panacea. The effects were like the work of magic, for we were, in the twinkling of an eye, converted into orthodox 'Republicans of '98. . . .' "[16]

As we have seen, the Antimasons employed the "federalist" and "aristocrat" epithets normal to New York political conflict. But they had also employed the richly imaginative, dread-full rhetoric normal to sectarian conflict; its effectiveness may be gauged by observing that in 1832 the New York Jacksonians paid their opponents

---

[15] *Working Man's Advocate*, November 9, 1830, p. 1.
[16] *Albany Evening Journal*, November 2, 1830, p. 3.

the highest compliment—imitation. In fact, the counterattack of the New York Jacksonians followed the Antimasonic-Working Men line so faithfully that it might have been as deliberate a parody as Weed's advertisement for the "Albany Regency Patent Republican Panacea."

For years, the Regency had been accused of protecting and being protected by the Monster Institution (Freemasonry). For years, the Regency had been accused of having created an "overgrown political monied monster" (Albany Mechanics' and Farmers' Bank). Short of the radical solution of overthrowing their Safety Fund System and advocating free enterprise for state banks, what could the Regency do to divert public attention from the "political and moneyed [sic] aristocracy" and Monster Bank based at Albany? After the veto message showed the way, the answer was obvious. Jump on board the antimonopoly bandwagon, guide it down the state rights road, and crush the Monster in its Greek temple on Chestnut Street, Philadelphia. To switch metaphors, the Regency adopted classic jiujitsu principles in the 1832 campaign. They took firm hold upon the egalitarian arguments developed by the Antimasons and Working Men and tried to floor their opponents by turning against them the power of their own arguments.

Masonry had been portrayed as a secret, sinister monster with powerful tentacles which reached everywhere and threatened everybody. Masonic leaders' extravagant and arrogant public boasts about its power had been artistically used to darken that portrait. But by 1832 Masonry had been reduced to a pathetic shadow of a monster. In contrast, the Monster Bank was flourishing and, through its branches, *influencing* economic development all over the country. (Of course, we need not take stock in Jacksonian charges that the Bank practically controlled the nation's currency, credit, and price level.) Moreover, like the Masonic leaders in their days of glory, the Bank's officers and supporters succumbed to the fatal sin of *hubris*. They boasted arrogantly of great power and thereby enabled the Regency to denounce their "dictatorial manner" and claim plausibly that the Bank's officers had issued this challenge: "The question for the decision of the American People, was whether they would have *Andrew Jackson and no Bank*, or the Bank without Andrew Jackson! This is the issue, made distinctly, and with an abundant want of respect, either for the government or the people of the U. States."[17]

17 See the Republican *Address* in *Albany Argus*, October 2, 1832, pp. 1, 4.

As the Regency skillfully portrayed the combatants and the issue, it was not the unprivileged masses against "rich and haughty" Masons; it was not Working Men against the "aristocrats" who controlled state "licensed monopolies"; it was "Old Hero" against the Monster Bank. Either deliberately parodying the Antimasons or unwittingly plagiarizing them, Old Hero's enthusiasts attacked the Bank as this "colossus, this Hercules, this Mammoth; this Beast with seven heads and ten horns; this dragon, this Hydra-headed monster." They praised the hero "who saved the wives and daughters of the citizens of New Orleans, from the Brutish lust of British soldiery." New York Jacksonians, it may be noted, did not overlook the changes that could be rung on the theme that this was a Philadelphia Monster whose "monopoly power" came from a federal charter.[18]

By emphasizing the Bank's federal charter, the Regency leaders could continue to rely upon the strategy of making state rights the principal doctrinal issue. But, in addition to directing public opinion against impersonal internal improvement projects, they now directed it against the Bank, the corporate personification of social, political and economic evil. Thanks in large measure to the Jacksonians, the corporation henceforth received high billing among the cast of characters in the American political morality play.

One set of comparisons suggests the impact of the Bank veto upon the Regency's strategy in 1832. Compared with the *Address* of the "Republican Delegates," published in June, the *Address* of the state convention held in September clearly and sharply reversed the emphasis upon the Maysville Road and Bank issues. It piled extravagant praise upon Jackson for "his adherence to the old constitutional landmarks, in relation to *the power of the general government over internal improvements. . . .* [He defended the] 'reserved rights of the states.' . . . This indeed may be regarded as the great conservative principle of the government. It is the dividing line between the Federalism and the Democracy of the country." Piling glory upon glory, the *Address* then invited attention to Jackson's heroic defiance of the "United States Bank": "But the high credit which was deservedly awarded to Gen. Jackson by an intelligent and vir-

---

[18] This was Jacksonian anti-monster rhetoric, Cincinnati style. I have quoted it to suggest that the phenomena described in the text reflected a general tendency and were not confined to New York. For the quotation from a speech reported in the *Cincinnati Democrat*, October, 9, 1832, see Daniel Aaron's illuminating study, "Cincinnati, 1818-1838: A study of Attitudes in the Urban West" (Harvard University, Ph.D., 1942), 223-224.

tuous people for his Maysville Veto, has been in some degree thrown in the shade by that sublime exhibition of moral courage and devoted patriotism which he has more recently displayed and which has literally electrified the Nation [that is, veto of Bank recharter]."

Among the more noteworthy features of the *Address* was its studied neglect of *state* reform issues (for example, abolition of monopolies, equal education). Despite the Jackson Party's policy of steadfast silence on such issues, however, it now had a doctrine and a mission as well suited to demagogic exploitation as those developed by its opponents. The democracy of the state—the phrase was now increasingly employed—could be rallied behind heroic General Jackson who defended state rights and warred against the Monster Bank. As Marvin Meyers helps us to see, Jackson's "party formed, or found its character in the Bank War."[19] But that conflict did more than form the character of Jackson's party: it helped to form the character of the party opposed to "King Andrew." More precisely, it speeded the formation in New York of a party opposed to the principle of state rights and the practice of executive usurpation.

3. The Bank War Shapes the Whig Party

Before the Bank veto "electrified the nation," the heterogeneous anti-Regency, anti-Jackson factions faced complicated, vexing organizational problems. In September 1831 an Antimasonic presidential ticket (Wirt and Ellmaker) had been nominated at a national convention largely controlled by Weed, Seward, and other New Yorkers who sought to establish their party on a permanent basis. But in December 1831, at a National Republican convention that wanted to establish its own party on a permanent basis, Henry Clay was nominated for president. Though the Antimasons in New York were now the most powerful faction opposed to Jackson, they could hope to carry the state only by rallying the full anti-Jackson strength behind their ticket. At best a difficult task to accomplish quickly, it was made more difficult because many Clay supporters were Masons, or ex-Masons who had abandoned the Order only under intense public pressure. But Weed and company faced still other problems. Clay, like Jackson, was a high Mason who insisted on publicly proclaiming his continued loyalty to the Monster Institution. Given these circumstances, how could the animosities between Antimasons and Clay Masons be played down so that Weed could successfully

19 Marvin Meyers, *The Jacksonian Persuasion: Politics and Belief*, 6-9.

implement his plan to "secure the votes of all who were opposed to the re-election of General Jackson?"[20]

What would have happened in the absence of the Bank War can only be conjectured. But it seems reasonable to conclude that its presence fused Antimasons and National Republicans into a more effective coalition than would otherwise have been possible. Meeting first in June 1832, the Antimasons nominated an electoral slate pledged to Wirt and Ellmaker, but chosen carefully to include prominent National Republicans. It renominated the 1830 state ticket which had been especially designed to please Working Men. And, it is worth emphasizing, the Antimasons' *Address* reaffirmed their solemn conviction that "the highest and most important political duty which they have to perform, consists in maintaining and transmitting to their posterity, *the supremacy of the laws* [italics added], over rich and poor, over the feeble and the powerful, over political combinations and over secret associations. To the accomplishment of this great purpose, the first step in their estimation, is the destruction of the political and moral influences of free-masonry."[21]

Thus the Antimasons held fast to their original franchise while adroitly extending its provisions to cover Jackson's attack upon the "supremacy of the laws" and the authority of the "people's representatives." Drafted before the Bank veto had been made public, their *Address* argued that Jackson's "executive usurpations" (for example, Maysville veto, refusal to enforce Supreme Court decision against Georgia) raised constitutional questions of the greatest magnitude: "If the monstrous pretensions on which they [Jackson's actions] are justified, find favor with the American people; if they are ready to substitute for written laws, the capricious will of a President; for the decisions of courts and juries, the unbridled discretion of an executive who assumes to himself the right of revising not only the judgments of the courts, but the *deliberate acts of the supreme authority, the Congress of the United States* [italics added], and of determining whether they shall be obeyed or disregarded; if our citizens are ready to sanction such pretensions, all is lost, and the fair inheritance purchased by the blood, and secured by the wisdom of our ancestors, is gone forever."

[20] Weed, 1: 389-391, 413-414; Seward, ed., *Autobiography*, 1: 89-91, 99-100; Hammond, *History of Political Parties*, 2: 397-398, 417-419; Samuel R. Gammon, *The Presidential Campaign of 1832*, 34-52, 60-71, 142-147; Charles McCarthy, *The Antimasonic Party*, 1: 410-418.

[21] *Albany Evening Journal*, June 29, 1832, p. 2.

The inference seems reasonable that, in order to sustain their crusade at a high emotional pitch and simultaneously win support from National Republicans, the Antimasons decided to shift their emphasis from Masonic "secret intrigues" to Jacksonian "monstrous pretensions." Then came the "electrifying" Bank veto. Seizing upon it to unite the opposition, Weed and other leaders quickly intensified their efforts to play down Masonry and play up Jacksonism.

During the 1832 campaign, however, substantial differences in program and emphasis continued to divide Antimasons and National Republicans. Analysis of their state and county addresses and resolutions reveals that they differed, at least in emphasis, on Freemasonry, internal improvements, the United States Bank, "licensed monopolies," tariffs, and other matters. But each group could be faithful to principle and call upon voters to preserve the "supremacy of the Laws and the Constitution." Antimasonic and National Republican documents, therefore, usually featured a passage paraphrasing the Declaration of Independence: "He [Jackson] has disregarded the voice of the people, as expressed through their representatives in issuing arbitrary Veto's upon wholesome and constitutional laws thus endeavoring to imitate the Ancient Monarchs of France, who used the *Veto* and the Bastille for the most arbitrary and tyrannical purposes, and in fine, he has shown himself 'Unfit to be the Ruler of a free people.' "[22]

Though the Antimasons and National Republicans could unitedly condemn Jackson and the Regency, the Bank War had not become hot enough to fuse the heterogeneous opposition into a single, well-organized party. In private, the National Republicans conceded their political debility. As one leader wrote in May 1832, "A wag observed to me a few days since he thought we were looking up, being flat on our backs we could look no other way."[23]

The National Republicans who gathered in July to endorse the Antimasonic ticket plainly indicated that they wanted a temporary coalition, not a merger. (I refrain from calling that gathering of "flat-on-our-backs" National Republicans a convention, because to do so gives an exaggerated impression of their organization and strength.) Their *Address* to the voters conceded that they endorsed

22 *Ibid.*, July 20, 1832, p. 1. To strengthen the ties between Antimasons and National Republicans, the paper carried lengthy accounts of the county conventions and meetings held by both factions during the campaign.

23 As quoted in Dixon Ryan Fox, *The Decline of Aristocracy in the Politics of New York*, 362. See also Weed, *op.cit.*, 2: 43-44.

the Antimasonic tickets only to prevent Jackson and Van Buren from carrying New York. It predicted that if the anti-Jackson electoral slate won, Clay's victory was assured. "We feel confident, that if chosen, these electors will never vote for Andrew Jackson, or Martin Van Buren, and we firmly believe that before being called upon to give their votes, the absolute necessity will be seen and acknowledged by every branch of the opposition party, of defeating the election of Andrew Jackson, in order to save the Union from dissolution."[24]

Available evidence provides little or no support for the confident prediction that the "Antimasonic Republican" electors—to use the official title of the convention that nominated them—would have deserted the Wirt-Ellmaker ticket and voted for Clay and Sergeant. After the election, Weed publicly affirmed that "everyone who had taken the least pains to be acquainted with the facts of its [Antimasonic electoral ticket] nomination perfectly understood that it would, if elected, as certainly vote for Mr. Wirt, as the successful ticket will now vote for Gen. Jackson." And the notion of a "plot" that would have resulted in the Antimasonic electors voting for Clay seems particularly untenable in the light of the following private letter, written by Weed to Francis Granger just after the returns had come in: "We are in a pretty boat. Our friends say we should have done better on our own hook; but this is not so, for the result would have been the same, and the opprobrium of producing that result would have been charged to obstinacy. Everybody would have exclaimed that Jackson, Van Buren, and Marcy owe their elections to Anti-Masons. Now we have done our duty to the country, and without wronging anybody. . . . It is a great calamity, so far as Anti-Masonry is concerned. *It seems peculiarly unfortunate that we have not the power of vindicating ourselves to the world by giving the electoral vote of the State to Wirt* [italics added]."[25]

Yet the candid admission of the National Republicans that they supported the Antimasonic ticket in the expectation that its electors

[24] *Albany Evening Journal*, July 31, 1832, p. 2.

[25] *Ibid.*, November 23, 1832, p. 2; Weed to Granger, November 11, 1832 in Weed, 2: 45-46. Despite Weed's disclaimer, if the New York Antimasons had won, their electoral votes would probably have gone to Clay under two conditions: if they were necessary to his election; *and* if Wirt had no chance of election. But if Wirt had won more electoral votes than Clay, the Antimasons would probably have demanded that the Clay electors cast their ballots for Wirt. As I reconstruct the situation, neither faction had to make firm commitments before the election returns showed which one had greater strength.

would be forced to vote for Clay instead of Wirt underscores the real lack of unity among anti-Jacksonians in 1832. To use the *Argus'* illuminating epithet, they were a "Siamese Twin" party, separate entities bound together more by common antagonisms than by common sympathies.

It would be a mistake, however, to underestimate the binding power of common antagonisms in American political history. In fact, the theory of the negative reference group supports the speculation that antagonism is a stronger unifying force than agreement in the formation, duration, and operation of American parties. Like the diverse groups who rallied around the symbol of "Old Hero" defending the Constitution and state rights against the federal Monster Bank, the diverse anti-Jacksonian groups soon subordinated their own differences in order to wage a more effective fight against the "tyrant" who defied the people's representatives, trampled on the Constitution, and helped the Regency to protect its *state* Monster Bank.

The *Argus*, trying to split the opposition, displayed considerable ingenuity in developing variations upon the "Siamese Twin," corrupt-bargain theme. Jacksonians reached new rhetorical heights as they contemplated the sublime virtues of Old Hero. All to little avail. *The Jacksonian rhetoric was ecstatic, but it lacked persuasive power.* The state election returns demonstrate that the anti-Jacksonian gubernatorial ticket registered a slight gain. In 1830, before the Bank issue arose, the anti-Jacksonians received 47.9 per cent of the vote; in 1832, after the issue arose, they received 48.8 per cent. And even though Van Buren's nomination gave the Jacksonians the considerable advantage of being able to offer the only presidential ticket boasting a "favorite son of New York" in 1832, their increase over 1828 was a scant 1.1 per cent.[26]

Weed woefully concluded that the defeat was caused by Jackson's "huzza strength," that is, his personal appeal. But Weed estimated the "huzza" vote at about 10,000, or 3 per cent of the total. If we accept his estimate, Jackson's personal appeal may have "won" the state and national elections for his party. At best, however, he decisively influenced only a minute fraction of the electorate. Moreover, we get a better estimate of Jackson's appeal if we recognize that Weed chose to ignore the "anti-huzza" votes, those cast against Jackson.[27] Systematic analysis of voting behavior forces us to reject

[26] Computed from the returns in the *Albany Argus*, November 23, 1832, p. 3.
[27] Weed, 2: 45-46.

the notion that Old Hero decisively influenced the New York electorate.

When we compare the 1832 *county* percentages with those from 1826 to 1860, we can draw two significant conclusions: 1) In 1832, New York voting behavior attained a state of equilibrium which lasted for two decades (this conclusion will be discussed in Chapter VII). 2) Although formal party organization was delayed until 1834, the anti-Regency, anti-Jackson voting bloc actually crystallized in 1832. Put another way, New York voting patterns crystallized two years before the formal restoration of the two-party system.

It is unnecessary here to trace in detail the complicated processes whereby anti-Regency, anti-Jackson factions subordinated their mutual antagonisms and fused into the Whig Party. For our purposes, we need only suggest that the fusion can be attributed to the Bank War, which intensified after 1832 and reached its political climax in 1834.[28]

B. Two New Parties, Not Two Old Parties in New Dress

Among other things, this chapter has tried to show that neither of the parties established in New York by 1834 represented a reincarnation, lineal descendant, or close replica of the Hamiltonian Federalists and Jeffersonian Republicans. Neither of the new parties could logically have derived from either of the old parties, because the Whigs and the Jacksonians both subscribed to principles of political democracy that were alien to the Republicans and the Federalists. (For convenience, hereafter we will call the Jackson Party the Democratic Party, although it apparently did not adopt that name until about 1840.)

Examination of the constitutional theories of the Whigs and Democrats also shows the invalidity of the Federalist-Whig, Republican-Democrat formula. It is true that the Whigs resembled the Federalists in affirming the broad power and clear responsibility of all organs of government to promote the general welfare. But it is equally true, as Chapter V will try to show, that the

---

[28] See the accounts in Hammond, *History of Political Parties*, 2: 433-442; McCarthy, *op.cit.*, 421-426; Fox, *op.cit.*, 366-371; E. Malcolm Carroll, *Origins of the Whig Party* (Durham, N.C., 1925), 71-128. Some interesting letters and reminiscences concerning the formal organization of the Whig Party are in Seward, ed., *Autobiography*, 1: 149-159, 230-241.

Whigs radically differed from the Federalists in their concepts of political economy. Moreover, a fundamental Whig principle, advertised and incorporated in the party's name, affirmed unrelenting opposition to the Federalist doctrine of a strong executive. In contrast, the Jackson Democrats affirmed the Federalist doctrine of a strong executive with almost as much fervor as they affirmed the old Republican doctrine of state rights.

Has the argument been overstated? Granted that significant differences existed, did not the Whigs strongly resemble the "conservative" Federalists and the Democrats the "liberal" Republicans? In my opinion, the superficial analogies drawn between the parties have warped American political historiography. They do not take into account the political transformations which populistic egalitarianism brought about, or the crucial differences which exist between the old parties and the new ones. We can say that the two-party system was formally restored *in New York* by 1834. But I do not believe we can say that *the two old parties were restored*.

Perhaps the best way to sustain that argument is: 1) to examine the course of New York political history between 1834 and 1844 with particular reference to the leadership, principles and policies, and mass support of the Democrats and the Whigs; 2) to ask such questions as, apart from the principles of state rights and strong executive, in what respects did the two parties differ, in what respects did they resemble each other?

CHAPTER IV

NEW YORK PARTY LEADERSHIP, 1834-1844

DURING the decade 1834 to 1844, the two major parties in New York displayed striking similarities and profound differences. This chapter will analyze the social composition of their leadership; the next one will analyze their political doctrines; and the following one will analyze the minor parties in order to highlight certain characteristics of the major parties.

A. Who Led the Democrats and Whigs?

If parties were characterized solely by the leaders they keep, it would be difficult to distinguish between the Democrats and Whigs. A composite account of their social and economic backgrounds reveals striking similarities. Perhaps their most significant difference is that several Democratic leaders claimed Dutch or German ancestry,[1] while the Whigs invariably claimed British ancestry (mostly by way of New England). And Democratic leaders tended to be more affluent than their Whig counterparts, or to have more affluent relatives who supported their political careers. Unless fine criteria are used, however, both parties can be said to have recruited their leaders from *the same social and economic strata.* That generalization seems warranted when we sketch the socioeconomic attributes of the half-dozen men who led each party.

Many important changes occurred in New York politics between 1827 and 1844, but major party leadership displayed remarkable continuity. Ranked somewhat arbitrarily, the top Democratic leaders were Martin Van Buren, Silas Wright, William Marcy, Edwin Croswell, Azariah Flagg, and John Dix. All were prominent members of the Albany Regency before 1834, and all maintained or improved their place in the hierarchy afterwards.[2] Their Whig counterparts were Thurlow Weed, William Seward, Horace Greeley, Francis

---

[1] In addition to Martin Van Buren who was of Dutch ancestry, William C. Bouck and Michael Hoffman were the leading representatives of the Schoharie and Mohawk Valley Germans in the Democratic Party.

[2] This rank order is based on the accounts of Jabez D. Hammond, *History of Political Parties in the State of New York*, 2: 157; Harriet A. Weed, ed., *Autobiography of Thurlow Weed*, 1: 103, 2: 36-37; De Alva S. Alexander, *Political History of the State of New York*, 1: 293-294, 2: 53; John A. Garraty, "Silas Wright and the Election of 1840 in New York State," *New York History* (July 1947), 28: 288-289; Robert V. Remini, "The Early Political Career of Martin Van Buren, 1782-1828," 318-342.

Granger, Millard Fillmore, and Luther Bradish. All six had been Antimasons, a significant indicator of the dominant role of that faction in the new party.[3]

1. Top Democratic Leaders, 1834, 1844

From the early 1820's to 1844, Martin Van Buren controlled the Albany Regency. His career might serve as the classic model for the self-made man in America. Though the Van Burens had settled on the Van Rensselaer Manor in the mid-seventeenth century, the Regency chief's father can best be described as a farmer and tavern-keeper of modest status and fortune. Despite his lower-class origin, and before he completed the course of study at Kinderhook Academy, Van Buren was articled to a leading lawyer of Columbia County. Once admitted to the bar, he rose rapidly in his profession and in politics. On his way up, he acquired polish and wealth. In 1829, when he assumed the governorship, he already had "a competence fairly earned, which his prudence and skill made grow into an ample fortune." Fulltime devotion to politics—Governor, Secretary of State, Ambassador to Great Britain, Vice-President, President— failed to diminish his fortune or lessen his financial skill. In 1837, when he assumed the presidency, the tavern-keeper's son was described as "a very rich man" whose understanding of business was "vastly better" than General Jackson's.[4]

Unlike the Regency's leader, Silas Wright came from Yankee stock, and his family ranked higher on the socioeconomic ladder than did Van Buren's. A moderately prosperous farmer, his father won election several times to the Vermont legislature. As befitted a "solid" citizen of Vermont, his son Silas attended Middlebury Academy and Middlebury College. Upon graduation, young Wright turned to the

[3] The chain of command was not as distinct among the Whigs as among the Democrats. Moreover, since they did not win any statewide election before 1838, the Whigs had fewer prominent leaders. The rank order was arrived at on the basis of several criteria, including nomination for office and my estimate of their influence upon the party's program. For a lengthy list of "prominent men" in the Antimasonic and Whig parties see, Weed, *op.cit.*, 1: 336-337, 451-453; Alexander, *op.cit.*, 2: 18-20, 31-33, 78-81; Glyndon G. Van Deusen, *Thurlow Weed*, 74-76, 134-135; Van Deusen, *Horace Greeley* (Philadelphia, 1953), 13-14, 50-56, 96-98. Greeley had been too young to play a role in politics during the Antimasonic period, but "became deeply suspicious of the Masonic Order as a menace to democratic institutions." *Ibid.*, 13, and *New York Tribune* (w.), November 15, 1851, p. 3.

[4] Dennis T. Lynch, *An Epoch and A Man: Martin Van Buren And His Times* (New York, 1929), 15-48; Remini, *op.cit.*, 2-63, 319-326; B. Hammond, *Banks and Politics In America*, 331-332. The quotation is from Hammond.

law for a career and had the good fortune to work in the office of a leading Regency politician. After his admission to the bar in 1819, with good political connections but little capital, he joined the Vermont trek to northern New York and opened a law office in Canton, St. Lawrence County.

Like many another young lawyer in New York, Wright polished up his politics while practicing law. He polished up his politics so successfully that from 1823 to 1846 he was never out of office. From the state senate he went to the House of Representatives, crossed over to the United States Senate, and wound up his career as governor of New York.

By the time he retired to private life, Wright was financially "comfortable." Compared to Van Buren and most Regency leaders, however, he had been uninterested in or had failed to take advantage of the many profitable opportunities open to politicians of note and power. In 1840, according to his own reckoning, he was "now worth about $8,000." His most recent biographer writes that, after losing his bid for re-election in 1846, "Silas undertook to become a fulltime farmer [in Canton]. His long career in politics had not made him rich, but he had accumulated a reasonable amount of property and a little money. His farm was run by several hired hands while he was away on political business at Washington or Albany, and he had interests in several local enterprises, such as grist-mills and saw-mills."[5]

William Marcy was born into a Massachusetts Federalist family, but grew up to become an ardent Jeffersonian whose views clashed sharply with those "of his family and . . . social class." He graduated from Brown University in 1808 and soon moved to the New England "colony" of Troy, New York. Like Van Buren and Wright, he practiced law and worked hard at politics. His devotion to Van Buren's Republican faction brought rich rewards. Appointed to an important state job in 1823, Marcy held a variety of offices during the next fifteen years. In succession, he served as state comptroller, judge of the state Supreme Court, United States senator, and governor. After Seward defeated him in 1838, he held important cabinet posts, including secretary of war and secretary of state.

Apart from his direct role in politics, Marcy's career symbolizes

[5] John A. Garraty, *Silas Wright* (New York, 1949), 11-23, 391; Franklin B. Hough, *History of St. Lawrence and Franklin Counties, New York* (Albany, 1853), 613-616; John Bigelow, *The Life of Samuel J. Tilden* (New York, 1895), 1: 102-103.

the intimate relationships enjoyed by the Democratic Party and the "business community." That he married the boss's daughter is not quite accurate, but by 1824 he had become the son-in-law and trusted associate of Benjamin Knower, a charter member of the Albany Regency and a wealthy, self-made entrepreneur. As Marcy's biographer puts it, a close bond developed between the two men, and "in a sense he had married not only Cornelia [Knower], but also father Benjamin as well." Knower, leaving his son-in-law to represent him in the Regency, "retired" from public life in 1824 and devoted himself to the job of expanding his business interests.

Knower had originally been a self-made man. Once on his way, he had ceased to depend solely upon his business acumen and is perhaps best described as a "political entrepreneur." Highly placed in Jacksonian ranks and president of the Albany Mechanics' and Farmers' Bank, he used his financial and political connections for grand-scale speculations in wool, real estate, water rights, and related enterprises. His "gambling proclivities" repeatedly landed him in financial hot water, however, and he "issued frequent calls for help and endeavored to warp Marcy's political course to suit his own business predilections." Marcy's intimate association with entrepreneurs on-the-make was not limited to his father-in-law, nor were his ties to the business community unusual. Among his "associates in the Democracy . . . ties with business were all too numerous."[6] With the Marcy-Knower connection in mind, this portion of the 1831 Antimasonic legislative *Address* takes on new significance: ". . . The political organization which controls this state is combined with a moneyed aristocracy . . . which owns the Mechanics' and Farmers' bank. We find the officers and large stockholders of that institution, and their immediate connections, the most prominent leaders in the dominant party. . . . We find them embarking with the highest officers of the state, in speculations where the power of government, or the influence of its officers, can be brought to aid their projects of aggrandizement."[7]

Edwin Croswell was another Democratic leader who enjoyed close and profitable "ties with business." Born of Yankee stock in 1797 in Greene County, New York, he rose rapidly in the Regency hierarchy after his appointment as editor of the *Albany Argus* in 1823.

6 This sketch is based largely on, and the quotations are from, Ivor D. Spencer, "William L. Marcy Goes Conservative," *Mississippi Valley Historical Review*, 31: 205-224 (September 1944). See also Hammond, *Political Parties*, 2: 114, 289, 346-347, 423-488; Alexander, *op.cit.*, 1: 292-294.

7 See pp. 48-49 above.

When Van Buren picked him to run the party organ at the state capital, Croswell already had considerable experience as a Republican editor. His father had founded and edited the *Catskill Recorder* and had made him an apprentice by 1811, a partner by 1818 or 1819. Apparently he was well educated, for he was respectfully referred to as "the cultured editor of the *Albany Argus*." Under his guidance, the *Argus* laid down the party line for the Van Buren press in New York and eventually became the most influential Democratic organ in the North.

One reward bestowed upon the editor of the *Argus* by a grateful party was the lucrative office of state printer. His long tenure from 1823 to 1840 proved so profitable, in fact, that a clutch of other Regency editors clamored for "rotation in office." Croswell later suffered serious financial reverses, but, while the Regency reigned, he found little difficulty in accumulating considerable wealth. Unlike Wright, he had a keen ear for opportunity knocking and "was up to his neck in the Canal Bank of Albany and other speculations."[8]

Azariah Flagg was another member of the Regency who started political life as a Republican editor. A Vermonter, he served his printer's apprenticeship with a relative and then "swarmed from the New England hive" to a Yankee colony in New York. Settling in Clinton County in 1811, he rapidly made the *Plattsburg Republican* his party's leading organ in northeastern New York. Skillful "politicking" and unrestrained attacks upon DeWitt Clinton brought him fame, Regency approval, and appointment as New York secretary of state. After 1826, his occupation is most accurately described as "government official." Seven years as secretary of state and ten years as comptroller established him as his party's expert on state finances and internal improvements.

Flagg was a leading member of the faction that later became known as "Radical Democrats," because they wanted to reverse the state's traditional policy of active intervention in the economy. He dedicated himself to strict construction, severely-limited government aid to enterprise, rigid economy, and the pay-as-you-go principle for

---

[8] The sketch of Croswell has been pieced together from a variety of sources. See Hammond, *Political Parties*, 2: 122-123, 524; Alexander, *op.cit.*, 1: 374-375, 2: 56-59; Herbert A. Donovan, *The Barnburners*, 20, 38-40; Beman Brockway, *Fifty Years In Journalism* (Watertown, N.Y., 1891), 15-18; Milton W. Hamilton, *The Country Printer* (New York, 1936), 105, n.42; Remini, 328-330; Spencer, in *MVHR*, 31: 214. (This last citation is the source of the quotation on Croswell's participation in speculative activities.)

internal improvements. True to the ascetic creed of the Radical Democrats, he was one of the few leaders of his party who "seem[s] to have stayed fairly aloof" from the "charter-mongering and melon-cutting [which] were rife" at Albany during the Regency's reign. Measured by the criteria of high political office or rich financial rewards, he apparently profited less than any other Jacksonian leader.[9]

John A. Dix completes our roster of the Regency inner circle. He belonged to the "gentlemanly" or, as critics dubbed it, the *"clean-shirt party of the Democracy."* His ancestors were "early New Englanders of English and Puritan stock. All were substantial though undistinguished citizens." New Hampshire born, Dix had been educated at Phillips Exeter, the College of Montreal, and St. Mary's College in Baltimore. An officer in the War of 1812, he had remained in the Army and been appointed aide-de-camp to the Commander of the Northern Military Department in 1819. Impressed with the prominent politicians he met during his tour of duty and having made an excellent impression upon them, Dix decided to become a lawyer. He was admitted to the bar in 1824. Two years later he married the daughter of John P. Morgan. Thanks to his father-in-law's generosity and his position as a prominent, wealthy Republican businessman and large landholder, "after his marriage . . . Dix no longer depended upon the law or upon office for life's necessities."

In 1828 Dix resigned from the Army and moved to Cooperstown, New York. There he opened a law office, served as Morgan's land agent, and started to climb the Regency ladder. His father-in-law was a close friend and political ally of Martin Van Buren, which, coupled with Dix's own charm and talents, made his swift rise almost inevitable. Appointed state adjutant-general in 1830, he succeeded Flagg as secretary of state in 1833 and held that post until the Whig victory in 1838 brought the long Regency régime to an end.

Dix had been so valuable a member of the Regency that Van Buren and other leaders were disturbed by the prospect of his leaving Albany. As a result, President Van Buren wrote a letter to Dix's father-in-law and speedily relieved the anxieties of the Regency. According to Dix's biographer, "Both Dix and Mr. Morgan appreciated the need of retaining an important defender of the Administration in Albany . . . [so] John stayed on with the aid and

[9] Remini, 330-331; Brockway, *op.cit.*, 44-45, 419; Donovan, *op.cit.*, 15-21; Hammond, *Political Parties*, 2: 214, 431; Spencer, *op.cit.*, 31: 214. (This last citation is the source of the information on Flagg's aloofness from speculation.)

blessing of his father-in-law and his wife. The President quickly voiced his great satisfaction with the decision [to Morgan]." Though without government office for several years, Dix continued to labor in the Democratic vineyards and, in 1845, succeeded Silas Wright as United States senator. Whatever else may be said of the Regency under Van Buren's aegis, it always remained true to its first principle—to reward men for faithful service to the cause.[10]

2. The Top Whig Leaders, 1834-1844

Of the dozen men who led the two parties, Dix's family probably ranked close to highest on the socioeconomic scale; Thurlow Weed's family certainly ranked lowest. The future "dictator" of the Whig Party—like Edwin Croswell, his journalistic counterpart among Democrats—was born in 1797 and grew up in Catskill, New York. Again like Croswell, he was of New England stock and Republican heritage. There similarity stopped.

Croswell's father was owner of the village newspaper; Weed's father was a cartman frequently imprisoned for debt. "I remember with a shudder," Weed wrote in his *Autobiography*, "a sad and sleepless night occasioned by the incarceration of my own father, who though a poor man was known to be an honest one, and for that reason was enabled to give bonds that he would remain on the 'gaol liberties' until the debt (of something less than $20) was paid."

To know of the contrasting family backgrounds of their editors gives a new significance to the contrasting positions taken by the *Evening Journal* and the *Argus* on the bill abolishing imprisonment for debt. The family backgrounds also help to explain Weed's vitriolic, personal attack upon Croswell in connection with that bill. Many years later, in a letter to the editor of a Catskill paper, Weed recalled his father's imprisonment for debt and gave this account of his relationship with young Croswell: "Your correspondent [the author of an article on early Catskill days] kindly refers to the circumstance that Mr. Edwin Croswell and myself 'were boys together at Catskill.' Though of the same age, we were not intimate as boys. He had the advantage of me in position, education, etc."[11]

According to Weed's later recollections, which may exaggerate

---

[10] This sketch is largely based upon, and the quotations concerning Dix's father-in-law are from Martin Lichterman, "John Adams Dix" (Columbia University Ph.D., 1952), 3-44, 103-140. See also Alexander, 2: 2-4; Spencer, 31: 207, n. 12.

[11] Weed, 1: 1-9, 379-380. The quotations are from pp. 8, 380.

the humbleness of his birth but which are probably essentially correct, he enjoyed less than a year of formal schooling. At any rate, he was a self-educated and self-made man and whatever learning he acquired as a boy undoubtedly derived from his years of wandering as a printer's apprentice and journeyman. By 1818 he had made up in experience what he lacked in schooling and Clintonian politicians set him up as a newspaper proprietor in Chenango County. Without financial resources and unable to make the paper pay, he sold out in 1820 and went to work as a journeyman printer. He knocked about for a couple of years and then settled in Rochester where he became the energetic but debt-ridden editor of an enthusiastically anti-Regency newspaper. By 1823, a local leader of the People's Party, Weed rose rapidly in politics. By 1828, he had become campaign manager of the Adams faction in western New York, Antimasonic leader, and editor of the Rochester *Anti-Masonic Enquirer*.

By 1828 Weed had worked his passage to political power but not to fortune. During his Rochester years he was poor and chronically in debt. When he moved to Albany in 1830 to edit the *Evening Journal*, however, his financial as well as political stock rose. While the 1835 to 1837 boom lasted, he dabbled modestly in real estate, railroads, and banks; he was aided in this by well-placed friends (Democrats and Whigs). During the Panic his campaign to get rich quick stalled temporarily, but started up again in high gear after the Whigs took power in 1839. By then he was firmly established in politics as "My Lord Thurlow," the "dictator" of the Whig Party. In addition to political power, he held the post of state printer, which his predecessor (Croswell) had estimated to be worth $30,000 a year. His actual income from the post can only be conjectured, but "it was enough so that after four years' possession Weed could bear witness that it had given him 'at least one man's fair proportion of this world's goods.'" Like Van Buren, his opposite number in the Regency, the humbly-born leader of the Whigs had not overlooked the possibility that the road to power could also become the road to riches.[12]

The middle man in the Whig triumvirate of "Weed, Seward, and Greeley" was born in Orange County, New York. He came of "good, plain" British stock who "stood well in the communities in which they lived." During the course of a many-sided career as physician,

---

[12] This sketch is based primarily upon Van Deusen, *Weed*, 3-109. The quotation is from p. 108.

landowner, merchant, and county judge, his father had improved the family's fortune and prestige. He had done so well, in fact, that in addition to owning a few slaves, he had been able to found an academy, name it after himself, and endow it with $20,000—a sizeable sum in early nineteenth century rural New York.

Blessed with a father of such academic tastes and financial acumen, William H. Seward received an excellent education and was admitted to the bar shortly after graduating from Union College. He accepted the offer of a law partnership in Auburn, county seat of Cayuga County. Located in the midst of a fertile region recently settled by New Englanders, Auburn offered many opportunities to a well-educated man of Seward's background and talents.

Politics was traditionally the high road to fame and fortune of ambitious young New York lawyers; Seward was off and running hard soon after arriving in Auburn. Dr. Seward had been a staunch Jeffersonian who had passed his Republican faith on to his son, and, like many other Republicans in 1824, young Seward joined the anti-Regency faction. He was active in the People's Party campaign and during the next four years became firmly identified with the "friends of Adams" while working discreetly with the Antimasons in Cayuga County. After the 1828 election, which left the Adams Republican faction "practically dissolved and in ruins," Seward openly joined the Antimasons and continued to battle against the Regency and Jackson. In 1830, after having been a delegate to several Antimasonic state and national conventions, he won election to the state senate from a district once counted as a Regency stronghold. Not yet 30, Seward was already a "full-fledged politician."

Seward took full advantage of the four-year term in the senate to display his political talents and to help consolidate the Regency's opponents. As a result, despite Seward's youth, Weed succeeded in making his protégé the first Whig candidate for governor. Defeated in the 1834 campaign, Seward won in 1838 and again in 1840, but did not stand for re-election in 1842.

During the next few years, Seward worked hard to repair his badly-battered financial position. By the time he took office in 1839, he had accumulated about $50,000 or $60,000 from his law practice and from investments in Auburn real estate and other speculations. In addition, he owned a substantial interest in the firm that had bought part of the Holland Land Company's remaining holdings; eventually it yielded rich returns, but not until years after he retired to private life in 1843.

Not only had Seward failed to make the governorship pay, but his "moderate personal estate had nearly melted away" as a result of "the general financial crisis and his large expenditures when in office." He owed so much money, in fact, that some friends suggested bankruptcy proceedings as the only alternative to life-long indebtedness. Refusing to take that way out, he continued to be hard-pressed to meet obligations for several years. Clearly, their joint rise to political power had not brought Seward the financial rewards that had come to his more humbly-born mentor and friend, Thurlow Weed.[13]

Like the senior member of the Whig triumvirate, Horace Greeley was a poor journeyman printer who travelled the editorial road to political influence. But Greeley had a somewhat better start than Weed. His father at least held title to the farm near Amherst, New Hampshire where Greeley was born in 1811. He later described himself as the "son of a poor and hard-working farmer, struggling to pay off the debt he had incurred in buying his high-priced farm."[14] This self-description is consistent with a recent biographer's characterization of his mixed English and Scotch-Irish ancestors as "undistinguished, middle-class, small town and country folk, mostly farmers and blacksmiths."[15]

Although "middle-class" might describe Greeley's father, that term has a remarkably elastic range in the United States and is frequently misleading. Never prosperous, his father was hard-hit by the Panic of 1819. Like many other Yankees, he lost his farm and literally had to take to the Vermont woods to escape debtor's prison. After the farm was sold to satisfy creditors, and after a traumatic hand-to-mouth interval as a woodchopper—this experience left an indelible impression on his son Horace—he started to farm again in another section of New Hampshire. The miserable, hard-scrabble place was called, appropriately enough, "Flea Knoll."

Throughout most of Greeley's boyhood, the family experienced

---

[13] A modern biography of Seward is badly needed, but some of the requisite information is found in Frederic Bancroft, *The Life of William H. Seward* (New York, 1900), 1: 1-134, and Frederick W. Seward, ed., *William H. Seward: An Autobiography*, 1: 19-159. The financial information is compactly presented in Bancroft, 1: 131-134.

[14] Horace Greeley, *Recollections of a Busy Life* (New York, 1868), 38.

[15] Van Deusen, *Horace Greeley*, 5. The present capsule account is based largely upon *ibid.*, 5-128. It also draws upon Greeley's reminiscences of his trials and troubles in *Recollections*, 22-143.

desperate poverty. In all, young Horace managed to get only 45 months of district schooling over a ten-year period. But formal education was an unnecessary luxury. A prodigy, he read remarkably well at the age of four. When he was thirteen, "an honest teacher confessed . . . that the boy knew more than he did and might as well stay home. This ended his formal schooling." Two years later he became a fulltime printer's apprentice.

Five years of hard work on a New Hampshire country weekly gave Greeley a trade. But at $40 a year the trade gave him little chance to acquire much of the world's goods. Actually, most of his scant wages went to help his family, who were then trying to make a go of farming in Pennsylvania. After about another year as a wandering journeyman printer, in 1831 young Greeley set out for New York to find his fortune, "twenty-five dollars in his pocket and his red-handkerchief bundle on his shoulder." He arrived there with ten dollars.

Like most poor farmers in their section of New Hampshire (and many other places) who were interested in politics, the Greeleys had been ardent Federalists. Not surprisingly, the newspapers that Greeley read as a boy and the one on which he served his apprenticeship were Federalist in tone. During his apprenticeship, though not yet old enough to vote, he considered himself an Adams Republican and strongly sympathized with the efforts of the People's Party to overthrow the Albany Regency. That campaign to win popular suffrage for presidential electors apparently instilled in him a deep and abiding distrust of Van Buren; thereafter, he identified himself with the anti-Jackson, anti-Regency political factions. In turn, he was Adams Republican, Antimason, and Whig.

But in August 1831 when Greeley arrived in New York, he was only a poor journeyman printer in search of a job. He worked on various papers for a couple of years, formed a partnership in 1833 with another young journeyman, and scrounged around for jobwork. Moderate prosperity spurred ambition. In 1834 the young printers turned publishers and brought out the *New Yorker*, a literary weekly. The partnership dissolved in 1836, however. As his share, Greeley took sole ownership of the magazine. Then came the Panic of 1837. Like many other enterprising men, he was on the verge of bankruptcy. At this critical juncture in his career, the proverbial good angel appeared in the guise of Thurlow Weed.

With Weed's assistance, Greeley became editor of a cheap political weekly which the Whigs founded to promote their cause in the 1838 campaign. Greeley, aided by two newly-acquired partners, hung on to the *New Yorker* while he edited the *Jeffersonian* for the Whigs. During the 1840 campaign, he edited the *Log Cabin*, a remarkably popular paper that replaced the *Jeffersonian*.

By the spring of 1841, Greeley enjoyed modest prosperity. Freedom from debt again spurred ambition. He abandoned both the *New Yorker* and the *Log Cabin* to found a new kind of journal, a cheap Whig daily in New York City. Together with a well-to-do partner who supplied some capital and managed the business end, Greeley rapidly established the *Tribune*—particularly its weekly edition—as one of the country's great papers. His intellectual and political influence grew with the growth of the *Tribune's* circulation and prestige. By the mid-1840's, Greeley ranked as junior partner in the famous firm of "Weed, Seward and Greeley."

Though he had experienced desperate poverty, Greeley, unlike Weed and Van Buren, showed little interest and less ability in improving his fortune. To quote the foremost historian of American journalism: "Greeley was never a moneymaker. . . . None of his various enterprises thus far [prior to 1841] had been profitable; and even in later years, when the *Tribune* was showing large profits, he received little more than a salary—having allowed nine-tenths of his proprietary stock holdings to pass into other hands."[16]

According to family position, Francis Granger can be ranked as the Whig equivalent of John A. Dix. Actually, he ranked higher on the social scale than any other major party leader, and stands out as the only Whig leader who had important family connections. Significantly, they were Jeffersonian Republican family connections.

The first Granger in America arrived in Massachusetts from England in 1652 and moved to Connecticut in 1674. Granger's father was born there and was educated at Yale. A successful lawyer, he served as a distinguished member of the Jefferson and Madison cabinets. After thirteen years in the nation's capital, he retired and settled in western New York, "whither his reputation had preceded him, and where he was at once accorded the station to which his abilities entitled him." Elected to the state senate, he "became conspicuous in cooperation with Governor DeWitt Clinton in promoting the [state's] great system of internal improvements. . . ."

16 Frank L. Mott, *American Journalism* (New York, 1950, rev. ed.), 269.

With remarkable fidelity, Francis Granger followed the pattern of public service set by his father. Born in Connecticut, educated at Yale, trained as a lawyer, he practiced his profession in Canandaigua, which might well be called his family seat. In Weed's words, he was "a gentleman of accomplished manners, genial temperament, and fine presence, with fortune, leisure, and a taste for public life." Beginning in 1826, admiring constituents gratified that taste and for a number of terms elected him to the legislature.

As might have been expected, given his father's career, his residence in western New York, and his "taste for public life," Granger emerged as a high-ranking Adams Republican and a prominent Antimason. He was narrowly defeated for governor in 1830 and 1832 and had no better luck in 1836 as the Whig candidate for vice-president. Since he had been the party's standard-bearer during its years of adversity, Granger felt entitled to head the state ticket in 1838 when a Whig victory was almost certain. But "my lord Thurlow" used his persuasive arts, and Seward received the Whig nomination; Granger contented himself with a seat in Congress. Re-elected in 1840, he resigned to become postmaster-general in Harrison's administration.

But Harrison's death and Tyler's succession to the presidency disrupted the first Whig cabinet, and, together with most of its other members, Granger resigned. Faithful constituents re-elected him to Congress in November 1841. He served that term but never again held a major public office, although he remained an influential Whig leader and eventually headed the faction opposed to the Weed-Seward-Greeley wing of the party.[17]

Millard Fillmore celebrated the arrival of the nineteenth century by being born in a log cabin in Cayuga County, New York. His autobiography records, with apparent accuracy, that he came from New England stock and "humble origins." As was true of many other pioneers, Fillmore's father lost his property because of a faulty title. He then moved to another part of that county and took a perpetual lease on a small "farm," wholly uncleared and covered

[17] George S. Conover, ed., *History of Ontario County, New York* (Syracuse, N.Y., 1893), 469-473; Weed, 1: 391-392; Alexander, 1: 358-377, 393-404; 2: 19-21, 47-51, 153-154; Seward, ed., Seward's *Autobiography*, 1: 171-172. No direct information is available concerning Granger's efforts or abilities to increase the family fortune. But if Seward's assessment in 1831 was accurate, it is highly likely that Granger had done so —or at least attempted to do so. Writing to his wife about Granger, Seward noted, "There is yet one quality of Granger's character which you do not dream of—he loves money almost as well as power." *Ibid.*, 1: 172.

with heavy timber. Following the typical pattern of poor boys on the New York frontier, Fillmore spent his first fifteen years learning "to do all kinds of work which is usually done in clearing and cultivating a new farm." (Poor boys do not necessarily become "friends of the poor" when they grow up, but Fillmore's background may partly account for his introduction of the bill to abolish imprisonment for debt and his leadership of western New York debtor-farmers in their fight against the Holland Land Company.)

During childhood Fillmore received some intermittent instruction in village schools, but his education was as sketchy as his father's means were sparse. Misfortune having given the elder Fillmore a "great distaste" for farming, he earnestly wanted his sons to take up some other occupation. "His means did not justify him or them in aspiring to any profession," however, "and therefore, he wished them to learn trades." In 1815 young Fillmore was apprenticed to a wool-carder on a part-time basis. From June to December he carded wool, "went to school some during the winters of 1816 and 1817, and worked on the farm during the spring."

Driven by the desire to rise above the station of a wool carder, Fillmore acquired additional schooling and, by the stroke of good fortune usually found in the careers of self-made men, became a lawyer's clerk. He intermittently taught school and clerked at law in Cayuga and Erie counties until he won admission to the Buffalo bar in 1823. "But not having sufficient confidence in myself to enter into competition with the older members of the [Buffalo] Bar . . . I opened an office at East Aurora, where I practiced till May, 1830; when I formed a partnership with Joseph Clary and removed to Buffalo, which has ever since been my place of residence [written sometime after 1858]."

Little detailed information is available about Fillmore's finances, but it seems likely that his law firm prospered as his political career advanced. The historian of Erie County, however, suggests that although Fillmore made the law "a stepping stone to public life," he was not greatly interested in making it "a direct route to the center of economic affairs."

After he met Weed at an Adams convention in Buffalo, in 1828, Fillmore's political career flourished. The young lawyer impressed Weed, who suggested his nomination for the state assembly. Fillmore was elected as an Antimason and represented Erie County for the next three years. Devotion to Antimasonry, support of bills to abolish imprisonment for debt, and political opposition to the Holland Land Company made Fillmore increasingly popular. Elected to Congress in 1832, he served four terms in the House of Representatives and by 1844 "was well known and at the height of his popularity."

Having been born in a log cabin and filling to perfection the role of the self-made American, the erstwhile wool carder's apprentice envisioned himself as the ideal Whig candidate for vice-president in 1844. For various reasons, his party chose to regard him as the most available Whig gubernatorial nominee, and in that year he was defeated for state rather than national office. In 1848, however, he was elected vice-president; when Taylor died in 1850, he succeeded to the presidency. More than Van Buren, perhaps even more than Jackson, Fillmore demonstrates how every American boy can grow up to be president.[18]

The family status of Luther Bradish can be compared with that of William Marcy. He was born in a small town in Massachusetts, the son of Colonel John Bradish. His father's rank, his own graduation from Williams College in 1804, and his subsequent activities, suggest that he came from at least a moderately well-placed and well-to-do family. Moving to New York City after graduation, Bradish studied law and was admitted to the bar. Apparently his first identification with Franklin County, New York, came in 1815 when he and several partners purchased approximately 30,000 acres in the town of Moira. Bradish eventually took over his partners' interests and continued to buy and sell lands in Franklin and nearby counties until 1859, although he had disposed of most of his holdings for $54,000 in 1835.

Bradish actually took up residence in Franklin County in 1826, and, as befitted the local landed proprietor, his establishment at Moira was "a pretentious one." According to Franklin's historian, since he was "of imposing presence, courtly manners, gracious and benign consideration for others, entertaining in reminiscences of extensive travel and public affairs, erudite in politics and law, and

18 Fillmore's brief autobiographical account of his life until 1828 is printed in Frank H. Severance, ed., "Millard Fillmore Papers," Buffalo Historical Society *Publications*, 10: 3-15. See also *ibid.*, 10: v-xxxv, 17-26, 43-65, and *passim*. Other sources on which this sketch is based are John T. Horton, et al., *History of Northwestern New York*, 1: 88-90, 93-94, 108-109; Alexander, 1: 371-372, 379, 2: 38, 79-89; Van Deusen, *Weed*, 93, 98-104, 127, 132-136. (The quotation concerning Fillmore's attitude toward money-making is from Horton, *op.cit.*, 1: 109.)

a master among men, he became with his first appearance in the county a popular leader and exercised a commanding influence. Whether he should be regarded as the ablest man that this county has ever given to the public service, no adequate record remains to form a basis for judgment, but it probably may be safely claimed for him that he was at least the most accomplished, and that no one here surpassed him in personal popularity and in the public estimation which it is worth while to gain and hold."

The popular Bradish, elected to the assembly in 1827 as an Adams Republican, served two more terms before the Antimasons nominated him for Congress. Although defeated, he continued to lead the Antimasons in his section of the state, and in 1834 helped to organize the Whig Party. From 1836 to 1838 he represented Franklin County in the assembly and served as speaker during his last term. Bradish attracted attention as "an unusually able speaker" whom the northern counties chose for Whig gubernatorial nominee in 1838. Like Granger, his political aspirations were frustrated when Weed artfully secured the prize for Seward. As consolation, Bradish was nominated for lieutenant-governor and served in that post from 1839 to 1842. In the latter year, he finally secured the gubernatorial nomination, only to be defeated by the Democratic resurgence.

The 1842 campaign represented Bradish's last bid for elective office, but he remained an influential figure in the Whig Party. Like Granger and Fillmore, he eventually identified himself with the Whig faction that opposed the Weed-Seward-Greeley triumvirate. And, though the appointment came several years after the time span covered by this chapter, it is worth noting that Bradish was named to the office of United States assistant treasurer for New York by "his early and much esteemed friend, President Fillmore."[19]

B. Middle-Grade Democratic and Whig Leaders: Who Were They?

To say that the major parties recruited their *top* leaders from essentially the same social strata only partially answers the question of who led the Democrats and Whigs. Partial answers frequently give rise to misleading or erroneous conclusions, and comprehensive analysis of the social structure of party leadership requires more

[19] This account is largely based upon the material in Frederick J. Seaver, *Historical Sketches of Franklin County* (Albany, 1918), 696-704. See also Alexander, 2: 18-21, 51; Hammond, *Political Parties*, 2: 263, 293, 480-485; Van Deusen, *Weed*, 134.

than a collective socioeconomic biography of the one or five dozen men who formally fulfilled that role. Political leadership is exercised in ways other than formal public activity. Political power is no less potent for being indirect.[20]

On the crudest level, one question relevant to political leadership is: where did the "sinews of war" come from? Posed more comprehensively: upon which groups did the top party leaders depend for financial, intellectual and moral assistance and stimulus? Did men of wealth strongly tend to give their resources, talents, and prestige to the Whigs rather than to the Democrats? Did a large proportion of the business community—however defined—adhere to the Whig faith?[21] Or, did a Whig orator describe the situation more accurately when, in 1844, he sarcastically rejected the Democratic charge that "the privileged orders," the "rich men," restricted their support to his party? "The rich men are divided;—*how* divided may be seen in the fact that the five largest landed proprietors of this State, each owning [or claiming] a large fraction of the counties in which they reside, are Loco-Foco—*ultra*-Loco-Foco [that is, Democrats]—and that a formidable number of the wealthy merchants of this city are Loco-Foco. *Many of the sons of rich men, ambitious of political preferment are Loco-Foco, though their fathers may be nominal, inactive Whigs* [italics added]."[22]

The last sentence is suggestive. By exploiting the clue it supplies, historans may be able to clear away the rhetorical rubbish and reveal the social structure of party leadership during the Age of Egalitarianism.

After Jackson's Bank veto message in 1832, and particularly after 1837, when Martin Van Buren awoke to the political possibilities of Locofocoism (discussed in Chapter V), Democratic rhetoric was designed to sound something like class war. One Whig response to that rhetoric was to portray the Democrats as "desperate and

---

20 See Charles E. Merriam and Harold Foote Gosnell, *The American Party System* (New York, 1949, 4th ed.), 146-163; Heinz Eulau, et al., *Political Behavior* (Glencoe, Ill., 1956), 175-204.

21 The thesis that they did seems to have received its first full statement in Dixon Ryan Fox, *The Decline of Aristocracy In The Politics of New York*, 285, 409-439, and *passim*. The evidence it adduces for dividing the parties along class lines is flimsy, where it is not erroneous. The basis for this conclusion will appear in Chapter VII through IX, where an analysis is made of 1844 group voting patterns. The fullest expression of the thesis that American political history has been an enduring struggle between the business community and "the other sections of society" is presented in Arthur M. Schlesinger, Jr., *The Age of Jackson*, 505, and *passim*.

22 *New York Tribune* (w.), October 19, 1844, p. 1.

revolutionary enemies of Law and Order" who would impose "agrarian and destructive legislation" and bring about "popular demoralization, ruin and revolution. . . ." But class war rhetoric need not reflect reality. In fact, it has frequently been used to conceal rather than to reveal the socioeconomic status and the political objectives of those who use it. Moreover, it cannot be automatically assumed that class war rhetoric actually influenced political reality and changed the social structure of political leadership.

After long years of Antimasonic frenzy and Jacksonian counter-frenzy, who listened, and who believed? More precisely, who from 1834 to 1844 took the campaign claptrap literally? Had not partisan rhetoric come to be regarded as another form of American folklore, an oratorical indulgence to be enjoyed at regular intervals and ignored once the election was over and the country again "saved"? Granted that party loyalties were passionate and deeply rooted and that politics intensely concerned Americans in that decade. It does not follow that *all* aspects of the political process were regarded with equal seriousness and that campaign rhetoric was treated as Holy Writ.

The relative stability of New York voting patterns from 1832 to 1844 (discussed in Chapter VII) suggests that later historians have been more vulnerable to partisan claims than were contemporaries who experienced them directly. Populistic rhetoric had become so standard a feature of election campaigns that voters may well have developed immunity to it. (Do American voters take American politicians at face value today?) Moreover, the daily experiences of contemporaries gave them a real-life basis for assessing how reliable were partisan claims. In short, political rhetoric is not a reliable source for inferences about the social structure of American political leadership.

But an 1845 *Tribune* editorial made specific claims, which are subject to verification. "The Whigs are by no means all wealthy, nor are the wealthy all Whigs. A large proportion of the Capitalists, Landlords, Bankers, Brokers, etc., belong to the other party. For instance, of the manors of this State, we observe that far more than half the leased lands are owned by those who belong to what is called the Democratic party.—Most of the Banks of our City were chartered by that party, and a good many are still controlled by its members and officered from its ranks. The present Collector of Customs at this Port stepped out of a Bank Presidency into the Collectorship.

There are many members of the so-called 'Democratic' party in this city who are worth from $100,000 each to $1,000,000 or over. [italics added]."[23]

The design of this study does not permit the research necessary to test all the claims made in the editorial quoted above. But testing one of them does provide a basis for assessing the *Tribune*'s claims about party divisions among economic elite groups in New York.

1. Ratification Meeting Officers Who Were "Wealthy Citizens"

In January 1845, the sixth edition of a fascinating social document was published; the lengthy title suggests its contents: *Wealth and Biography of the Wealthy Citizens of New York City, Comprising An Alphabetical Arrangement of Persons Estimated To Be Worth $100,000, And Upwards—With The Sums Appended To Each Name. . . .*[24] If the *Tribune*'s claims are verifiable, the men listed on that roll-call should not have displayed heavily disproportionate preference for the Whig Party. And for our purposes, the publication date could not have been better timed. If the much-advertised Democratic conversion to Locofocoism in 1837 to 1838 had really driven or frightened the "rich men" away, the purge should have been complete by 1844, when the sixth edition was prepared.

In order to carry out this test, some sampling procedure must be devised for an analysis of the register of approximately one thousand *Wealthy Citizens*. Since our aim here is to get at the social structure of party leadership, not the sources of mass support, it is desirable to find an objective basis for classifying as "middle-grade party leaders" a limited number of "Wealthy Citizens." I believe that the independent criteria used to draw up two separate lists satisfy that requirement.

In New York City, during the 1844 campaign, both the Democrats and Whigs held their customary great public meetings to "ratify" the nominees of their national conventions. Designed to heal intraparty wounds and to rally the faithful against the enemy, these meetings followed standard formats. Much the same considerations, we may assume, governed both parties in their choice of the

23 *Ibid.*, September 20, 1845, p. 3.
24 That document (as well as several precursors) is conveniently reproduced in Henry Wysham Lanier, *A Century of Banking In New York: 1822-1922* (New York, 1922), 151-184. It is alphabetically arranged.

president and many vice-presidents who nominally controlled them. Since the ratification meetings formed an important part of the campaign, in all likelihood politically active men, who can accurately be classified as middle-grade party leaders, were selected for these positions. Although the *Wealthy Citizens* register cannot be considered a comprehensive collective biography, we can learn from it how many of the men who made the honor list at Democratic and Whig ratification meetings also made its pages.[25]

Analysis of the register essentially supports the *Tribune*'s claim about party divisions among the "rich men" of New York City. Of the 54 Democrats honored by their party, the president and 13 vice-presidents, or 26 per cent, were "Wealthy Citizens."[26] Of the 35 Whigs honored by their party, 12 vice-presidents, or 34 per cent, belonged to the same class.[27] Not large enough to be significant in any case, the percentage difference disappears when *the same size sample is used*. Neither party list was alphabetical. Men's party status as well as their prestige in the community apparently determined their rank order position. Thus, of the first 10 names on each list, 60 per cent were "Wealthy Citizens." When we restrict analysis to the 35 highest ranking Democrats (the total number in the Whig sample), the proportion of Democratic rich men rises to 34 per cent. On this level of leadership, therefore, the Democrats and the Whigs had drawn upon rich men in the same proportion. Using another criterion

25 The Whig list is taken from the *New York Morning Express*, May 7, 1844, p. 2; the Democratic list from the *New York Morning News*, September 17, 1844, p. 2. The Democratic meeting in September was used because Van Buren's defeat for the nomination at the party's national convention had aroused bitter resentment in New York. It took several months for important sections of the New York party leadership to become reconciled to the Polk and Dallas ticket. Thus the *News's* headline for its story on the September meeting read, "Old Tammany in A Blaze Of Glory/Tremendous Re-Union Of the Democracy of New York."

26 John Targee, Stephen Allen, Preserved Fish, J. M. Bradhurst, Peter Cooper, Charles K. Ferris, Peter Smith, Walter Bowne, Abraham Van Ness, George Arcularis, Charles A. Clinton [DeWitt Clinton's son!], John B. Lasalla, Isaac L. Varian Beach, John Pettigrew. As printed, the list totaled 55 names, but one could not be identified positively. Several men who could have been "M. Burke" appear in contemporary directories and the widow of "M. R. Burke" was listed among the wealthy citizens in 1845. Abraham Van Ness's name was misprinted as "Abram Van Nest" in the *News*, but no such name appears in the city directories. From the description in the *Wealthy Citizens* register, it is clear that "Van Nest" was "Van Ness." See John Doggett, Jr., *The New-York City Directory for 1844-1845* (New York, 1844), 358. As was true of the top leaders, the Democratic list included more men of non-British stock than did the Whig list.

27 Stephen Whitney, William Adee, William H. Aspinwall, Robert Hyslop, John Haggerty, Abraham R. Lawrence, John Drake, Peletiah Perit, Philip Hone, William Samuel Johnson, James W. Gerard, Gardiner G. Howland.

to select a sample of rich, middle-grade party leaders, we get the same results.

2. "Wealthy Citizens" identified as Party Leaders

The *Wealthy Citizens* register provided widely varying information for each entry. It ranged from a bare listing of name and estimated worth ("McBrair James—100,000") to a lush, full-page biography celebrating John Jacob Astor's rise from furs to landed riches. But clearly, the compilers had not attempted systematically to ascertain or to list political affiliations. Only a small proportion of the entries contained such information and a number of well-known party leaders were not identified as such (for example, David Dudley Field, Samuel Ruggles, John Van Buren). Where political affiliations were noted, however, the descriptions suggest that they enjoyed at least some leadership status in their party. Typical characterizations read: "An influential man in the democratic ranks," "the democratic candidate for Mayor at the last election," "distinguished as a Whig politician," "the standing Whig candidate for Mayor."

Twenty five wealthy citizens were explicitly identified with the major parties: 13 Democrats (52 per cent) and 12 Whigs (48 per cent).[28] For all practical purposes, this finding parallels that obtained from analyzing ratification meeting officers. Because the two lists were based on independent criteria, it seems particularly noteworthy that they yielded the same results. (There was little overlapping; only five names appear on both lists.)

Aside from supporting the *Tribune*'s claims, our analysis of party divisions among New York's wealthy citizens is also consonant with our findings about the top Democratic and Whig leaders. I do not claim to have "proved" that the men who led and controlled both major parties in New York belonged to the same socioeconomic strata. I do claim, however, that the above data make that hypothesis appear potentially verifiable.[29] If subsequent research does verify

28 The Democrats were David Banks, Henry Brevoort, Benjamin F. Butler, Johnathan I. Coddington, Charles G. Ferris, Preserved Fish, Eli Hart, William Paulding, John Pettigrew, John Targee, Johnathan Thompson, William W. Todd, James R. Whiting. The Whigs were Henry Andrew, R. M. Blatchford, Richard F. Carman, Edwin B. Clayton, Moses H. Grinnell, Oliver T. Hewlett, Philip Hone, William Samuel Johnson, Robert Jones, Gulian C. Verplanck, Caleb S. Woodhull.

29 Additional support for the conclusions presented here is found in a study of New York party leadership during the 1850's. See an unusually thorough Master's Essay, Norman Dain, "The Social Composition of the Leadership of Tammany Hall in New York City: 1855-1865" (Columbia University, M.A., 1957), 94-99, and *passim*.

it, and if the same situation is found to have obtained elsewhere during the 1840's, American historians will be confronted by this interesting and difficult question: what, if anything, differentiated men who belonged to the same socioeconomic strata but who led parties that advocated different and directly conflicting theories of liberalism? For, as I shall now try to show, contrary to the concept of Jacksonian Democracy, party battles in New York cannot be viewed primarily as battles between "liberals" and "conservatives."

CHAPTER V

POSITIVE VERSUS NEGATIVE LIBERALISM

By 1834, the New York Whigs and Democrats had committed themselves irrevocably to a social order based on political equality (for white men). But the Whigs translated the post-1815 egalitarian impulse into a philosophy of the *positive* liberal state, the Democrats translated it into a philosophy of the *negative* liberal state. Thus when we focus upon political economy and social legislation, we find that the parties actually stood for competing concepts of liberalism. When we focus upon certain types of "moral legislation" (for example, Sunday laws, temperance), however, we find that the "conservative-liberal" dichotomy did tend to exist. (Party differences over "moral legislation" are discussed in later chapters.)

A. Federalist, Whig, and Democratic Theories
of the State

Federalist and Whig theories of political economy seem to present a clear example of continuity in American thought. Both parties subscribed to the doctrines that the state had the capacity as well as the right to exercise broad powers over the economy, and the duty to serve as a positive instrument to realize the Good Society. Historians have therefore traditionally treated the Whigs as neo-Federalists. But commitment to the positive state is not the only criterion of historical continuity. If it were, we would characterize the New Deal as the twentieth century version of eighteenth century Federalism, and the "Brain Trusters" as the ideological descendants of Alexander Hamilton.

As these analogies are designed to suggest, I believe that inquiry into historical continuity requires us to do more than ask whether political parties favored positive or negative government; we must also ask about their concepts of the Good Society, their major objectives, and their methods of achieving them. When we answer those questions systematically, if the New York results are representative, the similarities between Federalists and Whigs will show up as superficial and the differences as basic. (No implication is intended, of course, that all Federalists or all Whigs or all Democrats shared the same beliefs. The problem is to determine what parties stood for and practiced, not what individuals believed.)

The transition from Federalist to Whig theories of political economy fails to demonstrate straight-line continuity; it more nearly demonstrates history unfolding according to the Hegelian dialectic. Expressed summarily, the Federalist thesis was built on the foundation of the positive *paternal* state. Put another way, the Federalists practiced mercantilism. Mercantilism, which developed in a number of European countries after the breakdown of the feudal economy, was less a well-defined body of doctrine than "a set of theories which explained or underlay the practices of statesmen for a considerable time" after 1500.

Mercantilists agreed that a strong central state was necessary to progress and that its power could legitimately be exercised *in any manner* calculated to increase national wealth and prosperity. They regarded competition among nations pursuing the same objectives as part of the natural order of things. Within the nation, however, they regarded competition as less natural and desirable, and favored legal monopolies to gain their ends. But whether action took the form of monopoly, protection, regulation, subsidy, or direct participation in enterprise, mercantilists regarded the state as the best governor of economic development and growth.[1]

As practiced by the Federalists, mercantilism stressed government aid to enterprise and minimized regulation. "In matters of industry," Hamilton observed, "human enterprise ought doubtless to be left free in the main; not fettered by too much regulation; but practical politicians know that it may be beneficially stimulated by prudent aids and encouragements on the part of the government."[2] Like their European counterparts, Federalist politicians were prepared to grant monopolies—even to themselves, or to friends—whenever that seemed to be the best way to increase national wealth and prosperity.

Inevitably, troublesome questions arose: Who decided what *form* of government intervention was best, and how did they obtain and preserve the power to implement decisions? What criteria determined which areas of the economy should be free, which controlled or aided? On what basis were legal monopolies to be granted, and who was to get them?

[1] Eric Roll, *A History of Economic Thought* (New York, 1947, rev. ed.), 49-84.
[2] As quoted in Sidney Fine, *Laissez Faire and the General-Welfare State* (Ann Arbor, Mich., 1956), 15. I have profited considerably from reading this book, but disagree with its classification of the Whigs as Neo-Federalists.

To concede that the Federalists expected to profit personally from the state's direction of the economy does not require us to accept an economic determinist explanation of their program.[3] Their program derived from the traditional doctrine of state intervention which dominated the climate of opinion in late eighteenth and early nineteenth century America. Hamiltonians, it must be emphasized, only adapted to local conditions the doctrines that European statesmen had preached and practiced for centuries. *And mercantilist doctrines had worked.* The historical record showed that positive intervention by strong central states had brought about economic and social progress more effectively than had the earlier maze of regulation by local governments, feudal contracts, and canon law. Though feudal contracts and canon law did not govern the United States, the new nation did suffer from localistic regulation and parochial thinking.

It seems unnecessary, therefore, to rely upon economic determinism in order to explain the politico-economic program which Federalist leaders developed. Undoubtedly they had a strong, healthy concern for their own interests as well as for those of the groups to which they belonged or with which they identified. But the crucial consideration is that they did not feel compelled to choose between what was profitable and what was right. Their ideology derived from an elitist, paternalistic, antidemocratic concept of the Good Society in which all forms of enterprise, not only agriculture, flourished. In other words, while rejecting the notion that ideas are a direct reflex of economics, we can say that a reciprocal relationship existed between the ideology and interests of Federalists.

For our purposes, it is unnecessary to ask how or why Hamiltonian Federalists could believe simultaneously in a government by the "rich and the well-born" and a society characterized by an expanding, well-rounded economy beneficial to all. The point is that they did. Since their vision of the Good Society, their political theory, and their political economy were interrelated, the Federalists were *logically* consistent in advocating a program based upon the concept of the positive paternal state. The following Federalist propositions may be untrue in fact, but they are not contradictory: 1) Control over the economy by a strong central government is mandatory to the well-being of all members of the nation; 2) Only a limited number of people have the capacity to participate in the decision-making

[3] For the classic statement of the economic determinist explanation, see Charles A. Beard, *Economic Origins of Jeffersonian Democracy* (New York, 1915), *passim.*

process, a consideration that must be taken into account if state intervention is to aid, not impede, progress.

As the Hegelian dialectic demands, an antithetical concept arose to challenge and eventually transform the mercantilist thesis. Developed and summarized by Adam Smith, the new doctrine held that the economy would progress more rapidly if: a) legal monopolies were abolished; b) the state were reduced to the role of policeman; c) within broad legal limits, individuals were given the freest rein to pursue their self-interest. The new doctrine hauled down the old aristocratic slogan, *noblesse oblige*, and replaced it with egoistic slogans such as "enrichez-vous" and *laissez faire*. In short, not the positive paternal state but the negative liberal state would achieve the Good Society.[4]

If history really followed Hegel, the new concept of the negative liberal state would have transformed itself into reality before the final synthesis was reached. But, as a series of recent studies have demonstrated, in America the new concept was first honored in theory by some men (for example, Thomas Jefferson) and for the most part ignored in practice by all state governments.[5] Specifically, before the Democratic Party, which claimed Jefferson as its founding father, made any successful attempt to implement *laissez faire* in New York, the Whigs produced a new synthesis, the *positive liberal state*.

Perhaps the best way to trace the evolution of the new synthesis is to sketch the events that culminated in New York's famous "free banking law" of 1838. Apart from the intrinsic significance of the law, its legislative history dramatically highlights the differences between the Whig and Democratic models of the liberal state.

B. The Movement for Free Banking in New York

First organized in the late eighteenth century, banks were assumed to have a public character in New York and elsewhere throughout the country.[6] Although private individuals operated them for private profit, they were regarded as instruments to implement public policy

---

[4] For a cogent analysis of the rise of classical economics, see Roll, *op.cit.*, 84-211.

[5] See the recent series of studies sponsored by the Committee on Research in Economic History. They are conveniently listed in a perceptive and comprehensive review article, Robert A. Lively, "The American System," *Business History Review*, 29:81-96 (March 1955). For a discussion of state regulatory activities in relation to a specific segment of the economy, see Lee Benson, *Merchants—Farmers—And Railroads* (Cambridge, Mass., 1955), 1-28.

[6] Bray Hammond, *Banks And Politics In America*, 67-71.

and to advance the Commonwealth's interests. "Within reasonable limits," Hamilton maintained, "[banks] ought to consider it as a principal object to promote beneficial public purposes."[7] In exchange for the privileges written into their charters, banks were expected to perform certain duties and to observe certain regulations— also written into their charters. Whether the banks abused privileges and ignored duties and whether they were proper instruments to execute public policy is not significant here. What is significant is that bank charters were granted on the assumption that the public interest would be directly served and the state would exercise its right to regulate the institutions to which it gave corporate life.[8]

By 1804, banking had become so vital a concern of the state that a restraining law was passed which prohibited "all unincorporated associations from issuing notes or loaning money." Until then it had been possible to operate a bank without benefit of charter privileges. The restraining law abolished "free banking," however, and prohibited anyone from performing those functions without the express sanction of the legislature. To plug loopholes, another restraining law was passed in 1818 that even more effectively prevented private banking or note issue.[9] In essence, the restraining laws transformed banking into a legal monopoly and gave to the legislature the power to make final decisions concerning the establishment of banks. Neither the "laws of trade" nor the private judgment of entrepreneurs decided their number, size, or location. Thus, by the very terms of its existence, banking in New York constituted a public enterprise inseparably connected with party and factional politics.

1. Early Bank Charters and Politics

Since bank charters were highly prized but infrequently and irregularly bestowed, and since state action directly influenced their operations and profits, men interested in bank charters had to be interested in politics. If they were not politically active themselves, they had to have influence with active politicians. As a result, as early as 1799, banks ranked high among the prizes won in party battles.[10] The passage of time only increased the importance of bank-

---

[7] As quoted in *ibid.*, 76.

[8] Robert E. Chaddock, *The Safety Fund Banking System in New York: 1829-1866* (National Monetary Commission, Washington, 1910), 233-257.

[9] *Ibid.*, 234-235; Charles Z. Lincoln, *The Constitutional History of New York* (Rochester, N.Y., 1906), 2: 31-32; Hammond, *Banks and Politics*, 577-580.

[10] Chaddock, *op.cit.*, 234-235.

ing (and related) issues in New York politics. More charges of corruption were made than proven, but scandals were so commonplace that the 1821 Convention wrote into the state constitution a clause requiring a two thirds vote of the legislature to pass a bank charter. As might have been foreseen, instead of taking banking out of politics, the clause operated in reverse.[11]

New Yorkers interested in banking were forced to calculate the value of being on the winning political side during the 1820's. Since the Van Buren Republicans won almost all the time, it is not surprising that prominent bankers such as Benjamin Knower, Thomas W. Olcott, Erastus Corning, and Charles E. Dudley were also prominent members of the Albany Regency.[12] As was generally true of the "spoils system," it was not the Regency that inaugurated the practice of using the distribution of bank charters and stock to strengthen its political machine. But the Regency developed the practice to a high degree of efficiency. Moreover, despite the abuses it permitted, the Safety Fund System, sponsored and controlled by the Regency, represented a significant, positive innovation in New York and American financial history.

2. The Safety Fund Banking System

Recommended by Van Buren in his 1829 gubernatorial message, the law which established the Safety Fund had been worked out and steered through the legislature by Thomas Olcott, Benjamin Knower, and "a few other intelligent and patriotic bankers." Their intimate acquaintance with the financial world[13] enabled them to understand "that banks constitute a system, being peculiarly sensitive to one another's operations, and not a mere aggregate of free agents."[14] Under the provisions of the law, banks would contribute to a general reserve fund administered by the state; this fund would be used to redeem the notes of any institution that failed. According to Joshua Forman, the law's originator, "[Banks] enjoy in common the exclusive right of making a paper currency for the people of the state and by the same rule should in common be answerable for that paper."[15] The state, by making them liable for each other's operations,

---

[11] B. Hammond, *Banks and Politics*, 578-579.

[12] Jabez D. Hammond, *History of Political Parties in the State of New York*, 2: 157, 298-299; Ivor D. Spencer, "William L. Marcy Goes Conservative," *MVHR*, 31: 214.

[13] J. Hammond, *Political Parties*, 2: 297-302.

[14] B. Hammond, *Banks and Politics*, 556-559.

[15] Joshua Forman, quoted in *ibid.*, 557.

would simultaneously fulfill its responsibilities to protect the public and strengthen the banking system.[16]

Although opponents may have been correct in charging that political considerations influenced strongly the establishment of the Safety Fund System, the Regency deserves praise for having sponsored a significant banking innovation. It cannot be said, however, that the Safety Fund act derived from "Jeffersonian and Jacksonian liberalism." The Regency did not strike a blow for free enterprise. It improved upon the Federalist model of the positive paternal state.

Under the Safety Fund System, banking became to an unprecedented extent a tightly controlled legal monopoly. The legislature decided who could operate a bank, where it would be located, and how it would be operated. Commitment to the state rights doctrine had not yet led the Regency to embrace *laissez faire*, and its *Hamiltonian* response to the popular demand for a responsible and efficient banking system served to enlarge the powers, duties, and functions of the state. An example is the establishment of a board of bank commissioners—probably the most significant innovation of the Safety Fund act.

As noted above, bank regulation in the United States dates from the very beginning of bank operation under the charter system. And each charter contained provisions designed to guard against abuse of the public powers granted to private enterprisers. Prior to 1829, however, charters were regarded essentially as self-enforcing instruments, and no standing agency was charged with the responsibility of supervising banks. Now that banks had become mutually liable and would suffer from each other's errors and misdeeds, the fallacy of control by self-enforcing charter could no longer be tolerated. To protect the banks as well as the public, the "intelligent and patriotic bankers" who shaped the Regency's policy had the state resort to direct intervention.

The law called for three commissioners to supervise the operation of Safety Fund banks: one to be chosen by the governor and *two* by the banks. To insure compliance with the law's stringent provisions, the commissioners were given broad powers and responsibilities. They were required to visit each bank four times annually (more often, if three other institutions requested it); they could examine bank officials under oath and make as thorough an investigation as was

16 In addition to the works cited above in notes 8-15, for an enlightening discussion of the Safety Fund banking system, see Fritz Redlich, *The Molding of American Banking* (New York, 1951), 88-95.

necessary to determine a bank's solvency; and, by appropriate court action, they could even close a bank. Under the Regency-sponsored and written law, the state acted more positively and "paternally" than ever before toward New York banks. Not surprisingly, some of its opponents charged that the Safety Fund act interfered with enterprise and subjected banks to "inquisitors."[17]

No doubt, precursors can be found—historians traditionally assume that nothing is ever the beginning of anything—but establishment of the New York Bank Commission must be regarded as an innovation of prime importance in American political economy. It effectively initiated the independent regulatory agencies which thereafter played an increasingly dominant role in controlling and regulating the American economy. The point here, however, is that the politicians responsible for its creation in 1829 had won election in 1828, wrapped in what they claimed was the mantle of Thomas Jefferson, marching under the banner of Andrew Jackson.

3. The Whigs Campaign against State "Monied Monopolies"

Passage of the Safety Fund Act, we recall, was followed by a rising outcry against "licensed monopolies." Since the Regency continued to control the state that chartered and supervised the banks, the antimonopoly movement necessarily became an anti-Regency movement. Although the Jacksonian attack upon the Monster Bank, which really got underway in 1832, may temporarily have diverted attention from the homegrown "banking monopolies," it could not do so indefinitely—particularly after the Monster's charter expired in 1836. In one respect the Jacksonian campaign boomeranged. Clearly, the Bank War intensified interest in and concern about state banks. And it is primarily in this unintentional way that the Jackson Party contributed to the antimonopoly movement in New York. After Jackson's veto "electrified the nation," the Regency, having sponsored and profited from the Safety Fund System, waged all-out war against the "federal monopoly." But it recoiled from using the antimonopoly principle *on the state level.* Quick to see the political possibilities, Thurlow Weed found one consolation in the 1834 Whig defeat. By giving the Democrats control of Congress,

---

[17] Chaddock, *op.cit.*, 259-269; Redlich, *op.cit.*, 91-93; B. Hammond, *Banks and Politics*, 559.

he argued, the election "terminated the U.S. Bank War" and thus spiked the Regency's most powerful weapon. The Bank's disappearance from the political scene, however, did not mean that banks and exciting questions relating to banks had also disappeared. "The people have learnt that they can put down Monied Monopolies. This is a lesson which they will be slow to forget. Our State is literally groaning under the accumulating power of these *MONOPOLIES*. *Industry and enterprise, at every turn we take, are cramped and trammeled by INCORPORATED COMPANIES* [italics added]. Our Statute Books are filled with *CHARTERS* conferring advantages upon the *few* at the expense of the *many*. Our whole course of Legislation, for the last ten years, has tended to make the '*rich richer and the poor poorer*.' "[18]

4. The Locofoco Conception of "Equal Rights"

Effective termination of the Bank War in 1834 simultaneously intensified the Whig antimonopoly drive against the Regency and stimulated the antimonopoly movement within the Democratic Party. Like the Working Men in 1829, the "Locofocos" began as a small dissident faction in Tammany Hall. In 1835 they broke away, charging that "the Republican Party had become a monopoly aristocratic party." Convinced that reform was impossible within Tammany, they organized the short-lived yet influential Equal Rights Party.[19] Largely confined to New York City, it never attracted any mass following; its high-water mark was the twelve per cent it received in the 1837 mayoralty election.[20] But, as with many dissident movements in American history, the Equal Rights Party influenced the major political parties rather than having a direct impact on events.[21]

By the time the Locofocos appeared on the political scene, demands for equality had become a familiar theme in New York. But in the Locofoco interpretation, equality could be achieved only by a complete repudiation of the positive state. To the Locofocos, equal rights and the negative state formed inseparable concepts. Analysis of their "Declaration of Rights," "Proposed Constitution," and

[18] *Albany Evening Journal* (s.w.), November 18, 1834, p. 3.

[19] F. Byrdsall, *The History of the Loco-Foco or Equal Rights Party* . . . (New York, 1842), 13-54; Carl N. Degler, "An Inquiry Into The Locofoco Party" (Columbia University, M.A., 1947), 7-55.

[20] Calculated from data in the *Whig Almanac For 1838* (New York, 1838), 4.

[21] Apparently the Locofocos did not generally become known as the Equal Rights Party until 1836. Degler, *op.cit.*, 53-54.

similar documents reveals their overriding concern with the alleged inequalities inevitably resulting from any kind of positive state action.[22] They crystallized, codified, and extended the antistate doctrines preached by classical economists. Like the Antimasons, they invoked egalitarian values and demanded "equal rights." Unlike them, they converted egalitarianism into an ideological weapon to destroy the authority and prestige of the state and its officers.

According to the Locofocos, equal rights would be assured if no charters were granted to any corporate or "artificial" body; if no exclusive privileges, special advantages, or any form of monopoly were granted to any individual or company; if every member of the community could engage in any "profession, business, or trade not hurtful to the community," without "charter, license, impediment, or prohibition" (literally anyone could function as doctor, lawyer, banker, etc., but since they wanted to abolish license rather than encourage it, the Locofocos included the "not hurtful" clause); if no men or institutions were exempt from any tax imposed on the rest of the community; and if none but general and equal laws were passed, "declaring the duties and reciprocities of the community and its members to each other respectively; protecting individuals in the enjoyment of their natural rights of property, prohibiting aggressions on them, and specifying the redress for all aggressions and the mode of obtaining it."[23]

In sum, the Locofocos wanted to destroy the positive state which mercantilism had created, and allow every man to pursue his own self-interest, unrestricted by government unless he trespassed upon the "natural rights" of other men. In an age that antedated the rise of "Big Business," they expressed that variant of the small-producer ideology in which the state is regarded as the natural enemy of men who cannot hope to control it. After the Civil War, small producers increasingly came to regard belief in state action as a central tenet of the egalitarian ideology.

Since the Locofocos preached anticorporation, anticharter doc-

---

[22] These documents are conveniently reprinted in Byrdsall, *op.cit.*, 27, 39-42, 57-58, 68-69, 71-74, 147-152, 163-170. They show that the extraordinarily negative liberalism of the Locofocos derived essentially from a mechanical transference of ideas proclaimed during the French Revolution. To describe the Locofocos as radicals fails to recognize their intellectual shallowness; they believed that the "Declaration of the Rights of Man" invoked in France against a "despotic monarchy" could properly be invoked in the United States after it had achieved political democracy.

[23] *Ibid.*, 164-166.

trines, and particularly opposed any banking system based on paper currency, they inevitably broke with the Democratic Party built by Martin Van Buren. The intense desire of many entrepreneurs and would-be entrepreneurs to secure bank charters during the great boom that preceded the Panic of 1837 helped to precipitate that break. Since the Democratic Party controlled the state apparatus, it bore direct responsibility for the corruption and abuses that accompanied satisfaction of those desires.[24] Locofocos viewed such developments as absolute proof that positive state action resulted in the degradation of republican institutions. To quote the Antimasonic-sounding rhetoric of their first historian, they "regarded the Banking system of the State of New York, with its safety fund league and restraining law, as a hydra-headed monster whose overthrow was essential to human rights and human progress. They saw it was *absolutely vain to hope for any reform voluntarily* [italics added] from that party which had connected itself almost indissolubly with the system."[25]

Convinced that voluntary Democratic "reform" was impossible, the Locofocos exercised their option to try to speed reform by pressure from without. Thus in 1836, following the path broken for them by the Working Men in 1830, they formed a coalition with the Whigs. Aided by the Whigs, they elected one congressman and three members of the state legislature.[26] Then came the disastrous Panic and in May 1837 the suspension of specie payments by the New York banks. Events demonstrated daily that the Regency's Safety Fund System—"the best banking system in the world," according to its sponsors—could not cope with the economic situation. As crisis deepened, events also demonstrated that the Democrats faced serious political trouble on both the state and national levels. In some respects, the situation resembled 1832. Democratic political strategy again dictated a sharp turn to "radicalism"—if "radicalism" is understood to mean the extreme antistate and hard-money doctrines preached by classical economists of the David Ricardo school.

Whether from expediency, conviction, or both, the Democratic Party in 1837 adopted the same Locofoco "reform" program that it contemptuously rejected in palmier days. Particularly after President Van Buren surveyed the political prospects, decided to bring

---

[24] J. Hammond, *Political Parties*, 2: 447-448; Lester H. Rifkin, "William Leggett: Journalist-Philosopher of Agrarian Democracy in New York," *New York History*, 32: 51-52 (January 1951).

[25] Byrdsall, 140.   [26] *Ibid.*, 78-97; Degler, 55-64.

in his September bill of divorcement against the country's banks, and recommended establishment of an Independent Treasury system, most Locofocos saw little point in remaining outside the party fold. "Resolved, That the Message delivered by Martin Van Buren, to the present 25th Congress of the United States, for its able and convincing Arguments, and for its cogent, equitable, and constitutional objections to a National Bank, and for its clear, just, and practicable recommendation of dispensation with State Banks as fiscal agents, and the adoption of a governmental system of finance, predicated exclusively on the constitutional currency—gold and silver, awakens the admiration and deserves the applause of every friend of Equal Rights, and will elicit the approbation of the whole genuine Democracy of the Union."[27]

The Locofocos really applauded themselves. To the extent that their program applied to federal control over banking and currency, Van Buren had implemented it. On the state level, they won a less sweeping ideological victory in 1837. But in 1838 the New York Democratic Party abandoned the Safety Fund "hydra-headed monster" and adopted the Locofoco formula for the cure and prevention of banking and currency evils.[28]

5. Free Banking—Democratic and Whig Versions

Though the Locofoco formula differed in some respects from that of the "Radical Democrats" (their allies and, to a large extent, their rural counterparts), both the urban and rural Democratic antimonopolists essentially agreed that banking should be "left open to the free competition of all who choose to enter into that pursuit."[29] They agreed also that no charter should be granted that gave bank stockholders the vital privileges of limited liability and note issue. In fact, their whole-hearted distrust of and contempt for the state and their thoroughgoing commitment to *laissez faire*, can be deduced from the *New York Evening Post*'s prescription for a proper "free banking law." The *Post* opposed the bill which the Whigs had introduced early in the 1838 legislative session: "We regard all this

---

[27] Byrdsall, 161-162; Rifkin, in *New York History*, 32: 53-55. For an incisive analysis of the "radicalism" of the "hard-money Jacksonians," see Joseph Dorfman, "The Jackson Wage-Earner Thesis," *American Historical Review*, 54: 296-306 (January 1949).

[28] See the "Address and Resolutions" of the 1838 Democratic state convention in *Albany Argus* (s.w.), September 18, 1838, p. 2.

[29] This was the formula of William Leggett, the Locofoco's leading theorist. Quoted in Degler, 12-13.

lumber of restrictions, formalities, and ceremonies of supervision, as originating in a false principle, and pregnant with mischievous effects. The more completely you leave trade to itself, whether it be trade in money or goods, the more beneficially for the community will it be transacted."

Reliance should be placed not on the state but on the individual entrepreneur: "In our view, the simpler the provisions of such a law, the freer it leaves the individual in his pursuit, and the less it tampers with his doings in the way of supervision, the better."[30]

When we consider the actual nature of the New York Free Banking Act of 1838, it is ironic that American historiography has tended to credit the Locofocos and their Radical Democratic allies with its passage. That they strenuously agitated against monopoly and called for "free banking" is true. But they failed to originate, direct, or monopolize the agitation. In one form or another, "free banking" had been advocated in New York since 1825,[31] and, more significantly, the 1838 law violated some of their most cherished doctrines of political economy.

The free banking bill, introduced and passed by the Whigs, repudiated both the Hamiltonian doctrine of the positive paternal state (embodied in the Safety Fund System) and the Jeffersonian doctrine of the negative liberal state (embodied in the Independent Treasury). In effect, the *Tribune* emphasized those points some years later during a running battle with the *Evening Post* over party credit for "Our Free Banking System." According to the *Tribune*, a great popular uprising had occurred in 1837 and 1838 against "the unsoundness and general viciousness of the system of Political Monopoly Banking which had been matured and upheld by the supporters of Jackson and Van Buren. . . . As to 'the little band of Loco-Focos' to whom so much credit is awarded by *The Post*, their declared position was that of general hostility to Paper Money Issues or to any form of Banking which did not involve the unlimited Personal Liability of every stockholder in a Bank. They never devised nor proposed

---

[30] *Evening Post for the Country* (s.w.), March 22, April 16, 1838, p. 2.

[31] Redlich, *op.cit.*, 188-190, 200-201; B. Hammond, *Banks and Politics*, 573-584. Apparently both Redlich and Hammond were led astray by the published recollections of Abijiah Mann, Jr. Mann, a Radical Democratic leader from Herkimer County, claimed to have made a major contribution to the free banking bill. Actually, he opposed it relentlessly during the 1838 legislative session and voted against it. See the assembly vote on the bill, *Albany Evening Journal* (s.w.), April 6, 1838, p. 2. For the Reverend John McVickar's contribution to free banking theory, see Joseph Dorfman, *The Economic Mind in American Civilization* (New York, 1946), 2: 521-522, 657-659, 717.

any system of Banking at all resembling that created by our General Law.

"We [Greeley] were in Albany during the greater part of the Session of 1838 engaged in reporting the proceedings of the Assembly. We know that the General Banking Law was Whig in its inception, Whig in the character of a large majority of its supporters, and that the opposition it encountered, whether of a direct or of a guerilla character, came almost entirely from the self-styled 'Democracy' and especially from the Herkimer and St. Lawrence wing of the Democracy, whereof *The Post* is a disciple [that is, the 'Radical Democrats']."[32]

The 1851 claims of the *Tribune* on behalf of the 1838 Whigs are slightly exaggerated but essentially correct. They can be verified by examining the party vote on the bill in the assembly, by noting some of the bill's most important provisions, and by analyzing *contemporary* claims concerning party responsibility for its passage.

In 1837, Van Buren's public conversion to the negative liberal state brought the small band of Locofocos back to the party fold, but failed to impress the electorate. For the first time since 1824, the Regency was routed at the polls, and, especially in eastern New York, many "Conservative Democrats" openly went over to the Whigs. (A high proportion of these "Conservative" voters had probably been "Clay Masons" or "National Republican Masons" who had originally been driven into the Jackson Party by the Antimasonic campaign.) But the Whig tide was not confined to the Hudson River Valley. It swept over the Democrats in almost every county. The Whigs elected 100 of the 128 assemblymen and 6 of the 8 senators who were elected annually.[33]

The Whig victory, as Weed's *Evening Journal* interpreted it, reflected the voters' attitudes toward the conflicting party positions on the proper role of the state in a time of depression. "The electors have now placed power in the hands of Representatives to whom

---

[32] *New York Tribune* (w.), October 11, 1851, p. 2. For a contrary view, see *New York Evening Post*, October 6, 1851, p. 2. For earlier statements by the *Tribune* claiming that the Whigs had always been the antimonopoly party, see *ibid.* (w.), May 3, 1845, p. 5; January 3, 1846, p. 3; November 10, 1849, p. 3. The *Tribune's* 1851 statement concerning the *Evening Post's* position on free banking during the legislative session of 1838 is borne out by an analysis of the latter's editorials during that period. The *Post* at first attacked the Whig free banking bill, but reluctantly supported it later as the best one that could be obtained. It sharply criticized the Democratic leaders in the legislature who tried to block its passage. See *Evening Post for the Country* (s.w.), March 29, 1838, p. 3; April 16, 1838, p. 2.

[33] J. Hammond, *Political Parties*, 2: 472-479.

they will look for relief. Nor can they be turned off with the cold, unsympathising remark that 'communities expect too much from Government' when they ask for relief from distress 'created by revulsions in credit and commerce' [referring to Van Buren's message on the Independent Treasury]. That *unsocial sentiment* [italics added] has been signally rebuked."[34]

When the new legislature met in 1838, the Whigs acted as though they held a mandate to take positive action to relieve communities from distress. Since no state officers had been elected in 1837, and only 8 of the 32 state senators were elected annually, their control was limited to the Assembly. As a result, that chamber fought the crucial party battles over free banking (and other issues).

The Whigs were not alone in interpreting the 1837 election results as a mandate for positive state action, however. Governor Marcy, a Conservative Democrat and a "friend of the chartered banks," had become increasingly appalled by the "Hideous Monster of locofocoism" and disturbed by what he called "the 'spirit of destructiveness' that was abroad." Although he had previously opposed Whig attempts to pass a free banking law,[35] his 1838 gubernatorial message demonstrated his political realism and flexibility. Having already shifted his position somewhat in 1837, Marcy now went further and recommended that the legislature "open the business of banking to a full and free competition, *under such general restrictions and regulations as are necessary to insure to the public at large a sound currency* [italics added]."[36]

Soon after the legislative session began, the Whigs in the assembly introduced a free banking bill that was roughly along the lines recommended by Marcy.[37] The Radicals, making up nearly the entire Democratic bloc in that chamber, uncompromisingly fought it. As the *Tribune* later claimed, Preston King and Abijiah Mann, Jr., the

---

[34] *Albany Evening Journal* (s.w.), November 14, 1837, p. 2. This editorial should be read in conjunction with Weed's denunciation of the Regency for having defeated a free banking bill during the 1837 legislative session. "The Regency stand exposed before the People. They have insulted the public understanding and trifled with the people's welfare. Professing to be in favor of a General Bank Law, they first palmed an unconstitutional *bill* upon the Legislature, and when detected in that, they have defeated a bill which was free from Constitutional objections. How much of insult and injury the People will endure, remains to be seen." *Ibid.*, May 9, 1837, p. 3.

[35] Spencer, in *MVHR*, 31: 220-223; B. Hammond, 583.

[36] Charles Z. Lincoln, ed., *State of New York: Messages From The Governors* (Albany, 1909), 3: 655; Spencer, *op.cit.*, 31: 221-223.

[37] *Albany Evening Journal* (s.w.), February 6, 1838, p. 3.

experienced leaders of the "Herkimer and St. Lawrence wing of
... [the] Democracy," led the opposition to the bill. To quote King's
recent biographer, his strategy as minority leader was "to hamper
Whig measures by endless amendments and parliamentary maneuvers
designed to further disorganize the inexperienced majority, and to
use the chamber as a forum for the expression of the policies and
principles of the Radical Democracy. . . . Roll calls were increasingly demanded, not only to delay business, but also to place on
record the minority's opposition. It might prove useful in later years
when, as King firmly believed, the Whig policies would result in
disastrous public debts [from expanded internal improvements] and
a deranged banking system."[38]

Despite "endless amendments and parliamentary maneuvers" by
the "Radicals," a Whig bill to "authorize the business of banking"
passed the Assembly by a vote of 86 to 28.[39] According to the *Evening Journal* it "was most reluctantly passed by the Senate, at the
last hour under express instructions from Tammany Hall."[40] This
claim is supported by the course of action of the *Evening Post*. Over-
coming its strong disgust with many of the bill's features, it called
for its passage as the first step toward reform.[41]

The Radicals in the assembly refused to follow the tactics recommended by the *Post*, however, and did not limit themselves to parliamentary maneuvers designed to harass the Whigs and force them to
revise their free banking bill. Nineteen of the 28 Democrats voted
against it outright (including King and Mann), the votes of 2 were
not recorded, and 7 voted for it (presumably either Marcy-type Conservatives or men who agreed with the *Post*'s policy of choosing the
lesser evil). In contrast, 79 of the 100 Whigs voted in favor, the
votes of 12 were not recorded, and 9 voted against it. These unusually
distinct party divisions become understandable, and revealing, once
we analyze the provisions of the 1838 "General Banking Law."[42]

The law, in keeping with its antimonopoly character, authorized

---

[38] Ernest P. Muller, "Preston King" (Columbia University, Ph.D., 1957), 186-187,
187-191.

[39] *Albany Evening Journal* (s.w.), April 6, 1838, p. 2. The bill was signed by Governor Marcy on April 18. (*Ibid.*, April 24, 1838, p. 3.)

[40] *Ibid.*, April 20, 1838, p. 2.

[41] *Evening Post for the Country* (s.w.), January 8, p. 3; March 15, p. 2; March 22,
29, p. 3; April 16, p. 2 (1838).

[42] Compare the vote on the bill with the names signed to the Whig and Democratic
legislative addresses. *Albany Evening Journal* (s.w.), April 6, May 11, 1838, p. 2;
Albany Argus (s.w.), April 24, 1838, p. 2.

individuals or associations to engage in banking without any special charter—*provided they began with a paid-up capital of at least $100,000*. But the nonspecial charter provision represented the only feature of the bill at all consonant with Locofoco doctrines.

Designed to insure financial responsibility, the minimum capital requirement formed precisely the kind of "impediment" that Locofocos denounced as a limitation upon the freedom of any man to engage in "every profession, business, or trade, not hurtful to the community." Banks organized under the 1838 law, contrary to Locofoco and Radical ideas about how "the trade in money" should be conducted, had the essential powers and faculties of corporations and were empowered to issue paper currency. Moreover, the law granted stockholders freedom from personal liability for bank losses—a freedom that Locofocos devoutly did not desire bank stockholders to have. Finally, the law not only failed to implement *laissez faire* doctrines, but it laid down strict rules for banking operations, provided machinery for stringent regulation, and established a board of bank commissioners with broad supervisory powers and responsibilities.[43] Thus in 1838 the Whigs adopted the banking innovation sponsored by the Regency in 1829.

The procedure used to study the 1831 bill abolishing imprisonment for debt gives us another good indicator of party responsibility for the free banking law. When we examine the 1838 legislative addresses, we find the Democrats again maintained silence on the reform measure,[44] their opponents again pointed with pride. The Whig *Address* is particularly noteworthy because it cogently expressed the concept of liberalism developed by the party between 1834 and 1844.

In the Whig reading of political economy, the *paternal* state violated the egalitarian principles enshrined in the Declaration of Independence. Those sacred principles, according to the Whigs, required that all men have equal access to opportunity and the freest possible scope for enterprise. But, since the United States was a republican rather than a despotic country, since all men enjoyed political equality, government intervention in the economy could foster equal opportunity and free enterprise. Instead of abdicating responsibility,

[43] Analyses of the free banking law are presented in Chaddock, *op.cit.*, 369-381; Redlich, *op.cit.*, 196-201; B. Hammond, 580-592.

[44] *Albany Argus* (s.w.), April 24, 1838, p. 2. The Democrats were also silent about free banking at their state convention. (*Ibid.*, September 18, 1838, p. 2.)

as the Locofocos and Radical Democrats demanded, the state had a positive responsibility to act. It must regulate society so as to promote the general welfare, raise the level of opportunity for all men, and aid all individuals to develop their full potentialities. In discussing the free banking law, the Whig *Address* defined equality and liberalism as follows: "The great objects to be accomplished were in our judgments, to put an end to all political influence over our monied institutions—to do away with every thing like monopoly or special privilege in the hands of any favored class, *and to give free scope* [italics added] to the employment of capital and credit, whereever and by whomsoever they could be beneficially employed. On the other hand, we looked upon it to be a duty of the highest obligation *to protect every individual in the community from being imposed upon by a worthless currency—whether rendered worthless by speculation, imprudence or by fraud* [italics added]. These objects we hope and believe have been in the main attained in the General Banking Law. . . ."[45]

To quote other self-congratulatory passages on other issues underscores the differences between Whig and Democratic conceptions of liberalism: "We are proud and happy, fellow citizens, to have had it in our power to give the means of wider diffusion to useful knowledge and fresh energies to the great cause of Education. . . . Nor have we been discouraged by the gloomy aspect of commercial and political affairs from applying the resources and calling forth the energies of this great and powerful commonwealth, to renewed and increased efforts in promotion of its own best interests by works of internal improvements. . . . We hold it to be the wisest and soundest political prudence, to apply the means of the state boldly and liberally to aid those great public works of railroads and canals which are beyond the means of unassisted private enterprise. By judicious expenditure in this way, the cost of transportation and travel is diminished to the lowest point, and thus the profits of every producer are augmented, whilst expense is lessened to every community; labor finds full employment and just reward and youth and enterprise have opened to them new roads to independence or to wealth."[46]

Nevertheless, the differences between Whig and Democratic conceptions of liberalism are most clearly illustrated by their preach-

45 *Albany Evening Journal*, May 11, 1838, p. 2. In addition, see the *Address* adopted by the 1838 Whig state convention. (*Ibid.*, October 2, 1838, pp. 3-4.)
46 *Ibid.*

ments and practices on free banking. On other issues they did not draw their party lines so distinctly or consistently.

C. Whig and Democratic Models of the Liberal State

Under the free banking law which the Whigs passed and the Democrats fought, the state maintained its traditional responsibility for protecting and advancing the general welfare. In part, that responsibility was discharged by the creation of an independent regulatory agency that would supervise certain aspects of banking operations, and in part by the exercise of its traditional prerogative to confer valuable privileges upon men engaged in banking (for example, corporate powers, exemption from liability, note issue). In a revolutionary departure from mercantilist precepts, however, *the free banking law made the same opportunities and privileges legally, available to all men, and gave independent entrepreneurs, rather than the State, the option of determining where and when* "capital and credit . . . could be beneficially employed."

Seen in perspective, the New York Whigs' theory of the state represented a new synthesis; it combined the positive features of mercantilism with the liberal features of classical political economy. In the Free Banking Act, and in their overall program, which included positive state action to improve both the intellectual and material well-being of society, the Whigs anticipated the "positive liberalism" and "the General Welfare State" of the late nineteenth century.[47] Seward succinctly summarized the Whig position in his 1839 gubernatorial message which recommended liberal government expenditures for internal improvements and education: "To enlarge . . . national prosperity, while we *equalize its enjoyments* [italics added] and direct it to the universal diffusion of knowledge are the great responsibilities of our age."[48]

According to the Whig conception of sound political economy, a program to discharge "the great responsibilities of our age" did not require statesmen to choose *between* government and private enterprise. Both played important roles in achieving the Good Society. Properly conceived and executed, their activities complemented rather than competed with each other. To repeat this quotation

[47] Compare the Whig position on the role of government as stated, for example, by Horace Greeley in 1843 and 1852 with Professor Fine's summary of the anti-*laissez faire* movements after 1865. *Whig Almanac for 1843* (New York, 1843), 16-17; *Whig Almanac For 1852* (New York, 1852), 6-12; Fine, *op.cit.*, 167-168.

[48] Lincoln, *Messages From the Governors*, 3: 727.

from their 1838 legislative *Address*: "We hold it to be the wisest and soundest political prudence, to apply the means of the state *boldly and liberally to aid those great works of railroads and canals which are beyond the means of unassisted private enterprise* [italics added]." In other words, one major function of the state was to supply the "venture capital" necessary to remove the obstacles to progress that were either beyond the reach of private entrepreneurs, or did not afford them opportunities for profit.

1. Whig and Democratic Similarities

If we abandon the time-honored but ill-founded preconceptions about liberal Jacksonian Democracy and conservative Whiggery, we can more accurately locate the two parties in the stream of American historical development and more accurately assess the similarities and differences in their theories of political economy.

By 1838, both parties in New York had broken irrevocably with the mercantilist theories underlying the Federalist conception of the state. After Van Buren's conversion to Locofocoism in 1837, the Democrats as well as the Whigs stood committed to equal rights and antimonopoly. Neither party advocated the Federalist ideal of a highly centralized economic system, tightly controlled, administered, and operated by a relatively small elite group. Both parties now agreed that liberation of enterprise from mercantilist leading strings required that they repudiate the paternal state whose virtues and vices the Safety Fund banking system exemplified. Both parties had adopted programs whose *stated objectives* were to democratize American enterprise and enable men to respond swiftly and flexibly to the challenging opportunities that accompanied the transportation revolution. Here consensus ended.

2. Whig and Democratic Differences

The Whig modernists looked forward to an increasingly dynamic, complex, and industrialized society. To use twentieth century terms to state their conception of their party's mission: they thought the party should help to provide the political, social, and cultural conditions necessary to launch the United States on the "take-off" stage of economic growth. Accordingly, to cope with the problems inherent in achieving and sustaining such a society, they developed the theory of positive liberalism. Though they may have denied it, the Democratic traditionalists looked backward to the late eighteenth century and found inspiration in Jefferson's idyllic vision—anachronistic even in his own time—of the negative state functioning in Arcadia, that is, in a sparsely-settled, simple agrarian country.[49] Locofocos and Radical Democrats carried the doctrine of the negative state so far, in fact, that by comparison Adam Smith and the classical political economists look like ardent interventionists.[50] "The world is governed too much," the slogan credited to Amos Kendall (a guiding spirit of "Jacksonian Democracy"),[51] accurately summarized the Democratic response to the transportation revolution. But given their theoretical commitment to an extreme antistate doctrine, how could the Democrats logically support the program of social, cultural, and humanitarian reform that historians have recently come to associate with the Jacksonians?

There are two answers: 1) If Democrats supported liberal government expenditures for social legislation (for example, public education, aid to the handicapped, poor relief, care of the insane), or joined movements to secure such "moral objectives" as abolition of slavery and temperance through government action, their practice belied the principles of their party. 2) Individuals may have acted inconsistently with party principle, but the Democratic Party in New York did not; it stolidly opposed those reforms now commonly treated as manifestations of Jacksonian Democracy.

During the 1840's, John Bigelow served as a leading writer for the *Democratic Review* and the *New York Evening Post*. A Radical who both shaped and reflected his party's thinking, he exemplifies Democratic logical consistency.

In Bigelow's view, Weed, Seward, and Greeley resorted to despicable, opportunistic methods to win the 1840 Log Cabin compaign. More significantly, he regarded the Whig triumvirate's program of "government aid to canals, railroads, charities, and education [as]

[49] William Leggett, the Locofoco's leading theorist, was also the "leading exponent [in the 1830's] of a simple agrarian economy and way of life. . . ." Rifkin, in *New York History*, 32: 32-46. Implementation of the negative state would actually have required a simpler agrarian economy and way of life than had existed in the American colonies in the pre-Revolutionary decades. The irony of the Democrats' conversion to negative liberalism is that it occurred just when the transportation revolution was destroying any possible basis for a simple agrarian economy.

[50] For example, Smith believed that the government had a responsibility for education; in contrast, the Locofocos and Radical Democrats extended the do-nothing principle to this aspect of social development. See, for example, Rifkin, 32: 55, for Leggett's "faith in *laissez nous faire* and *pas troup gouverneur* [which] carried him to extremes."

[51] See the illuminating analysis of Kendall's position and role in B. Hammond, 332-334.

downright dangerous."[52] A cultivated man, Bigelow undoubtedly wanted to raise the standards of popular education as fervently as did Seward and Greeley. But for the same reason that he uncompromisingly and dogmatically opposed their program of state aid to internal improvements, he uncompromisingly and dogmatically opposed their program of state aid to education.

When, several years later, the question of whether to hold a state constitutional convention arose, Bigelow urged his party to take advantage of the opportunity to implement its egalitarian principles. According to his biographer, among other measures he urged "the extension of suffrage to all men eighteen years and over, be they black or white. . . . He believed that *the common-school fund should be applied to the present crippling state debt and that thereafter the state should cease to propagate any science, art, trade, or religion among any class of people* [italics added]. He wanted an end to the death penalty. He wanted individual liability clauses written into all corporation charters and all incorporations to be made under general laws. But in these, as in other measures, he was too radical for the Radical convention." (Though the Radicals controlled the 1846 Constitutional Convention, they apparently did not believe that they had been elected to enact changes that would probably liquidate the Democratic Party at the polls—a probable result had they taken Bigelow's advice.)

Shortly after the Convention ended, Bigelow wrote an article entitled the "History of Constitutional Government." In it he tried to prove the Democratic dogma that positive state action necessarily resulted in social inequality: "Too much government has a direct tendency to aid one man or one set of men in the 'pursuit of happiness,' and in the 'acquiring, possessing and protecting property,' if not at the expense of the rest at least without rendering them the like assistance. As far as the conditions of animal existence go, there is very little difference in the ability of all men to provide for themselves and families; and if all were left without any special aid from government, both land and the products of industry would be far more equally distributed than they are. . . . It is, however, the case, that four-fifths of the action of all legislation, is, by law, to promote the accumulation of prosperity in a few hands."

Bigelow was an urban "reforming publicist," Preston King was a

---

[52] Margaret Clapp, *Forgotten First Citizen: John Bigelow* (Boston, 1947), 31. The quotations below are from *ibid.*, 54, 55.

rural practising politician and legislative leader of the agrarian Radical Democracy. Though not as logically consistent as Bigelow (among other things, intense hostility to Negroes led him to reject extension of suffrage to "all men . . . be they black or white"), King, too, exemplified his party's commitment to the negative state doctrine. A resident of the North Country, remote from the Erie Canal and major transportation routes, he "was a Democrat from principle and from prejudice. He had grown up hostile, not only to canals, but to improvements of every description; the world, he said, was good enough for him as it stood, and would progress quite fast enough without the aid of legislation."[53]

Many years after the period under discussion, Thurlow Weed made that assessment of King. Its accuracy might be questioned, therefore, except that it is confirmed in every respect by King's recent and sympathetic biographer. "King was by this time [1838] a leading Jacksonian in the state. His orthodox political views, couched in the Jefferson-Jackson spirit, caused him to resist humanitarian reforms when they required an act or interference by government. During the previous winter in Albany he had opposed granting state financial support to the New York Eye Infirmary which gave treatment to all regardless of ability to pay. Likewise, he voted against aid to the New York Orphan Asylum Society. These, in his opinion, were worthy fields for private generosity but not to be confused with the proper service to be rendered by the state."[54]

If we searched diligently enough, no doubt we could find Whigs who preached the extreme antistate doctrines championed by Bigelow and King (and William Leggett, the main Locofoco theorist). No doubt we could also find Democrats who resembled Seward and Greeley in their conception of positive liberalism. But they would be exceptional men; Bigelow and King were *representative* men (that is, as the dictionary defines it, "exemplifying a class; typical"). Their views essentially reflected the position taken by the allied urban and rural Democratic factions that set the party line in the 1830's and 1840's. For example, King's biographer observed that in the late 1830's, "the county Addresses of St. Lawrence and Herkimer contained the most uncompromising presentations of the radical agrarian philosophy of that portion of the Democracy which was to become the Barnburners of the next decade. It is noteworthy

[53] Harriet A. Weed, ed., *Autobiography of Thurlow Weed*, 1: 471.
[54] Muller, "Preston King," 1: 176.

that these statements are all politico-economic in substance and none contain the faintest trace of the social and humanitarian ideals which recently have been attributed to the Jacksonian movement as a whole."[55]

What was the substance of these statements on political economy? "Government is necessary for the protection of the persons and property of the individuals, for whose benefits it is instituted, and that government is best, which is merely sufficient for that purpose. All attempts in any government, to do more than to protect the rights of those over whom its powers extend, must result in the enactment of partial and unequal laws; laws that operate, more for the benefit of some, than of others; and most frequently, all such attempts result in the enactment of laws, of such partial and unequal character that while they operate for the benefit of some, their inevitable tendency works positive injury to others. . . .

"In a Republic . . . the grand fundamental principle is equality; in such a government, a great regulator of business occupations, *or consciences of men* [italics added], not only is not required, but should not be tolerated."[56]

From this review of the doctrines preached and practiced by the major New York parties during the 1834 to 1844 decade, it seems reasonable to draw this conclusion: the Whigs come closer than the Democrats to satisfying the requirements of historians in search of nineteenth-century precursors to twentieth-century New Dealers.[57]

[55] *Ibid.*, 1: 176.　　　　　　　　[56] *Ibid.*, 1: 175.

[57] The similarities between the positions of Seward and Franklin D. Roosevelt on appropriate government action during an economic depression are briefly, but suggestively, noted in Dexter Perkins, "William H. Seward," *New York History*, 15: 166-167 (April 1934). For a different analysis of the Whig Party than the one presented in this chapter, see Van Deusen, *Thurlow Weed*, 22-24, 68-69, 86-113; *Horace Greeley*, 25-32; "Some Aspects of Whig Thought and Theory In The Jacksonian Period," *American Historical Review*, 63: 305-322 (January 1958).

CHAPTER VI

TWO MINOR "PARTIES"

BY HINDSIGHT we can see what contemporaries during the 1834 to 1844 decade could not see, namely, that two movements then emerged that were later to shape American society basically and disorder it drastically.

The Liberty and American Republican movements, called political parties by contemporaries, can best be described as pressure groups. Both were organized around a relatively limited range of issues; in fact, we can say that both were essentially organized around one issue. Like the Locofocos, they did not establish permanent new parties: they influenced the course of action of the major parties. If they could secure the balance of power at elections, they believed, they could force at least one of the major parties to adopt their policies. Unlike the Locofocos, however, they failed to make much impression upon either the Democrats or the Whigs. But their failure to do so deepens our understanding of New York politics, since it helps us to identify those ideas rejected, or at least not embraced, by the major parties during the 1830's and 1840's.

A. The Liberty Party

Although the Liberty Party found it necessary to take stands on other matters, its "great mission" was to make abolition of slavery the central issue of American politics. It was organized by one group of abolitionists who had become convinced that antislavery agitation would fail unless translated into political action. Accordingly, the October 1837 convention of the New York Anti-Slavery Society adopted a resolution calling for candidates to be questioned on certain issues related to slavery. The purpose was to force "public men" to make public their positions on those issues. Satisfactory answers would be rewarded with abolitionist support; unsatisfactory ones would be punished by abolitionist opposition. No machinery was established, however, for running independent tickets in the event that the candidates of neither party gave the right answers.[1]

[1] Ralph V. Harlow, *Gerrit Smith* (New York, 1939), 113-138; Whitney Cross, *The Burned-Over District*, 217-228; Betty Fladeland, *James Gillespie Birney: Slaveholder to Abolitionist* (Ithaca, N.Y., 1955), 175-178.

In 1847 Gerrit Smith attempted to organize a permanent, full-fledged antislavery party. He then summarized the Liberty Party's basic objective and strategy as fol-

Initial response to political abolitionism seemed to justify the innovation. By March 1838, so experienced an observer as Francis Granger had became convinced that they were "gaining converts by the regiment. . . . They will have one-fourth of the votes of the state before the grand contest of 1840, and before that day men who now say, 'D—'em, put 'em down!' will beg not to be put down by them. They are engaged in it with the same honest purpose that governed the great mass of the anti-masons."[2] New York abolitionists shared his flattering estimate of their power and sincerity. At their 1838 convention they adopted resolutions that formally bound members of the Anti-Slavery Society to withhold support from candidates who failed to endorse its stand on current issues. Unlike the previous year, however, the convention appointed a committee to prepare "interrogatories" to be answered by the Whig and Democratic candidates for major office. The only satisfactory reply came from the Whig candidate for lieutenant-governor, Luther Bradish. Passing the test handsomely, Bradish earned official endorsement and abolitionists were exhorted to vote for him alone and thereby vindicate the balance of power strategy.[3]

The election returns demonstrated, however, that Granger and the abolitionists had vastly overrated the political strength of the movement. Seward's evasive reply to the "interrogatories" earned him the abolitionists' contempt; Bradish's earned him their high praise. And yet, although they ran on the same ticket, when the cam-

---

lows: "The Liberty party was organized for only one purpose—that of contributing to overthrow chattel slavery. I admit it. I always contend for this interpretation. At the same time, I yield to the claims of candor, and admit that they, who take opposite ground, find no little authority for it in several places, and among them, the earliest national conventions of the Liberty party. I admit, I say that the Liberty party was organized for nothing else than to war on chattel slavery. It is however, but justice to me, for those who quote this admission, to couple with it, as I so frequently do, the declaration, that the principle, in the light of which the Liberty party was organized, and by the forces which it undertook to accomplish its object is THE EQUAL RIGHTS OF ALL MEN. But who can doubt that this principle points to free trade, land limitation, etc., etc., as well as to exemption from chattel slavery? And why should not the Liberty party follow all these pointings? There was reasons, why it should not, so long as it regarded itself as a temporary party, and believed that ere long, the great political parties would supersede it by inscribing the abolition of chattel slavery upon their banners. But, for years now, the Liberty party has seen, that these parties are past all cure, all hope, and that it must regard itself as a permanent party." (*Address of the Macedon Convention, By William Goodell and Letters of Gerrit Smith* [Albany, 1847], 16. I am indebted to Mr. John Hendricks, a graduate student at Fordham University, for calling this statement to my attention.)

[2] Thurlow Weed Barnes, ed., *Memoir of Thurlow Weed*, 2: 57. For convenience, this is cited as the second volume of Weed's *Autobiography*.

[3] Harlow, *op.cit.*, 138-141; Bancroft, *Seward*, 1: 59-62.

paign rhetoric settled and the ballots were counted, both men were elected by almost exactly the same margin. His strong antislavery stand had earned Bradish, on balance, a grand total of 43 votes more than Seward (192,925 compared to 192,882). In six of the state's eight senate districts, the two men received practically identical votes. And, from the statistics, it seems reasonable to infer that in the Fifth district (central New York) the abolitionist endorsement earned Bradish about 1,000 votes; in the First (largely New York County), it cost him about 1,000 votes.[4]

The 1838 election results revealed clearly the fatal flaw in the balance of power strategy. So long as only a relatively small number of men in New York cared *intensely* enough about abolishing slavery to be willing to desert their parties, no benefit would accrue to the major party which identified itself with that position. Gains acquired by propitiating abolitionists would be counterbalanced by losses suffered from antagonizing antiabolitionists. Under the circumstances, major party leaders in the North did not regard the antislavery gambit as a wise move. To identify their party with an advanced antislavery position would precipitate a southern bolt without gaining them any net advantage at home.

Disenchanted with the interrogatory-endorsement tactic, the New York abolitionists thereafter led the northern movement to organize an independent party and present a presidential ticket in 1840. Since the masses were most responsive to political argument during election campaigns, the abolitionists expected simultaneously to increase and demonstrate their vote-getting power. If the independent party tactic succeeded, they would secure the desired balance of power and vindicate their decision to embark on a course of political action. This vindication was an organizational necessity because many abolitionists, especially those associated with William Lloyd Garrison, opposed political action of any kind and demanded that the work of moral purification go on much as it had before 1837.

Abolitionists differed among themselves over more than strategy and tactics. As is usually true of dissident movements in their early stages, aside from conflicts over the wisdom of political action, the antislavery "crusade" suffered from intense sectarian quarrels, personal jealousies, and petty feuds. As a result, the extremely

[4] Edwin Williams, *The New-York Annual Register for . . . 1840*, 39-44. Analysis of the returns demonstrates that political abolitionism had some effect only in Oneida, Madison, and Lewis counties.

small vote received by the Liberty Party in 1840 (0.6 per cent) undoubtedly failed to measure accurately abolitionist sentiment in New York. By definition, however, it did accurately measure the movement's effective political strength. (Its total national vote was 6,784.)[5]

Liberty leaders, disheartened but undaunted by initial failure, spent the years between 1840 and 1844 building and extending their political organization. They ran candidates for local as well as state offices and carried out an unrelenting, intensive campaign to win men to political abolitionism. Gerrit Smith, Lewis Tappan, William Jay and others poured large amounts of money and energy into the work, party papers were established, thousands of speeches were made, and great quantities of reading material distributed. All to little political avail. Slight gains were registered, but the election results demonstrated that only a minuscule proportion of the voters felt strongly enough about abolitionism to support it at the polls. The Liberty Party's vote increased from 0.6 per cent in 1840 to 1.6 per cent in 1841, inched ahead to 1.8 per cent in 1842, jumped to 4.5 per cent in 1843, and declined to 3.1 per cent in 1844.[6]

After 1840, rather than converting new men to the cause, the intensive campaigning of the Liberty Party apparently only convinced a higher percentage of the New York abolitionists to vote for its candidates. (A very detailed study, I concede, would be required to support that impressionistic hypothesis.) Moreover, the "high" Liberty percentage in 1843 is in some respects deceptive. The vote was not cast for a statewide candidate. It represented the party's share of the small total vote cast for senators in the eight districts. And, to a considerable extent, the increased percentage seems to have resulted from an extraordinary concentration of effort in Gerrit Smith's home county. Weeks before the election, an "army" of lecturers and party workers invaded Madison County and turned it into "one immense cauldron of Abolitionism."[7] As the 1844 election returns showed, the Liberty percentage fell off substantially when

[5] Harlow, 142-162; Fladeland, *op.cit.*, 179-189; Margaret L. Plunkett, "A History of the Liberty Party with Emphasis upon its activities in the Northeastern States" (Cornell University, Ph.D., 1930), 79-102.

[6] Computed from "Record of State Canvass, 1828-1855," pp. 222-224, 227-229, 246-248 (New York State Library, Manuscript Collection). The highest vote ever obtained by the Liberty Party in New York was 4.8 per cent, in the off-year election of 1845.

[7] Harlow, 169-170.

statewide offices were at stake and it was more difficult to carry out the policy of concentrating forces in certain areas.

B. The American Republican Party

Movements that the American Republican Party typifies are usually described and dismissed as temporary outbreaks of "nativist" and "anti-Catholic" bigotry. Those epithets are accurate. Unfortunately, they tend to obscure the significance of the phenomena they stigmatize. Stripped of their peculiar characteristics, nativist and anti-Catholic movements illuminate the cultural conflicts and tensions inherent in a heterogeneous country such as the United States.[8] In New York, for example, essentially the same kind of phenomena might have been observed from the time the English and Dutch first came into contact and collision in the seventeenth century.[9] Between 1834 and 1844, however, the conflicts between "natives" of Protestant background and Catholic immigrants (and certain other "foreigners") developed much greater intensity than those that simultaneously existed among Yankees, Dutch, Palatine Germans, and Scots in the Hudson and Mohawk valleys. Though many factors influenced the result, their greater intensity owed much to the belief that the cultures of the new immigrants threatened the success of the American experiment in republican government.

Ethnocentrism, bigotry, ignorance, misunderstanding, political calculation, desire for "clean government," economic competition, status considerations—all substantially contributed to the movement for political action oriented around nativist, anti-Catholic appeals.[10] "Are we to derive *no* advantage on account of the 'accident' of being the children and heirs of revolutionary fathers? And is it of no account to be an 'American born'?"[11] Despite the implications of that typical quotation, a critical reading of the American Republicans'

---

[8] I am grateful to Professor John Higham for allowing me to read his unpublished paper, "Another Look At Nativism." That stimulating paper has helped to clarify my own ideas on the subject. I have also benefited considerably from the analysis in Richard Hofstadter, "The Pseudo-Conservative Right," in Daniel Bell, ed., *The New American Right* (New York, 1955), 33-35.

[9] See the suggestive analysis of New York group conflicts in Dixon Ryan Fox, *Yankees and Yorkers, passim.*

[10] The standard study remains Louis D. Scisco, *Political Nativism in New York State* (New York, 1901), 39-61. See also Robert Ernst's excellent article, "Economic Nativism in New York City During the 1840's," *New York History*, 28: 170-186 (April 1948); Ray A. Billington, *The Protestant Crusade: 1800-1860* (New York, 1938), 142-237.

[11] *American Republican*, July 20, 1844, p. 2.

publications supports the view that on the whole they *believed* they were motivated by patriotic principle rather than pride, prejudice or desire for personal advantage. We need not accept their self-assessment, but we would be mistaken, I believe, to discount the persuasiveness of this line of argument: "Our country presents many inducements to foreigners to come here; and the past policy of the government has given a too easy and indiscriminate admission to it. . . . If it is a fact that, as a class, they are more ignorant and more vicious and more corrupt than the native inhabitants, and bring with them habits and sentiments not congenial with our free system of self-government, it is certain that their prevailing influence is not favorable to the preservation and perpetuity of our institutions. . . . In the early period of our national existence, there may have been reasons for the free admission of foreigners which do not exist now; and if the reasons have changed or ceased to exist, the practice founded on them should also be changed. The United States have already, even in their infancy, become a great and prosperous nation. The natural ratio of increase is great, beyond precedent; and [it] is better for the strength, the stability, the perfection and the duration of our republican institutions, that the future increase should be from our native inhabitants. Let the generations that shall rise up to supply the places of those that pass away, as all must pass away, be born in the country."[12]

If we ignore their epithets and translate their rhetoric into neutral terms, we can say that the American Republicans fought to establish the principle that the United States should be a culturally homogeneous, not a culturally pluralistic, nation. Conflicts over that principle originate in or touch upon men's most primary emotions and needs. Of course, we might dismiss "Americanism" as little more than a patriotic euphemism resorted to by nativist, anti-Catholic scoundrels. But if we did so, we miss the movement's significance and fail to recognize that the desire for a distinctive American culture has powerfully shaped American history. As the "Americans" put it in 1844: "We wish, fully and entirely, TO NATIONALIZE THE INSTITUTIONS OF OUR LAND AND TO IDENTIFY OURSELVES WITH OUR COUNTRY; to become a single great people, separate and distinct in national character, political interest, social and civil affinities from any and all other nations, kindred and people on the earth, and to pledge our eternal, unyielding devotion to the country of our birth, the

12 *Ibid.*, August 10, 1844, p. 2.

[115]

altars of our fathers, and the home of our children; to declare an open and uncompromising war against all invasions of our right, as a people, or aggressions upon our institutions as a government. . . .

"We have all the elements of becoming a greater people, a mightier nation, and more endurable government than has ever held a place in the annals of time. The civilized countries of the old world will yet do homage to the wisdom and learning, the science and arts of our people; and the combined powers of all Europe shall bow before the majesty of our power."[13]

According to the American Republicans' reading of history, the country had begun to develop a truly national spirit and sense of purpose prior to the rapid increase in the number of immigrants. That spirit and purpose had arisen out of the Revolution and represented a healthy reaction against slavish copying of Old World institutions, customs, and habits. But "nationality in feeling" and a distinctive American culture were threatened by the hundreds of thousands of foreigners—particularly the Catholic Irish and Germans—now pouring in annually.

Instead of the "melting pot" image, which depicts immigrant cultures as contributing valuable ingredients to the national stock, the American Republicans projected the nightmare image of a witches' brew—a "great seething cauldron of society" which produced an increasingly debased people. Thus the *American Republican* viewed with alarm the influx of 230,000 foreigners in 1843: "At least *two hundred thousand* of these are *Catholics*—reared in the belief, daily and hourly inculcated that their priest is infallible, and can not only pardon all their offenses—theft, drunkenness, fornication, robbery and murder—in this world, but can pray them out of purgatory hereafter—and that the Pope, next to the Virgin Mary, is the most powerful and omnipotent being in the Universe—that to read the Bible is perdition, and to confess to the priest the only moral obligation that cannot be violated with impunity. Is it wonderful that with such impurities as those cast annually in such immense quantities into the great seething cauldron of society in America, public morals have become degenerated, pauperism and crime unendurably abundant, and religion and morality little better than idle words? But worse than all—that political virtue is rapidly becoming extinct beneath the hands of these vile, ignorant and superstitious hordes, and that the Elective FRANCHISE—that sacred palladium of our liberty—

13 *Ibid.*, November 7, 1844, p. 2.

is already polluted by the contaminating contact of these mental, moral and political slaves and helots! Fellow-countrymen, give these things your earnest thought!"[14]

That editorial illustrates the bigotry and chauvinism that expressed itself in the American Republican movement. But we must concede that Catholic immigrants did retard development of a culturally homogeneous nation (that is an observation, not a value judgment). As one leading Catholic historian has recently shown, the American Catholic hierarchy opposed rapid assimilation: "The native-born Catholics, including the older Irish, looked forward to the day when the immigrant would cease to be looked upon as a foreigner. [Orestes] Brownson, a militant Yankee [convert], wanted to eliminate this distinction at once. Archbishop Hughes [of New York] objected to Brownson's reasoning because he feared that the loss in Faith in a hasty adoption of American ways would outweigh any social gain. . . . In the case of the Irish immigrant, the absence of a language difficulty did not prevent Archbishop Hughes from realizing that there was a cultural difference between the immigrants and the native Americans. But like the defenders of later national groups he failed to see the advantages of a quicker Americanization. The cultural conflict in the forties and fifties . . . was the first great manifestation of a foreign nationalism in the American church. Culturally the policy of Hughes set back the progress of the Irish immigrant at least a generation. . . ."[15]

Recognition that Bishop Hughes (his rank in the early 1840's) was perhaps the most aggressive leader of "the most militant Catholic organization in the English-speaking world" helps to account for the intensity of American Republicanism in New York.

Hughes's policy of segregating the Catholic immigrants set in motion one chain of events which significantly contributed to the organization of the American Republicans in 1843. (The origins of the movement go back much earlier, of course, and its coming had been foreshadowed by the short-lived Native American Party of the mid-1830's.) In 1839, in his first gubernatorial message, Seward had recommended "establishing schools in which . . . [immigrant] chil-

---

[14] *Ibid.*, August 2, 1844, p. 2. See also editorials and articles in *ibid.*, July 3, 8, 23, August 10, 20, October 7, 31, November 7, 14, 1844, p. 2.

[15] Thomas J. McAvoy, "The Formation of the Catholic Minority in the United States, 1820-1860," *Review of Politics*, 10: 24-26 (January 1948). The nonintegration policy was also followed by the German Catholic hierarchy in the United States. See Colman J. Barry, *The Catholic Church and German Americans* (Catholic University of America Press: Washington, D.C., 1953), 9-19.

dren shall enjoy advantages of education equal to our own, *with free toleration of their peculiar creeds and instructions* [italics added]."[16] Having failed to arouse any positive response, he enlarged upon the separate but equal thesis in his next gubernatorial message, and thereby precipitated in New York City a bitter, enduring Protestant-Catholic struggle over educational policy.

Seward argued that the state's educational program should be based upon the principle of cultural pluralism and that parochial schools should be granted public funds. "The children of foreigners, found in great numbers in our populous cities and towns, and in the vicinity of our public works, are too often deprived of the advantages of our system of public education, in consequence of prejudices arising from difference of language or religion. It ought never to be forgotten that the public welfare is as deeply concerned in their education as in that of our own children. I do not hesitate, therefore, to recommend the establishment of schools in which they may be instructed by teachers speaking the same language with themselves and professing the same faith."[17]

Seward's message encouraged the trustees of the Catholic parochial schools in New York City. Acting under the direction of Bishop Hughes, they immediately applied for a share of the educational funds.[18] At the time, the Public School Society, a private organization, directed the city's school system. Controlled by Protestants, it called upon the Common Council to reject the Catholic request as unconstitutional and inexpedient. (The Society was consistent, for it had previously fought the same kind of request by Protestant groups.) Among other reasons, the officers of the Society claimed that the request was unconstitutional "because it is utterly at variance with the letter and spirit of our chartered rights, and with the genius of our political institutions, that the community should be taxed to support an establishment in which sectarian dogmas are inculcated, whether that establishment be a school or a church."[19]

16 Charles Z. Lincoln, ed., *State of New York: Messages From the Governors*, 3: 729.

17 *Ibid.*, 3: 768. Strong opposition from within his own party caused Seward to backtrack somewhat in his next two gubernatorial messages. See Bancroft, *Seward*, 1: 96-101.

18 John R. G. Hassard, *Life Of The Most Reverend John Hughes, D.D., First Archbishop of New York* (New York, 1866), 223-241.

19 William O. Bourne, *History of the Public School Society of the City of New York* . . . (New York, 1870), 178-181. This valuable source reprints many of the speeches, memorials, remonstrances, and documents related to the school controversy. *Ibid.*, 178-525.

The school-aid issue immediately spilled over into politics. Both sides brought intense pressure upon the Common Council and the state legislature. When Bishop Hughes organized a separate Catholic ticket in the fall of 1841, Catholic-Protestant tensions increased. And they increased still more when the election demonstrated that the Democrats depended heavily upon solid Catholic support; every Democratic candidate who had not been endorsed by the Bishop's "Carroll Hall ticket" was defeated.

Emergence of an organized Catholic pressure group did not go unnoticed by the 1842 state legislature, now controlled by the Democratic Party. Acting upon Seward's recommendation, it passed a bill that ended the Public Schools Society's control over public education in New York City. Under the bill's provisions, a Board of Education elected annually would govern the city's common schools. Although the Catholic trustees did not succeed in getting public money for parochial schools, the issue of cultural homogeneity versus cultural pluralism continued to find expression and stimulus in the annual school board elections.[20]

The Catholic Church was not the only institution in New York whose policies and practices worked against a "nationality of feeling." During the mid-1820's, Tammany Hall correctly envisioned the future, reversed its traditional nativist position, and began to cultivate the naturalized voters. At first, Tammany confined itself to offering mild encouragement to immigrants, but by 1840 it operated a permanent efficient bureau which quickly converted aliens into naturalized citizens and naturalized citizens into steadfast Democrats. Copying their rivals, the Whigs also pursued the immigrant vote on an organized basis, although their apparatus was less elaborate and effective.[21] As outraged natives saw it, the parties appealed to the Irish and Germans, not as Americans, but as foreigners. Appeals couched "in the brogue of the Patlander and in Teutonic gutturals," they believed, would perpetuate divisions rather than bring about homogeneity.[22]

[20] Hassard, op.cit., 243-251; Scisco, op.cit., 32-37; *New York Tribune* (w.), January 27, 1844, p. 6; *New York Herald* (w.), November 11, 1843, p. 5. Two Whig papers were sympathetic to the movement and published a great deal of material related to it. See *New York Morning Express* and *New York Courier and Enquirer*, during the latter part of 1843 and all of 1844.

[21] Gustavus Myers, *The History of Tammany Hall* (New York, 1917), 73, 128-130. For a vivid and penetrating analysis of the Tammany system, see Robert Ernst, *Immigrant Life in New York City: 1825-1863* (New York, 1949), 162-171.

[22] *New York American Republican*, August 30, October 11, November 1, 1844, p. 2.

Together with the heightened Protestant-Catholic tensions that resulted from the school question, the Tammany policy of aggressively courting foreign-born voters contributed strongly to the organization of the American Republican Party in the summer of 1843. It seems possible to identify the precipitating factor with reasonable certainty. Apparently as a reward for past support and as an earnest of future favors, the Democrats gave Irish Catholics unusual patronage in the form of market licenses and petty offices connected with the food markets. Resenting such "bribes" to their despised competitors, some native Protestant market men bolted Tammany and formed the nucleus of a new political organization. Like the Working Men in 1829, the new "party" polled a surprisingly heavy vote in the fall local elections and thereby demonstrated that it expressed an intense, widespread opinion. Significantly, contemporary analysts offered convincing evidence to support their estimates that two thirds of the approximately 9,000 men who voted the American ticket in 1843 normally cast Democratic ballots.[23] Nativist, anti-Catholic sentiments, therefore, cut across party lines and had roots other than Whig jealousy of the successful electioneering forays Tammany conducted among the foreign-born.[24]

To state summarily the political goal of the American Republicans: they sought to modify the naturalization laws and thereby end "the present connection between politics and religion, and the constant courting and buying of the votes of . . . [naturalized citizens] to settle our elections. . . ."[25] They proposed, therefore, that the right to vote be withheld from foreigners until they had lived in the country for 21 years. "We do not contend but that the foreign as well as the native-born citizen has a right to participate in the legislation and administration of the laws that govern him, but we *do* contend that the peculiar form and nature of our government require that that right should not be extended to the foreigner until he has resided among us, not only long enough to learn the letter of our Constitution and spirit of our laws, but until he shall have had sufficient time *completely* and *entirely* to divest himself of all prejudice for the government and country of his birth and education, and to have

[23] Scisco, 39-44; *New York Tribune* (w.), April 13, August 29, 1844, p. 5; *New York Morning Express*, April 13, 1844, p. 2.

[24] In the mid-1830's, for example, the Locofoco Democrats had developed an informal coalition with both the Native American Party and the Whigs. Degler, "Locofoco Party," 56-59.

[25] From an 1843 American campaign document quoted in Scisco, 42.

become so incorporated with the genius of our institutions, so imbued with a love for our country, and so identified with the welfare and perpetuity of our government, as to be in *spirit* and in *fact* as truly an American as though to the 'manor born.' *Then,* and *not till then,* should the foreigner be privileged to take a part in making our laws, maintaining our government, and conducting the great interests of our nation."[26]

The American Republicans' version of "the true science of politics" appeared to hold considerable appeal for New Yorkers. More precisely, the American Republicans, for one reason or another, held considerable appeal for New Yorkers. Although 1844 was a presidential year and the local spring elections traditionally represented an important phase of the state and national campaigns, the new "party" elected its mayoralty candidate and a majority of the Common Council. It received about 49 per cent of the vote, the Democrats about 40 per cent, and the Whigs the remaining 11 per cent. Except for the small group connected with the *Tribune,* the Whigs provided only token opposition to the Americans. The latter's vote, however, clearly cut across party lines. Contemporary estimates agreed that about 60 per cent of it came from Whigs and about 40 per cent from Democrats.[27]

The Americans, encouraged by their stunning success in New York City, began to organize in several Hudson Valley counties. A series of murderous riots in Philadelphia between "natives" and Irish Catholics spurred on this development by focusing excited attention upon the issues raised by the Americans. Convinced that wider and greener fields of political opportunity now beckoned, the organizers of the movement in New York City called a convention to consider nominating an independent state ticket. But, unlike the Liberty Party, the Americans decided against that tactic in a presidential year. Following the lead of the Americans in Philadelphia, they formed a coalition with the Whigs in New York City and in several other counties. The *quid pro quo* was clear and simple: the Americans would vote for the Whig gubernatorial and presidential tickets, the Whigs would vote for the American congressional and local tickets.

[26] *Address To The People Of The State Of New York, By The General Executive Committee of the American Republican Party Of The City Of New-York* (New York, 1844), 4.

[27] See the detailed analysis of the vote in the *New York Tribune* (w.), April 20, 1844. Its estimate agreed with the *Journal of Commerce,* a paper with Democratic inclinations, but which sympathized with the Americans. See attacks upon the *Tribune* and the *Albany Evening Journal* in the *Morning Express,* April 11, 13, 1844, p. 2.

If the coalition had been successful, if the Americans had demonstrated that they could substantially crack the Democratic ranks *during a major election*, they might have convinced the Whig Party to adopt their position on the naturalization laws. But, as Chapter VII will show, the election returns demonstrated that the Americans could not deliver the necessary votes. They elected a few local officials, but both parties to the coalition actually suffered heavily from it.[28] Like its numerous precursors, the nativist, anti-Catholic movement soon burned itself out. Phoenix-like, it was to rise again in the 1850's in another and more powerful form. But awareness of its earlier rapid rise and decline heightens our sensitivity to the climate of opinion that conditioned New York politics during the 1834 to 1844 decade.

[28] Scisco, 46-51. In my opinion, Scisco seriously misinterpreted the impact of the 1844 election. He accepted the Americans' evaluation of it as a great victory for their cause. Actually, election of some candidates who received their endorsement was a Pyrrhic victory. The Whig state leaders took alarm and openly fought the Americans thereafter; the Democratic leaders reformed their patronage practices, temporarily avoided making blatant appeals to the immigrant groups, and soothed their native-born adherents. Moreover, after 1844, the annexation of Texas and the Mexican War focused attention on questions related to slavery, and the nativist, anti-Catholic issues faded into the background until the early 1850's.

CHAPTER VII

CLASS VOTING IN NEW YORK

EADERSHIP, principles and policies, mass support—these categories help us to organize a study of New York political
parties in action.[1] Some aspects of the first two have been
discussed in previous chapters and we can now direct attention to
the group voting patterns that crystallized in the 1844 election. Although the introduction of some interpretive data cannot be
avoided, the primary objective of this chapter and the two that follow is to identify who voted for whom.

A. The 1844 Election in Historical Perspective

The 1844 campaign may rank as the most exciting and intensive
ever fought in New York. Writing in 1848, Jabez Hammond, the
classic historian of early New York politics, recorded his opinion
that "never was an electioneering campaign conducted with more
spirit and energy than that of 1844. Both parties entered the field
well organized and animated with high hopes. The recollection of
their success in 1840 inspired the whigs with courage; while a bitter
feeling of resentment for what they deemed the treachery of Mr.
Tyler, which had snatched from them the fruits of their victory at
the last presidential election, and their ardent attachment to their
chivalric and gallant leader [Henry Clay], kindled a zeal which
spread through all ranks of the party, which approached almost to
fanaticism. . . . On the other hand, the democratic party felt that
their all was at stake . . . [both Democratic factions had reasons]
to exert all their energies in support of the common cause. Mr. Van
Buren, too, had in several communications which were published,
declared his acquiescence in the nomination of Mr. Polk, and his determination to support him. Immensely large mass meetings were
held by the respective parties in all the large towns, and in almost
every county in the state. These meetings were addressed by the most

---

[1] Those three categories, of course, do not exhaust the list. The constitutional system
governing party battles, the partisan and nonpartisan machinery used to influence
voters directly or indirectly, and the consequences of election outcomes are significant
topics that warrant intensive investigation. But any study must select, concentrate
upon, and try to reconstruct certain aspects rather than the whole of historical reality.
The limited attention the present study gives to the topics cited in this note does not
imply a judgment that they are unimportant, only that they are relatively peripheral
to the problems it considers.

eminent orators in the state, and sometimes by distinguished states-men from abroad [that is, non-New Yorkers]."[2]

During the 1844 campaign, techniques used in the 1840 Log Cabin extravaganza were more widely applied and further refined—although "refined" is perhaps not the most appropriate word for the frenzied rallies, parades, "pole-raisings," "musters," picnics, and barbecues used to arouse mass enthusiasm. Estimates like Ham-mond's are intrinsically difficult to verify, but it seems accurate to say that the electorate was whipped into a state of unparalleled po-litical excitement. This estimate is supported by the turnout of 92.4 per cent of the eligible voters at the polls. If we assume only the normal amount of fraud in 1844, that turnout was never equalled in New York between 1826 and 1865, and probably never there-after.[3]

The extremely high turnout serves as an excellent indicator of the 1844 campaign's intensity and impact. It seems particularly significant, therefore, that comparison of the New York election returns from 1832 to 1844 reveals relatively little fluctuation in party percentages. This stability suggests the hypothesis that the frenzied 1840 and 1844 campaigns reinforced and deepened party loyalties but did not markedly alter party affiliations. To support that hypothesis and to support the general approach adopted in this book—that we can ascertain what happened in an election only by viewing it in long-range historical perspective—I shall try to demon-strate the existence of voting cycles in New York. (That we must acquire historical perspective to discover what happened in an elec-tion is a truism, no doubt. But the *ahistorical* character of American election studies suggests it is a truism not usually acted upon.)[4]

[2] Jabez D. Hammond, *Life and Times of Silas Wright* (Syracuse, N.Y., 1848), 495-496. For an informative treatment of party organization and campaign machinery, see G. W. Roach, "New York State in the Presidential Campaign of 1844" (Colum-bia University, M.A., 1937), *passim*.

[3] A table giving the percentage of eligible votes cast at annual elections from 1826 to 1865, inclusive, is presented in New York State, *Census . . . For 1865* (Albany, 1867), LXXXII. No doubt, thousands of illegal ballots were cast—particularly in the large cities—but a detailed analysis of the voting statistics over time indicates that the 1844 frauds were not significantly greater than in previous elections. Stated an-other way, the percentage of fraudulent ballots cast in 1844 probably was not sig-nificantly different than the norm in previous elections.

[4] That American election studies have tended to be *ahistorical* in character is the argument presented in Lee Benson, "Research Problems in American Political His-toriography," in Mirra Komarovsky, ed., *Common Frontiers of the Social Sciences* (Glencoe, Ill., 1957), 113-183.

1. Defining and Identifying New York Voting Cycles

Depending upon whether we take the state or the county as the unit of analysis, voting in New York appears to have followed markedly different courses between 1826 and 1900. Compared on the basis of statewide returns, the two major parties experienced little change in relative strength throughout the entire period and, except for brief intervals, show only a narrow percentage gap at any election. Moreover, within those narrow limits, their relative strength tended to shift from election to election. Particularly after 1860, victory banners were likely to wave over different party headquarters at successive presidential elections. To show that New York's major parties remained closely balanced, despite extraordinary changes in the size and composition of the electorate, the table below has been extended back to 1789.[5]

TABLE 1

NEW YORK STATE VOTE FOR GOVERNOR OR PRESIDENT, 1789-1900

| | Democratic Party[a] | | Major Anti-Democratic Party | | |
	No.	%	No.	%	Total
1789	6,391	51.7	5,962	48.3	12,353
1801	24,808	54.3	20,843	45.7	45,651
1816	45,412	54.0	38,647	46.0	84,059
1826	96,135	49.1	99,785	50.9	195,920
1832	166,410	51.5	156,672	48.5	323,082
1860	312,510	46.3	362,646	53.7	675,156
1880[b]	534,511	48.4	535,544	50.3	1,103,945
1900[b]	693,733	44.8	804,859	51.9	1,548,551

[a] For convenience, parties associated with the names of Jefferson and Jackson are treated here as predecessors of the modern Democratic Party. In bowing to convention, I do not imply agreement with it.

[b] Minor parties received the balance of the vote.

Table 1 accurately depicts the relative strength of the major parties over time, but it gives a distorted picture of political stability.

[5] For the election returns from 1789 to 1832, inclusive, the table presents the vote for governor; in 1860, 1880, and 1892 the presidential statistics were used to compute the party vote because of factional splits over state candidates, or because the intervals between gubernatorial elections were shifted or did not coincide with presidential contests. Though ticket-splitting increased in the 1890's, the practice was still confined to an extremely small minority of the electorate. The difference between the gubernatorial and presidential votes throughout the nineteenth century tended to be about one per cent. For the sources of all election statistics used in the present chapter, see Appendix I.

When the county returns are used to measure party strength, voting changes of great magnitude show up between 1826 and 1900. Those changes represent neither random fluctuations nor more or less regular oscillations from a base line. Because the patterns of change were fairly regular and had significant common characteristics, and because impressionistic data indicate that similar phenomena occurred at other times and places, it seems useful to suggest the concept of a voting cycle.

B. A Voting Circle and its Phases

If Wesley Mitchell's definition of a business cycle is adapted to political data, a voting cycle in New York can be defined as a *recurrent pattern of fluctuation in county party percentages.*[6] (In other states other political entities may be more appropriate units of analysis.) Fluctuation is measured by comparing a party's strength in a county at successive elections, for example, 1832 to 1836, 1836 to 1840, and calculating the arithmetic percentage change. (Towns and urban wards yield more precise results, but their large number makes them expensive to handle. For our present purposes, the county returns give sufficiently precise results.)

If we follow Burns's and Mitchell's procedures in handling economic data,[7] each voting cycle can be divided into a *fluctuation phase* and a *stable phase*. During the fluctuation phase which begins a cycle, marked changes in party percentages occur at successive elections in a large number of counties. By the end of the fluctuation phase, in many counties significant and lasting shifts in the relative strength of the major parties will have occurred. During the stable phase, comparatively little change occurs in most counties at successive elections and the relative strength of parties remains fairly constant.

Changes in New York voting patterns during the nineteenth century were so distinct that simple procedures suffice to identify cycles and phases. If we add the arithmetic percentage changes in a major party's vote in all counties (ignoring the plus and minus signs) and divide by the total number of counties, we find its average fluctuation between elections. And by comparing the average fluctuation of the major parties at successive elections *and inspecting both the*

---

6 Alvin H. Hansen, *Business Cycles and National Income* (New York, 1951), 4.

7 *Ibid.*, 7-16. In developing this definition of a voting cycle, I have adapted for my own purposes J. A. Schumpeter's concept of "neighborhoods of equilibrium." See *ibid.*, 7-8.

absolute and percentage county votes, we find natural "breaks" in the series. The breaks are sharp enough to warrant dating certain elections as the end of one phase and the beginning of another.[8]

I do not suggest that party percentages change markedly in all counties during a fluctuation phase and remain unchanged in all counties during a stable one, nor that an identical sequence of events occurs in the same phase of two voting cycles. On the contrary, it can be assumed that perceptible differences will exist between the *same phases* of *different cycles.* What I do suggest is that fluctuation phases resemble each other more closely than they resemble stable phases, and vice versa. Put another way, the concept of a voting cycle assumes *some degree of repetition* in the sequence of events, not exact duplication. Several other definitions may help to clarify that concept.

1. Equilibrium Years and Voting Cycles

The two phases of a voting cycle are separated by *equilibrium years.* Equilibrium is defined as the *absence of change* in county party percentages. There would be perfect equilibrium if no change occurred at successive elections in any county within a state. This, of course, never happens. Granted that they denote relatively little change rather than no change, two types of equilibrium years can be distinguished. An election that registers simultaneously the end of a fluctuation phase and the beginning of a stable phase is called an *overlapping* equilibrium year; the last election in a stable phase is called a *nonoverlapping* equilibrium year.

Other definitions deal with the shifts in county party percentages that occur during a stable phase. Those shifts are called "oscillations" because the party percentages *tend* to approximate the level reached in the equilibrium year that began the phase. But in some counties there is a tendency for slight changes *in the same direction*

---

[8] A deliberate attempt was made to avoid using elaborate statistical procedures to identify the voting cycles from 1826 to 1900. The objective was to devise a simple procedure which could be used by historians like myself who are innocent of the higher mathematical learning. But as a check upon the validity of those procedures, the same data were subjected to elaborate analysis by a trained statistician, Dr. Lee Wiggins of the Bureau of Applied Social Research, Columbia University. His findings paralleled those obtained by the elementary procedures noted in the text.

Specifically, I used four criteria to develop an "index of fluctuation" that permitted me to date the cycles and phases: 1) average fluctuation of each party; 2) number of counties whose fluctuation was more than ± 5.0 per cent; 3) impact of temporary party factionalism on fluctuation; 4) extent to which fluctuation resulted in longtime changes in party percentages in counties.

to become cumulative over a long period. This phenomenon is called a *secular trend*.

With definitions out of the way, New York's voting cycles from 1826 to 1900 can now be identified. In that period there were two complete cycles and the fluctuation phase of a third. If we begin with 1826 as a nonoverlapping equilibrium year, the first cycle went from 1827 to 1853, the second from 1854 to 1892, and the fluctuation phase of the third began in 1893 and ended in 1900.[9] (A subsequent study will collect and analyze the statistics for New York voting in the twentieth century.)

Examining the two complete cycles more closely, we find that the fluctuation phase of the first cycle ran from 1827 to 1832 and that its stable phase lasted from 1832 to 1853. The fluctuation phase of the next cycle began in 1854, ended in 1860, and its stable phase lasted until 1892.

2. Major Characteristics of New York Voting Cycles

The statistics for two representative counties illustrate the sequence of events in New York voting cycles and suggest several of their major characteristics. Table 2 below is based on the Democratic percentages in Allegany and Oneida counties.[10] Although they rep-

[9] From 1826 to 1858, inclusive, the table is based on the vote for governor or highest ranking state officer; in 1860 and 1880 the presidential returns were taken as the party vote, either because of factional splits over state candidates or because the gubernatorial election did not come in presidential years.

[10] To my knowledge, no comprehensive study has been published which closely examines New York politics during the confusing decade from 1816 to 1826. But the traditional assumption that Federalist-Republican party alignments continued unbroken seems to have no basis in fact. Though both factions in 1826 claimed to be "Republican," they are distinguished here as "Clintonian" and "Republican." The former takes its name from Governor De Witt Clinton, the main leader of those groups and voters opposed to the "Bucktail" and "Tammany Hall" factions of the Republican Party. The Clintonians of 1826 undoubtedly formed the greater part of the Antimasonic and "National-Republican" parties. Similarly, it appears to be a reasonable assumption that most "Republicans" *of 1826* went into the Democratic-Republican Party which rallied around Andrew Jackson after 1828. The 1826 election was the first one which can be said to have been fought along distinct factional lines after the Constitution of 1821 went into effect.

The 1821 Constitution extended the suffrage considerably and, for various reasons, factional distinctions were blurred for some time after its ratification. That factional alignments were firm in 1826 is demonstrated by a comparison of the votes for governor and lieutenant-governor. Ticket-splitting on any substantial scale was confined to a few counties in the Southern Tier. It seems evident that the unusually heavy support received by the Van Buren Republican nominee for lieutenant-governor in Allegany, Cattaraugus, and Steuben was caused by his widely advertised support for the State Road projected through the Southern Tier. On a lesser scale, he also

resent counties with distinctly different types of voting patterns,
no two counties had exactly the same pattern, of course. It is important to observe that the arithmetic percentage changes in the
table are for the successive elections listed; for example, they show
the change in the Democratic vote from 1826 to 1827 and from 1832
and 1853, the equilibrium years of the first cycle. Some oscillation
occurred between 1832 and 1853 in both counties, but, as the table
shows, the Democratic strength remained about the same.

TABLE 2

ARITHMETIC PERCENTAGE CHANGE IN THE DEMOCRATIC PARTY
VOTE, 1826-1900, ALLEGANY AND ONEIDA COUNTIES

| | Allegany | | Oneida | |
	%	Arithmetic % Change	%	Arithmetic % Change
1826	56.6	——	42.7	——
1827	57.2	+0.6	49.2	+6.8
1828	44.9	—12.3	46.6	—2.6
1830	39.4	—5.5	58.1	+11.5
1832	46.0	+6.6	52.2	—5.2
1853	48.5	+2.5	50.2	—2.0
1854	27.7	—20.8	49.7	—0.5
1856	18.2	—9.5	33.3	—16.5
1858	25.8	+7.6	41.1	+7.8
1860	28.2	+2.4	41.9	+0.8
1892	28.7	+0.5	45.6	+3.5
1893	22.1	—6.6	40.7	—4.9
1894	26.3	+4.2	41.3	+0.6
1896	30.0	+3.7	38.5	—2.8
1898	30.4	+0.4	46.3	+7.8
1900	31.2	+1.3	40.6	—5.7

Close inspection of the table reveals the most significant characteristic of a voting cycle. At the end of a fluctuation phase, the
strength of a major party tends to *stabilize* around a level markedly
higher or lower than in the preceding equilibrium year. In Allegany

attracted support from some Clintonian voters in Chautauqua, Delaware, Sullivan,
Tioga, and Yates, all counties which hoped to benefit from the State Road. As a result, though Clinton was re-elected governor by a narrow margin, the Van Buren
Republican nominee for lieutenant-governor won, also by a narrow margin. The
leading Van Buren journal misrepresented the results as a great victory for its
faction by focusing attention upon the *outcome* of the contests for the legislature; the
vote for governor is a far more accurate measure of the relative strength of the opposing factions in 1826. See the *Albany Argus* (s.w.), November 21, 28, 1826, p. 2.
Even at this late date, the most comprehensive, detailed account of New York politics from 1816 to 1826 is found in Jabez D. Hammond's 2 vols., *The History of
Political Parties in the State of New York*. For the details of the 1826 contest see
Hammond, 2: 208-236.

the net arithmetic percentage change was −10.6 per cent from 1826 to 1832; in Oneida the change was +9.5 per cent. Oscillation occurred in both counties during the stable phase, 1832 to 1853, but the long-time change in Democratic strength was negligible. Comparing 1853 to 1832, the net shift in Allegany, after two decades, was +2.5 per cent, in Oneida, −2.0 per cent.

But the fluctuation phase beginning in 1854 resulted in spectacular and lasting changes throughout the state. (The phase dates from 1855 in Oneida and a few other counties.) The sequence of events in Allegany was typical of many counties from 1854 to 1860. In those counties, the Democrats were reduced to their permanent status (as of now) of a weak minority party. If we compare 1860 with 1853, we see that their net *decline* in Allegany was 20.3 per cent; their net decline in counties like Oneida was also substantial (8.3 per cent).

As was true of voting patterns during the 1832 to 1853 stable phase, oscillation occurred in both counties from 1860 to 1892. But again the net shift of the Democratic Party was fairly slight. In Allegany it registered a gain of 0.5 per cent; in Oneida, a gain of 3.5 per cent.

We observe that the three fluctuation phases from 1826 to 1900 began in nonpresidential years (1827, 1854, 1893). This significant characteristic of New York voting cycles suggests a tentative hypothesis: that the structure of the American political system makes it more likely for a voting cycle to get underway in an "off-year" than in a presidential election year. When attention is not focused on a national contest for presidency, discontented voters may find it easiest to break the bonds of party discipline. But if party discipline is effectively broken and if the bases of discontent are not quickly removed or do not quickly remove themselves, the process of change accelerates and intensifies. Thus the same pattern can be observed in all three fluctuation phases. The first marked change occurred in an off-year contest, fluctuation continued during the next presidential election, and a new equilibrium was attained four years later. To what extent the pattern sketched here holds for other times and places is a question that remains to be investigated.

Unlike fluctuation phases that lasted from five to eight years, stable phases tended to last considerably longer (1832 to 1853, 1860 to 1892). This suggests that one (or both) of the major parties responded quickly to the discontent manifested by voters during a fluctuation phase and altered itself sufficiently to accommodate the voters. But during the relatively long stable phase that followed, discontent built up again and found expression in a new fluctuation phase.

During the stable phase, county party percentages tended to become *less* dispersed. Both major parties tended to lose some support in counties where they were strong and to gain some support in counties where they were weak. In other words, the range between a party's strong and weak counties tended to narrow and its median county approached *closer* to 50 per cent.

The final characteristic of the stable phase discussed here is the tendency for secular trends to emerge. One trend was for a major party opposed to the Democrats to suffer moderate decline in some counties where minor parties appeared. The Democrats also lost voters to minor parties, but in a number of counties their losses seem to have been counterbalanced by gains that stemmed from the changing composition of the electorate. Since the most solidly Democratic groups (identified below) cast increasing percentages of the total vote, the changing composition of the electorate produced small but cumulative Democratic gains in certain counties. The significant point is that secular trends appear to have stemmed more from shifts to minor parties and from changes in the composition of the electorate than from a sizeable number of voters gradually deserting one major party to support another.

Having identified and described nineteenth century voting cycles in New York, we are now in a better position to find out what happened in the election of 1844.

C. What Happened in the 1844 Election?

From 1827 to 1832 the Antimasonic Party was formed, enjoyed a remarkably swift growth, and abandoned independent existence to coalesce with segments of the National Republican and Working Men's "parties." Although the Whig Party was not formally organized and named until 1834, by 1832 the anti-Democratic voters in New York had been effectively united in support of one electoral slate.[11] That voting patterns had reached an equilibrium point in 1832 is apparent from the state and county party percentages. In the table below, Allegany and Oneida are again used as representative counties.

[11] See Chapters II and III.

At first sight, the 1836 figures for Oneida appear to contradict the claim that a stable phase began with the Antimasonic-National Republican coalition of 1832. Closer examination shows that the 1836 election is considerably out of line with those preceding and following it. Moreover, analysis of the actual returns suggests that in-

TABLE 3

NEW YORK PARTY PERCENTAGES, 1832-1844

| | New York State | | Allegany | | Oneida | |
	Dem.	Whig	Dem.	Whig	Dem.	Whig
1832	51.5	48.5	46.0	54.0	53.0	47.0
1834	51.8	48.2	48.8	51.0	52.3	47.7
1836a	54.3	44.6	50.0	50.0	60.0	36.9
1838	48.6	51.4	44.6	55.4	54.7	45.3
1840b	49.0	50.2	45.3	53.7	51.5	46.3
1844b	49.4	47.4	44.6	51.2	49.5	43.8

a In this election, in some counties, Democratic *percentages* increased sharply—but temporarily. When 1832 is compared with 1838, or 1840, or 1844, the fluctuation is normal for a stable phase.

b Minor parties polled a small vote in this election.

stead of deserting to the Democrats, many Whigs chose to "sit out" the election and not vote at all. Although the Democratic Party scored *percentage* gains, the *number* of voters who supported it was considerably less in 1836 (a presidential year) than in 1834 (an "off-year"). In 1834 the Democratic statewide gubernatorial vote was 181,905; in 1836 it dropped to 166,122. But the Whig numerical vote fell off even more sharply (from 168,969 to 136,648), and the Democratic *percentage* in Oneida and many other counties therefore rose from 1834 to 1836. Perhaps there is no better example to underscore the point that a comprehensive analysis of what happened in an election must use both the numerical and the percentage data as well as the data for a long series of elections.

In addition to showing when county voting patterns stabilized, Table 3 indicates how systematic collection, ordering, and analysis of voting data helps us to see political developments between 1832 and 1844 in perspective. For example, the traditional explanation of the Whig victory in 1840 becomes highly questionable. That election is usually treated as a triumph of demagogy over principle. Allegedly, the Whigs won because they nominated a military hero (General William Harrison), forbade him the use of "pen and paper," unleashed a torrent of songs and slogans, and effectively concealed their real goals. "Conservatism had carried the election, but it had to assume the banner of the popular [Democratic] party in order to do it. The champions of inequality were forced to take over the slogans of the new dispensation."[12]

But as Table 3 demonstrates, it is misleading to term the Democrats "the popular party" in New York, if that term means the party of the majority of the people. (Inspection of the national and state election returns indicates that the term is equally misleading for the country as a whole.) Except for the untypical 1836 election, when the Jackson administration basked in the sunshine of a great business boom and the Whigs nominated weak candidates in New York, the Democrats won by such slight margins that a shift of two per cent would have made their opponents "the popular party." Actually, the Whigs became the majority party in New York without benefit of the 1840 Log Cabin hullabaloo about "Tippecanoe and Tyler Too."

Sometime in mid-1837, Democratic supremacy ended in New York. The Democrats won the spring elections, were routed in the fall, and did not win again on the state level until 1842. By examining the election statistics over time, we can see that the Whigs won after 1837, whether or not they followed the Democratic lead and nominated military heroes. Moreover, detailed examination on state and county levels suggests that the Whigs' failure to become the "permanent" majority party after 1837 must largely be attributed to the Liberty Party.

1. Net Turnover on State and County Levels

In 1832 and 1834 a shift of less than two per cent of the total vote would have made the Democrats the minority party. By 1840 such a shift had occurred and the Whigs won the gubernatorial election by a narrow margin. But they could not maintain their lead in 1842 nor again in 1844. What happened in 1844 is seen more clearly, however, when the party percentages are viewed as part of a time series.[13]

The table demonstrates that on the state level there were relatively small changes in party strength between 1840 and 1844, that is, in the *net turnover* of all voters. And it suggests that the changes

[12] Arthur M. Schlesinger, Jr. *The Age of Jackson*, 305.

[13] The sources used for the voting statistics presented in this chapter are cited in Appendix I.

[133]

that did occur resulted mostly from abolitionist rather than Democratic inroads into Whig strength. Although the net turnover on the state level is frequently a misleading measure of what happened, in this instance it accurately reflected *gross turnover* from 1840 to 1844, that is, changes in voting behavior on all levels.

With minor exceptions, the Democratic *county* percentages in 1844 remained almost unchanged from 1840, and the median unit

TABLE 4

NEW YORK STATE PARTY PERCENTAGES, 1832-1844

	Democratic %	Whig %	Liberty Party %
1832	51.5	48.5a	—
1834	51.8	48.2	—
1840	49.0	50.2	0.6
1844	49.4	47.4	3.1

a Antimasonic coalition vote.

(the middle one in the series) registered almost the same arithmetic percentage gain (0.6) as the state (0.4). Moreover, the range of fluctuation was unusually narrow.[14] The greatest gain was in Erie (4.6 per cent), the greatest loss in Madison (5.0 per cent), and a figure of ±2.0 per cent covers the Democratic percentage changes in about 80 per cent of the counties. The Whig County percentages tended to fluctuate within a narrow range, also. The median was −2.8 per cent, but *where declines of 5 per cent or over were registered, the shifts were largely to the Liberty Party.*

2. Net Turnover on Town and Ward Levels

Carrying the analysis down to the rural town and urban ward level strongly confirms the state and county findings. Again, with few exceptions, aside from areas in which the electorate's composition had changed (Erie County provides the clearest example), the Whig declines almost equalled the Liberty totals.[15] Systematic analysis of the relevant data on state, county, and town levels, therefore,

14 Comparison of the county and town voting statistics in 1840 and 1844 indicates that ex-Democrats could have constituted a substantial percentage of the Liberty Party vote only in Madison County; there the Democrats registered a net loss of 5.0 per cent.

15 On the town and ward level the 1844 vote is for president; no source could be located for the Liberty Party's gubernatorial vote.

supports the Whigs' postelection claim that about 90 per cent of the Liberty voters had formerly "drilled" in their ranks; it invalidates the Democrats' counterclaim that the "great body" of political abolitionists had formerly "drilled" with them.[16] And when a time series is constructed for the Liberty vote from 1840 to 1847, what happened in 1844 can be seen even more clearly than if the analysis were restricted to the presidential years. (The series ends in 1847 because in 1848 the Liberty Party was swallowed up by the Free Soilers and it never recovered from that traumatic experience.)

TABLE 5

NEW YORK STATE, LIBERTY PARTY VOTE, 1840-1847

	Number	Percentage
1840	2,662	0.6
1841	5,936	1.6
1842	7,263	1.8
1843	16,097	4.5
1844	15,136	3.1
1845	15,754	4.7
1846	12,844	3.2
1847	13,429	4.1

Table 5 is most meaningful, perhaps, when used to assess the traditional claim that Henry Clay's letters on slavery during the 1844 campaign cost the Whigs the election in New York and the nation. That most political abolitionists would have voted Whig, if Clay had remained silent, is what logicians call a "contrary-to-fact-conditional" statement.[17] Like all such statements, by its nature it can be neither empirically verified nor discredited. Obviously, no one can ever demonstrate what would have happened had Clay forbidden himself the use of pen and ink. Nevertheless, aside from other considerations noted below, the table strongly suggests that the 1844 abolitionist vote was not a product of campaign "accidents" or tactical

[16] *New York Tribune* (d.), December 24, 1844, p. 2; *Albany Argus* (w.), November 23, 1844, p. 381; *New York Morning News*, December 24, 1844, p. 2. A nominally independent, generally anti-Whig paper agreed with the *Tribune* that ex-Whigs overwhelmingly predominated in the Liberty Party. *Herald* (w.), October 26, 1844; p. 337.

[17] Historians also frequently make statements of this kind, sometimes not fully aware of their logical implications. For an illuminating discussion, see Roderick M. Chisholm, "The Contrary-to fact Conditional," in Herbert Feigl and Wilfrid Sellars, *Readings in Philosophical Analysis* (New York, 1949), 482-497.

mistakes. The Liberty Party's gains had actually been scored *between presidential years,* and the party's *numerical* vote remained relatively stable between 1843 and 1847, inclusive, whether cast in a state or national election. Moreover, the table strengthens the view that the small turnover between 1840 and 1844 is more significant than the actions of a relatively few voters who might conceivably have remained with the Whigs had Clay substituted prudence for publicity.

Despite the extraordinary intensity of the campaign, compilation and analysis of the relevant data indicates that roughly 95 per cent of the participants voted in 1844 as they had in 1840.[18] Perhaps the basis for that estimate is most clearly suggested by presenting the data for three long-settled towns *whose electorate remained practically unchanged in size and composition.*

TABLE 6

THREE REPRESENTATIVE TOWNS, PARTY VOTE, 1840-1844

| | | Democrat | | Whig | | Liberty | | |
		No.	%	No.	%	No.	%	Total
Blooming Grove,	1840	179	45.0	219	55.0	—	—	398
Orange County	1844	180	45.1	208	52.1	11	2.8	399
Plattekill,	1840	188	43.2	252	56.8	—	—	440
Ulster County	1844	196	44.0	252	54.4	7	1.6	445
Root,	1840	363	60.4	238	39.6	—	—	601
Montgomery County	1844	352	58.0	254	41.8	1	0.2	607

No implication is intended that all units in the state had the same fluctuation pattern, but the figures for these three towns accurately suggest the *central tendency.* Of course, the party percentages conceivably could have remained unchanged even though many voters switched parties. This could have happened if the number of voters who switched from one major party to the other had been approximately the same in each town or ward. That possibility can almost certainly be ruled out for 1844, however. Given the widely different composition of the electorate in approximately 1,000 towns and wards, if many voters had switched parties, only a most remarkable

18 This figure takes into account changes in the electorate's size and composition. Of course, it cannot be established that exactly 95 out of 100 voters cast the same party ballot in 1840 and 1844; but fluctuation was relatively so slight on the town, county, and state levels that the figure seems approximately accurate.

set of circumstances could have produced as little net turnover as actually occurred on that level. In relation to fluctuations in voting behavior, therefore, the most revealing thing that happened in the 1844 election was that so little happened.

3. Gross Turnover, 1840 and 1844

Allowing for a reasonable margin of error, the data seem to warrant the conclusion that from 1840 to 1844 about 25,000 voters switched allegiances. About half of them, I estimate, switched to the Liberty Party; most of the other switches can be attributed to the American Republicans. Probably as a result of heightened group tensions and the Whig-American coalition in several counties, from 2,000 to 3,000 erstwhile Democrats switched to the Whigs in 1844. Yet the coalition boomeranged for the Whigs, because about 4,000 to 5,000 "adopted citizens" abandoned them and switched to the Democrats.[19]

Aside from changes associated with the Liberty and American movements, the close working relations between Whigs and Anti-renters (organized tenant farmers) probably won hundreds of Democrats away from their traditional party.[20] Similarly, though precise estimates are not possible, it seems clear that in the northern counties bordering Canada, hundreds of Democrats who had switched to the Whigs in 1840 because of temporary local issues *returned* to their party in 1844.[21]

After totaling the changes cited above, we can estimate with *rough* accuracy and *reasonable* certainty that no more than one per cent (about 5,000) of the voters in 1844 could have switched from one major party to the other because of campaign issues.

[19] In 1840 the Liberty Party received 2,662 votes for governor; in 1844 its vote had risen to 15,136. The estimates about "desertion" by "adopted citizens" presented in antinativist Whig papers after the election are borne out by a detailed analysis of the voting statistics for local, state, and national offices. See the *New York Tribune* (d.), November 6, 9, 11, 26, 1844, p. 2; *New York Express*, November 30, 1844, p. 2. The latter was a pronativist paper, but, arguing against the contention that the Whigs had suffered from the coalition, it merely claimed that the losses and gains counterbalanced. To support that argument, however, the *Express* had to juggle statistics and distort their meaning.

[20] *New York Morning News*, November 11, 1844, p. 2; *New York Evening Post for the Country*, December 21, 1844, p. 2.

[21] *Albany Argus* (w.), November 23, 1844, p. 379. Even while the campaign was on, the Whigs conceded that they would lose some votes in the border counties because the issues arising out of the 1837 to 1838 "Patriot War" had died out. (*New York Tribune* (w.), August 3, 1844, p. 6.

4. Party Strength, 1844 Compared to 1832

Fluctuation was at a low ebb between 1840 and 1844, but greater fluctuations in party strength become apparent when the time span is lengthened. Compared to 1832—the year that marked the beginning of the stable phase of the 1827 to 1853 voting cycle—the 1844 percentages reveal a more even distribution of party strength. Both major parties tended to register declines in counties where they had been "very strong" (defined below) and gains in counties where they had been very weak. The extreme cases exaggerate the magnitude of change but suggest the central tendency. In Ulster the Democrats declined from 66 to 50 per cent; in Erie they rose from 29 to 41 per cent. Although in most counties the fluctuation from 1832 to 1844 was relatively small, as Table 7 shows, it resulted in a less *polarized* distribution of party strength.

Two different processes caused the Democratic county percentages to cluster around the 50 per cent mark. Erie County offers the most

TABLE 7

DEMOCRATIC AND WHIG STRENGTH, DISTRIBUTION OF COUNTIES
BY PERCENTAGE CATEGORIES, 1832 AND 1844a

Category	1832	1844
DEMOCRATIC		
Very strong Dem. (65.0—)	2	1
Strong Dem. (57.5-64.9)	15	2
Moderate Dem. (52.5-57.4)	11	16
Neutral (47.5-52.4)	13	21
Moderate anti-Dem. (42.5-47.4)	5	10
Strong anti-Dem. (35.0-42.4)	6	5
Very strong anti-Dem. (0.34.9)	3	0
	55	55
ANTIMASONIC-WHIG		
Very strong Whig	3	0
Strong Whig	6	2
Moderate Whig	5	6
Neutral	13	14
Moderate anti-Whig	11	21
Strong anti-Whig	15	11
Very strong anti-Whig	2	1
	55	55

a To keep the table consistent, Chemung, Fulton, and Wyoming counties, which did not exist in 1832, were excluded from the 1844 calculations.

striking example of the first—changes in party percentages stemming from changes in the composition of the electorate; Ulster County the most striking of the second—changes in party percentages stemming from changes in group voting behavior. Detailed analysis of the town and ward data shows that the Democratic gains in Erie occurred gradually and were confined almost exclusively to communities where large numbers of Irish and German immigrants settled after 1830; Democratic losses in Ulster largely occurred from 1837 to 1838 in communities where the composition of the electorate remained stable.[22]

But when the voting patterns for 1832 and 1844 are compared, continuity is much more evident than discontinuity. In 1844, as in 1832, the strongest Democratic counties are found to be in the lower Mohawk and Hudson valleys, the Southern Tier, and the North Country. Similarly, the Whig strongholds are found to be the Antimasonic counties of western New York, and Washington and Essex again form isolated, anti-Democratic bastions in the northern part of the state. Completing this description of the spatial distribution of party strength in 1844, we find that the Liberty vote was highly concentrated in a few central New York counties. The party's strength tended to radiate out from its hub in Madison County (15.4 per cent), Gerrit Smith's home and center of operations.[23]

Finally, absence of rural-urban cleavages constitutes an extremely significant aspect of the distribution of party strength in 1844. Both major parties had considerable strength in rural counties and both parties had considerable strength in almost all counties; neither party was largely dependent on the cities. The Whigs tended to lead the Democrats in urban areas, but the differences generally were not wide. Moreover, the larger total vote in New York City, where the Democrats ran ahead by several percentage points, counterbalanced the Whigs's numerical superiority in other cities.

[22] The large influx of Germans and Irish into Erie County after 1832 is reflected in the fact that foreign-born inhabitants made up 29.8 per cent of the total population in 1845. In contrast, Ulster had 7.7 per cent foreign-born in 1845, an unusually low figure for a Hudson Valley county. Computed from data in the New York State *Census For 1845.* For discussion of the population changes in Erie County and the solid German and Irish support for the Democrats, see the excellent account in John T. Horton, et al., *History of Northwestern New York,* 1: 132-133, 143-158.

[23] In descending order, the ten highest ranking Liberty counties were Madison (15.4 per cent), Clinton, Cortland, Oswego, Cattaraugus, Herkimer, Oneida, Wayne, Jefferson, Niagara (5.0 per cent).

TABLE 8

CITY VOTE IN NEW YORK STATE, 1844

	Dem. %	Whig %	Lib. %
Albany	47.8	51.2	1.0
Brooklyn	46.3	53.1	0.6
Buffalo	50.0	48.3	1.7
Hudson	48.0	52.0	—
New York	51.7	48.2	0.2
Rochester	43.9	53.7	2.4
Schenectady	42.1	57.9	—
Troy	41.4	56.4	2.2
Utica	41.5	52.5	5.9

D. Who Voted for Whom in 1844?

In the North the Whigs represented primarily the owners of accumulated property, the business community, the "squirearchy," and the prosperous farmers living on better soils or along good transportation routes. In contrast, the Democrats represented primarily the "common men," the poor or less-well-to-do farmers, the artisans, mechanics, small businessmen, urban workers, and "rising entrepreneurs."

Through constant repetition by historians, those assertions have achieved the status of verified facts.[24] To trace the processes which led to that development would require a long essay in historiography,[25] but for our purposes it suffices to say that the traditional claims, summarized above, are not applicable to New York. (Without attempting to justify the conclusion in the present book, I do not believe New York is an exceptional case.)

1. A Method of Analyzing Voting Behavior

Since the traditional claims about American voting behavior derive essentially from economic determinism, they rely upon a logi-

[24] See, for example, the accounts in Wilfrid E. Binkley, *American Political Parties* (New York, 1943), 120-180; Arthur M. Schlesinger, Jr., *The Age of Jackson*, 132-143, 177-209, 251-305; Bray Hammond, *Banks and Politics*, 326-368.

The treatment in a provocative recent study indicates that such assertions are no longer automatically accepted by historians. However, since that study does not provide any comprehensive substitute for the traditional economic class analysis of party affiliation, in a later section it actually restates it in somewhat modified form. (Marvin Meyers, *The Jacksonian Persuasion*, Stanford, Cal. 1957, 4-6, 215-217.)

[25] Though the article only examines the historiography of the Jacksonian Democracy concept, see the illuminating discussion in Charles G. Sellers, Jr., "Andrew Jackson versus the Historians," *Mississippi Valley Historical Review*, 44: 615-634 (March 1958).

cally fallacious method of analysis. It is logically fallacious because, in formal terms, it tries to discover the relationships between two variables (economic class and political affiliation) without considering the possible influence of other variables.[26] To discover the relationships between economic class and political affiliation, we must consider not only the possible influence of *all* aspects of economic class (that is, we must not confine our attention to self-interest), but also the possible influence of other variables, such as membership in ethnic groups, membership, or lack of it, in religious groups, previous partisan affiliations, and level of education. Thus to sustain the position that the traditional claims accurately describe the Whig-Democratic cleavage in New York, it is necessary to show that when other attributes are considered, a strong relationship continues to exist between economic class and voting behavior.

For example, it is logically insufficient and may be seriously misleading to ask only whether "workers" supported or failed to support the Democrats. Suppose that the great majority of workers belonged to religious and ethnic groups whose members voted Democratic, *independently of their economic class position.* Under those conditions, a strong, positive relationship between workers and the Democratic Party might turn out to be spurious, that is, their affiliations with the Democrats would be related to their religious and ethnic affiliations, not to their class position.

To discover the relationships between New York workers and the Democratic Party in 1844, questions of this order must be posed and answered: Did workers belonging to different religious and ethnic groups all vote strongly Democratic, or did they vote differently, depending upon their membership in those groups? An extreme case dramatically suggests the need to consider other variables in testing alleged relationships between class and voting behavior: Did Catholic Irish workers and Protestant Irish workers vote alike in 1844? Or did the Catholics vote overwhelmingly Democratic, the Protestants overwhelmingly Whig?

Unfortunately, few of the data needed to answer this type of question have been collected for the country at large. But as will be shown later, convincing evidence can be offered that, in New York at least, Catholic Irish and Protestant Irish workers did vote in

---

[26] In my opinion, the section on "multivariate analysis," in Paul F. Lazarsfeld and Morris Rosenberg, eds., *The Language of Social Research* (Glencoe, Ill., 1955), 109-199, could be of great value to studies in history.

diametrically opposite ways. Similarly, by considering additional variables, the present study tested other claims about strong relationships between economic class and voting behavior. With a few revealing exceptions (noted below), the alleged relationships were found to be either nonexistent in fact or tended to *disappear* when additional variables were considered. In short, if the New York results are at all representative, as I think they are, voting behavior during the 1840's did not follow economic class lines and the traditional historical interpretation lacks foundation.

2. Were the Whigs the Party of the "Classes"?

On the face of it, the data presented in Section *C*, *What Happened in the 1844 Election?*, refute the assumption that the Democrats were primarily the party of the "lower classes." If the Democrats had had significantly disproportionate support among the lower classes, how could the two parties have been evenly balanced on the state, county, and city levels? (It is instructive to note that the same close balance existed on the national level. In 1844 the Democrats received 49.5 per cent, the Whigs 48.1 per cent, and the Liberty Party 2.3 per cent of the total vote.)[27] For example, the "lower classes" must have greatly outnumbered the "upper classes" in the cities. Yet the Whigs had a majority in all but two cities (Table 8 above), and even in New York and Buffalo the Democrats had only a small majority or an even split (51.7 per cent and 50.0 per cent, respectively).

A. CLASS AND PARTY IN THE CITIES. During the 1844 campaign, a Whig orator sardonically noted that the realities of American voting refuted the Democrats' claim that they represented the masses while their opponents represented the "aristocrats." "Who are the Whig voters?" he asked rhetorically: "Who are the millions that arise at the call of such a leader [Clay] to follow him to the LAST great struggle for beneficial Liberty, for Progressive Democracy, for Protective Government? Are they the *aristocracy* of America—merely the men of possession, of wealth and ease? Who believes it? What Tory [Democratic] demagogue does not smile and sneer at the lie when he utters it? But, look at the composition of the two parties, either throughout the nation, or merely in this city; and see how baseless and shadowy the fiction. Of the 22,000 votes in this city conceded

[27] Computed from data in *The Whig Almanac . . . For 1845* (New York, 1845), 53.

to Mr. Clay even by Loco-Foco [Democratic] estimates, how many are to be given by rich men, by 'the privileged orders,' so-called? Are there 22,000 *aristocratic* voters in New York? Wonderful country,—wonderful city,—where more than half the population constitute *aristocracy*! . . . Who crowd these vast assemblies and throng on our streets by day and night in legions, with 'Clay and Protection' on their banners? Not one in a hundred of the men of wealth will leave his dwelling for the fatigue of such an exertion. The attachments of such men to Whig principles are few and feeble, cold and light, compared with the enthusiastic affection, the desperate interest, the laborious, almost convulsive energy, with which the poor, the industrious cling to the cause and its leader as their best, last hope in life."[28]

We need not take all its claims at face value, but, as the quotation suggests, the narrow margin between the parties shows that voting in New York City could not possibly have followed strict class lines. Certainly the contemporary Democratic assertions, echoed by later historians, cannot be accurate. "The Democratic party in the cities was the party of the little man, the day worker, and the millhand."[29] If that claim and its implications were accurate, and if voting had followed strictly class lines, the Whigs would have trailed far behind the Democrats in New York City. Actually, they received 48.9 per cent of the total vote in 1840 and 48.2 per cent in 1844. The data are conceivably consonant, however, with a drastically modified version of the traditional class analysis of voting behavior. Although voting may not have followed rigid class lines, the Democrats may have received *somewhat stronger support* from the lower classes than from the entire city electorate. By analyzing the ward data, we can test that possibility.[30]

[28] *New York Tribune* (w.), October 19, 1844, p. 1.

[29] This typical quotation is from Dixon Ryan Fox, "The Negro Vote in Old New York," *Political Science Quarterly*, 32: 274 (June 1917).

[30] For contemporary descriptions and for those made by later historians of New York City wards, see *New York Tribune* (d.), November 6, 1844, p. 2; *New York Tribune* (w.), November 24, 1849, p. 3; November 14, 1854; *New York Herald* (d.), November 8, 1852, p. 1; November 7, 1855, p. 1; Dixon Ryan Fox, *Decline of Aristocracy In The Politics of New York*, 430-432; Robert Ernst, *Immigrant Life in New York City: 1825-1863*, 39-47, 82-83, 167; Carl N. Degler, "Labor In The Economy And Politics Of New York, 1850-1860" (Columbia University, Ph.D., 1952), 332-337. Degler presented an excellent critique of the pioneering methods Fox used to establish the economic class character of urban wards. Though his own method represented a considerable improvement, it rested primarily upon census data. In my opinion, because of the large size and heterogeneous character of New York wards, such statistical data permit only very gross distinctions between wards. The present

At first glance, the ward returns appear to support the claim that the Whig-Democratic cleavage followed economic class lines. The weakest Democratic ward (the Fifteenth, 33.0 per cent) undoubtedly had the largest percentage of wealthy men among its voters; the strongest Democratic ward (the Eleventh, 65.6 per cent) undoubtedly had a high percentage of poor, working-class voters.

To stop the analysis here would give credence to the traditional claim. But further analysis shows that the Democrats received only 52.5 per cent in the *median* ward and scored higher than 53.5 per cent in only six of the seventeen wards. Moreover, five of those six high Democratic wards contained very high percentages of Irish or German-born inhabitants who were, for the most part, Catholics. In contrast, the lowest Democratic wards tended to contain *relatively* low percentages of foreign-born inhabitants. (Every ward contained large *numbers* of immigrants. Ranked according to that criterion, the lowest contained 22.3 per cent, the median had 36.5 per cent, and the highest 52.0 per cent. These percentages considerably understate the proportion of non-native Americans, as that term is defined below, for they do not include immigrants' children who were born in the United States.)[31]

The data cited above show that the moderate to strong Democratic percentages in six of the seventeen wards did *not* necessarily relate to their economic class composition. Instead, they suggest that the high Democratic Party percentages may actually have reflected the overwhelming support of Irish Catholic, German, and French voters, as well as Catholics in general, regardless of class, for the Democratic Party. That members of those groups did vote Democratic everywhere throughout the state will be shown later; here the point is that when we consider other attributes, we find that the Democrats in New York City cannot be said to have received disproportionate support from the lower classes.

Mechanics comprised such a large proportion of the Tenth ward's population that it was popularly known as the Mechanics' Ward.[32] Although many immigrants of Irish or German birth lived there,

---

study relied upon both impressionistic and statistical material in estimating the economic character of the several wards.

[31] All urban ward and rural town percentages of native and foreign-born are computed from data in the New York *Census for 1845*. Contemporary descriptions, and the material in Ernst, *Immigrant Life In New York City, passim*, were used to identify the ethnic composition of immigrants in New York City wards.

[32] *New York Tribune* (w.), September 28, 1844, p. 2.

compared to the composition of the electorate in other wards, they formed a *relatively* small proportion (26.1 per cent) of its inhabitants. Thus it is significant and revealing that this almost completely lower-class ward gave the Democrats only 53.5 per cent of its total vote. If we grant overwhelming Irish, German, and Catholic support for the Democrats, it logically follows that *a majority of the natives of Protestant background* in the Mechanics' Ward must have supported the Whigs. And the same observation can be made about the Fifth and Eighth wards. Both wards were overwhelmingly lower class and both had *relatively* low (though substantial) foreign-born percentages. Yet the Democrats received only 45.7 per cent of the vote in the Fifth, and 49.6 per cent in the Eighth. Since they contained a sizeable proportion of "adopted citizens" who, according to our assumption, voted Democratic *en masse*, it again follows that the Whigs received a clear majority among their native Protestant lower-class voters.[33]

[33] Dixon Ryan Fox conceded that "the fifth and eighth wards, the majority of whose inhabitants were poor mechanics, several times presented Whig majorities." Attempting to salvage his class interpretation, he then claimed that "the residents here who actually voted were in more comfortable circumstances than would at first appear; for reference to another column [of a table] will disclose that here a considerable proportion of these workingmen were colored, and hence without the ballot, except for those who were possessed of property worth two hundred and fifty dollars. And the negroes who were thus qualified, as we have seen, were likely from historic reasons to support the Whigs."

This can only mean that the Whig majorities reflected the presence in those wards of a large number of relatively well-to-do, qualified Negro voters. Though a considerable number of Negroes did live in the fifth and eighth wards, Fox cited no evidence or logical reason for the assumption that they contained a large number of *eligible Negro voters*. I believe that in this and similar instances Fox fell victim to the well-known dangers of the "dominant hypothesis." Finding that the data frequently contradicted his economic determinist interpretation, he either made untenable assumptions, or was unable to perceive the contradiction. Actually, an informed contemporary observer estimated that only about 1,000 Negroes voted in the entire state in the mid-1840's—or about two per cent of the Negro population. Even if the same proportion of Negroes qualified and voted in the lower-class fifth and eighth wards, they numbered about 50 and 40, respectively, a minuscule fraction of the wards' electorate.

Compare Fox, *Decline of Aristocracy in New York*, 431-436, with the remarks of Federal Dana, *Debates and Proceedings in the New York State Convention . . .* [1846] (Albany, 1846), 790. Dana's estimate seems reasonable, since only about 2,000 free Negroes in New York paid *any* taxes, while the suffrage requirements called for a freehold valued at $250. As late as 1860, the *Albany Evening Journal* estimated the total Negro vote in the state to be about 1,500. *Ibid.*, February 13, 1860, p. 2.

All of Fox's attempts to use the "witness of statistics" to support his thesis are open to similar criticisms. To cite but one example: using circulation figures of cheap daily newspapers as an indicator of lower class party affiliation, he noted that the *Tribune* was the only Whig paper in that category. He then estimated that the *Tribune* had about 10,000 of the 62,500 lower class "readers" of cheap dailies, "rep-

Similarly, systematic examination of the data reveals that if certain groups of "foreign" voters, as well as Catholics in general, are separated from the rest of the electorate—I estimate that those groups provided from one third to one half of the Democratic strength in the city—the Whigs must have been supported by the majority of native Protestants *in every ward*, whether upper or lower class in economic character. Even the "aristocratic" Fifteenth ward probably contained only a small proportion of voters who belonged to the upper classes. Therefore, its strong support for the Whigs fails to discredit the postelection estimate of a leading anti-Whig newspaper that "a large portion of the monied men and capitalists of this city and throughout the State, voted the Democratic ticket. . . ."[34]

The data cited above sustain these summary conclusions: although it may be literally true, it is thoroughly misleading to assert that the Democratic Party had strong lower class support in New York City. As will be demonstrated below, its strength was actually concentrated among voters who belonged to certain religious and ethnic groups, not among lower class voters per se. The observation that groups that voted overwhelmingly Democratic also happened to be largely lower class in composition reflects a casual rather than a causal relationship.

To reinforce the argument that traditional claims about Democratic strength among the urban lower classes rest upon spurious relationships, attention is directed to Buffalo, the only other city in the state where the Democrats were the majority party. Like New York, the Buffalo ward returns have been cited as contributing support to "the economic interpretation" of voting behavior.[35] No doubt, the Fourth and First wards which registered the highest Democratic percentages (63.9 per cent and 61.6 per cent) also contained the

---

resenting, probably, the proportion of Whig strength there to be found." This implies that the other cheap dailies were Democratic organs. Actually, the large circulation papers were careful to proclaim their neutrality and the *Plebeian* was the only avowedly Democratic cheap daily. The source Fox used for his estimate of the *Tribune's* circulation gives the *Plebeian's* as 2,000. If this criterion were accepted as valid and applied systematically, the Whigs had about five times as many lower class supporters as the Democrats. That finding, of course, is nonsensical; I use it only to show the weaknesses in Fox's use of "statistics" to bolster the "economic interpretations." Compare *ibid.*, 426-427; Frederick Hudson, *Journalism In The United States* (New York, 1873), 525; *New York State Register For 1843* (Albany, 1843), 146-147.

[34] *New York Herald* (w.), November 9, 1844, p. 356.

[35] Fox, *Decline Of Aristocracy*, 436-437, 445-446.

highest percentages of lower class voters. But, as in New York City, they also contained the highest percentages of Irish and German-born voters who, for the most part, were Catholics.[36] In fact, in the five Buffalo wards, a near perfect rank order relationship can be seen between Democratic strength and foreign-born percentage; this is made clearer when we compare the 1840 and 1844 returns, which neatly suggest the extent to which the Democratic vote varied with the proportion of "adopted citizens" in each ward.

In 1840 the Democrats carried only the First ward, which was heavily Irish Catholic. Except in the closely-balanced Fourth ward, the area of German concentration where the Whigs received only 50.2 per cent, the Whigs overwhelmed their opponents. Between 1840 and 1844, however, as the influx of Germans continued, the size and composition of the electorate in the Fourth changed greatly, and it swung sharply to the Democrats. That is, the number of Whigs remained practically the same (316 in 1840, 325 in 1844), but the number of Democrats nearly doubled (313 in 1840, 602 in 1844). Apart from the inferences we may draw from the statistics, contemporary expert observers of both parties agreed that the Germans voted Democratic *en masse*. And there is no reason to doubt the Whig postelection estimates—made both privately and publicly—that the 1,400 foreigners naturalized since 1840 in Erie County (mostly in Buffalo) voted "against us almost to a man."[37]

Thus detailed analysis of the returns in Buffalo, New York City, and every other city in the state not only fails to support the traditional claims about voting behavior, but it demonstrates that the lower class-Democratic relationship is a spurious one.

B. CLASS AND PARTY IN RURAL AREAS. If for the cities the traditional interpretation of voting behavior rests upon spurious relationships, for the rural areas, where the great bulk of the electorate lived, it simply lacks factual basis. To test the economic interpretation, a quantitative measure was devised to classify rural towns in

---

[36] "Roman Catholicism was the denominational preference of most of the Germans and practically all of the Irish" in Erie County. Horton, *Northwestern New York*, 1: 132, 143-153.

[37] "Contrary to all our anticipations the foreign vote of this county went almost unanimously against us, and as near as I can calculate our majority on the electoral ticket is 1838, when we should have had 2800." Millard Fillmore to Thurlow Weed, November 6, 1844, in Frank H. Severance, ed., "Millard Fillmore Papers," 11: 267. See also *ibid.*, 11: 268; *New York Express*, November 12, 1844, p. 1; *Albany Argus* (w.), November 1, 1844, p. 370.

five economic categories, "unusually prosperous," "very prosperous," "prosperous," "marginal," and "poor." Constructed from the average value of dwelling per family, the measure, when judged by a variety of independent quantitative and qualitative criteria, proved to be highly reliable.[38] Taking the state as a whole, we find that no significant relationship existed between *wealth* and voting in 1844, whether or not other attributes were considered. (The relationships between *occupational groups* and party affiliation will be discussed later.)

With few exceptions anywhere in the state, it was found that, in the same county, numerous towns with roughly the same degree of prosperity *varied widely in their voting patterns,* and that towns with the same voting patterns *varied widely in their degree of prosperity.* In some counties a tendency existed for economically low ranking units to be the low ranking Democratic units, but in others, economically low ranking units tended to be the high ranking Democratic units. At best, in only a few counties could there be found any clear-cut relation between wealth and party affiliation; and even those disappeared when other variables were considered.

Three counties from different parts of the state can serve as representative examples of the general tendency. Beginning with southeastern New York, we find that the "marginal" towns of Davenport and Hamden in Delaware County were practically identical in respect to economic status (average value of dwelling per family was $305 and $302, respectively). Despite this similarity, the former gave the Democrats 82.1 per cent of its vote, and the latter 31.8 per cent. On the other hand, Delhi and Masonville cast about the same Democratic vote (48.5 per cent and 46.8 per cent, respectively), yet they stood at opposite ends of the county's economic scale ($613 compared to $258). The table below illustrates the kind of analysis made for all counties (except urban areas, where the average value of dwelling per family could not be accurately constructed from the available data, and did not constitute a valid measure of wealth.)

Located in the Mohawk Valley, Montgomery County shows the same more-or-less random relationship between wealth and voting behavior as Delaware. Actually, the "prosperous" agricultural town of St. Johnsville ($567) bordered the Mohawk River and was the

[38] The procedures used to classify political units according to their economic characteristics are described in detail in Appendix II.

TABLE 9

DELAWARE COUNTY, RANK ORDER, 1844 DEMOCRATIC PERCENTAGE
AND ECONOMIC STATUS

Town	Democratic Vote Rank Order	%	Economic Status[a] Rank Order	Av. Val. Dwell. per Family
Davenport	1	82.1	12	$305
Tompkins	2	75.9	7	378
Sidney	3	74.9	11	325
Colchester	4	73.8	16	203
Franklin	5	72.9	5	441
Middletown	6	64.4	15	204
Meredith	7	54.9	10	332
Walton	8	54.7	9	343
Kortright	9	52.9	3	453
Hancock	10	51.5	–	na
Delhi	11	48.5	1	613
Harpersfield	12	47.9	6	428
Masonville	13	46.8	14	258
Roxbury	14	46.3	4	447[b]
Stamford	15	44.9	2	473
Bovina	16	40.9	8	377
Andes	17	32.5	–	na
Hamden	18	31.8	13	302

[a] The data are for 1855, the first year for which these statistics are available. But convincing evidence in county histories shows that the *relative* economic status of towns changed little between 1844 and 1855.

[b] The data are for 1865; the 1855 data are not available.

county's banner Democratic unit (65.6 per cent); the "poor" agricultural town of Charlestown ($268), the only one in the county not along the river route, was the second lowest Democratic unit (46.0 per cent).

The pattern repeats itself in the western New York county of Wayne. Wolcott was the highest Democratic town with 59.5 per cent, Marion the lowest with 29.2 per cent. Yet, both occupied almost the same position on the county economic scale ($389 compared to $420). In contrast, Palmyra, an important distribution center along the Erie Canal, one of the very few "unusually prosperous" ($971) towns in the state, ranked highest economically in the county and cast the second *highest* Democratic vote (58.7 per cent). The second *lowest* Democratic town (32.6 per cent), Ontario, a long distance from the canal, was among the poorest in the county ($275).

Perhaps the most dramatic way to illustrate the inaccuracy of the traditional claims about voting behavior is to present the data for the two towns in the state that received the highest and lowest Democratic vote. Clarkstown in Rockland County was a "very prosperous" ($629) Hudson River town, but its 89.9 per cent Democratic vote established it, by a considerable margin, as that party's banner unit. The second highest Democratic unit (83.9 per cent) was an extremely "poor" ($94), isolated interior town (Croghan in Lewis County). The lowest Democratic unit was Putnam, a "marginal" ($339) town in Washington County, where the Democratic vote was 18.5 per cent of the total. West Bloomfield, the next lowest unit, gave the Democrats 19.3 per cent. Though "prosperous" ($477), it ranked economically among the lowest in Ontario County.[39]

3. Where Did the Traditional Interpretation Go Wrong?

How can we account for the startling gap between the traditional claims about New York voting behavior and the findings revealed by systematic collection and ordering of the data? Without attempting to answer that question fully, and without going into the historiography of the economic determinist interpretation, we can identify two closely related contributing factors. One is the time-honored but fallacious assumption concerning the impact of the Erie Canal on rural prosperity in central and western New York; the other is the lack of an intensive study of the Antimasonic movement and Party, particularly of its socioeconomic composition.

It may have seemed plausible to assume that the Erie Canal brought prosperity to the farmers in all the counties along its route, particularly the "commercial farmers" in western New York, and that *they therefore voted Whig*.[40] But it did not happen that way. Though the canal spectacularly benefited many places and individuals, its completion in 1825 did not signal the beginning of general prosperity throughout central and western New York—and the prosperous places did not necessarily vote Whig. The roseate picture that is traditionally painted of those regions after 1825 is not consistent with the bitter, enduring conflicts that actually were fought between hard-pressed tenant or debtor-farmers and great

---

[39] In every case cited in this section, the classification based on the criterion, average value of dwelling per family, was consonant with the description of the town in county histories.

[40] See, for example, Fox, *op.cit.*, 302-310; Frederick Jackson Turner, *The United States: 1830-1850*, 116-119.

landlords or land companies. Before 1844, western New York in particular had been wracked by agrarian struggles for decades.[41]

Thus, accounts describing the attack upon an "oppressive" company's land office in Mayville, Chautauqua County resemble accounts describing the attacks upon *chateaux* in France during the Revolution.

Early in 1836, the successors to the Holland Land Company imposed severe terms on debtor-farmers. Great excitement developed and spread throughout western New York.[42] "The owners had grown wealthy by the industry of the settlers, and their agents rolled in fatness; to impose such terms at a time and under such circumstances as, in a majority of instances, would deprive the settlers of their farms and compel them to abandon their possessions, while a course of fair dealing and equitable requirements on the part of the owners would enable them, after a few more years of toil, to call the soil on which the fire and vigor of their manhood had been expended, their own, was more than they would submit to or endure."[43]

Indignation swept the entire region, but reached its highest pitch in Chautauqua County. The more the "oppressive" exactions of the new "Genesee Tariff" were discussed, "the more were the people incensed and inclined to resort to harsh measures." Angry village gatherings fanned resentment and a call for a public meeting soon circulated through the county towns. It was generally understood that the climax of the meeting would be destruction of the company's Mayville land office.

"On the 6th of February, from 300 to 500 people assembled at Barnhart's inn at Hartfield. They were principally from Gerry, Ellery, Charlotte, Stockton, Poland, Ellicott, Busti, and Harmony. Roland Cobb of Gerry was chosen chairman. Gen. George T. Camp was solicited by several to become their leader in the contemplated enterprise, but he declined and in an earnest speech endeavored to induce them to abandon their violent intentions. The chairman also said that the Land Company might yet be willing to make terms, should another conference be had with them. Nathan Cheney, an intelligent and resolute old settler,

41 A systematic study of agrarian conflicts in western New York remains to be made, but see the accounts in Paul D. Evans, *The Holland Land Company*, 305-427; Neil McNall, *An Agricultural History of the Genesee Valley, 1790-1860* (Philadelphia, 1952), 32-51, 210-227.

42 Evans, *op.cit.*, 398-404.

43 Georgia Drew Merrill, ed., *History of Chautauqua County, New York* (Boston, 1894), 338.

who stood leaning upon a sled-stake while the speeches were being made, now abruptly and effectively addressed the meeting in these words: 'Those who are going to Mayville with me fall into line.'

"The whole assemblage at once obeyed the order, chose Cheney for their leader . . . [and marched in double file to the Land Office in Mayville] admittance was first demanded to which no response was given. Cheney, in a strong voice, then gave the order to strike, which was obeyed, and all the windows came out with a crash. The door was broken down, and an entrance to the building effected. A costly clock was disposed of by the blow of an ax. A valuable map of the county, upon which every farm was delineated, was destroyed. The axmen made light work of the furniture and woodwork. They cut the posts and canted the building over. They found some difficulty in opening the vault that contained the safe, which was made of solid mason-work of cut stone. Van Pelt pried out the keystone with an iron bar; others took one of the pillars of the building and used it as a battering ram, and strong arms soon battered down the door of the vault. The iron safe enclosed was pried open, *and half a cord of the books and papers of the company were taken out, placed on a sleigh and carried to Hartfield where a bonfire was made and they were burned* [italics added]. Some of them, however, were carried away by the people and have been preserved. The party dispersed and went to their homes about midnight.

"The most of those engaged in this affair held contracts for the purchase of land, and, in many instances, would have suffered ruinous consequences from the Company's exactions."[44]

Copied from a county history that was warmly sympathetic to the settlers, this account undoubtedly relates the version of the Mayville riot that is celebrated in the local folklore. Fortunately, letters from the company's agent to his superior have been preserved which enable us to view the same events through his eyes. The first letter, dated at Mayville, five o'clock in the morning, February 7, 1836, might almost have been written by an estate bailiff to his lord at Versailles in August, 1789: "My office is destroyed last night by a mob of about 300 Men from the East part of the County, they came armed with guns, Rifles & Clubs. I just made my escape—they have burnt, carried off & destroyed all the Books, Land Ledgers and every paper almost of any value—they have threatened death to the whole of us—It was given out by them that all the offices would share the same fate last night if nothing prevented it—I feel indeed bad, very bad—My heart is sick & my office is in ruins. . . ."[45]

[44] *Ibid.*, 339-340.   [45] Evans, 404; the quotation below is from p. 405.

The next letter, dated Ripley, February 8, conveys the sense of terror that drove the agent to flight: "I had to flee last night from my House & cannot tell what has happened to it—My life is threatened, & since the destruction of my office & Books, they seem to be more bold—god knows what it will end in—The only thing that I can find out, which has caused this state of things, is the [Genesee] *Tariff.* . . . I press it upon you to keep a good lookout for your safety —as we are all under the same danger by this horrid mob—There is in my opinion an absolute necessity for the military arm to step out & seize these persons—or our persons or property are not safe."

Contrary to the impression given in both accounts quoted above, the riot did not attain its immediate objective of destroying the company's records in order to prevent it from proceeding against the settlers. In time, documents that permitted an exact reconstruction of each man's obligations were recovered. The Mayville riot and similar outbreaks elsewhere, however, indirectly resulted in the settlers' achieving their main goals. Shortly afterwards, a regional agrarian convention was held in Buffalo at which Millard Fillmore and other Whig leaders played prominent roles. It created an executive committee to carry on the fight against the company, appointed town committees to widen the struggle and collect funds, and formed a committee to bring pressure upon the legislature to investigate the validity of the company's title.[46]

Legislative attacks upon the company by leading politicians, assaults by settlers upon its offices, and growing financial difficulties convinced its directors that its best course of action was to reorganize and adopt new policies. One partner in the resulting new enterprise, William Seward, soon took over general management of its affairs. According to the historian of the Holland Land Company, Seward's "administration was completely successful. By a well-judged mixture of indulgence and firmness he soon established both friendly relations with the settlers and a satisfactory situation [*sic*] of the debts [owed by the settlers to the new proprietors]."[47]

Aside from helping us to reconstruct the relationships between Whig leaders and debtor-farmers, the violent agrarian conflicts in western New York also help to demolish the traditional assumption that general prosperity ruled the region after 1825. An unusually

---

[46] *Ibid.,* 405-423.

[47] *Ibid.,* 424-425. See also the brief account of Seward's role in Frederic Bancroft, *The Life of William H. Seward,* 1: 57-59.

good history of Chautauqua County gives a more accurate account of the condition of the *average* farmer during the "early farming period," 1825 to 1851. "The population of the county in 1835 was forty-four thousand eight hundred sixty-nine, an increase of ten thousand two hundred twelve in five years, showing the effect that the Erie Canal had upon the prosperity of the County, and also showing in what high esteem the County was held abroad. Yet the inhabitants of the County were still poor, their lands in most instances unpaid for, and all that they had was represented by the labor that they had expended in clearing and improving their lands. . . . In the early part of the period that elapsed between . . . [completion of the Erie Canal in 1825 and completion of the Erie *Railroad* in 1851] the wealth of the County was small. The stores and principal buildings were unpretentious. The dwellings along the straggling and poorly worked roads often stood among the stumps in the open fields, or a few yards from the highway in irregular yards fenced with rails or logs. The log houses were in the majority except in the north part of the County. Upon the back roads they were universal. . . . The farming was rude and primitive. The farms having been but recently cleared, the farmers had to contend with stumps, roots and cradle knolls. The fields were usually enclosed by brush or log fences, and the cattle and sheep often had no other screen from the weather than a straw stack or rude shed. The hogs were often turned into the woods to fatten upon beechnuts [homely details of simple residence]. . . . The tall well-sweep standing guard over all completes the picture of the house and its surroundings of the *average citizen* [italics added] of Chautauqua County in the period immediately preceding the building of the Erie Railroad [that is, until 1852]."[48]

Yet in 1844 Chautauqua was the highest ranking Whig county in the state (59.6 per cent), and had given that party heavy majorities ever since its formal organization in 1834. Moreover, most of the towns that supplied the men for the Mayville riot belong in the category, "very strong anti-Democratic." As the table below demonstrates, only one of the eight towns cited in the quotation above

---

[48] The quotation actually is spliced together from different pages, but it is in context. See Obed Edson, *Centennial History of Chautauqua County* (Jamestown, N.Y., 1904), 136, 154. In 1849 a letter from "Chautauqua County" noted that it was settled "by men of very small means" who still had difficulty in paying for their lands. In the town of Clymer, for example, a large portion "of the soil is not paid for by the occupants, consequently the 'Land Office' acts as a constant drain upon the industry and energies of the county." *New York Tribune* (w.), June 9, 1849, p. 6.

(p. 151-152) gave the Democrats more than 36.5 per cent of their vote—several registered much lower percentages.

TABLE 10

CHAUTAUQUA COUNTY TOWNS PARTICIPATING IN
MAYVILLE RIOT, 1836; PARTY PERCENTAGES, 1834, 1844

| TOWN | 1834 | | 1844 | | |
	Whig %	Dem. %	Whig %	Dem. %	Liberty %
Busti	73.1	26.9	68.6	24.9	6.6
Charlotte	56.4	43.6	54.4	44.9	0.7
Ellery	65.5	34.5	63.9	36.1	—
Ellicott	59.0	41.0	56.3	35.3	8.3
Gerry	69.7	30.3	65.9	28.3	5.7
Harmony	74.4	25.6	72.9	26.6	0.4
Poland	69.1	30.9	64.4	31.2	4.4
Stockton	59.5	40.5	63.3	36.4	0.3

The Mayville land agent, I suspect, would not have been easily convinced that the Whig debtor-farmers who sacked his office, or who approved that action (majority opinion in the county apparently favored the rioters), were devoted to a neo-Federalist, conservative doctrine of property rights. Yet that is the impression of "Whiggery" given by historians who stand committed to the Jacksonian Democracy concept.[49]

It may be true that by 1844 economic conditions had probably improved somewhat in Chautauqua (and elsewhere in the region), as compared to 1836 when the Mayville riot occurred. It would still be misleading to argue that the Whigs in western New York were primarily the party of the prosperous farmers. Other considerations aside, by 1832 the hot iron of Antimasonry had branded the region with its permanent (to-date) voting pattern. A perceptive local historian who had been active in Chautauqua County politics noted correctly that "one familiar with the history of the politics of the county during successive years of struggle between Democrats and Whigs, and the still later contests between Democrats and Republi-

---

[49] Compare the account in the present study with the chapter, "The Whig Counter-Reformation," in Schlesinger, *Age of Jackson*, 267-282. According to the leading student of western New York land history, "The majority of the citizens of Chautauqua County seemed to look upon the [Mayville] attack as a just reprisal for the oppressive measures of the new proprietors and the author suspects that they winked knowingly at one another over the expressions of deep regret and righteous indignation which appeared in the local papers." (Evans, 405.)

cans, can trace to the present time [1904] in the vote of the county and in each of the towns of the county the strong impress that anti-masonic sentiment made upon the minds of the people. . . ."[50]

As noted earlier, although an intensive study of Antimasonry remains to be made, all available evidence indicates that the "blessed spirit" was most fervent among the poorer farmers belonging to the evangelical sects. Thus even assuming that most Whig voters in western New York were prosperous by 1844—and little basis exists for that assumption—the crucial point remains that they had been Antimasons and Whigs *long before they became prosperous*. Moreover, as will be shown below, the Democrats tended to find their strongest support in eastern New York among groups living in long-settled areas and enjoying considerable prosperity. Systematically examined, therefore, the data reveal that the traditional economic interpretation of voting behavior breaks down in the rural areas as well as in the cities.

4. Occupational Group and Party

To reject the traditional claims does not force us to conclude that *no* relationships existed between economic class and voting during the 1830's and 1840's. On the contrary, I assume that such a relationship tends to exist in some form and to some extent at all times in American history. But I maintain also that historians must try to develop a theory that will *specify the conditions under which different types of economic factors are most likely to exercise determining influence upon the voting behavior of specific classes or groups of men*. Concretely, although I reject an interest group theory of politics, I assume that economic factors are most likely to determine voting behavior when direct, significant, and clearly perceived relationships exist among government action, party policy, and material interests. Stated in that abstract, general form, the assumption seems obvious enough, perhaps even tautological. Yet a survey of the literature suggests that its implications have not been readily grasped.[51] In effect, the traditional interpretation expresses an economic determinist bias and implicitly assumes that the requisite con-

---

[50] Edson, *op.cit.*, 160.

[51] Actually, the survey revealed that, as a rule, American historians have made little attempt to specify the conditions under which any type of voting determinant has operated in any election. The findings of that survey were partially reported in Benson, "Research Problems in American Political Historiography," in Komarovsky, ed., *Common Frontiers of the Social Sciences*, 113-183.

ditions are almost always present and that economic factors almost always significantly and *directly* influence the voting behavior of most Americans. I do not believe that assumption is well-founded.

In general, the literature presents findings based upon one or the other of two different types of economic analyses of voting behavior; one stresses economic class as measured by wealth, the other stresses occupational group as the criterion of class. But wealth and occupation are frequently lumped together indiscriminately, with little effort made to discover their joint or individual relation to voting behavior, or their relationships to social status. For example, though he was trying to correct loose generalizations made by earlier historians, Frederick Jackson Turner offered this typically vague description of urban voting patterns in the Middle Atlantic states; ". . . It is unsafe to generalize as to the attitude of large cities in this section, for, while (with the single exception of 1848) New York City was consistently Democratic in its Presidential vote, Philadelphia was steadfastly Whig. One may say, however, that, as in New England, Democracy found its strength among the poorer people, while the capitalists, bankers, merchants, and manufacturers, and their following, were usually Whigs."[52]

Such formulations do not recognize that great differences in wealth and size of enterprise existed among men who engaged in the same type of business or belonged to the same occupational group. Moreover, within a broad group such as "merchants" or "manufacturers," functional differences existed, differences, for example, between importing merchants and merchants acting as agents for domestic manufacturers, as well as between textile or iron manufacturers and coach or wagon makers. Once the potential significance of such differences in wealth or function is recognized, we can see that, even if we ignore social status, economic categories must be identified fairly precisely before *causal relationships* between voting behavior and class can be discovered.

Having challenged the interpretation that uses wealth as the indicator of economic class, we can turn our attention to the interpretation that uses occupational group. For example, one authority on American political parties, summarizing a widely-held view, asserted that ". . . wool-growers [in Vermont and Massachusetts] were protectionists and their communities show up on election maps as Whig."

[52] Turner, *United States: 1830-1850*, 117.

Essentially the same claim has been made, less succinctly, about voting behavior in New York.[53] Perhaps that claim is accurate and states a causal relationship in New England, but for New York it has little factual basis.

David Ellis' excellent history of New York agriculture covers the period under consideration and singles out Otsego, Dutchess, and Washington as leading wool-growing counties.[54] Yet the 1844 Whig vote in those counties encompassed *almost the entire range of the party's strength within the state*. It varied from 41.9 per cent in Otsego, to 49.7 per cent in Dutchess, to 57.6 per cent in Washington. Fortunately, a study of agriculture in Otsego County ranks the *towns* according to their relative number of sheep in 1845,[55] which permits us to test the relationship between wool-growing and party affiliation. Using the Democratic vote since some Whigs supported the Liberty Party in 1844, we see that the eight towns that contained large numbers of sheep exhibited a wide range of party strength. Ordered by political category, one town falls into the "very strong Democratic" category, two "strong Democratic," another "moderate Democratic," two "neutral," and two others "strong anti-Democratic." This negative finding is particularly convincing because the Democrats were the majority party in Otsego, and because the county's ethnic composition was unusually homogeneous. (New Englanders constituted an extremely high proportion of Otsego's population.)

Contemporary observers support the conclusions derived from the statistical data. For example, in 1844 Columbia County divided narrowly between the two parties (52 per cent Democratic, 48 per cent Whig). One disappointed Whig analyzed the returns and commented sardonically upon his party's failure to obtain strong support from sheep raisers. The farmers in Austerlitz, he claimed, were extensive wool growers who had benefited from the Whig tariff of 1842: "In view of its direct interest in this matter, wool-growing Austerlitz gave a Whig majority of eighteen, instead of increasing her majority of 1840, which was seventy-two. Hillsdale—Adjoins Austerlitz, and has the same interest in the perpetuation of the tariff,

53 Binkley, *op.cit.*, 163; Fox, *op.cit.*, 325-326.
54 David M. Ellis, *Landlords and Farmers in the Hudson-Mohawk Region: 1790-1850* (Ithaca, N.Y., 1946), 196.
55 Alexander Joss, "An Economic Study of Land Utilization in Otsego County, New York," Cornell University Agricultural Experiment Station, *Bulletin 791* (Ithaca, N.Y., 1943), 12.

being also a wool-growing town; and to show how well she understood her interest, she declared in favor of no duty on wool by giving Mr. Polk a majority of 147! being an increase of 51 votes over Mr. Van Buren's majority in 1840."[56]

Why did the tariff issue not induce wool-growing towns to cast heavy Whig majorities? One obvious explanation is that in areas where the issue was salient, Democrats also endorsed a pro-tariff policy, thus blurring the differences between the parties.[57] Another and more fundamental explanation is that the term "wool grower" misleads us, except when applied to a very small group of voters. As Ellis has observed, "Wool never became the most important business for most farmers. It was merely an item in mixed husbandry, with the average farmer keeping from one hundred to two hundred animals."[58] That is, contrary to traditional assumptions, the tariff could have had relatively little direct, immediate effect on the fortunes of most "wool growers." Perhaps if we considered the possible effects of a number of variables—in other words, if we used "multivariate analysis"—we would find that large-scale sheep farmers voted solidly Whig. Such a finding would be consonant with the theoretical assumptions of this study, but to my knowledge no one has demonstrated it empirically. Moreover, since large-scale wool growers constituted only a small fraction of the electorate, they could not have accounted for the strong Whig vote in many farming towns and counties.

"Bankers" can more reasonably be regarded as a distinct occupational group during the 1840's. It is useful, however, to recognize that in an era dominated by unspecialized entrepreneurs, many "bankers" might easily be classified under other headings. For example, Erastus Corning, an Albany Regency leader, wore many hats, including bank president, iron manufacturer, railroad president, and large-scale hardware merchant.[59] But if we ignore their

---

56 Letter signed "V," *New York Courier and Enquirer*, November 21, 1844, p. 2.

57 "In New York, Pennsylvania, and other portions of the middle and eastern states, both parties claim to be tariff, whatever their candidates may be by this or that declaration of their position." *New York Herald* (w.), October 12, 1844, p. 325. For Whig charges that in pro-tariff areas the Democrats disguised their real position on the tariff and particularly tried to pull the wool over voters' eyes in "sheep counties," see *New York Tribune* (d.), November 8, 23, 25, 1844, p. 2; *New York Morning Express*, January 16, 1844, p. 2.

58 Ellis, *Landlords and Farmers*, 196.

59 Allen Johnson and Dumas Malone, eds., *Dictionary of American Biography* (New York, 1930), 4: 446-447.

other occupational ties, how accurate is the claim that, in New York state, bankers "and their following were usually Whigs?"

To assess that claim, as well as the more comprehensive hypothesis from which it derived, an attempt was made to discover the party affiliations of the presidents and cashiers of every bank in the state in 1844. Although the study did not obtain the information required for a *comprehensive* collective biography of the 300 men involved, sufficient data were collected to make this conclusion seem credible: "It is not correct to say that . . . [New York] bankers were members of one particular party as opposed to another . . . the bankers in 1844 were not prone to be Whigs any more than they were to be Democrats." For example, of the seven bankers in Albany County whose political affiliations were definitely established, four were Democrats and three were Whigs.[60]

Abandon the a priori assumption that the Whigs represented the "business community" and the Democrats the "other sections of society," and that finding should cause little surprise. Why should the occupational interests or associations of bankers have led them to join the Whig Party, particularly in states like New York where long Democratic control of the legislature had made that party the best political investment for prudent entrepreneurs? A comprehensive analysis would require that similar questions be asked and answered about every occupational group that has been particularly identified with one party or the other.

For example, why, simply because of their occupational interests or associations, should "merchants" have voted either Whig or Democratic? I do not believe that any answer to that question has ever been given that is either logically compelling or factually correct. It is true, however, that if we analyze more precisely the broad category, "merchants," we may find a causal relationship between occupational group and party affiliation. "Yesterday the Whigs passed through Pine Street [in New York City], *calling upon all the commission merchants who deal with domestic goods* [italics added], and all traders of other descriptions, known to be Whigs, to make contributions of money for the approaching [1844] elections."[61]

[60] Leonard Zivitz, "The Political Affiliations of Bankers in New York State in 1844" (Columbia College, unpublished seminar paper, 1958), 3, and *passim*. This paper was undertaken at my suggestion and written in Professor James Shenton's senior seminar in American history. It was designed to test the Beard-Fox thesis as elaborated in Schlesinger, *Age of Jackson*, 505, and *passim*.

[61] *Evening Post For The Country*, October 19, 1844, p. 3; October 26, 1844, p. 1.

The nuances of this editorial observation in the *New York Evening Post*, an ardent free trade Democratic paper, suggest the type of merchant most likely to vote Whig on economic grounds.

Similarly, the *New York Tribune's* protectionist attacks upon the *Post* as the organ of importers dealing in foreign goods—"the British Importers are Free Trade men, and read and swear by the Post" —indicate the type of merchant most likely to vote Democratic on economic grounds. Thus the *Tribune* incessantly attacked the "Locofocos" (that is, Democrats) who benefited from "British Money in our Elections," and the "British importers," the "allies and hired instruments of British manufacturers." Its chief target was "Mr. Edwin Hunt [of Edwin Hunt & Co.] . . . whom the tariff appears to trouble more than any other man in the country [and who] thinks it very hard that he must pay six cents a yard duty on muslins." The following *Tribune* editorial observation points up one economic basis for political divisions within the New York mercantile community: "There is a good deal of sparring back and forth between the British Importers and the Domestic Goods men, with regard to the prices and values of their respective goods, in which the advantage seems to us entirely on the side of the Americans [*sic*]."[62]

A comprehensive, intensive study might perhaps demonstrate that a majority of "merchants" voted either Whig or Democratic because of their occupational interests or associations. But at present, the question of how New York "merchants" voted must remain open. The available impressionistic evidence merely suggests that certain types of merchants, directly interested in the tariff question, probably were more likely to vote for one party than the other.

Unlike the traditional claims about wool growers, bankers, merchants, and capitalists, the traditional claims about men engaged in certain types of manufacturing appear well grounded. Use of the method of "multivariate analysis," particularly among voters associated with the textile, iron, and other industries affected by foreign competition, led to the conclusion that direct, significant, and clearly perceived relationships existed, or were believed to exist, among government action on the tariff, party policy, and material interests.

For example, although a "manufacturing town" was not the top Democratic town in any county, such towns registered the lowest Democratic percentages in Columbia, Essex, Fulton, Montgomery,

---

[62] *New York Tribune* (d.), September 17, 19, 24, 25, 26; October 1, 3, 1844, p. 2.

and Orange.[63] Thus the contemporary observer whom we quoted
above on the failure of Columbia County's wool-growing towns to
reward the Whigs praised the clear-thinking voters of Stockport:
"One of the greatest manufacturing districts in the United States;
and true to her interests, Stockport increased her Whig majority
from 93 to 146, as compared with 1840."[64] In that cotton and woolen
textile center where Whigs hammered away at the advantages of the
"home market" for farmers as well as workers, they received 76.4
per cent of the total vote in 1844. And to cite an example from
another tariff-oriented industry: the Democrats tended to win majorities in northern New York, but in Moriah, Essex County, where the
mining and working of iron was "the most important branch of industry in town,"[65] the Whigs won 68.1 per cent of the total vote.

The estimate cannot be verified at present, but the assumption
seems reasonable that in manufacturing towns the Whig vote among
men actually engaged in tariff-oriented industries was much higher
than among the remainder of the electorate. But it cannot be automatically assumed that *workers* in those industries supported the
Whigs *as strongly as did their employers*, or that all employers were
Whigs. Thus Horace Greeley bewailed the "irrational" behavior of:
". . . many of our Workmen [who] are taught in the grogshops they
frequent that it is a test of independence and spirit to vote right
or wrong, contrary to those whom they work for; and "*You* won't
be controlled by your boss?" has impelled many a man to vote against
what was clearly his own interest and patriotic duty."[66]

Greeley did not know the term, of course, but he was invoking the
negative reference group concept to account for the voting behavior
of Democratic workers. Like the Masons and Antimasons, whose
party choices were influenced by their mutually hostile relations,
some workers, according to Greeley, voted Democratic because it

[63] The manufacturing towns and their Democratic percentages were: Stockport,
Columbia County (23.2 per cent); Moriah, Essex County (25.6 per cent); Johnstown,
Fulton County (31.6 per cent); Amsterdam, Montgomery County (45.5 per cent);
Monroe, Orange County (39.8 per cent). These were classified as "manufacturing
towns" on the basis of the relatively high percentages of their labor force engaged
in "Manufactures and Trades" in 1840, *and* the description in county histories and
gazetteers. The 1840 Federal census statistics of the labor force's composition by
town and county are conveniently found in J. Disturnell, *A Gazetteer of the State of
New York* (Albany, 1842), 448-472.
[64] Letter signed "V," New York *Courier and Enquirer*, November 21, 1844, p. 2.
[65] H. P. Smith, ed., *History of Essex County* (Syracuse, N.Y., 1885), 575.
[66] *New York Tribune* (w.), August 3, 1844, p. 4.

represented one way of expressing hostility to their Whig employers, *not because the Democratic party's program benefited them.*

A partial explanation at best, Greeley's observations nonetheless point up the inadequacies of an economic determinist explanation of party affiliation. Surely we can agree that material self-interest is not the only aspect of class position that influences men's behavior, that voters are members of many groups simultaneously, and that men are subjected to cross-pressures when the several groups to which they belong have contradictory voting patterns. As yet, little empirical work dealing with these important and difficult problems has been reported: 1) How do voters resolve different types of cross-pressures? 2) Under what conditions are one set of pressures likely to exert more influence than others upon voting behavior?

Analysis of voting statistics in a "deviant" iron-manufacturing town illustrates the effect of cross-pressures upon voting behavior, however, and suggests a tentative proposition of potential significance. One of relatively few nonurban communities in the state, where, during the 1840's, a majority of the labor force engaged in non-agricultural pursuits,[67] Phillipstown in Putnam County contained Cold Spring, "a thriving village supported mainly by the mammoth iron foundry." The West Point foundry, "the largest in the United States . . . employs more than four hundred men."[68] Phillipstown differed from the other manufacturing towns cited above in that it gave the Democrats 73.9 per cent of its total vote. But it also differed from them in ethnic and religious group composition. Its "native" inhabitants were "Yorkers" (defined later), and from the foundry's beginning in 1813 most of its workers had been Irish Catholics.[69] Irrespective of class, members of both those groups tended to vote Democratic (although not to the same degree).

This deviant case and several similar ones suggest that, particularly in the absence of severe economic depression, party loyalty and ethnic or religious pressures influence voters more powerfully than membership in tariff-oriented occupational groups or in any other kind of politically-sensitive occupational group. Gouverneur Kemble illustrates the point. Founder and part-owner of the West Point company, he came of high-prestige Yorker stock and was "a

[67] Disturnell, *New York Gazetteer*, 464.

[68] J. H. Mather and L. P. Brockett, *A Geographical History Of The State Of New York* (Utica, 1848), 362-363.

[69] William S. Pelletreau, *History of Putnam County, New York* (Philadelphia, 1886), 518-628. Information about the workers' religious affiliations is given on p. 572.

[163]

strong adherent of the democratic party," which sent him to Congress for two terms during the Van Buren administration.[70] The example of Kemble supports the argument that the complexities of political behavior cannot be satisfactorily explained by the simplicities of an interest group theory of politics.

[70] *Ibid.*, 362-363.

CHAPTER VIII

ETHNOCULTURAL GROUPS AND POLITICAL PARTIES

THE present study rejects the economic determinist interpretation that Frederick J. Turner and Charles A. Beard impressed upon American political historiography.[1] It also rejects the proposition that American political differences are random in character, that they reflect not group patterns, but the clashing ideas held by individual voters about the "community interest." And it rejects the proposition that socioeconomic cleavages are the obvious place to begin a study of American voting behavior. A counterproposition is advanced here: that at least since the 1820's, when manhood suffrage became widespread, ethnic and religious differences have tended to be *relatively* the most important sources of political differences. No attempt is made to "prove" that sweeping proposition, but this chapter and the following will try to show that it holds for New York in 1844. (Since the United States is highly heterogeneous, and has high social mobility, I assume that men tend to retain and be more influenced by their ethnic and religious group membership than by their membership in economic classes or groups.)

To anyone familiar with the literature, it will come as no surprise to read that the Democrats were the party of the immigrants and of the Catholics, the Whigs of the native Protestants, particularly those of New England stock. Unfortunately, that statement is almost as inaccurate and misleading as it is unoriginal. Collection and analysis of the relevant data reveal that the sharpest political cleavages occurred, not between immigrants and Yankees, *but between different groups of immigrants.*

By 1844, New York's population was remarkably heterogeneous. Thus before the relationships between ethnocultural group and voting

---

[1] See Lee Benson, *Turner and Beard* (Glencoe, Ill., 1960), *passim.* The systematic errors that the traditional economic determinist interpretation makes are less harmful than the confusion which results when voters are identified haphazardly according to a variety of attributes, for example, when "workers" are identified as Democrats and then Catholics are identified as Democrats, but little or no attempt is made to identify the voting patterns of different social strata of Catholics. In short, I accept Francis Bacon's observation: "Truth emerges more easily from error than from confusion."

behavior could be ascertained, it was necessary to work out a detailed classification system. The term ethnocultural is used in preference to ethnic, because the latter term lumps together men who came from the same "stock" but who, like the English in New England and New York, had developed considerably divergent cultures in the New World.[2] Classifying men according to their membership in ethnocultural groups, however, enables us to uncover significantly different voting behavior patterns—patterns that are hidden or obscured when men are grouped according to ethnic attributes only.

Brevity was sacrificed to clarity when it came to labeling the two main categories of the classification system: "Groups in United States by 1790" (hereafter called "natives") ; "Groups arriving in significant numbers after 1790" (hereafter called "immigrants"). Both the natives and the immigrants are subdivided, but our present concern is with the latter groups. For convenience, they are labeled "New British" and "New non-British." The former consisted of the Northern or Protestant "Irish," the Welsh, Scots, and English. Among others, the New non-British included the Southern or Catholic Irish, the Germans, French, and French-Canadians. (The "Irish" religious divisions actually corresponded closely with ethnic divisions, but the traditional terms of Protestant and Catholic Irish will be used hereafter.)[3]

1. How Did the Immigrants Vote?

If the Democratic Party really had been the party of the immigrants, the ethnocultural groups identified above should have voted more or less alike. But they did not. Except for the Negroes, the New British were by far the strongest Whigs of any group in New York, the New non-British by far the strongest Democrats.

[2] For a brilliant analysis of the cultural differences between people of English stock living in New England and New York, see Dixon Ryan Fox, *Yankees and Yorkers*, *passim*. By the time Fox came to deliver these lectures, he had sharply revised the views concerning "the economic interpretation" of American history which he had expressed in *Decline Of Aristocracy In The Politics Of New York*. Unfortunately, that doctoral dissertation has tended to be treated as Fox's last word on the subject of New York history. In my opinion, *Yankees and Yorkers* corrects many of the oversimplifications and errors in his pioneer (and pioneering) study which have seriously misled later historians.

[3] For a succinct, informative discussion of the different ethnic stocks included in the "British" migration to the United States, see Rowland T. Berthoff, *British Immigrants in Industrial America* (Cambridge, Mass., 1953), 1-11.

A. PROTESTANT IRISH AND WELSH. Numerically the smallest of the New British groups,[4] the Protestant Irish and the Welsh were probably the most homogeneous politically. Because the Protestant Irish failed to constitute a distinct, significant group in rural towns or urban wards, it is necessary to rely primarily upon contemporary observations for estimates of their party affiliation. Although precise estimates obviously cannot be verified, because contemporary observers agreed so unanimously, it seems safe to say that about 90 per cent of the Protestant Irish voted Whig. (As is true of all such estimates presented below, that figure is not intended to be taken literally. Assigning groups a specific percentage enables us to indicate their *relative* party support.) The *Tribune* claimed "almost every Protestant Irishman" for the Whigs;[5] the *New York Plebeian* (Democratic), the *Evening Post* (Democratic), and the *Freeman's Journal* (official Catholic organ) emphasized the "nativist," "anti-Catholic" proclivities that led the members of the group to vote against the Democrats.

According to the *Plebeian*, "every Orangeman" in the city voted American Republican in the 1844 mayoralty election, when the Whigs deserted their own nominees and voted for that party.[6] Commenting upon this election and the 1844 anti-Catholic Irish riots in Philadelphia, the *Freeman's Journal* argued that "the most active, although not the most prominent of the Native Americans in New York, and probably in Philadelphia also, have been Irish Orangemen. They alone have been capable of furnishing the anti-social views

[4] The New York State *Census for 1845* listed under one heading all inhabitants born in Great Britain or its possessions; the 1855 *Census*, however, had a much more precise breakdown. Impressionistic evidence suggests that the totals for 1855 accurately indicate the rank order of the several groups in 1845; Ireland, 469,753; England, 102,286; Scotland, 27,523; Wales, 8,557. According to an analysis made by the Irish Emigrant Society of the immigrants arriving in New York in May and June 1844, the Irish numbered 10,668, the English and Scots combined, 3,992. (*Freeman's Journal*, August 24, 1844, p. 60.) The Protestant Irish were not listed separately in the census data. For informed estimates concerning them and other British immigrants, see Berthoff, *British Immigrants*, 1-11.

[5] A sizeable group of Protestant Irish had settled in Lisbon, St. Lawrence County. Out of 28 towns in that traditionally Democratic county, Lisbon ranked 26th on the party's list, with 42.2 per cent. Actually, that figure is somewhat misleading, for Silas Wright's popularity in his home county undoubtedly swelled the Democratic vote. Without Wright on the ticket, the Democrats received only 34.0 per cent in 1834 and 28.4 per cent in 1840. See also *New York Tribune* (w.), March 22, 1845, p. 5.

[6] See Louis D. Scisco, *Political Nativism In New York State*, 47.

with which our young *Natives* have been inoculated."[7] The *Post* agreed that the "Orangemen" stood in the forefront of the "nativist" movement and, in effect, it wrote them off for the Democrats.[8] Actually, as early as 1832 a Catholic Irish paper in Albany, which was devoted to the Republican (that is, Jacksonian) cause, claimed that any "Orange Irish" who may once have been attached to that party were now "apostates."[9] There seems to be no reason to doubt that claim or to believe that it was less accurate after 1832, particularly not in 1844 when the Whigs coalesced with the American Republicans in several counties and the Democrats identified themselves more closely than ever with the Catholic Irish.[10]

Although the Welsh had outposts throughout the state, they were most heavily concentrated in Oneida County. The first Welsh families came to the Oneida hills in 1795, and by 1808 they had formed a significant element in the population of the area.[11] The high Whig vote in the predominantly Welsh agricultural town of Remsen bears out the *Tribune's* claim that "hardly one of them [was] a Loco-Foco." Remsen was the lowest ranking Democratic town in the county, and in 1844, when the median Democratic unit registered 50.8 per cent, Remsen gave that party only 32.8 per cent; in 1840, 25.6 per cent. Since many voters in Remsen belonged to groups that did not strongly support the Whigs (including some

[7] *Freeman's Journal*, May 11, 1844, p. 364. A week later, the paper printed a letter charging that the "Native American Party" was the "spawn" of the American Protestant Association, an "Orange" organization. Letter signed "A Catholic Native American," *ibid.*, May 18, 1844, p. 373. See also the quotation from a Pittsburgh Democratic newspaper asserting that on July 12, the anniversary of the Battle of Boyne, the Orange amended their traditional slogan and cried out "For King William and [Henry] Clay." *Ibid.*, August 3, 1844, p. 37.

[8] *Evening Post For The Country*, March 29, 1845, p. 3.

[9] Letter to the editor of the *Irish Republican Shield*, quoted in the *Albany Argus* (s.w.), September 21, 1832.

[10] *Albany Argus* (w.), June 15, 1844, p. 205; November 2, 1844, p. 356; November 9, 1844, p. 366; *Brooklyn Eagle* (d.), October 16, 18, 26; November 6, 9, 1844, p. 2.

[11] Millard F. Roberts, *History of Remsen . . . Including Parts of Adjoining Steuben and Trenton* (n.p., 1914), 1-18, 116-117; Pomeroy Jones, *History of Oneida County* (n.p., 1851), 306-307.

To quote Jones: "The reports of these early foreign immigrants to their friends in Wales, of the cheapness and fitness for dairying of the lands in this section has induced these ancient Britons to emigrate in such numbers that competent residents of the town [Remsen] believe that at least three-fourths of its population are Welsh. It is said that Remsen, Steuben, Trenton, and portions of Deerfield, Marcy and Boonville, are almost as well known in Wales as in Oneida County." Jones's estimate is probably essentially correct, but somewhat exaggerated; Roberts estimated that in 1857 "they comprised nearly, if not quite, two-thirds of the community," *Remsen*, 116-117.

Catholic Irish), the *Tribune* apparently was not exaggerating Welsh anti-Democratic sentiment.[12] A reasonable estimate seems to be that about 90 per cent of them *usually* cast Whig ballots (that is, unless abolitionist candidates were running).

B. ENGLISH AND THE SCOTS. It is not possible to estimate precisely the number of voters of English and Scots descent, but they almost certainly constituted a much larger proportion of the electorate than the other two New British groups. The *Tribune* claimed nearly all the Scots and a "large portion" of the English for its party.[13] Significantly, the *Evening Post* conceded the accuracy of that claim in a campaign editorial which argued that nativism would cost the Whigs many votes: "There is a large number of naturalized citizens in the interior counties of the state, and in all the western states, mostly English or Scotch by birth, who have hitherto [1844] voted with the Whigs. Not being gregarious in their manner of settlement, like the Irish and Germans, they do not pass for so large a portion of our population as they are found upon enquiry to make."[14]

The *Post* erred in one respect, for the Scots were markedly "gregarious in their manner of settlement," and formed a respectable proportion of the population in counties as far apart as Washington, Fulton, Delaware, and Livingston. "Scots" towns comprised the lowest Democratic units in three of those counties and the second lowest (33.7 per cent) in Fulton; the Scots were also well represented in the lowest (Johnstown, a manufacturing area). Putnam was the lowest ranking Democratic town (18.5 per cent) in Washington as

[12] *New York Tribune* (w.), March 22, 1845, p. 5. The Welsh probably comprised about 65 per cent to 75 per cent of Remsen's electorate in the mid-1840's. (See n. 11). Since political abolitionism attracted some of them (Roberts, *Remsen*, 128), the town's devotion to the Whig Party is best seen by presenting the percentages for 1834 (69.4 per cent) and 1840 (69.5 per cent), as well as 1844 (57.0 per cent). Moreover, as will be shown below, Irish Catholics throughout the state voted overwhelmingly Democratic and the New Englanders tended to be closely divided; the Whig vote among the Welsh in Remsen must therefore have been extremely high. Fortunately, it is not necessary to rely solely on logical deduction. Long agitation by the Welsh finally paid off in 1869 when the northern half of Remsen was set off as the town of Forestport; it contained most of the Irish Catholics. The party percentages before and after the division tell their own story: In 1868 Remsen voted Republican 62.5 per cent, Democratic 37.5 per cent. Four years later, Remsen voted Republican 85.4 per cent, Democratic 14.6 per cent; Forestport voted Republican 48.2 per cent, Democratic 52.8 per cent. See Roberts, *Remsen*, 37-38, 108, for the division of the town in 1869. As a Democratic newspaper noted during the 1844 campaign, the Whigs published a Welsh paper in Utica and "wooed" the Welsh with pamphlets in New York City. *Morning News*, October 29, 1844, p. 2.

[13] *New York Tribune* (w.), March 22, 1845, p. 5.

[14] *Evening Post For The Country*, October 12, 1844, p. 2.

well as in the state. In 1844 it was overwhelmingly a community of Scots, as was York in Livingston, where the Democrats received only 23.0 per cent of the total vote. Perhaps the clearest indication of the group's voting pattern is this; not a single town in which the Scots were clustered gave the Democrats a majority, *even in the strongest Democratic counties.*[15]

Delaware County, for example, was a longtime Democratic stronghold. Yet the towns in which the Scots formed either a majority or a large minority of the population were the highest-ranking Whig units in the county. Hamden gave the Whigs 68.2 per cent of its vote, followed closely by Andes which gave them 67.5 per cent. Even Bovina, with 59.1 per cent, was a "strong anti-Democratic" town. Such figures in traditionally Democratic Delaware County support the observations of the *Tribune* and *Evening Post* and justify the estimate that, like the Protestant Irish and the Welsh, about 90 per cent of the Scots voted Whig.

The *Post* noted that the English were not "gregarious," and it has been possible to locate only two towns in which they formed a significant proportion of the population. Stockport in Columbia County and Stafford in Genesee were both "very strong Whig" communities. But they had voted much the same way before the English came and might well have continued to do so whether or not they contained any sizeable number of English "adopted citizens." As noted previously, Stockport was a manufacturing town; and Stafford had been an Antimasonic stronghold prior to the arrival of immigrants from Devonshire. But it is at least suggestive that both towns were even more strongly Whig after sufficient time had elapsed for the English to make their presence felt. In Stockport, the Whigs received 69.6 per cent of the vote in 1834, and 76.8 per cent in 1844. In Stafford they received 69.0 per cent and 70.1 per cent, respectively. Thus there is no reason to doubt the *Post*'s and *Tribune*'s description of the English as Whig sympathizers. Moreover, other contemporary observers agreed that they shared the antipathy to the Catholic Irish that was characteristic of all the New British

15 Together with the leads provided by the 1845 and 1855 Census data, the detailed description of settlement patterns and churches in the appropriate regional, county and town histories and gazetteers made it possible to estimate the ethnocultural composition of the towns identified in this section. The New York Public Library and the New York Historical Society have excellent collections of these histories and gazetteers. They vary greatly in quality, but at least one useful history has been published for every county in the state.

groups, and that they voted their antipathies.[16] Nevertheless, there are nuances in *Tribune* editorials that suggest the English were *relatively* less homogeneous politically than the Protestant Irish, Welsh, and Scots. Since the *Tribune* editorials indicate that workers of "Radical" (Chartist) background tended to support the Democrats, it seems safer to estimate that only [*sic*] about 75 per cent of the English voted Whig.[17]

c. CATHOLIC IRISH. Though precise figures are not available, by 1844 the Catholic Irish undoubtedly formed the single largest immigrant group in New York.[18] Contemporary observations suggest that about 95 per cent of the Catholic Irish who participated in the 1844 election cast Democratic ballots.[19] But that group had not always formed so solid a bloc. During the late 1830's, enough Catholic Irish supported the Whigs to raise the expectations of men like Weed, Seward, and Greeley. Their expectations were badly blighted in 1840, however, when even Seward conceded that "the Irishmen ... voted against us generally, and far more generally than heretofore."[20] Desertions increased after 1840, and by November 1844 the *Albany Evening Journal* was printing letters that claimed, for example, that out of about 100 Catholic Irish voters in the city of

16 See, in particular, the calculated attacks upon the English and the defense of the Irish in a leading Democratic newspaper, the *Brooklyn Eagle* (d.), August 9; September 16, 19, 28; October 26, 1844, p. 2. The paper noted that "no exception" was taken to the English or Scotch by nativist Whigs; the Irish in particular, not British immigrants in general, were the targets of Whig fury. *Ibid.*, November 9, 1844, p. 2. See also the praise for the "intelligent English naturalized citizens" in the *American Republican*, November 4, 1844, p. 2; the attacks upon the Protestant Irish, English, and Scotch merchants of New York in the Irish Catholic organ, the *Freeman's Journal*, October 15, 1844, p. 108, and the answer to this in the *American Republican*, December 12, 1844, p. 2, letter signed "Junius."

17 For example, the *Tribune* (w.) claimed that some workers were Democrats because "a good many of our workmen in factories, forges, etc., are English Radicals, who have been led to attribute the depression of the Laboring Classes in Europe to Protection, and who never ask nor think whether the circumstances and the essence of the thing are the same here as there, but cry out for this 'Free Trade' here which would inevitably reduce their own wages to the European standard." August 3, 1844, p. 4. See also *ibid.*, September 12, 1846, p. 3. Moreover, as noted below, free thinkers strongly tended to vote Democratic, and in the 1830's English immigrants were stigmatized as the "worst atheists in the country." Albert Post, *Popular Freethought in America, 1825-1850* (New York, 1943), 86, 32-33.

18 See n. 4 above.

19 *New York Herald* (d.), November 9, 1844, p. 4; *Evening Post For The Country*, November 23, 1844, p. 1; *New York Express*, November 6, 1844, p. 1; *New York Tribune* (w.), November 16, 1844, p. 5; *New York Courier and Enquirer*, November 18, 1844, p. 2.

20 William Seward to B. S. [Benjamin Squire?], November 12, 1840, in George E. Baker, ed., *The Works of William H. Seward*, 3: 386-387.

Hudson, all were "against us except 2 or 3."[21] (Whether the Catholic Irish voted along ethnocultural or religious lines will be discussed later.)

Affiliation of the *urban* Catholic Irish to the Democratic Party has long been noted, although little attention has been given to changes in their voting behavior over time. What has tended to be overlooked is that the Catholic Irish voted Democratic in New York State, whether they lived in urban or rural communities, whether they were day laborers or freehold farmers—in short, their voting pattern represented an ethnocultural or religious group, not a place or class, phenomenon.

Most Catholic Irish lived in cities and large villages, but by 1844 many could be found in rural areas scattered throughout the state. Wherever they constituted a substantial proportion of the population, they voted as a bloc and made their presence felt politically. For example, in Franklin County "Irish [Catholic] settlers began to swarm into Bombay about 1825 . . . Mr. Hogan, the younger [the town's landowner], is said to have received these [settlers] with great kindliness, and to have located them upon what was then regarded as the very best lands in the town, which location came to be known as the 'Irish ridge.' "[22] As the local historian noted, thanks to the solid Irish attachment to the Democrats,[23] Bombay was a "strong Democratic" town in a traditionally Whig county.

Similarly, in 1844 in the Antimasonic and Whig county of Wyoming in western New York, the only town that gave the Democrats enough support to place it in a category above "neutral" was Java (58.6 per cent). After the advance guard of Catholic Irish arrived in 1829, its farmlands began to attract many others. By 1844 substantial numbers of Irish Catholics must have lived there, for by 1855 the *Freeman's Journal* was proudly claiming that in Java and the adjoining town of China, *"there are one thousand Catholic families engaged in farming, most of whom have already paid for their land."*[24] Though concentrated in Java, enough of those families lived in China to make it another high-ranking Democratic town.

[21] *Albany Evening Journal* (d.), November 15, 1844, p. 2. See also *ibid.*, November 8, 1844, p. 2.

[22] Frederick J. Seaver, *Historical Sketches of Franklin County* (Albany, 1918), 186-187.

[23] *Ibid.*, 104-106.

[24] F. W. Beers and Co., *History of Wyoming County, N.Y.* (New York, 1880), 204-211; *Freeman's Journal*, October 27, 1855, p. 4.

Few agricultural towns contained as heavy concentrations of Catholic Irish as Bombay and Java. But the *Evening Journal* and the *Tribune* emphasized that the Catholic Irish were sufficiently numerous to aid the Democrats materially in about half the counties of the state.[25] Thus, once it is recognized that the Catholic Irish voted overwhelmingly Democratic wherever they lived and whatever their occupation, it follows that their voting behavior cannot be attributed to conditions peculiar to urban areas or to particular occupations.

D. GERMANS. Of the New non-British groups, the second largest, the Germans, were also strongly attached to the Democratic Party. Unlike the others, however, they divided into three distinct religious segments, Catholics, Protestants, and "Rationalists," or free thinkers. A credible source estimates that nearly one half the German settlers in New York State before the Civil War were Catholics; the remainder were divided among the Protestants and Rationalists.[26]

Pending an intensive study, firm statements are unwarranted, but the available data suggest that the Protestant Germans, particularly the Prussian Lutherans, voted less strongly Democratic than the other two groups.[27] Yet in the 1840's this difference in German voting behavior was apparently only a matter of degree, and Democratic papers claimed the Germans almost exclusively for their party. In Syracuse, for example, during the 1844 campaign, the *Argus* reported that "no Dutchman [*sic*] could be found to carry Gen. Granger's Banners, at the recent coon [Whig] celebration."[28] Even before the nativist issue developed intensity, the Whigs conceded that the "great majority" of German voters were arrayed against them. From the *Tribune*'s admission—and it appealed strongly for Ger-

[25] *Albany Evening Journal* (d.), November 11, 1844, p. 2; *New York Tribune* (w.), November 16, 1844, p. 5.

[26] Alexander Flick, *History Of The State Of New York* (New York, 1933), 7: 43-44; Carl Wittke, *We Who Built America* (New York, 1940), 222-229; Post, *Popular Freethought In America*, 197-198.

[27] Both Clarence in Erie County and Wheatfield in Niagara County contained large settlements of Prussian Lutherans. Unlike other towns in which Germans made up a large or significant proportion of the population, they cast very low Democratic votes: 22.9 per cent and 36.3 per cent, respectively. See Truman White, *Erie County* (Boston History Company, n. p., 1898), 1: 516-519; William Pool, ed., *Landmarks of Niagara County, New York* (D. Mason Company, n. p., 1897), 338-359. For an interesting discussion of the conflicts between German and Irish Catholics, and between Protestant and Catholic Germans, see John T. Horton, et al., *History of Northwestern New York*, 1: 143-148.

[28] *Albany Argus* (w.), August 3, 1844, p. 261; July 27, 1844, p. 253; October 5, 1844, p. 327; October 26, 1844; p. 348; November 16, 1844, pp. 369, 370, 372.

man support—as well as from other evidence, it seems clear that they voted Democratic irrespective of religious affiliation.[29] Nonetheless, the Catholic Germans probably voted most Democratic, the Protestants probably least Democratic.[30]

A highly "gregarious" group, the Germans are easily detected in the rural areas. In Croghan, Lewis County, they appear to have constituted a larger proportion of the population than in any other New York town.[31] Croghan was the highest ranking Democratic unit in the county (83.2 per cent), and the second highest in the state. As part of its campaign to get the vote of "adopted citizens," the *Albany Argus* highlighted the presence of naturalized German citizens from Croghan at the Democrat's main rally in Lewis County. They were assigned a prominent place in the parade and their float's banner emphasized a favorite party theme: "The Naturalized Citizens of Croghan—Have Not We the same rights as Natives?"[32]

Croghan, with its large proportion of Germans, was an extremely "poor" town in a Democratic county; Tonawanda (in Erie) and Irondequoit (in Monroe), each with large numbers of Germans, were "prosperous" agricultural towns in Whig counties. Both were the highest-ranking Democratic units in their counties, giving sizeable majorities to the party (65.6 per cent and 58.6 per cent, respectively), even though Erie and Monroe were longtime Antimasonic and Whig strongholds. With the exception of two towns settled by Prussian Lutherans,[33] all towns in New York containing significant numbers of Germans were found to be high-ranking Democratic units. The estimate that approximately 80 per cent of the Germans voted Democratic is based upon my analysis of the statistical data and the impressionistic evidence of contemporary observers, for ex-

[29] *New York Tribune* (w.), April 6, 1844, p. 6; *New York Herald* (d.), November 9, 1844, p. 4.

[30] Immediately after the election, Millard Fillmore wrote that the "foreign vote" went against the Whigs in Erie County; several days later he was more precise and twice referred to the "foreign Catholics" as the cause of the Whig defeat in New York. Fillmore to Weed, November 6, 1844, Fillmore to Clay, November 11, 1844, in Frank H. Severance, ed., "Millard Fillmore Papers," 11: 267-268.

[31] "In 1849, this town had a population of 1,168 of whom 646 were Americans and Irish, and 522 French, Germans, and Swiss." These designations refer to country of origin. Actually, the immigrants were from German areas then under French domination, and from the German cantons of Switzerland. A large majority were Catholics. Franklin Hough, *History of Lewis County* (New York, 1860), 74-79.

[32] *Albany Argus* (w.), October 19, 1844, p. 340.

[33] See n. 27 above.

ample, "The victory of the Loco-Focos is not that of *Americans* but a triumph of *Irishmen* and *Germans* over *Americans*."[34]

E. CATHOLIC FRENCH. Though few in number and concentrated largely in New York City,[35] the Catholic French also contributed to the 1844 Democratic victory. Under the headline, "A New Foreign Ally Brought Into the Field," the *American Republican* added the French to the Catholic Irish and German "foreign battalions," long mustered under Tammany banners. According to the *Express*, an ardently nativist Whig paper, the French as a group "since time immemorial," had abstained from political participation. But "this year they have wakened," the paper observed; and its tone suggested that the awakening would not bring joy to Whig politicians. Unwilling to concede the French to the Locofocos before election, the *Express* included them afterwards in its angry denunciation of "the avalanche of Germans, Irish, Swiss, Prussians, French, Russians, and Poles" that had rolled over the Whigs on election day. The *Herald*, an independent paper, also presented evidence sustaining the view that the French voted *en masse* for the Democrats in 1844.[36]

Perhaps the most significant aspect of the solid French support for the Democrats relates to their socioeconomic status. In his illuminating study of New York immigrant life, Robert Ernst has noted that, unlike the Irish and the Germans, "there were few laborers or shanty dwellers among them [the French]." Also unlike those groups, a relatively sizeable percentage of the French were merchants, some of whom "grew rich from the increasing trade between New York, Le Havre and Paris."[37] Since they probably voted as solidly Democratic as the Catholic Irish, and since their socioeconomic status was much higher than the latter's, French voting behavior strengthens the claim that in 1844 the New non-British acted along ethnocultural (and religious) rather than economic group lines.

F. FRENCH CANADIANS. The smallest of the New non-British groups, and the latest to arrive in the United States (after 1837),

---

[34] *New York Express*, November 9, 1844, p. 2.

[35] In 1855, of the state's 18,366 residents born in France (including the Germanic provinces), more than one third lived in New York City. New York State, *Census For 1855*, 175-176.

[36] *American Republican*, November 1, 1844, p. 2; *New York Express*, October 29; November 11, 1844, p. 2; *New York Herald* (w.), November 2, 1844, p. 346.

[37] Ernst, *New York Immigrant Life*, 44-45, 94-95.

the French Canadians were highly concentrated in a few Northern Tier counties.[38] Their small number and late arrival makes it difficult to estimate their 1844 party allegiance from statistical data. But the *Tribune* in effect conceded them to the Democrats.[39] An impressionistic estimate that they voted along the lines of the Catholic Irish (95 per cent Democratic) is probably not far off the mark. The 1852 data support that estimate, since by then enough time had elapsed for the voting statistics to reflect their presence. Clinton, where they were more highly concentrated than anywhere else in the state, gave the Democrats 74.1 per cent of its vote and thereby became the party's banner unit in the county. (By 1860 the French Canadians comprised an even higher proportion of the electorate in Clinton, and the Democrats received 85 per cent of the town vote in that strong Republican county.) Similarly, Chateaugay in Franklin County was another French Canadian center, and its Democratic vote (72.7 per cent) in 1852 was even higher than Bombay's (60.1 per cent), where many Catholic Irish lived.[40]

G. SUMMARY. As noted above, the purpose of estimating group percentages is to suggest the relative rather than actual support given the major parties by different groups. The group estimates appear to be roughly accurate, at least, and they discredit the claim that the Democratic Party was the party of the immigrants. That claim may be literally accurate, but it is thoroughly misleading. The New non-British strongly supported the Democratic Party; the New British just as strongly opposed it. Because the former considerably outnumbered the latter in the state, it is undoubtedly true that many more "adopted citizens" voted Democratic than Whig.[41] But that statistic is a demographic accident. Had migration been larger from New British areas than from New non-British, it seems reasonable to assume that the reverse situation would have developed in the state—as, in fact, it did in many localities.

[38] Marcus L. Hansen, *The Mingling Of The Canadian And American Peoples* (New Haven, Conn., 1940), 115-126. Using the data for 1855 as a guide, the three counties with the highest proportion of French Canadians were Clinton, Franklin, and Essex.

[39] *New York Tribune* (w.), August 3, 1844, p. 6; September 13, 1845, p. 3.

[40] See D. H. Hurd, compiler, *History of Clinton And Franklin Counties* (Philadelphia, 1880), 300-302; Seaver, *Franklin County*, 238-249. According to the *Freeman's Journal*, October 19, 1844, pp. 124-125, the Catholics in Chauteaugay were principally French-Canadian.

[41] My estimate is that the Democrats outnumbered the Whigs among the immigrants by about two to one.

2. How Did the Natives Vote?

Shifting attention to differences in voting behavior *between immigrant groups and native groups*, we find a significant phenomenon that will be noted here and commented upon in later chapters. Although all immigrant groups voted as solid blocs, the natives divided *relatively* closely between the two major parties (except for two small groups identified below).

A. YANKEES. Contrary to the traditional view that voters of New England descent voted strongly Whig, the estimate here is that for the state as a whole they split about 55 per cent Whig, 45 per cent Democratic. (This estimate counts Liberty Party voters according to their previous affiliations.) That the generic term "Yankee" refers to men who derived from heterogeneous social and cultural backgrounds is suggested by this finding: unlike every immigrant group, and to a greater extent than any other native group, the Yankees varied widely in their voting behavior in different parts of the state and in different towns within the same county.

The small Whig margin among the Yankees actually derived from the original Antimasonic strength in western New York. That extensive region constituted a "colony from New England,"[42] and the party that dominated it politically contained necessarily a large proportion of Yankees. But in many New York counties where the Antimasonic movement had failed to penetrate or had produced a counterreaction, the Democrats received strong Yankee support.

Since Yankees constituted about 65 per cent of the state's electorate,[43] it follows logically that they must have been closely divided in their party allegiance. Had the Whigs received much more than 55 per cent of that group's vote, their opponents would invariably have been beaten badly on the state level, unless all other groups cast solid Democratic ballots. But logical deduction need not be relied on; "New England" counties and towns are easily located.

For example, the county of Suffolk, directly across Long Island Sound from Connecticut, was "completely Yankee in population."[44] Traditionally a Democratic stronghold, in 1844 it ranked as the third-highest Democratic county and gave the party 57.8 per cent of its total vote. Within the county, however, the descendants of

[42] David M. Ellis, "The Yankee Invasion Of New York, 1783-1850," *New York History*, 32: 3 (January 1951).
[43] The basis for that estimate is given in Appendix III.
[44] Ellis, in *New York History*, 31: 4.

Connecticut Yankees differed widely in political allegiance. East-hampton, an "unusually prosperous" agricultural town ($883), was the banner Democratic unit with 75.7 per cent of the vote; South-hampton, a "very prosperous" agricultural, whaling, and fishing town ($632) was the lowest-ranking Democratic unit with 34.0 per cent. (The voting record of the latter nicely illustrates the prop-osition stated in Chapter VII about the conditions under which economic interests are most likely to influence political behavior. A local Democratic newspaper explained its party's poor showing in Southhampton by citing the specific attractions that Whig policies held for its substantial nonagricultural interests.)[45]

Much the same situation obtained in Delaware County (south-eastern New York) as in Suffolk on eastern Long Island. Except for the Scots (and some Dutch in a couple of towns), Delaware was overwhelmingly Yankee. And yet, despite the solid Scots support for the Whigs, Delaware was the sixth-highest Democratic county in the state (57.3 per cent). Again, striking variations in Yankee voting patterns appear on the town level. For example, Franklin, unmis-takably a transplanted Connecticut community, gave the Democrats 72.9 per cent of its total vote. Stamford, just as clearly an outpost of Fairfield County, Connecticut, gave them only 44.9 per cent.[46] Contrary to what the economic determinist interpretation of voting behavior would lead one to expect, both Franklin ($441) and Stam-ford ($473) were "prosperous" agricultural towns.

To an even greater extent than Delaware, Otsego County in cen-tral New York was settled by Yankees. The historian of that area noted, as late as the Civil War, that "the vast majority of the in-habitants traced their ancestry to New England."[47] Yet "wool-growing" Otsego was traditionally Democratic and gave that party 54.5 per cent of its vote in 1844. Moving up to the North Country, we find that Warren and St. Lawrence were other Yankee counties that traditionally voted Democratic. The former trailed Delaware closely in the party's honor roll with 55.1 per cent, the latter ranked just above Otsego with 54.7 per cent. And even in western New York many New England towns voted strongly Democratic. Pratts-

[45] See the *Greenport Watchman*'s analysis reprinted in *Brooklyn Eagle*, Decem-ber 3, 1844, p. 2.

[46] David Murray, ed., *Delaware County, New York* (Delhi, N.Y., 1898), 48-49, 120; Jay Gould, *History of Delaware County* (Roxbury, N.Y., 1856), 199.

[47] James P. Frost, *Life On The Upper Susquehanna: 1783-1860* (New York, 1951), 99-100, and 7-16.

burg in Steuben County serves as a good example, since its settlers "were peculiarly a homogeneous population." Its pioneers were nearly all of Congregational background and "originally from Connecticut, of the best Puritan stock."[48] In this "prosperous" agricultural town, the Democrats received 61.3 per cent of the total vote.

Other examples would only belabor the point. The data, I believe, warrant these conclusions: 1) In no county did Yankee voting behavior resemble the bloc pattern characteristic of all immigrant groups. 2) In some counties the Yankees voted strongly Whig. 3) In other counties they divided more or less evenly. 4) In still others they voted strongly Democratic. Contrary to traditional assumptions, the group's voting behavior shows no significant class differences. Put another way, unless one knew *where* well-to-do or poor Yankees lived, or knew certain other information noted below, one would have little basis for predicting party affiliations. Yankee voting in New York during the 1830's and 1840's was heterogeneous, suggesting that so wide a variety of factors over time and space had influenced them that easy generalizations are exceedingly dangerous.[49]

B. NEGROES AND HUGUENOTS. Aside from the Yankees, I estimate that only two native groups cast Whig majorities in New York, the Negroes and the Huguenots (Protestant French). Unlike all other natives, members of each of these small groups had experienced or were experiencing "persecution," and each voted as a solid bloc.

Because of the property restrictions upon Negro suffrage which the Van Buren faction had written into the 1821 State Constitution, only about one thousand "persons of color" were eligible to vote in 1844.[50] An analysis of the parties' opposing positions during the 1840's on the proposed constitutional amendment removing Negro suffrage restrictions strongly confirms Dixon Ryan Fox's conclusion that Negroes voted solidly Whig.[51] To estimate that they supported

[48] W. W. Clayton, *History of Steuben County* (Philadelphia, 1879), 355-363; James H. Hotchkin, *A History Of The Purchase And Settlement Of Western New York* (New York, 1848), 463-467.

[49] Even a cursory study of the county statistics in New England indicates the scant basis which exists for the notion of a solid "Yankee" vote. See, for example, the 1844 returns in *The Whig Almanac . . . For 1845* (New York, 1845), 42.

[50] See n. 33 in Chapter VII.

[51] Fox, in *Political Science Quarterly*, 32: 263-275. Compare *New York Tribune* (w.), January 4, 1845, p. 5; June 14, 1845, p. 3, March 25, 1846, p. 5; April 4, 1846, p. 3; November 28, 1846, p. 5; *New York Morning News*, June 2, 7, 11, 1845, p. 2; *Evening Post For The Country*, September 23, 1845, p. 3; *Albany Atlas* (s.w.), October 27, 1846, p. 2.

the Whigs as solidly as the Catholic Irish supported the Democrats (95 per cent) does not appear to be an overstatement.

Like the Negroes, the Huguenots were among the earliest inhabitants of New York province. An estimate based upon the best available study indicates that they comprised about three per cent of the state's population in 1790. By 1844, however, as a result of the influx of native and foreign migrants to New York, they probably comprised less than one per cent of the electorate and cast about 4,000 votes.[52] Though it seems reasonably certain that they strongly supported the Whigs, the estimated figure of 75 per cent is frankly impressionistic. Clusters of Huguenots lived in Ulster, Richmond, Westchester, New York and Kings counties, but only in the town of New Paltz, Ulster County, did they form a substantial part of the population. Unfortunately for our purposes, that town also contained many Dutch—a group that tended to vote Democratic. It is difficult, therefore, to draw any credible inferences from the 52.3 per cent the Whigs received in New Paltz. Contemporary references to enthusiastic Huguenot participation in the 1844 anti-Catholic campaign suggest, however, that the 75 per cent Whig figure is not too inaccurate an estimate of their group voting pattern.

The *American Republican* carried frequent and glowing reports concerning "the progress of Americanism" in the "old Huguenot county of Ulster." Both New Paltz and Hurley (another Huguenot center) were "all right" and ready to do their part at the polls. An editorial hailing the group's contribution to the success of an "immense" Fourth of July party rally in Ulster is revealing. "That county may be considered as the Huguenot county of the State. It is filled with a class of people who appreciate all the blessings of liberty, and are sensitively alive to anything that threatens danger to the Protestant faith." Although resolutions passed at the July rally denounced the Whigs as well as the Democrats for "truckling to papal interests,"[53] the *Tribune* later revealed that before the campaign was over the Whigs and American Republicans had practically merged in Ulster.[54] Nonetheless, a not insignificant proportion of Huguenots must have voted Democratic or that party's vote would have been lower in New Paltz.

[52] These estimates are discussed in Appendix III.
[53] *American Republican*, July 9; September 2, 5; October 30, 1844, p. 2.
[54] *New York Tribune* (w.), November 16, 1844, p. 5.

C. OTHER "YORKERS." The Huguenots comprise one of four native groups classified here as "Yorkers," the descendants of men who came directly to the province of New York rather than migrated to it after first settling in New England, New Jersey, or elsewhere. The Dutch, the Palatine Germans, and the "Old British" complete the list. This latter group is really a composite and includes the English, Welsh, Scots, and Scotch-Irish living in New York by 1790. Long residence in the country as well as behavior patterns and traditions associated with Revolutionary and early national struggles differentiated them from the post-1790 "New British."

Like the Huguenots, the other Yorker groups were largely clustered in eastern portions of the state that had been settled before the Revolution, particularly in the Hudson, Mohawk and Schoharie valleys.[55] But, contrary to the Huguenot pattern, I estimate that roughly 60 per cent of the Dutch, Palatines, and Old British voted Democratic. (Only a study that examined the evidence microscopically could isolate their separate voting patterns.) The estimate, 60 per cent is supported by the comfortable Democratic majorities in most Yorker counties and communities. Thus they comprised either a majority or a substantial minority of the population in the *highest-ranking Democratic towns in 14 counties; they comprised either a majority or a substantial minority of the population in the lowest ranking Democratic towns in only two counties.*

Dutch, Palatine, and Old British majorities for the Democrats powerfully discredit the traditional assumption that the Whigs represented primarily the prosperous farmers living on better soils or along good transportation routes. Having arrived early, the Yorker families had decades, often centuries, to pick out the best sites, accumulate wealth (and status), and pass it along to descendants. This is not to imply that all Yorkers in 1844 were well-to-do. But as a group, their early arrival had given them relatively high places on the economic scale. For example, as a local historian observed, long devotion to agriculture by the Dutch in Rockland County had paid off handsomely. "Wealth brought with it grand and comfortable homes. Money begat money. 'Money saved is money made' was the Dutchman's motto. It was not an unusual thing for a farmer, a generation ago [that is during the 1850's], to be worth from $50,000

[55] David Ellis, et al., *A Short History Of New York State* (Ithaca, N.Y. 1957), 60-67.

even up to $100,000 in cash, besides a fine farm to leave to his posterity."[56]

As noted previously, the solidly Dutch, "very prosperous" agricultural community of Clarkstown in Rockland County was the state's leading Democratic unit (89.9 per cent). In contrast, the "prosperous" agricultural town of Ramapo, settled largely by twice-transplanted Connecticut Yankees from Hempstead, Long Island, was the county's lowest ranking Democratic unit (56.5 per cent). Another "very prosperous" Dutch agricultural community, Coeymans in Albany County, cast 71.4 per cent of its vote for the Democrats. The predominantly Yankee "marginal" town of Knox in the same county cast only 34.0 per cent for the Democrats. (It is worth noting here that the pattern of high Yorker and low Yankee support for the Democrats was not limited to Rockland and Albany, but tended to persist in almost all counties where "restless" Yankees came to disturb the peace of "conservative" Yorkers.)

Other "Dutch" towns heading their county's Democratic list were Lexington in Greene (79.1 per cent), Deerpark in Orange (67.7 per cent), Greenbush in Rensselaer (64.7 per cent), Newton in Queens (60.3 per cent), Shawangunk in Ulster (60.1 per cent), and Sullivan in Madison (53.1 per cent). In every case, these towns were "prosperous" or "very prosperous" agricultural communities. The two Yorker communities at the tail-end of their county's Democratic list were Catskill in Greene (42.3 per cent) and Esopus in Ulster (32.7 per cent). Catskill, a "very prosperous" commercial and agricultural town on the Hudson, was settled originally by the Dutch, but the heavy Yankee influx after the Revolution makes it difficult to determine whether the Yorker element actually predominated by 1844. Similarly, Esopus on the Hudson was a "prosperous" old Dutch agricultural town, but it contained many Huguenots who may have been responsible for its low Democratic vote.

Arriving in the lower Hudson Valley early in the eighteenth century, many of the "poor German Protestants" from the Palatine migrated soon afterwards to the "fat lands" along the Mohawk and Schoharie rivers.[57] Although by 1844 the post-Revolutionary Yankee invasion had drastically changed the ethnocultural composition of Herkimer, Schoharie, and Montgomery counties, the Palatines still

[56] David Cole, *History of Rockland County* (New York, 1884), 99.
[57] Walter A. Knittle, *The Early Eighteenth Century Palatine Migration* (Philadelphia, 1936), 144-210.

formed at least a substantial minority element in those reliably Democratic counties. Certainly they formed the numerically dominant element in the highest ranking Democratic towns in all three counties.

The town of Herkimer in the county of Herkimer, named after the Palatine's revolutionary hero (General Nicholas Herkimer), was "unusually prosperous" and contained the "German Flats," widely renowned for their enduring fertility. It gave the Democrats 70.5 per cent of its vote, slightly more than the "prosperous" Palatine agricultural towns of Sharon in Schoharie (66.0 per cent) and St. Johnsville in Montgomery (65.6 per cent) gave them. Of the highest ranking Democratic towns dominated by the Palatines (and Dutch), Taghanic in Columbia County (70.1 per cent) was the only one of "marginal" status.

As was true in general of the three Yorker groups we are now considering, not all Palatine towns voted heavily Democratic. For example, although the "very prosperous" town of Schoharie in Schoharie County strongly resembled Herkimer in socioeconomic composition and other characteristics, it voted only 52.0 per cent Democratic. Schoharie shows that the group's voting pattern varied somewhat in different areas, but does not weaken the finding that Palatine communities characteristically gave the Democrats comfortable majorities.

Yonkers, an Old British (English) town, led the Democratic ranks in Westchester (70.3 per cent). Nearness to New York City had long given its farmers an excellent market for produce, and land values soared after 1842 as Yonkers increasingly became a suburban community. The "marginal" town of Putnam Valley in adjoining Putnam County presented an exception to the general rule of Yorker prosperity, but it was another Old British community long devoted to the Democratic cause (83.2 per cent). Across the Hudson in Orange County, the flourishing agricultural towns of Crawford (Scotch-Irish), Hamptonburg (English and Scotch-Irish), and New Windsor (English and Scotch-Irish) also registered comfortable Democratic majorities (65.8, 59.3, and 57.5 per cent, respectively).

Although I estimate that the three groups voted about 60 per cent Democratic, undoubtedly differences existed among the Dutch, Palatine, and Old British patterns. The significant point, however, is that those groups enjoyed relatively high socioeconomic status in their communities and definitely sided with the Democrats in the political wars.

D. PENN-JERSEYITES. Like the Old British, the last ethnocultural group to be considered here is a composite one. Particularly after the Revolution, Scotch-Irish, Germans, and Dutch from Pennsylvania and New Jersey came to take up unoccupied lands in New York. Although they tended to locate in southeastern and Southern Tier counties, many of them pushed father north. Seneca County in western New York, for example, was as much a Penn-Jersey center as Chemung on the Pennsylvania line and Orange on the New Jersey line.[58]

Analysis of county and town statistics leads to the conclusion that the Penn-Jerseyites tended to divide evenly between the parties. Unlike the Yankees, however, this native group leaned to the Democratic side, and I estimate that about 55 per cent of them voted "Locofoco." Thus the Democrats had a majority in counties such as Chemung (58.1 per cent) and Steuben (55.0 per cent), and the Whigs had a majority in no Penn-Jersey county. Even in Seneca, where the Antimasonic "blessed spirit" had manifested itself, the Democrats received 51.6 per cent of the total vote. Nevertheless, both the highest and the lowest ranking Democratic towns in Seneca, Tioga, and Tompkins counties were Penn-Jersey centers that resembled each other in many respects; it seems clear, therefore, that the group was closely divided politically.[59]

SUMMARY. Perhaps the most dramatic way to summarize and delineate the ethnocultural basis of party divisions in New York in 1844 is to bring together the estimated group voting percentages. The table below illustrates the main point: party affiliations were extremely polarized among immigrants, and native voters tended to be relatively evenly divided. It is worth noting that the "deviant" behavior of Negroes and Huguenots strengthens rather than weakens the conclusion that native groups had not yet developed polarized

[58] Whitney R. Cross, *The Burned-over District*, 67-68; McNall, *Agricultural History of Western New York*, 68-69. New York State *Census For 1845* provided an excellent clue to the location of the Penn-Jerseyites by dividing native migrants in New York according to their birth in "New England" and "Other States." Research in county and town histories revealed that the latter category consisted overwhelmingly of Penn-Jerseyites.

[59] The highest and lowest ranking Democratic towns in the three counties were: Lodi 67.7 per cent, Ovid 36.9 per cent (Seneca); Barton 74.1 per cent, Nichols 39.0 per cent (Tioga); Lansing 68.8 per cent, Ulysses 37.4 per cent (Tompkins).

voting patterns. Like the immigrants, members of those two groups were influenced by certain ethnic and religious factors that differentiated them from the great bulk of the native electorate.

TABLE 11

ESTIMATED PARTY PERCENTAGES,
NEW YORK ETHNOCULTURAL GROUPS, 1844

	"Natives"			"Immigrants"	
	Whig %	Dem. %		Whig %	Dem. %
Negroes	95.0	5.0	Catholic Irish	5.0	95.0
Huguenots	75.0	25.0	French Canadian	5.0	95.0
Yankees	55.0	45.0	French	10.0	90.0
			New German	20.0	80.0
Penn-Jerseyites	45.0	55.0			
Old British	40.0	60.0	English	75.0	25.0
Dutch	40.0	60.0	Scots	90.0	10.0
Old German	40.0	60.0	Welsh	90.0	10.0
			Protestant Irish	90.0	10.0

CHAPTER IX

RELIGIOUS GROUPS AND POLITICAL PARTIES

ORTUNATELY for the race, unfortunately for the historian aspiring to be "scientific," refractory human beings frequently refuse to arrange themselves in neat, distinct categories. Thus the overlapping of religious and ethnocultural groups in 1844 complicates the task of identifying and classifying voting patterns. In which category, for example, should we place the voting patterns of the Protestant and Catholic Irish or the Huguenot (Protestant) and Catholic French? Any decision can be questioned, but the heavy stress placed upon defense of their "faith" during the 1844 campaign suggests that, for members of those groups, factors associated with religion operated as *more than normally significant determinants of voting behavior.* For non-Catholic voters, however, the data indicate that sectarian religious affiliations or backgrounds would not have provided a significant basis for political differentiation.

In certain areas, it is true, politics "plainly [was] becoming a controversy between Protestants and Catholics,"[1] and appeals were made "calling forth the Protestant feeling against the Catholics, and producing an altogether new element in the great election of this country."[2] As the *Freeman's Journal and Catholic Register* saw it, one religious issue centered around the Whig nomination of a prominent Protestant layman for vice-president (Theodore Frelinghuysen). This Catholic organ charged that Protestant religious journals hailed him as the "Bible candidate," and that "ultra-Protestantism" used his candidacy to drag religious prejudices into party politics.[3] Countering this charge, Whigs claimed that their opponents successfully appealed to Catholic religious prejudices *against* Frelinghuysen.[4] Nevertheless, the highly localized and unsuccessful activities of the American Republicans showed that although sectarian arguments figured more prominently in the 1844 campaign than ever before, they remained confined to limited areas and, at most, sig-

[1] *New York Tribune* (w.), March 22, 1845, p. 5.
[2] *New York Herald* (w.), October 12, 1844, p. 325.
[3] *Freeman's Journal*, June 22, 1844, pp. 412-414.
[4] *New York Tribune* (d.), November 9, 11, 1844, p. 2; *Morning Express*, November 12, 1844, p. 2.

nificantly influenced the voting behavior of only a small fraction of the non-Catholic electorate.[5]

A. Catholic Voting Patterns

Probably about 95 per cent of the "Catholic voters" supported the Democrats in New York State, but a "Protestant voting bloc" had not yet crystallized. As shown above, the Protestants, the overwhelmingly dominant religious group, had split along ethnocultural lines. (Intra-Protestant divisions will be discussed later.) Moreover, perceptive contemporary observers noted significant differences in the voting patterns of "foreign Roman Catholics" and "native Roman Catholics." Thus, preaching revision of the naturalization laws, the *New York Courier and Enquirer* warned the Whigs against adopting policies that would convert *all* Catholics into opponents: "We cheerfully admit that a great majority of the Roman Catholics of this city act with those who take pride in considering themselves *foreigners* instead of American citizens; but this is the *consequence*, not the *cause* of the evil. Were our adopted citizens Protestants, or Mohammedans, or Greeks, the result would be the same. A majority —a very large majority of them—happen to be Roman Catholics; and having fallen into the error of acting together as Foreigners instead of Americans, it would appear to the unreflecting that their religion is their bond of union, when in fact religion has nothing to do with it.

"In illustration of this position, we have only to point to the Roman Catholics of Maryland, and the *native born* Roman Catholics wherever they may be found. . . . At least four-fifths of the native born Roman Catholics of the United States are *Whigs*, because they have grown up with our institutions, are intelligent and patriotic, and know what are the true interests of our country. If, as is undoubtedly the case, nineteen twentieths of the Roman Catholics of this city vote with, and sustain, a party more unprincipled and corrupt than any other that ever existed in the country, it is not because they are Roman Catholics, but because they are *naturalized*

[5] The anti-Catholic American Republican Party made progress only in New York, Kings, Richmond, and Ulster counties. Moreover, as noted earlier, relatively few Democrats switched over to the Whigs on this issue. See Louis D. Scisco, *Political Nativism In New York State*, 48-51; *Albany Evening Journal* (d.), November 15, 1844, p. 2; *New York Tribune* (w.), March 15, 1845, p. 5.

foreigners and *ignorant* of the principles of our institutions and of the true interests of our country."[6]

Anxious to prevent the Whigs from embarking on a politically perilous anti-Catholic crusade, the *Courier* minimized the impact of the religious issue and probably exaggerated the strength of its party among "native-born Roman Catholics." But in relative terms, as the paper claimed, native Catholics apparently did vote more heavily Whig than "foreign Catholics."

Reformulated, the *Courier* (and other Whig journals) claimed that people who happened to be Catholics followed ethnocultural rather than religious lines. Distinct native-foreign divisions among Catholic voters in Maryland, Kentucky, Pennsylvania, and Louisiana support that claim.[7] The recent historical researches of Father Thomas T. McAvoy support it also. His study emphasizes the high social and cultural position of the "Anglo-American Catholic group" before 1835, and the antagonisms that developed between its members and the Irish and German Catholic immigrants who poured in after that date.[8] And to buttress further the *Courier*'s position, we can note that non-Catholic or anti-Catholic New Germans and other New non-British voters formed a material part of the "foreign" avalanche that rolled over the Whigs in 1844. Perhaps the most convincing evidence, however, is that leaders of the Catholic hierarchy did not want their Church to become identified with one party and they worked to break the Democratic hold on their parishioners.

One of Seward's private letters, written shortly after the election of 1840, testifies to the close relations between Bishop Hughes and the leaders of his Whig faction. It also suggests why Seward, Weed, and Greeley clung to the hope that naturalized Catholic voters eventually would cease to go *en masse* for the Democrats. "From one end of the state to the other, the complaint rings that Bishop Hughes and his clergy have excited the Catholics against us [Whigs]. I *know* this to be untrue, totally untrue . . . Bishop Hughes is my friend. I honor, respect, and confide in him. When I read the charges you preferred against him, I felt as I should, if he, or

---

[6] *Courier and Enquirer*, November 4, 1844, p. 2.

[7] *Freeman's Journal*, October 19, 1844, p. 124; *New York Tribune* (w.), November 23, 1844, p. 6.; letter signed "T.F.," March 22, 1845, p. 5; *Albany Evening Journal* (d.), August 30, November 11, 1844, p. 2; *Morning Express*, December 14, 1844, p. 3.

[8] Thomas T. McAvoy, "The Formation of the Catholic Minority in the United States 1820-1860," *Review of Politics*, 10; 13-34 (January 1948).

any other friend, had written to me unjustly concerning you."[9]

Events that occurred four years later suggest that Seward did indeed *"know"* Bishop Hughes's position on party politics.

Hughes's organ was *The Freeman's Journal.* During the 1844 campaign it attacked Frelinghuysen's nomination by the Whigs. Though it did not mention the Democrats by name, it also denounced politicians who stimulated "nativism" by appealing to Catholics and to "adopted citizens" as blocs. The paper emphasized its authoritative knowledge of the Catholic Church's position: "We say then—and in this we *know* we speak for our entire body throughout the country—*the politicians must let us alone.* They must not profane our religion by mixing it up with their intemperate and often unprincipled strife, nor must they drag it and us, singled out from the nation, into the arena to become targets for mob-fury."[10]

A month later, the weekly edition of the *New York Tribune* printed on its front page a long, unsigned article under the heading, "The Position of Catholics and Adopted Citizens in the Present Political Contest." If I accurately interpret the *Tribune's* comment, it hinted that Bishop Hughes was the anonymous author.[11] That interpretation is consonant with a *postelection* editorial in the *Albany Evening Journal* which defended Hughes against the charge that he had defeated the Whigs by ordering Catholics to vote Democratic. On the contrary, the *Journal* asserted, "Several of the Bishops, and many of the Clergy of the Catholic Church have been laboring to rescue their people from party thralldom."[12] Whether or not Hughes actually wrote, inspired, or approved it, this theme—the necessity of breaking the solid attachment of naturalized Catholics to the Democrats—dominated the *Tribune* article written by "A Catholic and an Adopted Citizen":

"It requires but little reflection to be convinced that there is no position more unfavorable to the permanent well being of any class of citizens in a free community than to stand, or even seem to stand, banded together between contending political parties, alternately courted and flattered, calumniated and insulted . . . to maintain it permanently, al-

9 Seward to B.S. [Benjamin Squire?], November 15, 1840, in George E. Baker, ed., *The Works of William H. Seward*, 3: 389-390.

10 *Freeman's Journal*, September 21, 1844, p. 93.

11 *New York Tribune* (w.), October 26, 1844, pp. 1, 3.

12 *Albany Evening Journal* (d.), November 16, 1844, p. 2. See also the interesting letter by Bishop Hughes attacking a nativist Whig editor who claimed that he had ordered naturalized Catholics in the North Country to vote Democratic. *New York Courier and Enquirer*, November 23, 1844, p. 2.

ways so to move and act together as that the separate existence of the class can be seen and felt; habitually to be regarded as a distinct body, with peculiar feelings and special objects to consult and provide for, is a course of conduct fraught with the most serious evil consequences. Such a class may be *in* and *among* the community, but is *not of it*; and it will soon come to find itself more frequently the object of hatred than of love—more generally deprived of the just measure of its rights by the pressure of public ill-will than enriched with favors, by the hand of public liberality. And yet this position—unenviable, unprofitable and pernicious in every respect is the one which the great body of adopted citizens have long occupied, and which it is painful to observe, designing men would still seek to keep them in. . . . They [Irishmen, Germans, French, Swiss, Catholics] have been addressed in a mode which implied that they were not identified in interest and feeling with the American People, but existed as a distinct race, who should be approached and incited to action by motives wholly selfish and personal, if not absolutely alien, to the spirit of American Republicanism; and with a weak and most unwise credulity they have listened to these sordid appeals, and gone on pertinaciously, year after year and almost *en masse*, in support of one political party, the party which had plied them most unscrupulously and most dexterously with these base arguments. . . . [The Whigs do not favor the intolerant policies charged upon them 'by so-called Democratic electioneers.']

"And what have you gained by this course [voting 'in almost solid mass with the Loco Foco party']? You supposed that by it you were fortifying and strengthening your position in your adopted country— but has it been so? Are you more respected by the American people now than when you first began this course? Do you hold a more elevated place socially or politically? Have you more influence? Is there less hostility manifested towards you? Or are your rights and privileges more secure or more favorably regarded? We all see and feel that to each and every one of these interrogations a painful negative must be returned . . . [attack on the appeals made by the *Albany Argus* to Irish, Germans, Swiss, and Catholics, and defense of Whigs].

"I do not desire that you should be all Whigs any more than I would desire that you should be all Democrats. But I do ask you to reject with disdain all efforts of partisan politicians to excite your prejudices or to alarm you for the safety of your rights and interests as Catholics, or as Citizens of foreign birth. I do ask you to trust those rights, if they shall be menaced, to the keeping of the WHOLE AMERICAN PEOPLE and not to the worse than questionable protection of any mere PARTY. I do ask you to judge for yourselves of the measures proposed by the two great parties of the day for your support, and then to vote with an eye directed solely to the public good, and as you may think the welfare of the Republic shall demand."

A decade later, as I will try to show in a subsequent book, Catholic leaders reversed the policy of nonalignment with "any mere party." But in 1844 a sharp distinction must be made between the party affiliations of the Catholic "immigrants" and the political position taken by the Catholic hierarchy and the Anglo-American Catholics.

B. Protestant Voting Patterns

When we concentrate attention upon "Protestant voters," we can see even more clearly that party cleavages did not yet significantly correspond to sectarian religious cleavages. Actually, so inclusive a category impedes rather than aids research designed to identify the social bases of American voting behavior. Sectarian rivalries and conflicts were hardly confined to Catholics versus Protestants; in some respects, they raged more fiercely among the Protestant groups themselves.[13]

If we ignore the complex questions involved in determining whether and to what extent they represented cause or effect, we can see intra-Protestant rivalries, associated with *doctrinal disputes*, as significant bases of *social differentiation* also. Thus Dixon Ryan Fox, when he commented upon the emergence of a "Yankee Culture in New York," noted the far-reaching, subtle impact of religious associations. "The New England migration after 1783 did not bring religion as a fresh gift to New York. . . . Nevertheless, the new settlers greatly strengthened the religious interest in the state and gathered into it a great part of the social life. The church in the earlier years of the nineteenth century *was the place where people met* [italics added]. Mora Adams, writing to his father in Massachusetts from West Almond on the Genesee in 1837, remarked, 'As for society, we have three kinds—Baptist, Methodist and Presbyterian—and a few others, but not much note.' "[14]

Social divisions and Protestant doctrinal divisions may have been closely intertwined, but during the 1840's the same cannot be said

[13] For example, an unusually good history of Chautauqua County noted that "many of the early settlers were from New England or were of Puritan descent, and thoroughly imbued with the old and established Calvinistic doctrines of that people. Between them and the Methodists, who were of a later and then of a more liberal faith, there existed a strong antagonism and a polemic warfare was waged for many years." Obed Edson, *Centennial History of Chautauqua County*, 132.

[14] Dixon Ryan Fox, *Yankees and Yorkers*, 210-211.

of Protestant doctrinal divisions and political divisions. Some impressionistic evidence does suggest that Congregationalists tended to vote more strongly Whig than did members of sects that had once fought to disestablish the "standing order of Congregationalists" in New England.[15] And, according to Whitney Cross's social and intellectual history of western New York, the "New York descendants of Yankee Congregationalism . . . inherited a bias against Freemasonry not shared by their companion evangelical sects"; in contrast, Universalists in the same region were often "aligned with both Masons and Democrats."[16] Broadly speaking, however, the relevant data indicate little causal relation between sectarian and political affiliations.[17] Except for Catholics, knowledge of men's *sectarian* background would not have provided a good basis for predicting their voting behavior in New York during the 1840's. But knowledge about another type of religious cleavage would have provided a good basis for prediction.

C. Free Thinkers Versus Orthodox Believers or Conformists

In addition to Protestant-Catholic and intra-Protestant conflicts, the period between 1825 and 1850 was notable for bitter and widespread conflicts between adherents of orthodox religion and of "popular free-thought" (that is, men either indifferent or hostile to institutionalized religion based upon "divine revelation and overruling Providence"). Precise figures are not possible, but all available evidence indicates that the number of "skeptics," "deists," "rationalists," "infidels," and "atheists" multiplied considerably after 1825, and that they constituted a substantial minority of the population.[18] *Classifying the electorate solely according to formal religious affiliation or background, therefore, is incomplete and may be misleading.* Despite the obvious difficulties, it seems clear that systematic historical studies of voting behavior in this period (and others) must try to determine whether differences can be detected between the voting

---

[15] See the extremely interesting editorial in the *New York Tribune* (w.), March 22, 1851, p. 5.

[16] Whitney R. Cross, *The Burned-over District*, 122, 323. Such vague generalizations, however, must be treated with caution. For example, Prattsburg was a strong Congregational town and it also voted strongly Democratic. See pp. 178-179.

[17] This statement is based upon a close analysis of the voting patterns of towns which can be credibly identified as associated with specific sects. The analysis attempted to hold other factors constant (for example, ethnocultural group, section of the state).

[18] Albert Post, *Popular Freethought In America*, 7, 11-33, 187-198.

behavior of free thinkers and orthodox believers or conformists. Were Whig Yankees in given localities, for example, more likely to attend church or profess adherence to some sect than were Democratic Yankees of approximately the same socioeconomic status or occupation?

It would be easier to answer such questions if political units could be systematically classified according to their relative proportion of free thinkers. Since religious censuses and other available sources neglected to collect those data, we must rely on impressionistic evidence. Yet the evidence points so unmistakably in one direction that we must conclude that the Whigs were the "religious party" and the Democrats the "free thought party." No implication is intended that all, most, or a majority of Democrats were free thinkers; I estimate that most free thinkers were Democrats and relatively few were Whigs. Some were neither. Like so many other aspects of New York (and American) politics during the 1830's and 1840's, to understand the basis for that phenomenon, we must understand its relation to the Antimasonic movement. For, unless we recognize that religious enthusiasm has frequently accompanied social radicalism (for example, the English Levellers), *Democratic and Whig differences about the proper relationships between State and Church may be automatically and erroneously equated with "liberal" and "conservative" differences on other issues.*

A major "charge" against the Masons, it will be recalled, was that they belonged to an "infidel society" at war with true Christianity. Broadcast by religious enthusiasts in the frenzied rhetoric so normal to them, the charge and the missionaries contributed significantly to Antimasonry's crusade-like character.[19] Moreover, the Antimasonic crusade got under way during the years that "marked the serious beginning of a drive for an orthodox reinterpretation of the concept of religious freedom."[20] Logically enough, the two movements soon joined in holy union.

William Morgan had been kidnapped from Canandaigua jail on September 12, 1826. Less than a year later, "in a Fourth of July

---

[19] "Particularly with rural sectarian audiences who were firm believers in a literal interpretation of the Bible, the Antimasons had no difficulty in demonstrating that Freemasonry was not sanctioned by Holy Writ. . . . Whoever was not for Christ was against Him; and Freemasonry was not for Christ since it admitted the fellowship of Jews, Mohammedans *and deists* [italics added]." Leslie Griffen, "The Antimasonic Persuasion," 345. See his interesting chapter, "The Antimasonic Orator in the Pulpit," 332-359.

[20] Joseph L. Blau, "Freedom Of Prayer," *Review of Religion,* 15: 250 (March 1950).

sermon delivered in the Seventh Presbyterian Church of Philadelphia, Ezra Stiles Ely, pastor of the Third Presbyterian Church of that city founded in the spirit of liberty and brotherhood by William Penn, gave utterance to one of the boldest expressions of 'spiritual intolerance and oppression' that have been heard in the United States."[21] Reduced to essentials, Ely's sermon demanded formation of "a Christian Party in Politics." According to him, the criteria for choosing "civil rulers" required drastic change: "Let it then be distinctly stated and fearlessly maintained IN THE FIRST PLACE, that every member of this Christian nation, from the highest to the lowest ought to serve the Lord with fear, and yield his sincere homage to the Son of God. Every ruler *should be* an avowed and a sincere friend of Christianity. He should know and believe the doctrines of our holy religion, and act in conformity with its precepts. Our civil rulers ought to act a religious part in all the relations which they sustain."[22]

Ely's proposed party would transcend sectarian divisions and serve as a pressure group to prevent election of all "opponents of Christianity"—as he and other orthodox Protestant ministers defined them. His definition of these opponents would have excluded from office every president of the United States up to 1827—which may partly explain the national furore his sermon aroused when it was circulated in printed form.[23]

Ironically, at the time Ely delivered the sermon, Andrew Jackson rather than John Quincy Adams received his political preference "because Jackson was a churchgoing man and a fellow Presbyterian."[24] Although Ely did not become directly involved in the Antimasonic movement until 1830, Antimasons enthusiastically endorsed his call to Christian political arms. By 1830, "the Antimasons felt that they had translated Ely's dream into reality—that in launching the Antimasonic party they had created a new sort of union, a 'Christian party in politics.' "[25] Thus one resolution of the first National Antimasonic Convention (1830) warned that "freemasonry exerts a dangerous influence upon the Christian religion,

[21] Joseph L. Blau, " 'The Christian Party in Politics,' " *Review of Religion*, 11: 22 (November 1946).

[22] As quoted in *ibid.*, 23.

[23] *Ibid.*, 22-35; Cross, *Burned-over District*, 134-137; John R. Bodo, *The Protestant Clergy and Public Issues: 1812-1848* (Princeton, N.J., 1954), 46-48.

[24] *Ibid.*, 46.

[25] Griffen, "Antimasonic Persuasion," 238-239, and n.55.

affecting thereby the dearest interests and hopes of man." It invited "all professing Christians, of every denomination, to investigate that subject."[26]

Jacksonian presses quickly reported the results of their own investigations. The *Albany Argus*, the leading party organ, set the tone by attacking the "Antimasonic contrivance" at Philadelphia, "which with characteristic hypocrisy opened with prayer!"[27] Under the heading "Bigotry and Intolerance Revived," it also reprinted from another Jacksonian paper, a scorching anticlerical editorial which claimed that the new party's real purpose had been revealed at the Philadelphia convention. Unlike the Jacksonians, who stood on a Jeffersonian platform of genuine religious freedom and complete separation of church and state, the Antimasons wanted "to inquire into every man's religious opinions, and to reduce all to a particular creed." This reactionary proposal must be combatted, for it threatened to negate the Revolution's victory for freedom of conscience: "For the first time since our glorious independence was declared, do we see a party marshalled under the presidency of Francis Granger of Ontario, making a solemn and deliberate effort to renew the age in which men were burnt at the stake for religious belief— in which the spirit is invoked that condemned to the faggot the poor old women for witches and banished the peaceable Friends out of the community into the wilderness."[28]

Jacksonian presses were not the only ones to warn against old inquisitors in Antimasonic disguise. The *Working Man's Advocate*, spokesman for the small Working Men's faction that refused to join the anti-Regency coalition in 1830, charged that "political Anti-Masonry is neither more nor less than a Church and State intrigue." Antimasonic leaders, it claimed, denounced opponents of Sunday laws as "the most wicked of sinners" and ranked "the crime of Sabbath-breaking before that of murder." An "anti-Masonic party in politics," the *Advocate* declared, could just as well achieve Ely's bigoted dream as "a Christian party in politics." The passionate anticlericalism of the *Advocate* and its emphasis upon the importance of the Working Men's principle, "No legislation on religion," suggest that the issue strongly influenced the eventual decision of

26 *Albany Evening Journal* (s.w.), September 24, 1830, p. 2.

27 *Albany Argus* (s.w.), September 21, 1830, p. 1, and October 5, November 5, 1830, p. 2. On the eve of election, the paper stressed the argument that the "bigoted" Antimasons were "at war with Civil, Religious and Political Liberty."

28 *Ibid.*, September 21, 1830, p. 2.

its faction to join the Jacksonians.[29] For on this issue there is no doubt that the Jacksonians took a strong, unequivocal liberal position. According to a recent penetrating study, Richard M. Johnson's 1830 "Report to the Senate" on the Sunday mail question "remains to this day [1954] a classical defense of the American system of separation of church and state."[30]

Battlegrounds shifted over time, but the lines drawn in 1830 between "the Church and State Party" and the "Jackson Party" held fast. Struggles over Sunday laws, the sustained effort to open public assemblies with prayer, Jackson's refusal to act against Georgia for imprisoning missionaries to the Cherokees—on these and like issues, party differences were distinct, passionate, and enduring.[31] As a result, anti-Jacksonians presented themselves as "the party of all the 'religion' and all the 'decency,' " a claim that the *Argus* scorned as ridiculous in fact and hypocritical in manner. After the 1832 election returns were in, it conceded that "appeals to religious classes, and attempts to excite religious prejudices" against the Jacksonians had partially succeeded, but predicted that the time was "not far distant when the delusion under which a respectable portion of the religious community have been laboring, will have passed away."[32]

Fulfillment of the *Argus'* prediction was retarded, however, by the free thinkers' "notorious" affinity for the Jackson Party. As Arthur M. Schlesinger, Jr. has noted, "Most of the professional agnostics and atheists of the day . . . were active Jacksonians."[33] That the "moral philosophers," the longest-lived of the free thought societies in New York City, made Tammany Hall their headquarters and meetingplace, lends credibility to the Whig charge that the ranks of their opponents included "the infidels and sceptics of all the states."[34] Whether or not that claim had validity everywhere, comparison of the highest and lowest ranking Democratic towns in the strong Antimasonic-Whig county of Ontario suggests its essential accuracy in New York.

As noted previously, the town of Phelps gave the Democrats 60.1

[29] *Working Man's Advocate*, October 30, 1830, p. 1; November 6, 1830, p. 3; November 13, 1830, p. 2; December 11, 1830, p. 1; February 5, 1831, p. 2.

[30] Bodo, *Protestant Clergy and Public Issues*, 42.

[31] *Ibid.*, 35-60; Blau, in *Review of Religion*, 15: 250-264; Cross, *op.cit.*, 126-137; Schlesinger, Jr., *The Age of Jackson*, 350-359.

[32] *Albany Argus* (s.w.), November 9, 1832, p. 1; November 27, 1832, p. 2.

[33] Schlesinger, *op.cit.*, 356.

[34] Post, *op.cit.*, 89-99, 197, 213; Dixon Ryan Fox, *The Decline Of Aristocracy In The Politics Of New York*, 388-390.

per cent of its vote in 1844. It enjoyed much greater prosperity than West Bloomfield, which gave them only 19.3 per cent of its vote. Since, for the most part, both towns had been settled by New Englanders, their significant differences in other respects point up the dangers of treating Yankees as a homogeneous group. In recounting the outstanding events, institutions, and individuals in the history of Phelps, its chronicler noted that "one of the prominent organizations of the early days was the Masonic Lodge, organized May 7, 1811. It was doubtless organized by General Philetus Swift, the first district deputy in this section." Swift "was probably the most prominent character in the early days of Phelps and through his persevering industry he acquired a large fortune. Among the offices he held were those of County Judge and Senator."[35] Not only was Phelps a Masonic stronghold, but Reverend James H. Hotchkin's famous religious history of western New York (published in 1848) recorded disapprovingly that "a very large proportion of the community attend no public worship."[36]

Unlike the chronicler of Phelps, the chronicler of West Bloomfield made no mention of a Masonic lodge and emphasized the church's dominant role in the community. "The Congregational Church of West Bloomfield is one of the fixed institutions of the village and has a history almost as interesting as that of the town itself. The Society of Bloomfield, as it was originally called, had its beginning as early as the year 1796, and is therefore to be numbered among the first religious societies of Western New York." By 1846—almost exactly the time when Hotchkin noted Phelps' indifference to organized religion—"the congregation had become so large that a new Church was necessary. It was accordingly built—a large brick structure, costing about $5,000."[37] Together with other impressionistic evidence derived from many town and county histories, as well as the impressions of other researchers, the illuminating contrast between the piety and politics of Phelps and West Bloomfield lends credence to the Whig contention that "the infidel party" occupied a prominent place in the Democratic ranks during the 1830's and 1840's.

35 Charles F. Milliken, *History of Ontario County, New York And Its People* (New York, 1911), 445.

36 James H. Hotchkin, *A History Of The Purchase And Settlement Of Western New York* (New York, 1848), 378-379.

37 George S. Conover, ed., *History Of Ontario County, New York* (Syracuse, N.Y., 1893), 443-448; Milliken, *Ontario County*, 502.

D. Puritans versus Nonpuritans

The Whigs claimed not only that they were the party of "all the religion," but also that "decency" and "respectability" marched to the polls armed with their ballots. Writing a letter of condolence to Henry Clay after the latter's defeat in 1844, Philip Hone, the prominent New York merchant, observed that "nine tenths of 'our respectable citizens,' the merchants, the professional men, the mechanics and workingmen, those who went to church on Sunday," voted Whig. And a correspondent from Pittsburgh struck the same consoling note: "You had nine-tenths of the virtue, intelligence, and respectability of the nation on our side."[38] There is little doubt that Clay's correspondents took their theme from Horace Greeley. So overwhelmed by grief and disappointment that he literally broke into tears, Greeley had abandoned all restraint and charged that the Democratic victory resulted largely from successful demagogic appeals to the dissolute and the ignorant:

"Loafers around the grog-shops of our Manufacturing villages! subsisting on the earnings of your wives and children in the factories —give an extra glass and an extra yell for Polk and Dallas, and down with Cooney Clay! The time will come when you can no longer riot thus on the wages of your families; therefore make the most of the present, in venting curses on those who have earned and saved while you have idled and squandered, rejoicing in the hope that your victory will soon bring all to a common level of bankruptcy. What if there be sadness and despair among the thrifty, the thoughtful, the industrious—is there not illumination, revelry and extra blue ruin at the Five Points [notorious slum and vice district] and in nine-tenths of the three thousand drunkard-manufactories of our city? Does not ignorance and vice exult, if only to see Intelligence and Virtue perplexed and afflicted? Let Universal Rowdyism strain its throat on one more execration of Clay, and three cheers for *Polk* and Dallas!"[39]

Accused by the editor of the *Eastern Argus* (Maine) of slandering the Democrats, Greeley renewed the attack several weeks later: "The

[38] Clement Eaton, *Henry Clay and the Art of American Politics* (Boston, 1957), 178-179.

[39] *New York Tribune* (w.), November 16, 1844, p. 5. This editorial and the one quoted below bear all the hallmarks of Horace Greeley productions. For his reactions to Clay's defeat, see Glyndon G. Van Deusen, *Horace Greeley*, 95.

Argus is right in supposing that we believe that there is a great moral difference between the two parties, and that we quoted the vote of the Five Points and Corlear's Hook [another 'den of vice'] to show it . . . It was by . . . ['incendiary appeals to Poverty to array itself against Wealth'] that nine-tenths of those broken down by dissipation and degraded by their own profligacy were combined in a solid and powerful phalanx against the Whigs. Upon those Working Men who stick to their business, hope to improve their circumstances by honest industry, *and go on Sundays to church rather than the grog-shop* [italics added] the appeals of Loco-Focoism fell comparatively harmless; while the opposite class were rallied with unprecedented unanimity against us."[40]

Were such outbursts designed to conceal the real cause of the Whig defeat? Did they inadvertently support Democratic charges that the Whigs were the party of the classes and had scarcely disguised contempt for the masses? I do not believe so. Instead of indicating differences in the class composition of parties, Greeley's editorials indicated party differences in *moral attitudes and ways of life*.

Stripped of their more extravagant features, scaled down and reformulated, Greeley's tirades are consistent with the impressionistic evidence reported in the historical literature.[41] To recognize the existence of *something like* "a great moral difference between the two parties" does not, of course, require literal acceptance of his description of "intelligence and virtue" at war with "universal rowdyism." In effect, Greeley asserted that differences in men's attitudes and opinions concerning moral issues cut across class and ethnocultural lines and formed a significant basis for party divisions. This does not seem surprising when we recall that the Antimasons translated Reverend Ely's dream of "a Christian Party in Politics" into reality. Among other things, Ely demanded "the application of Christian principles to the exercise of the suffrage, viz. 'never wittingly to support for any public office' anyone possessing a 'bad moral character,' which includes not only 'confirmed sots and persons judicially convicted of high crimes,' but also 'all profane swearers, notorious

---

[40] *New York Tribune* (w.), December 21, 1844, p. 6.

[41] See, for example, Fox, *Decline of New York Aristocracy*, 368-372; Frederick Jackson Turner, *The United States: 1830-1850*, 19-38, 96-99, 481-483; Wilfrid E. Binkley, *American Political Parties*, 131-133, 159-176; Schlesinger, *op.cit.*, 408-410.

Sabbath-breakers, seducers, slanderers, prodigals, and riotous persons, as well as the advocates of duelling.' "[42]

No one has yet studied the subject systematically, but it seems that on all class levels—particularly the "lower-class"—and among all ethnocultural groups, Whigs were more likely than Democrats to share puritanical attitudes and to disdain the antipuritanical qualities that were esteemed on the American frontier and among urban "lower-class radicals."[43] As conceived here, puritanical attitudes are independent of theological creed. They connote a related set of definitions and values—piety, sobriety, propriety, thrift, "steady habits," and "book-learning."[44] (No implication is intended that all people who valued book-learning were puritans by any definition, nor that approval of book-learning implied approval of free inquiry.)

"Great personal courage, unusual physical powers, the ability to drink a quart of whiskey or to lose the whole of one's capital on the turn of a card and without the quiver of a muscle"[45]—these hell-of-a-fellow, individualistic characteristics suggest the qualities most likely to be valued in American frontier or frontier-like regions. (Indeed, the frontier displayed a strong tendency to insist that all men possess those qualities.) My impressionistic estimate is that in most localities, more Democrats than Whigs valued or possessed those qualities or their *urban equivalents and manifestations.*[46] The spirit of the "Protestant Ethic" may have contributed to capitalist development in long-settled areas. But in a relatively undeveloped, rapidly expanding economy that presented many opportunities to the bold and the adventurous, individualistic, antisocial frontier

[42] Bodo, *Protestant Clergy And Public Issues,* 46. I have found this book very helpful, but its confusion of support for puritanical and theocratic doctrines with support for antidemocratic, conservative political doctrines illustrates the misconceptions fostered by the Jacksonian Democracy concept. *Ibid.,* 48-52.

[43] "The free thought societies and their activities were sustained mainly by the [urban] lower class; rarely did a person of substance and standing in the community associate himself with the militant infidels." Post, *op.cit.,* 32-33. Granted the champions of orthodoxy's strait-laced definitions of "immorality" and "depravity," freethinkers undoubtedly were "immoral and depraved." See *ibid.,* 199-204.

[44] See the succinct summary of the virtues "possessed and admired by puritans" in Ralph Barton Perry, *Puritanism And Democracy* (New York, 1944), 297-320.

[45] Although focussed on the South, W. J. Cash's penetrating discussion of "the frontier tradition" has much wider application. See *The Mind Of The South* (Garden City, N.Y., 1956, Anchor Books ed.), 42-56.

[46] Note the essential similarities between Cash's description of the qualities admired by Southern frontiersmen and Schlesinger's description of the qualities admired by Mike Walsh's "Bowery b'hoys." *Ibid.,* 42-56; *Age of Jackson,* 408-409.

[200]

qualities might frequently have been more economically functional than puritanical qualities which stressed responsibility to the community and conformity to "respectable" values. Antipuritans, therefore, might well have flourished on upper class levels and found Democrats more congenial company than Whigs.

Frederick Jackson Turner's equation of Jacksonian Democracy with an idealized concept of frontier democracy no doubt pushed oversimplification beyond reasonable bounds. But at least he appreciated that Jacksonians flavored their rhetoric to the taste of the frontier and the back country. Although both parties depicted themselves as anti-aristocratic and pro-producer, until the Whigs went out of character and infringed on the Democratic patent in the 1840 Log Cabin campaign, the Democrats held a near monopoly on the rhetoric designed to conjure up a muscular, horny-handed image of their party.[47]

Drawing distinctions between "producers" and "parasites" was not original with Americans. What did make the Jacksonian rhetoric relatively original was its imaginative merger of the theme of the virtuous producer with that of the lusty Western pioneer.[48] If we could hold other factors constant, we would find that the Democrats tended to have their greatest success among voters who bragged about their fondness for hard liquor, fast women and horses, and strong, racy language. By this conjecture we need not grant the Antimasons and Whigs anything like their claimed monopoly on all the decency, respectability, and religion. It is even debatable whether such a study of Democratic voters could be made. But we can adduce some support for the conjecture by again contrasting the political and "moral" characteristics of two towns in the same county.

The town of Burke in Franklin County was settled "mostly from

---

[47] To quote Turner on the campaign: " 'We have taught them how to conquer us!' declared a prominent Democratic organ. Huge processions with floats of log cabins, coonskins, canoes, etc., and gatherings of thousands of supporters, were features of Harrison's campaign. This 'mummery' aroused the indignation of Jackson and his friends. One of them wrote to him that the United States had become worshipers [*sic*] of the most imbecile animals of the forest; and he himself, forgetful of the emotional aspect of his own contests, virtuously contrasted the decorum of the Democratic campaign with the Whig mode of electioneering." *United States: 1830-1850*, 482. In my opinion, recent historians have overreacted against Turner's overemphasis on the role of the frontier in shaping the character of Jackson's Party.

[48] Daniel Aaron's study of the relationships between what might be called the "Cult of Old Hickory" during the 1820's and 1830's and the "Cult of the Proletariat" during the 1920's and 1930's is, in my opinion, one of the most interesting and significant projects now underway in American intellectual history.

Vermont." Other places with a higher proportion of non-British immigrants supported the Democrats more strongly, but Burke gave them 60.2 per cent of its vote, although the county's median unit registered only 45.4 per cent. During the pre-Civil War period, it clearly was a "poor" lumbering and tanning town. Significantly, after it paid the standard tributes to the sterling qualities of its settlers, the local county history described them in unusual terms for a work of that genre. Along with good citizens, "bad ones came also or developed there, and at one period the hamlet of Burke, known also as the 'Hollow' and for a time as Andrusville, was exceedingly tough."

That period must have included July 4, 1861, for it was described as one of the "two days of great excitement" in the town annals. The first was in 1856 when the great tornado struck: "The other day in question [Fourth of July, 1861] was when Hiram Cartwright and other secession sympathizers raised a secession flag at the Hollow. The flag had been painted by William Hollenbeck. The time was when the Hollow was deemed one of the hardest places in the county, and the day was doubtless the wildest that Burke ever knew. It is said that there were two hundred men drunk there on that day, and drunk in no ordinary degree, but raving so. The men who were back of the flag raising armed themselves, assembled at the foot of the pole, and declared that they would shoot any one who should attempt to haul down the flag. Word of the affair reached Malone, and a company of sober men, quite as thoroughly in earnest as the rabble at Burke, was recruited, largely from the railroad machine shops, to go to Burke for the purpose of tearing down the rag."

But just as the train reached Burke, frantic admonitions by the county's leading Democratic editor prevailed, the secession flag was lowered, and the rumble never came off.[49]

From the description by the same historian elsewhere in the volume, it can be inferred that the phrase "company of sober men" is a good indicator of Malone's moral climate. According to one nostalgic inhabitant, in 1824 it had been "the most perfect representation of the ideal puritanical village." Malone probably had retained much of that character, for the outcome of local option referendums in 1846 and 1847 made it a nominally "dry" town. Like Burke, nearly all its settlers came from Vermont, but they "were mostly of the

[49] Frederick J. Seaver, *Historical Sketches of Franklin County* (Albany, 1918), 216-230.

Puritan type and of what Deacon Jehiel Berry used to call the 'white oak' strain, and of whom generally Gail Hamilton strikingly wrote: 'Every church, every school house, every town house from the Atlantic to the Pacific has Plymouth Rock for its foundation. Wherever Freedom aims a musket, or plants a standard, or nerves an arm, or sings a song, or makes a protest, or murmurs a prayer, there is Plymouth Rock.' "[50]

Mostly of the puritan type, they were also mostly of the Whig Party. In 1844 the prosperous farming town of Malone was the lowest ranking Democratic unit (36.0 per cent) in Franklin County. In 1834, before sizeable numbers of Irish Catholics and French-Canadians arrived, the Whigs had received 69.3 per cent, the Democrats 30.7 per cent, of its vote.

Like Phelps and West Bloomfield, the contrast between politics and piety in Burke and Malone supports the impressionistic finding that there were significant differences in Whig and Democratic moral attitudes. Fortunately, that finding is also supported by systematic data. But the inferences drawn from those data rest on certain assumptions that should be made explicit.

The key assumption here is that men engaged primarily in farming tended to have a different set of values, beliefs, and attitudes from those engaged primarily in lumbering and its allied pursuits (for example, tanning, charcoal-burning, shingle-making). By their nature, it is assumed, the two occupations retained or developed or attracted men who differed in psychological makeup. Other considerations aside, the environment in which they were carried out and the personal qualities necessary to their successful pursuit made belief in the value of education, religion, and temperance more functional and more likely to flourish in farming than in lumbering areas.

Except for certain specialized crops, farming was a slow process of growing things that sharply restricted men to their home boundaries and reserved its rewards for men capable of planning, self-discipline, and long adherence to a daily routine that varied little over the years. In contrast, lumbering required quick spurts of great exertion during which men destroyed things under conditions of constant physical danger, followed by long periods in which they were free to act as the spirit moved them and the spirits flowed. Moreover, it tended to bring quicker returns with more fluctuation than did farming, giving it something of the allure and excitement of gambling.

[50] *Ibid.*, 36-38, 397-493. The quotation is from p. 318.

Rafting logs down the Delaware, the Susquehanna, or the Allegheny in high-water season was a world away from the dull routine of hoeing weeds in home cornfields. Whatever the reasons for the difference in attitudes, if we hold ethnocultural group constant, I make the assumption that a much larger proportion of farmers than lumbermen shared puritanical views and possessed "intelligence and virtue," as defined in Greeley's and Hone's lexicon.[51]

If the assumption is granted, the systematic data presently available indicate the existence of heavy Democratic majorities in 1844 among rural "nonpuritan" voters. One set of statistics makes the point. Twenty lumbering towns constituted the *highest-ranking* Democratic units in their counties, but lumbering towns fell into the *lowest-ranking* Democratic category in only seven counties. (Half the top towns registered Democratic tallies of 71.2 per cent or better, only one under 60.0 per cent). The strong positive relationship between lumbering and heavy Democratic majorities is not spurious, for it persists when other variables are considered and held constant. For example, despite the Yankee tendency as a group to vote Whig, they were either the numerically overwhelming or the dominant element in 15 of the 20 highest Democratic lumbering towns.[52] In fact, partisan sympathies were so pronounced in lum-

[51] The account of lumbering in Chautauqua County during the period from 1825 to 1851 is evocative and suggestive: "The raftsmen were often rough men, accustomed to hard fare, and not averse to hard blows. No vigorous young man within the lumbering districts regarded his education as complete until he had had a taste of the rough life of a raftsman; had a pull at an oar, and had encountered the hardships and sometimes the perils of the river. Most young men desired at least once to look upon the beautiful and picturesque scenery of the Allegheny, to descend with its smooth flowing current, now gliding in the shadow of some lofty headland, now drifting along some gently-sloping shore, finally to float out on the broad waters of the Ohio and the Mississippi." (Edson, *Chautauqua County History*, 125.) Lumbering, it should be noted, sometimes paid rich rewards and "was a school in which a host of energetic business men were educated." Though no systematic study has yet been made of successful lumbermen, my impression, based upon county histories, is that Reuben Fenton's career was not untypical: He was both "a successful and leading operator in lumber on the Allegheny and the Ohio" and a leading Democratic politician. (*Ibid.*, 170-171, 194-195.) Similarly, in Greene County in eastern New York, Col. Zadoc Pratt owned what at one time was said to be the largest tannery in the world; he was also a Yankee Episcopalian, a Mason, and a prominent Democratic politician. Beers, *History of Greene County, New York*, 383-389. See also Greeley's typically polemical but perceptive analysis of why lumbering regions voted overwhelmingly Democratic. *New York Tribune* (d.), April 18, 27, 1844, p. 2.

[52] Of course, some farming was practiced in "lumbering towns." The term connotes areas where lumbering and allied activities were at least a relatively important source of income for most or many inhabitants, where population tended to be sparse and scattered, and where basic community institutions (for example, churches, schools) tended to be impermanent or crudely developed. The twenty highest rank-

bering towns that an estimate of 75 per cent Democratic appears reasonable for members of that occupational group. Since I can think of no "economic" reason why men engaged in lumbering should prefer one party to the other, I relate their voting to moral attitudes and values commonly held by lumbermen. In this respect, the argument differs radically from traditional occupational group interpretations of politics, and discredits rather than supports economic determinism.

Additional support for the finding that puritans tended more than nonpuritans to vote Whig can be inferred from the opposing views of the two parties concerning the proper role of the state in the Good Society. Committed to the doctrine of the negative state, the dominant wing of the Democratic Party in New York drew the logical conclusions and took a clear-cut liberal position on religious and moral issues. (In this context, "liberal" refers to the word's literal meaning and is free from value connotations.) As noted earlier, its official creed held that in a republic, "A great regulator of business occupations, *or consciences of men* [italics added], not only is not required, but should not be tolerated."[53]

In 1844, the Whig Party had not yet officially gone on record as favoring legislation to regulate the consciences of men or to improve their minds and refine their society. Nevertheless, semiofficial organs of the party, as different from each other as the *New York Express*[54]

---

ing Democratic towns were: Scio, Allegany (78.4 per cent); Sanford, Broome (64.0 per cent); Hinsdale, Cattaraugus (60.2 per cent); Carroll, Chautauqua (62.1 per cent); Southport, Chemung (71.5 per cent); Davenport, Delaware (82.1 per cent); Schroon, Essex (77.1 per cent); Moira, Franklin (65.5 per cent); Northampton, Fulton (65.2 per cent); Ossian, Livingston (53.3 per cent); Bolystown, Oswego (71.2 per cent); Unadilla, Otsego (67.3 per cent); Putnam Valley, Putnam (83.2 per cent); Russell, St. Lawrence (74.3 per cent); Day, Saratoga (64.6 per cent); Troupsburgh, Steuben (74.2 per cent); Cohecton, Sullivan (74.4 per cent); Warrensburg, Warren (81.8 per cent); Dresden, Washington (61.8 per cent); Italy, Yates (67.2 per cent).

The seven lowest ranking lumbering Democratic towns were Genesee, Allegany (25.2 per cent); Mooers, Clinton (25.2 percent); New Haven, Oswego (32.7 per cent); Hadley, Saratoga (33.7 per cent); Campbell, Steuben (25.6 per cent); Fallsburgh, Sullivan (41.9 per cent); Luzerne, Warren (23.0 per cent).

53 See p. 109, above.

54 The *Express* quarreled with the *Tribune* about most things, but it shared the general Whig disdain for the doctrines and values of "the Democracy." According to the *Express*, among the latter's "cardinal doctrines" were "opposition to all refinement in society;—opposition to education,—opposition to all charities, such as hospitals, asylums,—opposition to anything that tends to alleviate the sufferings of the poor;—etc. . . . Amongst those things which they hold, are, that ignorance is a better qualification for a legislator than intelligence. At every election they endeavor to arouse all the prejudices of the ignorant against the intelligent. Their

and the *New York Tribune,* in effect proudly confirmed Democratic charges that the Whigs were dedicated to what has been called the puritanical Yankees' "holy enterprise of minding other people's business."[55] In a sense, that witticism is slanderous, for as the *Tribune* viewed the social order, no such thing existed as other people's business.

According to the assumption underlying the *Tribune*'s doctrine, the righteous had no choice but to save the world from evil, and evildoers from themselves. Contrary to the Democratic position that men should be left free to make individual choices on religious and moral issues, the *Tribune* essentially argued that the state was a proper instrument for the regulation of every "evil" in society—as its editor and other "righteous" men defined evil. That doctrine was consonant with populistic doctrine and with the Antimasonic-Whig position on the positive state—but not, by any reasonable definition, with a liberal State. In respect to issues of this type, therefore, the Whig Party can accurately be described at best as "conservative" and at worst as "reactionary."

Perhaps the best way to illustrate concretely the real differences between Democratic "liberalism" and Whig "conservatism" is to cite the *Tribune*'s analysis of a Democratic pamphlet entitled, *Loco-Focoism Displayed, or Government for the People; in a Dialogue between a Whig and a Loco-Foco.*[56] Why analyze this particular pamphlet? Because it is a significant index of how Locofocoism is propagated and of "the considerations which . . . [won] men to its support." Substitute "Whiggism" for "Loco-Focoism" and the *Tribune*'s analysis serves precisely the same function—although the primary concern here is to identify the kinds of men won to the support of the two parties, rather than to understand their motives. "The leading idea of the writer is that popularly expressed by the current Loco-Foco axioms, 'The world is governed too much'; 'The best government is that which governs least'; etc. There is nothing new in these doctrines, and we have found them more ably set forth by Bentham, Hazlitt, and some of the modern Politicial Economists than by our 'Loco-Foco.' . . . Our 'Loco-Foco' of course contends

---

presses praise their candidates on account of their vulgarity and want of education, and ridicule their opponents for possessing these things." *(New York Express,* July 10, 1844, p. 2.)

[55] Fox, *Yankees and Yorkers,* 2-3. See the penetrating observations in Cross, *op.cit.,* 81-82.

[56] *New York Tribune* (w.), August 2, 1845, p. 5.

that Governments have no rights and duties beyond the prevention and punishment of palpable invasions of one man's rights by another —that, consequently, all laws against Gambling, Grogselling, Debauchery, Bigamy, Brothelkeeping, etc., etc., are gross usurpations. . . . The fallacy here, as in all similar arguments against the punishment of Seduction and Licentiousness in general, lies in the assumption that the perpetrators 'injure nobody but themselves.' They do injure others; they bring scandal and reproach to their relatives; they are morally certain to prove unfaithful to their duties as parents, children, etc., and they corrupt and demoralize those around them. . . . The general doctrine of this 'Loco-Foco' is more precisely set forth in another passage:

" 'W.[hig]. Then I suppose of course you think that all legislation for morality alone is useless.

" 'L.[oco]. Not only that, but that *all legislation* having any other object but the protection of rights is not only injurious to morality, but is in itself immoral and wicked.' "

Even if we knew nothing except the two parties' conflicting views about the state's role as a regulator of the "consciences of men," we could reasonably infer that, other factors held constant, puritans would be more likely to vote Whig, nonpuritans to vote Democratic. No implication is intended, of course, that all or an overwhelming majority of Whigs and Democrats were puritans and nonpuritans, respectively. The inference refers to central tendencies, not to perfect or near perfect relationships. To draw that inference in no way denies that attitudes and opinions related to other issues, interests, loyalties, and antagonisms exerted cross-pressures upon voters. Nor is it denied that some men who might be classified as puritans opposed the Whigs on the ground that the state had neither the right nor the ability to legislate morality. But, together with the other evidence cited above, the contrasting attitudes of the two parties on such issues support the finding that puritan and nonpuritan divisions strongly corresponded to Whig and Democratic divisions.

CHAPTER X

WHO VOTED FOR THE MINOR "PARTIES"?

MEMBERS of the Liberty and American Republican movements in New York shared at least one attribute: they felt passionately enough about "one idea" to break away from old political associates and old political associations. Moreover, they tended to share the same old associations.[1]

Analysis of the election statistics lends support to the *Tribune*'s claim that the Democrats "fanned political abolition" to injure the Whigs: "Right well does the *Argus* understand that any third party based on convictions of moral duty must naturally draw ten recruits from the Whig ranks to every one taken from the other side. Thus the right always suffers by these eccentric third parties."[2]

In more restrained moods, the *Tribune* estimated that ex-Whigs cast roughly 90 per cent of the Liberty votes; in any event, the campaign editorials of the *Argus* support the *Tribune*'s claim that the Democrats confidently expected political abolitionism to injure their opponents while leaving them relatively unscathed.[3]

Although American Republicanism drew supporters from both parties, it drew more heavily from the Whigs. Available evidence

---

[1] The most detailed analyses of the Liberty Party vote were presented in the *New York Tribune* (d.), November 9, 26, p. 2; December 25, p. 2 (all 1844); *Tribune* (w.), July 5, p. 5; 12, p. 3; 19, p. 5 (all 1845). See also *New York Herald* (w.), November 9, 1844, p. 357; Thurlow Weed to Francis Granger, June 19, 1845, in Thurlow W. Barnes, ed., *Memoir of Thurlow Weed*, 230-231. For the American Republican vote, the best available analyses deal with the 1844 mayoralty election. See the *New York Journal of Commerce*, April 12, 1844; *Tribune* (w.), April 20, 1844, p. 5.

[2] *Ibid.*, November 23, 1844, p. 6. With few exceptions, Democratic percentages remained relatively constant between 1840 and 1844 in towns where the Liberty Party received more than a scattering vote; Whig declines almost equalled the Liberty percentages. The exceptions tended to cluster in and around Madison County. Smith's policy of concentrating Liberty forces in his home county apparently dented the Democratic ranks. But the results in Putnam, Washington County, can be regarded as typical. In 1840 its total vote was 140; the Whigs received 113 (80.7 per cent), the Democrats 27 (19.3 per cent). In 1844 the total vote was 135; the Whigs received 68 (50.4 per cent), the Democrats 25 (18.5 per cent), and the Liberty Party 42 (31.1 per cent).

To argue that a substantial proportion of Democrats voted Liberty in 1844, one must assume that a substantial proportion of Democratic votes in 1844 were cast by erstwhile Whigs—an incredible assumption. We can reinforce the inferences drawn from the Putnam voting statistics for 1840 and 1844 by noting that, after the collapse of the Liberty and Free Soil parties, the Whig and Democratic percentages returned to almost precisely their 1840 levels. In 1850, the Whigs received 79.1 per cent of the total vote, the Democrats 20.9 per cent.

[3] *Albany Argus* (w.), September 14, p. 296; October 26, p. 348; November 2, p. 355 (all 1844).

concerning the political ties of American Republicans is impressionistic; little reason exists, however, to doubt contemporary newspaper estimates that they divided about 60 per cent Whig, 40 per cent Democratic. But despite their resemblance in political background and intensity of conviction, Liberty and American Republican voters differed in other major respects.

A. Liberty Party Voters

To my knowledge, no one has yet made a systematic, detailed study of the social composition of the Liberty Party in any state. The available data, however, appear to warrant several generalizations about New York.

That political abolitionism was overwhelmingly a rural movement is clear from the voting statistics. Except for Utica, no city in New York gave the Liberty Party as much as five per cent of its total vote. In every other city it received less than the state average (3.1 per cent), and in most, far less. The inverse relationship between political abolitionism and "urbanity" particularly shows up in the almost nonexistent Liberty Party vote in larger eastern cities, such as New York (0.2 per cent), Brooklyn (0.6 per cent), and Albany (1.0 per cent).

Although abolitionism was overwhelmingly a rural movement, its appeal was actually limited *to certain types* of rural areas. A prominent abolitionist, Henry Stanton, later noted that "for many years an influence on behalf of the slave radiated from the central counties of New York which was felt beyond the borders of the state. . . ."[4] But analysis of voting statistics and other data show that political abolitionists' hammer blows struck responsive chords in central, western, and northern New York communities containing few Negro inhabitants, or in cities serving those communities—and in those areas almost exclusively.[5] Considerable numbers of free Negroes lived in eastern and southeastern New York, areas which expressed intense hostility to antislavery "agitators" and to antislavery "agitation." Like the eastern cities, many rural counties, such as Ulster, Rockland, Dutchess, Suffolk, and Orange, registered either no Liberty votes or less than one per cent of the total cast.

Locating the towns that gave 15 per cent or more of their votes

---

[4] Henry B. Stanton, *Random Recollections* (New York, 1887), 65.

[5] As noted earlier, the ethnocultural composition of political units in New York can be ascertained from the State *Census* for 1845 and 1855. Among other forms of identification, individuals were listed "by color."

to the Liberty Party supports Stanton's observation that antislavery influence radiated out from central New York. Significantly, Smithfield in Madison County gave the highest Liberty vote (48.5 per cent) of any town in the state. The town had been founded and named by Gerrit Smith's father, and served as his family seat. Together with the energy and money concentrated upon the work in Madison County,[6] Smith's personal influence probably accounted for its position as the strongest Liberty county (15.4 per cent). In addition to Smithfield, five other Madison towns cast more than 15 per cent of their votes "on behalf of the slave." Just across the county border, Plainfield, in Otsego, ranked as the second highest Liberty town, with 32.3 per cent. Altogether, a 50 mile radius drawn from the Smithfield center would encompass 17 of the party's top 35 towns.[7]

Whether located near or far from the geographic center of Liberty influence, the top antislavery towns strikingly resembled each other in socioeconomic and ethnocultural composition. With few exceptions, they were small, moderately prosperous, Yankee farming communities. And impressionistic evidence suggests that the men who voted the Liberty ticket tended to have considerable standing in their communities and much better than average education.[8] Study of county histories suggests that the following description of Erie County abolitionists might be applied generally: "The slimness of the Abolitionist vote [in 1844] could not be blamed altogether upon political inexperience. In the Anti-Slavery societies of both city [Buffalo] and county the reformers had organizations to support their efforts. Certain of the members to be sure were unworldly idealists little used to the hustings and the rough and tumble of political contest. Among them was a merchant's clerk named Douglas Williams; a former schoolmaster in East Aurora, a Dartmouth man, named George W. Johnson; a New School Presbyterian Deacon, Abner W. Bryant; a few ministers like the Reverend Mr. Parmalee of Griffin's Mills and the Reverend Calvin Grey of Wales. More were substantial farmers or men of affairs in rural towns and to that

---

[6] Ralph V. Harlow, *Gerrit Smith* (New York, 1939), 4-17, 168-171.

[7] Listed in rank order, these towns cast Liberty votes of 15 per cent or higher: Smithfield, Plainfield, Putnam, Mooers, China, Georgetown, Birdsall, Linclaen, Winfield, Lawrence, Champlain, Leon, Alexandria, Franklinville, Williamson, Cazenovia, Volney, Litchfield, Marion, Rose, Parish, Richmond, Randolph, Scott, Hadley, Otisco, Cicero, Sullivan, Amity, Nelson, Norway, Madison, Salisbury, Walworth, Theresa.

[8] See the discussion and maps in Whitney Cross, *The Burned-over District*, 217-228. Cross's conclusions are supported by capsule descriptions of Abolitionists in county histories.

number belonged Joseph Plumb of Collins; Elihu Rice of Sardinia; Gideon Barker of Wales; Dwight Needham and Archibald Griffith of Concord. Here and there the roster of membership bore the name of a prominent professional man like Dr. Caleb Austen of Buffalo. Of these men very few were politicians; yet politicians there were who played conspicuous parts in the movement. Of this description were Isaac Phelps of Griffin's Mills, in whose bailiwick the Erie County Anti-Slavery Society had been organized; Joseph Freeman of Alden, William Mills of Clarence, and Colonel Asa Warren of Eden. These gentlemen, sometimes supervisors, magistrates, or members of the legislature, understood politics from long experience. So did the ex-Congressman and prominent member of the Buffalo bar, Thomas C. Love."[9]

Though we must again rely on impressionistic evidence, it seems reasonable to say that most Liberty voters shared a common set of "radical religious beliefs." During the 1830's and 1840's, those beliefs inspired numerous related reform and benevolent movements, and political abolitionism represented only one manifestation of religious ultraism. "The ultraist state of mind," according to Whitney Cross, "rose from an implicit, even occasionally an explicit, reliance upon the direct guidance of the Holy Ghost." Ultraists assumed and acted on the assumption that God directly intervened in human affairs by revealing the truth to certain souls. Once it had been revealed to them, once they saw "the inner light," men had no choice but to reveal God's will to others and thus bring about the ultimate perfection of mankind in this world. A victory over slavery might launch the millennium, these optimistic Calvinists believed—a belief likely to give great energy and sense of mission to men caught up in the antislavery crusade.[10]

Ultraists dedicated to antislavery carried the Yankee "holy enterprise of minding other people's business" to its logical extreme. No doubt they appeared intolerably self-righteous to contemporaries less convinced than they that eradicating the "sin of slavery" was God's will, or that abolitionists were His chosen instruments. And twentieth century psychologists and psychiatrists might see guilt and hyperactive superegos where ultraists saw "the spirit [that] has power to arouse the conscience and make it pierce like an ar-

[9] John T. Horton, et al., *History of Northwestern New York*, 1: 133.
[10] Cross, *op.cit.*, 198. My discussion of religious ultraism and antislavery is largely based on Cross, 173-237, 277-282.

row. . . ." However we account for them, antislavery ultraists clearly acted as righteous men compelled to follow God's inner light, wherever it led them and whatever personal vicissitudes they encountered along the way.

Read literally, rather than as a blatant expression of self-righteousness, this rhetorical question catches the ultraist essence: "For why should a good man stop," asked one minister in all innocence, "who knows certainly that he is right exactly, and that all men are wrong in proportion as they differ from him?"[11] Whether abolitionists really were "right exactly" could not be more irrelevant here; what is relevant here is to identify the kind of men who voted for the Liberty Party, not to assess the "rightness" of their doctrines.

All political abolitionists were not religious ultraists, but it seems reasonably certain that few, if any, were not intensely religious. True, antislavery appeals were sometimes phrased in economic terms. Those were arguments, not reasons. Economic arguments for abolition actually were most relevant in areas that rejected abolitionism most fiercely and ejected abolitionists most forcibly.[12] Given the nature and program of the Liberty Party, it is hardly surprising that its strongest support came from areas most likely to respond to the doctrines preached by New York rural evangelical sects. During the early forties, Baptists apparently led the antislavery hosts; Presbyterians and Methodists followed closely. That ranking is strictly relative, because at best only a very small minority of any major denomination cast Liberty ballots.[13]

For our purposes, the most illuminating aspect of the Liberty Party's composition is what it reveals about the Whig and Democratic parties. As suggested earlier, Whigs tended to respond more favorably than Democrats to the "church and state" concept. Moreover, the Whig political philosophy postulated an activist, positive state, responsible for improving the material and moral well-being of society and capable of wielding broad national powers. In contrast, the Democratic philosophy postulated a negative, passive state in general, and a restricted, passive federal government in particular. Since abolitionists belonged to economic and ethnocultural groups

11 Quoted in *ibid.*, 205.

12 The economic arguments employed by abolitionists are sketched in Julian Bretz, "The Economic Background of the Liberty Party," *American Historical Review*, 34: 250-264 (January 1929). A point made earlier is relevant here: a political party's rhetoric does not necessarily permit accurate inferences to be drawn about its social composition.

13 Cross, 222-224.

which did not vote strongly Whig, it is significant that the overwhelming majority of Liberty voters were ex-Whigs. From these two sets of facts, the deduction seems logical that they had been originally attracted to the Whig Party, in part at least, because its activist political doctrines closely corresponded to their activist religious doctrines; that is, they believed that the state must act to purge society of moral evils. This line of reasoning can be pushed further.

Antislavery ultraists "believed progress to be attainable by human effort and practically inevitable; but they derived from their Calvinist traditions an equally powerful suspicion that the natural tendency, *unaided by willful diligence* [italics added], was toward degeneracy."[14] Translated into nonreligious terms, this suspicion corresponds to the belief that egoistic individual action must fail to produce the beneficial results envisioned by *laissez faire* political economists. That abolitionists almost invariably had Whig histories lends support, therefore, to a conclusion developed further in succeeding chapters: Whatever the source of their inspiration, other things being equal, men convinced that organized, collective action contributed to human progress tended more to vote Whig than Democrat. Deliberately oversimplified to make the point, Whigs tended toward collectivism, Democrats toward individualism.

B. American Republican Voters

Unlike the abolitionists, the American Republicans failed to form an independent third party in the 1844 national and state elections. In some New York areas, local branches practically merged with the Whigs; in others, they maintained their independent identity. But invariably, some form of coalition developed between the two parties. It is difficult, therefore, either to distinguish "true" American Republicans from men who simply voted their local tickets as part of a political bargain, or to estimate the number of men who sympathized with American Republican doctrines but remained loyal to old associates and associations. Nomination of an independent state ticket in 1846, however, enables us to construct a rough indicator of American Republican strength in 1844. If the assumption is accurate that American Republican strength remained relatively constant during those two years, as did Liberty Party strength, we

14 *Ibid.*, 199.

can estimate that the party polled between one and two per cent of the total state vote in 1844.[15]

Though the number of American Republican voters in 1844 can be only roughly estimated, their location and social attributes can be more readily established. Political abolitionism was overwhelmingly rural and limited to certain central, western, and northern New York communities; political American Republicanism was overwhelmingly urban and limited to eastern and southeastern New York. Judged by the 1846 results, its strength was concentrated in New York City and Brooklyn where large numbers of Irish and German Catholics lived.[16] Put another way, Liberty voters clustered in areas where relatively *few* foreigners, Catholics, and Negroes lived; American Republicans clustered in areas where relatively *many* foreigners, Catholics, and Negroes lived.

Catholic and Democratic attacks upon the nativist "proclivity" of Protestant Irish, English, and Scots naturalized citizens, and "nativist" praise for them, suggest that some New British actually voted for American Republicanism.[17] And Huguenot support for the single avowedly anti-Catholic party has previously been mentioned. Although sympathy for American Republicanism undoubtedly cut across class and ethnocultural lines, a large majority of its adherents apparently were urban, native Protestants of skilled worker, mechanic, or lower middle class socioeconomic status, who resented competition and contact with immigrants of "strange" cultures, faiths and languages.[18] Perhaps the best clue to the movement's social composition is provided by the *Freeman's Journal*; the Catholic paper sarcastically referred to the skill at illegal voting displayed by "the fire boys [members of volunteer fire companies], market men, and

[15] The best available treatment of the American Republican movement is in Louis D. Scisco, *Political Nativism In New York State*, 39-61. A modern study building on Scisco's pioneer work is badly needed. In my opinion, the "American" movement of the 1840's represented the first significant expression of a major theme in American history and requires much closer study than it has received to date.

[16] *Ibid.*, 58-59. The party's county percentages were: Dutchess 11.2, New York 9.0, Putnam 5.2, Kings 5.0, Queens 3.3, Richmond 1.0, Suffolk 1.0, Ulster 0.8, Westchester 0.6, Rockland 0.5, Albany 0.4, Columbia 0.4, Orange 0.4, Greene 0.3, Oneida 0.3, Sullivan 0.3.

[17] *Freeman's Journal*, August 3, 1844, p. 37; *Brooklyn Eagle*, September 16, 28, 1844, p. 2; *Evening Post For The Country*, March 29, 1845, p. 3; *American Republican*, November 4, 1844, p. 2.

[18] For a detailed, illuminating discussion, see *Robert Ernst*, "Economic Nativism In New York City During The 1840's," *New York History*, 28: 170-186 (April 1948).

other irregulars who form so very large a portion of the original 'native Americans.' "[19]

Figuratively speaking, the "threat to Americanism" may be said to have sparked the "religious crusade" that impelled the "fire boys" and "market men" to independent political action. Together with the Liberty voters, they shared the conviction that neither major party adequately supported or expressed their "crusade." That they felt impelled to resort to independent political action, I suggest, deepens our understanding of the Whig and Democratic parties during the 1840's. Neither major party was yet prepared to embrace openly either one of the minor movements—a conclusion further supported by the analysis that follows.

[19] *Freeman's Journal*, April 13, 1844, p. 333.

CHAPTER XI

PARTY PROGRAMS, CHARACTERS,
AND IMAGES

WHAT a political party claims to stand for and what it actually represents are closely related but significantly different. Aside from the principles and policies it adopts and advocates, a party radiates an aura that influences the way the electorate appraises and responds to its principles and policies. A useful distinction can be made, therefore, between a party's *program* and its aura, or *character*. The program is concrete and refers to known actions or proposals; the character is intangible and connotes general qualities. Though the program of a party is more easily and reliably determined than is its character, historians cannot concentrate on the former and ignore the latter; the combined impact of program and character form the *image* which is projected to the electorate.[1]

But political parties do not confine themselves to projecting their own images; they also try to influence the electorate by projecting an image of their opponents. Thus parties create both an *official self-image* and an *official image of opponents*. Many different means are used to project official images, but, at least for the period studied, the platforms, addresses, and candidates adopted at formal conventions constitute the most important and revealing ones.

Particularly because intraparty battles frequently influence the adoption of platforms, addresses, and candidates, they require careful handling when we use them to draw inferences about voting behavior. Carefully handled, I believe that they can be useful in interpreting voting. Skeptics may hold that American party platforms and addresses do not invariably express the deepest convictions of their architects; no one can deny, however, that to some extent they usually reflect what their architects think the voters want to hear. Of course, all planks in a platform are not expected to be equally pleasing or important to all voters, but the overall structure is expected to be pleasing to the majority of voters.[2] Similarly, and

[1] See the suggestive comments in Graham Wallas, "Human Nature In Politics," in Heinz Eulau, et al., *Political Behavior* (Glencoe, Ill., 1956), 9-14.

[2] A fuller discussion of the value of political platforms for historical research is found in Lee Benson, *Research Problems in American Political History* (Bureau of Applied Social Research, Columbia University, 1954, dittoed), 134-136.

particularly in closely contested areas or closely contested elections, the selection of candidates is usually influenced by the party's assessment of the kind of image most likely to please the electorate. (Emphasis is given here to the officially avowed characteristics of candidates, not the sometimes less roseate realities.)

Studied systematically by analysts who "saturate" themselves in the source materials, the official images projected by political parties can serve two related but separate functions: 1) They permit analysts to ascertain the grounds on which political parties appealed for support and they help them to draw inferences about why men voted as they did. 2) They also permit analysts to draw inferences about the arguments and appeals that practicing politicians believed would win support from certain groups of voters.

A. Projecting and Reconstructing Party Images

Because of the federal nature of the American political system, party images are projected on a variety of geographic levels, such as national, state, and county. As a result, in addition to comparing the different official images of the different parties, it is possible to compare the images projected by the same party on different levels. Such comparisons are particularly revealing when, for example, variations between national and state platforms are seen to correspond with variations in the electorate's composition.

As party images can be differentiated by geographical level, they can be differentiated by degree of officiality. The agencies and agents officially charged with responsibility for projecting party images do not, of course, represent all the influences upon the electorate. During the 1830's and 1840's, for example, such newspapers as the *Albany Evening Journal, Albany Argus, New York Tribune*, and *New York Evening Post* worked hard to win support for their parties and helped to shape their party images. Since formally and legally even the *Argus* and *Evening Journal* were independent organs, they had more latitude in their arguments and appeals than did the official agencies and agents of their parties.

Unlike platforms and addresses adopted by conventions, candidates' speeches, or publications bearing the state committee's imprimatur, editorials by such powerful leaders as Thurlow Weed and Edwin Croswell did not necessarily state authoritatively their parties' positions. On the other hand, during the 1830's and 1840's, newspapers affiliated with a given party could not be considered free agents. Depending upon the paper, it occupied to a greater or lesser degree a semiofficial role in its party's table of organization. Similarly, a variety of other means and media, such as legislative addresses, speeches by noncandidates and by nonofficials at party meetings, publications by campaign committees functioning outside the official orbit, all contributed to a party's *semiofficial image*.

A party also has an *unofficial image*. A few of the many sources of this image are nonparty newspapers, individuals' speeches and publications, groups or institutions that are ostensibly or really nonpartisan, and day-to-day informal conversations and associations. It is not possible for historians to secure any direct or indirect data about the way all such instrumentalities influence voters' perceptions, but recognition of their existence at least militates against our concentrating exclusively upon official and semiofficial agencies and agents.

Even if attention were confined to a single campaign in a single state, the historian who tried to reconstruct the sum total of *all* the party images projected during its course would face a herculean task. And this is to say nothing about the previous campaigns and events which, to paraphrase Walter Lippmann's illuminating observations on stereotypes, helped to form the "pictures" inside the voters' heads.[3] Inevitably, therefore, the historian has to exercise judgment and restrict his attention to the data he believes are required by the specific situation and problem dealt with, the kinds of conclusions drawn, and the degree of precision and certainty desired. But if the data are systematically examined and the inferences drawn from them are explicitly stated, interpretations of voting behavior need not remain exercises in subjective relativism. These procedures not only enable the historian to check the adequacy of his data and the logic of his reasoning, but they expose them to analysis by other specialists who are perhaps more alert to factual errors or to weak links in the chain of argument. Thus the chances improve that disagreements can be resolved without recourse to personal philosophies, values, or intuitions.

Our examination of party images is not designed to explain the Democrats' narrow victory over the Whigs in New York in 1844— a task which would require a much different kind of study than this book reports upon. Instead, it helps us to explain the group voting

[3] Walter Lippmann, *Public Opinion* (New York, 1922), 59-70.

patterns previously identified, for example, why Irish Catholics voted overwhelmingly Democratic and Yankees divided closely.

In view of the objective sought here, I believe it can be achieved by a systematic "content analysis"[4] of the official images projected in 1844 by the Democratic and Whig parties on the national and New York State levels. Careful study of such sources as "semiofficial" and "unofficial" editorials, speeches, reprinted pamphlets, letters to the editor, and other sources, led to this conclusion: by 1844 the similarities and differences between the major New York parties had not only crystallized but were reflected in the platforms and addresses adopted at national and state conventions.

B. National Democratic Party: Official Images

Although the presentation of state party platforms and addresses goes back almost to the inception of the American party system, it is significant that national platforms did not become a standard political feature of election campaigns until 1844.[5] The Transportation Revolution, by accelerating the conquest of time and linking all parts of the country more closely, indirectly contributed to that development. Formal restoration of the two-party system, on a *national* basis, contributed more directly. Among other things, the long and enthusiastic 1840 Log Cabin campaign stimulated national and state parties to perfect their organizations and to crystallize their programs and characters. Other factors exerted influence, but the Transportation Revolution and the restoration of the two-party system did much to make it both easier and more necessary for the hitherto loose aggregation of state parties to try to present *a unified national image*.

In 1840 only the Democrats adopted a national platform, which they reaffirmed in 1844, also adding several more resolutions to the original nine.[6] The principles and policies they advocated can be

[4] The method is discussed in Bernard Berelson, *Content Analysis* (Glencoe, Ill., 1952).

[5] Ironically, the drafting of national platforms became a standard feature of American politics just before open factional warfare broke out and put increasing strains upon intraparty harmony. But, as so frequently happens in history, the clock could not be turned back. Once the precedent was set, failure to present a platform thereafter would have amounted to admission that a party seeking control of the national government was divided over what it would do with that control.

[6] Both the Democratic and Whig national platforms are conveniently reprinted in Kirk H. Porter and Donald Bruce Johnson, *National Party Platforms: 1840-1956* (Urbana, Ill., 1956), 1-9. All the quotations from the 1844 national platforms are from this source.

analyzed under four headings, which can also be used in analyzing Whig principles: 1) the general and specific role of government in a democratic republic; 2) the locus of government power (county, state, nation) ; 3) the role and power of the three branches of government; 4) foreign policy. Those four headings encompass the party's program; its character will be treated separately.

1. General and Specific Role of Government in a Democratic Republic

Analysis of the program adopted by the national Democratic Party in 1844 strongly supports the conclusion that the party built its church upon the rock of the negative liberal state. Regarding domestic affairs, the platform consisted of a long list of "Thou Shalt Nots." Significantly, the only resolution that can be construed as positive in nature did not deal with political economy; it ringingly affirmed that the "liberal principles embodied by Jefferson in the Declaration of Independence, and sanctioned in the Constitution, which makes ours the land of liberty and the Asylum of the oppressed of every nation have ever been cardinal principles in the Democratic faith; and every attempt to abridge the present privilege of becoming citizens, and the owners of soil among us, ought to be resisted with the same spirit which swept the alien and sedition laws from our statute-book."

By adopting that resolution, which encouraged unrestricted immigration, the Democrats implicitly endorsed the principle of cultural pluralism attacked by the American Republicans. Rather than place restrictions on immigration, they positively welcomed "the oppressed of every nation" and hailed the doctrine as one of the traditional "cardinal principles in the Democratic faith. . . ." They not only welcomed all immigrants, but they avowed opposition to any measure designed to hasten or force rapid "Americanization," linking such measures to earlier repressive laws.

Apart from the resolution on immigration, the Democrats called upon the federal government to do nothing positive. That is, although their first numbered resolution conceded that the federal government had some undefined "limited powers," none of their resolutions called for positive action under those powers.

As the Democrats interpreted the Constitution, it permanently prohibited the federal government from commencing or carrying on "a general system of internal improvements," or assuming "the debts of the several States, contracted for local internal improvements or other State purposes. . . ." Invoking the latter principle, they attacked the Whig Distribution Act of 1841 because, among other things, it distributed proceeds from the sale of federal lands to "the several States" for use as they saw fit. Since they claimed that "the proceeds of the Public Lands ought to be sacredly applied to the national objects specified in the Constitution," the Democrats avowed opposition to *any* distribution law "as alike inexpedient in policy and repugnant to the Constitution."

The Democrats claimed that the Constitution also prohibited Congress from chartering "a United States Bank" or from interfering with "the domestic institutions of the several States." The states "are the sole and proper judges of everything pertaining to their own affairs, not prohibited by the Constitution." Logically, the Democrats concluded that "abolitionists or others" pressuring Congress "to interfere with questions of slavery, or to take incipient steps thereto" endangered the Union; such efforts "ought not to be countenanced by any friend to our Political Institutions."

In addition to specifying what the federal government could not do, the platform specified what it *should* not do: enact a protective, discriminatory tariff. The relevant resolutions (4, 5) were slightly ambiguous. But read in historical context, they clearly invoked the equal rights doctrine to oppose a tariff for any purpose other than raising the revenue "required to defray the necessary expenses of the government."

The actions that the Democrats asserted the federal government should take followed logically from the actions they asserted it could not or should not take. Opposed to tariffs except for revenue, they held it to be "the duty of every branch of the government to enforce and practice the most rigid economy in conducting our public affairs. . . ." And opposed on policy as well as constitutional grounds to a United States Bank, they implicitly endorsed Van Buren's 1837 Independent Treasury system (without mentioning it by name): "Resolved, that the separation of the money of the government from banking institutions is indispensable for the safety of the funds of the government and the rights of the people."

In one sense, the only positive function the Democrats assigned to the federal government was that of providing all citizens and sections with "complete and ample protection of person and property from domestic violence or foreign oppression." And, it is worth noting, that function was mentioned in a subordinate clause of the resolution which held that "justice and sound policy forbid the Federal Government to foster one branch of industry to the detriment of another, or to cherish the interests of one portion to the injury of another portion of our common country. . . ." In short, if the Democratic prescription were swallowed, the federal government would be purged of all functions other than to preserve order.

Aside from the issues discussed above, the platform did not refer to past, present, or proposed federal or state actions on domestic issues. For our purposes, it is immaterial whether its position concerning the proper role of government in a liberal capitalist society was pragmatically wise or constitutionally sound. The point is that the 1844 Democratic national platform logically derived from the concept of the negative liberal state.

2. Locus of Government Power

Practice may occasionally have belied principle, but the Democrats postulated a rigid division between the powers of the federal government and of the states. Thus their 1844 resolutions logically conformed to their principle of rendering to the federal government what belonged to it and rendering to the states what belonged to them. The platform recognized the existence of a disputed boundary area, however, and dealt with it in revealing fashion. Resolved, "1. That the Federal Government is one of limited powers, derived solely from the Constitution and the grants of power shown therein ought to be strictly construed by all the departments and agents of the government, *and that it is inexpedient and dangerous to exercise doubtful constitutional powers* [italics added]."

In other words, doubts over the constitutionality of federal actions should be resolved either in favor of the states or in favor of *inaction*. Other resolutions specifically underscored the general principle that federal powers were limited to those explicitly given by the Constitution. For example, the Public Lands resolution emphasized that proceeds "ought to be sacredly applied to the national objects specified in the Constitution"; the slavery resolution emphasized that the "states are the sole and proper judges of everything pertaining to their own affairs, not prohibited by the Constitution." Unmistakably and unequivocally, the Democrats located the center of power deep within the constitutional territory occupied by the states. Moreover, they insisted that the federal government could not step across the boundary line, whether or not a state welcomed the invasion.

3. Role and Power of Three Branches of Government

From the nation's inception, political party battles have been fought not over federal and state powers only, but over the location of power among the executive, legislative, and judicial departments. As is well known, although their actions in office did not necessarily conform to their theoretical principles, the Jeffersonian Republicans sharply attacked the strong executive doctrine of the Federalists. "The Federalists," Leonard D. White has written, "were steady supporters of a strong executive branch, believing it essential to the vigor of government and fearing it would be overborne by Congress."[7] And yet, despite their general denunciation of "the creed and practice of Federalism," and despite their claimed descent from the Republicans, on this issue the Democrats applauded and extended the Federalist's doctrine—in all but name: "Resolved, That we are decidedly opposed to taking from the President the qualified veto power by which he is enabled, under restrictions and responsibilities amply sufficient to guard the public interest, to suspend the passage of a bill, whose merits cannot secure the approval of two thirds of the Senate and House of Representatives, until the judgement of the people can be obtained thereon, and which has thrice saved the American People from the corrupt and tyrannical domination of the Bank of the United States."

Before the first Jackson administration, only nine vetoes had been handed down in forty years—and those primarily on grounds of alleged unconstitutionality. In sharp contrast, by his frequent resort to the veto power Jackson helped to legitimate its use as a means of defeating bills on grounds of expediency. And, although John Tyler had been elected on the 1840 Whig ticket, after succeeding to the presidency in 1841 he followed Jackson's practice.[8] Despite the implication that could be read into the Democrats' resolution about the president's "qualified veto power," after a national election was held he could again veto a bill that he had vetoed before the people expressed their "judgement." Thus the Democrats formally endorsed Jackson's and Tyler's sweeping extensions of presidential power vis-à-vis the legislature and asserted that the presidential office constituted the substantial equivalent of two thirds of both Houses of Congress.

[7] Leonard D. White, *The Federalists* (New York, 1948), 509-510.
[8] Leonard D. White, *The Jacksonians* (New York, 1954), 20-49.

4. Foreign Policy

If the Democratic platform demanded federal inaction on domestic matters, it sounded the bugles for an uncompromisingly dynamic, expansive foreign policy: "Resolved, That our title to the whole of the Territory of Oregon is clear and unquestionable; that no portion of the same ought to be ceded to England or any other power, and that the re-occupation of Oregon and the reannexation of Texas at the earliest practicable period are great American Measures, which this Convention recommends to the cordial support of the Democracy of the Union."

Though contrasting dramatically, Democratic policies on domestic and foreign affairs were logically consistent. Territorial expansion fell within the federal government's province and the Democrats explicitly emphasized the legality of the proposed action: "Our title to the whole of the Territory of Oregon is clear and unquestionable. . . ." In certain respects the nationalistic emphasis of the resolution was its most significant aspect. Having opposed protective tariffs on the ground that the federal government could not foster the interests of one geographic section at the expense of others, the national Democratic Party had to depict the "re-occupation of Oregon and the re-annexation of Texas . . . [as] great American measures." As we shall see later, New York Democrats failed to share this view.

5. Character Self-Portrait

Because it is more tangible, a party's program is more easily ascertained and delineated than is its character. For that reason, historians will probably never agree completely on the character self-portrait drawn by the Democratic Party in its 1844 national platform. But most specialists, I believe, would not quarrel significantly with the broad description that follows. And, for our purposes, a credible broad description suffices.

Employing a variety of devices to achieve emphasis, the platform depicted the Democratic Party as fulfilling three roles: 1) it preserved the Constitution undefiled; 2) it protected the masses; 3) it championed the American liberal political tradition.

Unmistakably, the Democratic platform emanated reverence for the Constitution as the ark of the American covenant and the source of all government authority. For example, because they came under the Constitution's jurisdiction, even cash receipts from public land sales took on a sacred character: "The proceeds of the Public Lands ought to be sacredly applied to the national objects specified in the Constitution. . . ." Similarly, while applauding the liberal principles of the Declaration of Independence, the Democrats carefully noted that they were "sanctioned in the Constitution. . . ." Since they treated the Founding Fathers' principles of government as sacred, immutable truths, compatibility with strict constitutional construction was their first test for any proposal requiring federal action. In effect, the Democrats portrayed themselves as the high priests of the Republican Book, traditionally entrusted with the task of guarding it from blasphemers who advocated departures from the letter of its Law.

Not only were the Democrats the custodians of the Book: they were the warriors traditionally charged with the mission of saving "the American People" from their enemies. Who were the enemies of the people? Three resolutions identified threats to the "liberties and rights of the people," to "republican institutions," to "the business of the country." In all three cases the dangers sprang from "a concentrated money power." Specifically, the United States Bank, gone but not forgotten, was identified as the institution deadly hostile "to the best interests of the country" from whose "corrupt and tyrannical domination" presidential vetoes had "thrice saved the American People." Since heroic chiefs invariably lead warriors fighting off powerful enemies, it does not force the material to observe that once the Democrats portrayed themselves as battling on behalf of "the American People" against "a concentrated money power," presidential aggrandizement logically followed.

In addition to guarding the Book and protecting the People, the Democrats portrayed themselves as the champions of liberty. They hailed, as a distinctive feature of the "Democratic" political creed, reliance upon "the intelligence, patriotism, and the discriminating justice of the American masses," and described it as "the great moral element in the form of government springing from and upheld by the popular will. . . ."

As the Democrats conceived America's mission, the benefits from living in a "land of liberty" that was guided by "the liberal principles embodied by Jefferson in the Declaration of Independence" should be available to all peoples; the country should serve as a place of refuge for "the oppressed of every nation. . . ." Among other things, the Democrats used the immigration resolution to claim in effect that their party's history began with the Jeffersonian Republicans. Thus they emphasized support for the liberal principles that "have ever been cardinal principles in the Democratic faith." They contended that restrictions upon immigrants "ought to be resisted with the same spirit which swept the alien and sedition laws from our statute-book."

Several minor features can be sketched to put the final touches to the 1844 Democratic national self-portrait. Instead of adopting some variant of the traditional "Republican Party" title, the Democrats for the first time explicitly referred to themselves as "The American Democracy." Staunch advocates of state rights as the best guarantee of the "stability and permanency of the Union," they depicted themselves simultaneously as staunch, nationalistic defenders of American rights vis-à-vis other countries. And in one clause of the resolution that attacked discriminatory tariffs, they added an egalitarian line to their self-portrait, arguing that "every citizen and every section of the country had a right to demand and insist upon an equality of rights and privileges. . . ." Finally, though they maintained strict silence concerning their candidates, the Democrats sought to remove any blemish from the unified party image by stressing that their delegates came together "in a spirit of concord."

6. Official Image of Opponents

Though the national Democratic platform gave relatively little attention to opponents, it stigmatized the abolitionists as enemies of the Union's stability and implicitly identified the Whigs as old Federalists in new disguise.

Ignoring their own enthusiastic contributions to the process that turned American political campaigns into wildly unreflective spectacles, the Democrats portrayed themselves as placing their trust in the intelligence, patriotism, and discriminating justice of the American masses, "not in factitious symbols, not in displays and appeals insulting to the judgement and subversive of the intellect of the people. . . ." Antithetical to the American form of government, those tactics were typical of "the creed and practice of Federalism, under whatever name or form, which seeks to palsy the will of the constituent, and which conceives no imposture too monstrous for the popular credulity." In their reference to the alien and sedition laws, the Democrats clearly were trying to strengthen the Federalist-Whig identification. Finally, they linked the Whigs implicitly to the United States Bank and the "concentrated money power" that threatened the People's liberties.

C. New York Democratic Party: Official Images

The Democratic state convention met in September, three months after the national convention. It adopted a lengthy address which, together with resolutions, covered over two full pages in the *Albany Argus*.[9] An analysis of the document, such as was made of the national platform, yields suggestive similarities and differences.

1. General and Specific Role of Government in a Democratic Republic

Men who draft American national political platforms have the delicate task of differentiating their party from opponents without stirring up internal discords; men who draft state platforms have the same task, but they must accomplish it within the framework of their local situations and without appearing to alter the national images of their parties. Because national and state platforms show a marked tendency toward logical consistency, systematic comparisons frequently yield good indicators of public opinion. That is, it seems reasonable to assume that state leaders' assessments of their electorate's frame of mind will influence them in drafting documents that depart from or adhere to the national platform.

In respect to domestic affairs, New York Democratic leaders agreed emphatically with the national party's conception of the proper role of government. Their *Address* can also be characterized as a sermon on the text, "Thou Shalt Not. . . ." It claimed that "on no previous occasion have the lines of party been more clearly drawn than they are at the present moment" and it denied both the constitutionality and expediency of the three "principal measures" that it ascribed to the Whigs. Forcefully, lengthily, it denounced a national bank, protective tariffs, and distribution of the public land cash receipts to carry out "a magnificent scheme of internal improvements."

Though the *Address'* treatment of the tariff question could be read as approval of the "incidental protection" doctrine, it justified tariffs solely on the ground that they provided necessary revenue. And, in an omnibus resolution quoted and discussed below, the New

---

[9] *Albany Argus* (w.), September 14, 1844, pp. 300-302. All quotations from the New York Democratic *Address* and *Resolutions* are from this source.

Yorkers endorsed all the principles and policies adopted at the national Democratic convention. Moreover, they made no independent proposals for federal action. In short, as far as the federal government was concerned, they pledged that their party would do nothing other than operate "a simple and economical administration" and reduce the public debt, now risen "to the enormous sum of twenty-eight millions of dollars."

It would not be quite accurate to assert that the Democrats asked state government to play a do-nothing role. But if compatibility with a strict interpretation of the Constitution served as their first test of any action, their second was whether the action would increase government costs, tend toward creation of a public debt, and require new taxation. For example, in discussing the related issues of public debt and enlargement of the Erie Canal after 1835, they maintained "this marked difference in the policy of the two parties in regard to the enlargement—the Whigs were in favor of completing the work in five years and creating a debt for the purpose; while the democratic policy was to make use of the surplus revenues, and not create any new debt for this object."

In effect, the *Address* endorsed the principle that the primary role of the state was to preserve public order while avoiding public debt and taxes. Logically enough, they advocated suspension of internal improvements "until the heavy embarrassment and debt into which whig functionaries have plunged us shall be removed. . . ." Although in principle they approved enlarging the Erie Canal, they emphasized that it should proceed only as it could be paid for by "the surplus [canal] revenues," that is, after all debt charges and current expenses had been met. "With a wise husbandry of our resources, and a frugal management of every department of the government, after the debts which are immediately pressing upon the State are paid, we may anticipate a surplus of several hundred thousand dollars annually applicable to the purposes of internal improvements."

To guarantee that future state administrations would operate strictly within their conception of the proper role of government, the Democrats proposed two constitutional amendments. They first wrote into the state's fundamental law their famous "Stop and Tax" Act of 1842 (halt work on internal improvements and levy taxes to pay debts); the second provided that "the legislature shall not create any liability of the State, exceeding in the aggregate a million of dollars (except in case of invasion or insurrection) without submitting the law to the approval of the voters at a general election." Apart from the page-long argument for a pay-as-you-go-slow policy on internal improvements, and support for unrestricted immigration, the *Address* proposed no positive government action. Thus, in respect to *both* levels of government, the 1844 New York Democratic program derived essentially from the concept of the negative state.

2. Locus of Government Power

If there was any difference between the two documents on the location of government power, the New York Democratic *Address* gave stronger support to the state rights doctrine than did the national platform. For example, while urging resistance to the Distribution Act on grounds other than inexpediency, the *Address* proclaimed: "We hold it to be in its tendencies, a violation of the spirit of the political compact between the states. The framers of the Constitution designed to create a confederate, in contradistinction to a consolidated government. It is only necessary to look into the proceedings of the convention in which that *sacred* [italics added] instrument was framed, to be convinced of the unshaken determination of the democracy to fortify the system they were building up against the fatal error of consolidation. They designed, by the reservations of sovereignty, for which they made the most careful provision, to render the states independent of the general authority in respect to matters of internal concern; and in pursuance of this design the democratic majority in that body resisted all attempts, numerous as they were, and sustained by men of the highest talent, to consolidate the states into one great central government."

According to the New York Democrats, acceptance of federal funds would degrade the states and destroy their independent spirit. Since it is "through gradual approaches that the citadel of popular liberty, in all countries and in all ages, has been gained by the mercenary phalanx of money interests," "let us . . . resist this corrupt scheme at the threshold, assured that it is only by a rigid adherence to the constitutional compact in its spirit and intention, as well as in its formal distribution of power, that it can be handed down, untarnished and unimpaired, to our descendants."

Throughout the *Address*, the Democrats emphasized their role as guardians of the Constitution against "all speculative and constructive extensions of its powers and provisions as at war with the intention of its wise and patriotic framers." In the only section that even indirectly touched upon slavery, they praised themselves for having "adhered with patriotic firmness and unflinching tenacity to the constitution and its compromises, regarding it as the charter of our rights and liberties and the bible of our political salvation. . . ."

3. Role and Power of Three Branches of Government

Perhaps because Martin Van Buren lost the presidential nomination, perhaps because it was not considered good tactics to focus attention upon a strong executive when their candidate was a Southerner hot for immediate annexation of Texas, the *Address* ignored the perennial issue of which branch of the federal government held what powers. Since the *Address* paid great attention to problems and issues that had long been resolved, and since one of the national platform's strongest resolutions dealt with the relative powers of Congress and President, the omission does not seem accidental. In one sense, of course, the position of the national party on the issue received endorsement in the omnibus resolution discussed below. Nonetheless, it seems reasonable to infer that the silence of New York Democrats said much.

4. Foreign Policy

Whether or not the *Address'* silence on the strong president issue was accidental, its failure to refer explicitly to the "re-occupation of Oregon and the re-annexation of Texas at the earliest practicable period" clearly was not. Placed in historical context, the phrasing of the omnibus resolutions indicates that the New York Democrats considered that public opinion was opposed to the position taken by their national party. "Resolved, that we agree to the resolutions adopted at the Democratic National Convention at Baltimore, as being in substantial accordance with the long established principles of the Democratic party, as assented to in all their material facts by the great body of the democracy throughout the Union, and as containing no declaration of principles, *which rightly understood* [italics added], can be regarded with just exception by any portion of the Democratic party."

We can reasonably infer that by adopting an omnibus resolution which permitted their *Address* to avoid direct allusions to Texas, New York Democrats hoped simultaneously to preserve the unified national party image and to play down the issue. Actually, the national platform's resolution was difficult to misunderstand. As anti-Texas Democrats insisted, "rightly understood" it supported the immediate annexation policy of Secretary of State John Calhoun. Calhoun's proposed treaty with the Lone Star Republic not only defied Mexico's claims and admitted the territory as a slave state, but he publicly advocated admission as a slave state on the ground that the preservation of slavery required the annexation of Texas.[10]

Martin Van Buren, who strongly opposed annexation on such terms and for such an objective, had unequivocally and publicly proclaimed his stand in April 1844. Other factors contributed, but his Texas stand probably constituted the most important reason for his defeat at the Democratic national convention in May. Since Calhoun's treaty was then before the Senate for action, the convention's resolution on Texas in effect put the Democratic Party on record as favoring the policy of the South Carolinian and rejecting the policy of the New Yorker. Though neither the views nor the candidate of the New York Democrats prevailed at the National convention, Silas Wright shortly thereafter helped to defeat the treaty by voting against it in the Senate.[11]

Defeat of Calhoun's treaty failed to dispose of Texas. On the contrary, it only increased the political importance of the resolution that hailed annexation as a "great American measure" and urged its implementation at the "earliest practicable period." Long sensitive to the Whig "doughface" charge, influential New York Democrats decided to revolt against the "southern dictation" evident both in Van Buren's "humiliation" and in the adoption of the Texas plank.

During the summer, one group of New York City leaders sent out a circular designed to spark the revolt: "CONFIDENTIAL. Sir—You will doubtless agree with us that the late Baltimore Convention placed the democratic party at the North in a position of great difficulty. We are constantly reminded that it rejected Mr. Van Buren and nominated Mr. Polk for reasons connected with the immediate

[10] Jabez Hammond, *Life and Times of Silas Wright*, 438-439. Hammond's comment is particularly illuminating because he was a leader of a movement to get Van Buren to publicly oppose annexation. After citing several grounds on which annexation was urged, he wrote: "But Mr. Calhoun, the official organ of the government, and a bold, frank, and honorable man, who despised subterfuge, in his correspondence with Great Britain put forth other and different reasons for the treaty of annexation; which were,—that annexation was indispensable, in order to *preserve and perpetuate slavery in the slave-holding states*." See also James C. N. Paul, *Rift In The Democracy* (Philadelphia, 1951), 94-143; John A. Garraty, *Silas Wright* (New York, 1949), 232-286.

[11] Garraty, 245-289; Paul, *Rift In The Democracy*, 62-168.

annexation of Texas—reasons which had no relation to the principles of the party. Nor was that all. The convention went beyond the authority delegated to its members, and adopted a resolution on the subject of Texas (a subject not before the country when they were elected, upon which, therefore, they were not instructed) which seeks to interpolate into the party code a new doctrine, hitherto unknown among us, at war with some of our established principles, and abhorrent to the opinions and feelings of a great majority of northern freemen."

The circular invited state leaders to cooperate with William C. Bryant, David Dudley Field, and others, in achieving two objectives: "*1st.* In the publication of a joint letter, declaring our purpose to support the nominations, rejecting the resolutions respecting Texas. *2nd.* In promoting and supporting, at the next election, the nomination for Congress of such persons as concur in these opinions."[12]

The proposed joint letter was never issued but the "secret circular" did not remain secret for long. Word spread quickly if somewhat circuitously, and in July the *Evening Post* brought matters into the open by publishing the circular. Arguing that anti-Texas sentiment was widespread, the *Post* maintained that many longtime party members were either going to vote Whig or abstain unless New York Democrats disassociated themselves from the immediate annexation policy.[13] Read in this context, it seems reasonable to infer that the state Democratic *Address* and resolutions deliberately tried to blur the Texas feature of the national party image.[14]

5. New York Democratic Party: Character
Self-Portrait

With two exceptions—its Texas plank and its failure to reaffirm support of a strong president—the Democratic Party's character

---

[12] Hammond, *Silas Wright*, 497-501.

[13] *Evening Post For The Country*, July 27, 1844, pp. 1, 2, 3; August 21, 1844, pp. 2, 3.

[14] "By the resolutions adopted by the [Democratic state] convention, they denounced a high tariff, a national bank, the distribution of the proceeds of the sales of public lands, etc., and they approved the resolutions adopted by the Baltimore Convention. They do not allude to the annexation of Texas, other than by expressing their approbation of the principles put forth by the Baltimore Convention. They probably designedly avoided any express allusion to that '*great American measure*,' because, among other reasons, their candidate for governor had voted against the Texas treaty in the senate, and since his return from Washington, and since the Baltimore Convention, had declared in a speech delivered at Watertown to a mass meeting that he was opposed to annexation." Hammond, *Silas Wright*, 493-494.

portrait, as presented in its New York *Address*, agreed in all major respects with that of the national platform. By adding several minor features and retouching others for state presentation, however, it subtly altered the national portrait. It seems clear that the alterations were designed to maximize its appeal for the New York electorate, distract attention from Texas, direct attention to long-settled issues, and *thereby reinforce party loyalty.*

The New York Democratic Party, more than the national party, emphasized its Jeffersonian lineage. Addressing its message to the "Democratic Republican Electors of New-York," and claiming to stand "forth in prominent relief as a political party from the time of Jefferson to the present," the party maintained that in 1844 "the prominent questions, on which the country has been divided from the foundation, are brought distinctly into controversy. . . ." It placed its faith "in the virtue and intelligence of the people and in their capacity for self-government" and claimed that it had abolished property qualifications for office and the right of suffrage in "all practicable cases." The party also pointed with pride to its record of opposition to a life term for President and long terms for Senators; restrictions upon individual liberty and freedom of the press; and the alien and sedition laws.

By focusing attention upon ancient conflicts, the *Address* undoubtedly hoped to arouse political loyalty and overcome the damaging effects of Van Buren's defeat for the presidential nomination. It acknowledged disappointment that New York's "first choice" had not been selected, but it pledged ardent support to the national ticket. "We have unbounded confidence in the purity of JAMES K. POLK, in his inflexible integrity of purpose, his firmness, and his talents. His whole life has been devoted like that of General Jackson and Mr. Van Buren, to the vindication of democratic principles. Under no circumstances should New York, wielding as she does a preponderating power in the democratic scale, allow her strength to be frittered away by division or by the disappointment of an ardently cherished hope. . . . In his [Polk's] hands she feels that the great interests to be committed to his care will be cherished with devotedness, justice, and impartiality."

While appealing to party loyalty and calling upon voters to rally to the defense of first principles, the New York Democrats emphasized the personal qualities of Silas Wright, their candidate for governor. "Firm in the opinions which his strong judgment has coolly matured, he is never tempted to resort to the compromising fluctuations of expediency." If we weigh Wright's devotion to Van Buren, his refusal to accept the vice-presidential nomination conferred upon him by the national convention, and his vote against Calhoun's treaty, he was, no doubt, the best candidate to repel the charge that Democratic "doughfaces" could not honorably defend the rights of "northern freemen." Moreover, his reputation as the "Cato of the Senate," his residence on a farm in St. Lawrence County, his simple style of life and lack of wealth or large-scale business interests[15] all lent an authentic touch to the Democratic Party's portrait of itself as the warm-hearted champion of the common man: "Accustomed for years, in his youth, to rural occupation, his sympathies are identified with the great mass of his fellow men, because from early and continued associations he regards himself as one of them. His principles have been formed and his efforts directed for the promotion of the greatest good of the greatest number. Such are the principles of his head and the qualities of his heart which have attracted upon him the public regard."

In addition to highlighting Wright's rural associations, the *Address*, in its treatment of the tariff question, identified the Democratic Party with "the great interest of the country—the agricultural" and with the "mechanical [skilled craftsmen, not factory workers] interest, which embraces in its diversified pursuits the great majority of the working classes, aside from those engaged in agriculture. . . ." To indicate how important they regarded identification with the "industrious classes," particularly the farmers, the Democrats stigmatized the manufacturing interest as the "favorite interest with the Federal Party, and upon which they lavish all their favors. . . ."

By explicitly identifying their opponents with the "few favored manufacturers" who reaped "exorbitant profits" from the tariff of 1842, the Democrats obviously hoped to intensify the portrait of themselves as the champions of farmers and consumers as well as of skilled craftsmen who increasingly felt disturbed by the growth of factories.[16] Unlike the national party, which had to reckon Pennsylvania's industry in its political calculus, the New York Demo-

---

[15] Garraty, *op.cit.*, 304-313.

[16] For a perceptive discussion of the agrarian bias which spurred the Democrats' resistance to tariffs and large-scale factories, see Ernest P. Muller, "Preston King," 272-275.

crats must have believed that on balance it paid to add the "manufacturing interest" to the "concentrated money power" that oppressed the people. Though they softened (and confused) their indictment by arguing that a "moderate" and "fair" revenue tariff actually would benefit manufacturers, their willingness to concede the "manufacturing interest" to the Whigs suggests how much importance they attached to the agrarian party image.

It is crucial to note, however, that the Democratic agrarian image in no way connoted an *antibusiness* orientation. The *Address* proclaimed unrelenting opposition to "the mercenary phalanx of money interests" and the "few favored manufacturers" (or "privileged classes"), but it argued that Democratic economic policies accorded with the views of "every sound businessman in the State, whether democrat or whig. . . ."

6. New York Democratic Party: Official
Image of Opponents

Much more than the Democratic national platform, the New York Democratic *Address* sought to project an horrendous image of the program and character of their opponents. Unprincipled, deceitful, antidemocratic Federalists in disguise, the Whigs appealed to the worst instincts of men and sought to gain objectives dangerous both to "the prosperity of the country and the purity of the government."

Creation of a national bank, the *Address* charged, was a foremost Whig objective. But instead of candidly avowing their desire "to establish a moneyed institution of gigantic powers and corrupting tendencies," the Whigs insulted the people's intelligence by calling only for a "well regulated National Currency." Why had their national convention resorted to such deceptive language? Clearly, so that they could deny "in some sections of the Union, that they had any intention of creating a Bank, and to assure the friends of such an institution in other sections that their wishes would be gratified."

As with the national bank, so with tariff and distribution. Unlike the Democrats, the Whig Party sought power "by holding out false professions to the people, changing its positions with every change of public opinion, and yet retaining in spite of its declarations, the same secret designs." Contrary to their professions on both the federal and state levels, the profligate Whigs would engender corruption and bankruptcy, rend the constitutional compact, destroy the inde-

pendence of the states, and allow "the mercenary phalanx of money
interests" to conquer "the citadel of popular liberty." Once the
Whigs took power and implemented their schemes, "with what confidence could we hope that any effort to retrieve and restore the
fallen standard of democracy could, in the midst of all these elements
of corruption, be made with success?"

Perhaps the best way to describe summarily the New York Democrats' official image of the Whigs is to quote at length the Democrats'
first resolution. Avowedly designed to furnish "to every elector abundant means of exercising the right of suffrage with intelligence and
discrimination," the resolution looked at the Whigs and saw ". . .
a distrust of the people, a demand for a lengthened residence among
us, a condition of naturalization; an attachment to a strong consolidated and central, and in the early history of parties, to a monarchical form of government; a disposition to prolong and perpetuate official power, a fondness for excessive legislation, an ambition unduly to interfere by the strong arm of legislation in the
monetary affairs of the country, to regulate the currency, to establish a moneyed institution of gigantic powers and corrupting tendencies, to project and carry out a magnificent scheme of internal
improvements by the exercise of powers doubtful and dangerous; to
raise a large surplus of funds in the national treasury beyond the
just wants of the government, to encourage special and particular
interests at the expense of others equally entitled to favor and protection, to collect the means for an administration, lavish in its expenditures, anti-republican in its tendencies and spirit, and departing from the economy and simplicity of our early history; to bring
that great and national fund, the public lands, consecrated by solemn
compact to national purposes, within the vortex of the same spirit
of lavish, corrupt, unrestrained expenditure; to distribute the proceeds among the several states in violation of the pledges of its original cession and of the national objects to which it should be applied,
and thus to fritter it away among an army of officials taking part
in its distribution; a demand of property qualifications for the exercise of the right of suffrage; a disposition to involve the state in a
wild and profligate career of unlimited expenditures for internal improvements, based upon prospective and imaginary revenues, selfish
appeals to the people addressed to their pecuniary, local and private
interests, and to the most mercinary [*sic*] propensities of their nature, and a contemptuous disregard of their intelligence and patri-

otism evinced by the mode in which their suffrages are attempted to
be procured and influenced. These are in brief some of the general
characteristics which have distinguished the action of our opponents
from the earliest period of our political history."

D. National Whig Party: Official Images

The Whig national convention met at Baltimore on May 1, 1844,
several weeks before the Democrats assembled. The tradition that
national conventions should take positions on current issues had not
yet been established, but it is significant that the Whigs did not try
to project more than a broad image that might be easily altered
to show up best according to local lights. United as much by opposition to Democratic principles and policies as by agreement on
general principles of political theory and political economy, the
Whigs always had difficulty in drafting a national platform. Moreover, unlike the Democrats in 1844, the Whigs had agreed overwhelmingly on their presidential nominee and thus did not have to
beat the doctrinal drums to drown out discord over candidates. As
a result, their platform was general—and brief.

1. General and Specific Role of Government in a
Democratic Republic

Claiming that "all the great principles of the Whig party" were
well-known, the platform simply summarized them in a single resolution. The Whigs, like the Democrats, faithfully observed the ritual
of promising "such an administration of the affairs of the country as
shall impart to every branch of the public service the greatest practicable efficiency, controlled by a well regulated and wise economy."
In addition, their candidates would maintain and advance ". . . a
well-regulated currency, a tariff for revenue to defray the necessary
expenses of the government, and discriminating with special reference to the protection of the domestic labor of the country; the distribution of the proceeds of the sales of the public lands. . . ."

Doctrinal poles apart from the Democrats, the Whigs imposed no
limitations upon the power of the federal government to act. Viewed
in the context of the party battles during the 1830's and early 1840's
which had made known all their "great principles," the Whigs assigned the federal government responsibility for providing a safe
and reliable currency that would have the same value throughout
the country; speeding the country's economic development by pur-

poseful action; assisting the states to undertake large-scale internal improvements. Political expediency no doubt dictated the Whig resort to generalities, but their generalities derived from the text, "Thou Shalt. . . ."

One exception to the general rule of Whig positivism and Democratic negativism stands out. Unlike the Democrats, the Whigs offered no encouragement to immigrants to find asylum in the United States and thereby help to speed its development. In fact, the Whig platform failed to refer to immigration or to naturalization. Since those issues had been treated in the 1840 Democratic platform, since the emergence of American Republicanism increased their saliency in 1844, it seems reasonable to infer that Whig silence testified to lack of support for a policy to speed immigration. Nothing in the Whig platform warranted the charge that they advocated immigration restriction, but on this issue the Whigs and Democrats can be said to have reversed their usual do-nothing—do-something positions.

One other Whig omission merits notice. Unlike the Democrats, who explicitly condemned "abolitionists or others" attempting "to induce Congress to interfere with questions of slavery," the Whig platform maintained eloquent silence on those questions. In matters related to the role and power of the federal government, the national Whig Party tried to steer clear of all but politicoeconomic issues.

2. Locus of Government Power

Though the Whig platform did not refer explicitly to the division of power between the federal and state governments, implementation of its three general "principles" dealing with currency, tariff, and distribution required a broad construction of the Constitution. The position of the Whigs was perhaps best indicated by their enthusiastic endorsement of Henry Clay's well-publicized "American System" (although their platform did not refer to it by that title):

"*Resolved*, That in presenting to the country the names of Henry Clay for president, and of Theodore Frelinghuysen for vice-president of the United States, this convention is actuated by the conviction that all the great principles of the Whig party—principles inseparable from the public honor and prosperity—will be maintained and advanced by these candidates . . .

"*Resolved*, That the name of Henry Clay needs no eulogy; the history of the country since his first appearance in public life is his history; its brightest pages of prosperity and success are identified with the principles which he has upheld, as its darkest and more disastrous pages are with every material departure in our public policy from those principles."

As Clay's most recent biographer has put it, after the War of 1812, "Gallant Harry of the West" consistently advocated "a planned national economy through legislative interference. . . ." Contrary to the Democratic conception of a rigid division of powers between rival federal and state governments, Clay maintained that they should operate as well-coordinated agencies to execute "a beautifully integrated and harmonious system of political economy. . . ." Rather than allocate government powers and responsibility according to an unchanging construction of the Constitution, he employed this criterion: would proposed actions contribute to national and state prosperity? The American System, in contrast to the Democratic system based upon state rights, assumed that the interests of the several states were complementary, not competitive. Actions that benefited one area more than another did not necessarily violate egalitarian principles; all areas and groups would eventually benefit from government action that contributed immediately to the prosperity of any area or group.[17]

During Clay's long career, his American System underwent considerable modification, and, contrary to contemporary Democratic charges, his 1844 program did not include restoration of a national bank.[18] But despite abandonment of that measure, his System rested upon a flexible, nationalistic concept of the division of government powers and responsibilities. Thus by nominating Clay and enthusiastically endorsing his principles, the Whigs unmistakably proclaimed their belief that the federal government had great powers and enjoyed a complementary rather than competitive relationship with the states.

3. Role and Power of Three Branches of Government

The Whigs also opposed Democratic views about the division of powers among government departments. As noted earlier, the party name Whig originally symbolized opposition to a strong executive and had been designed to identify "King Andrew Jackson" with King George III and other "tyrants." Subsequent events only con-

[17] Clement Eaton, *Henry Clay and the Art of American Politics*, 34-37.
[18] *Ibid.*, 172.

firmed the Whigs's determination to resist the sweeping extension of executive power by the Jacksonians. Though they elected their ticket in 1840, most of the fruits of victory had been denied them by Tyler's vetoes and use of presidential patronage. Convinced that ambitious executives desiring renomination represented a threat to orderly government, they included in their "great principles" a "single term for the presidency [and] a reform of executive usurpations." (Neither party, it is worth noting, paid any attention to the role of the judiciary in 1844.)

4. Foreign Policy

What parties fail to say is sometimes more revealing than what they say. As I interpret it, the failure of the 1844 Whig platform to mention foreign policy is best attributed to their desire to lessen intraparty tensions concerning Texas. Emphasis upon domestic issues, which since 1834 had divided the two parties, would strengthen Whig unity; but any stand on Texas would inevitably increase intraparty tensions by increasing the pressures upon northern and southern Whigs to assume sectional rather than national positions. Like the Whigs's silence on immigration, their silence on foreign policy significantly differentiated the major parties in 1844. The phrase was not actually coined until 1845, but in effect the Democratic national platform enthusiastically endorsed "manifest destiny."[19] At the very least, the silence of the Whig national platform represented lack of enthusiasm for that aggressive foreign policy. Significantly, when Calhoun's treaty of annexation subsequently came up for Senate approval, with but one exception every southern and northern Whig voted against it.[20]

5. Character Self-Portrait

None of the fifteen resolutions of the national Democratic platform even mentioned the candidates by name; three of the four Whig resolutions eulogized Henry Clay and Theodore Frelinghuysen. The Whigs depended heavily upon their candidates to project their official self-image.

I have already noted that the resolution that endorsed Clay also

[19] For the setting and circumstances under which the "Manifest Destiny" phrase was coined, see Julius W. Pratt, "John L. Sullivan and Manifest Destiny," *New York History*, 14: 213-234 (July 1933).

[20] Ray A. Billington, *The Far Western Frontier: 1830-1860* (New York, 1956), 150-151.

identified the Whig Party with his American System and thereby contributed to the image of a vigorous, progressive party unfettered by the past and bounding forward to the future. Pledged to government planning and action, the Whigs promised that by collective design they would bring material blessings to all sections and to all groups. And yet, it seems extremely significant that the resolution that eulogized their vice-presidential nominee occupied more than twice as much space as the eulogy for Clay. The resolution's length and contents suggest that the Whigs operated on the principle that self-interest constitutes only one determinant of voting behavior.

"*Resolved*, That in Theodore Frelinghuysen we present a man pledged alike by his revolutionary ancestry and his own public course to every measure calculated to sustain the honor and interest of the country. Inheriting the principles as well as the name of a father who, with Washington, on the fields of Trenton and at Monmouth, perilled life in the contest for liberty, and afterwards, as a senator of the United States, acted with Washington in establishing, and perpetuating that liberty, Theodore Frelinghuysen, by his course as Attorney-General of the State of New Jersey for twelve years, and subsequently as a senator of the United States for several years, was always strenuous on the side of the law, order, and the Constitution, while as a private man, his head, his hand, and his heart have been given without stint *to the cause of morals, education, philanthropy, and religion* [italics added]."

We can see that the Whigs used Frelinghuysen's revolutionary heritage to discredit the Democratic image of them as lineal descendants of Tories; the reference to Washington specifically linked their party with the Revolution and liberty. And through their character portrait of Frelinghuysen, the Whigs, like the Democrats, depicted themselves as "always strenuous on the side of law, order and the constitution." No feature in the Democratic self-portrait, however, even slightly resembled the Whig depiction of their candidates as dedicated "to the cause of morals, education, philanthropy, and religion. . . ."

The Whig vice-presidential candidate had inherited the name of Theodorus J. Frelinghuysen, a prominent minister and organizer of religious revivals during the early eighteenth century. He had also inherited the intense religiosity of his ancestor and was famous as one of the country's leading Protestant laymen. "His head, his hand, and his heart" had been given to the American Bible Society, the American Tract Society, the American Sunday School Union, the American Board of Commissioners for Foreign Missions, and the American Temperance Union. Active in the "crusades" against slavery, for Sabbatarian legislation, for national fast days, he was undoubtedly "the special champion of religion in politics." To quote one of his friends, "I doubt if any layman in the land, or if few or any ministers of the gospel, ever made so many personal appeals on the subject of religion as during his life he did." Frelinghuysen was also active in educational affairs and in 1839 became chancellor of New York University.[21]

By publicly identifying themselves with Frelinghuysen's private convictions and activities, the Whigs reinforced the image of themselves as the party dedicated to moral as well as material progress. Put another way, the nomination and eulogy of Frelinghuysen reinforced the image of the Whigs as the orthodox Protestant "Christian Party," called for by Reverend Ezra Ely in 1827 and subsequently realized by the Antimasons.

6. Official Image of Opponents

Unlike the Democrats, the national platform of the Whigs ignored its opponents. As we shall soon see, however, the New York Whigs did not display similar reticence.

E. New York Whig Party: Official Images

The New York Whigs met at Syracuse on September 11, one week after the Democrats had met there. Since they were having the last official word, they could add substance and detail to the self-portrait of their national party, as well as subject to scathing review the Democratic national and state conventions.[22]

1. General and Specific Role of Government in a Democratic Republic

Like the Democrats, the New York Whigs asserted that in 1844 great issues were at stake, that distinct party differences existed upon

---

[21] Arthur M. Schlesinger, Jr., *The Age Of Jackson*, 351; Lucius Q. C. Elmer, *The Constitution And Government Of The Province And State Of New Jersey . . . And Reminiscences Of The Bench And Bar, During More Than Half A Century* (Newark, N.J., 1872), 440-456. See also John A. Krout, *The Origins of Prohibition* (New York, 1925), 135-137, 177, n. 58; Albert Post, *Popular Freethought In America*, 13.

[22] An account of the Whig convention, including the resolutions adopted, appears in the *New York Tribune* (w.), September 21, 1844, p. 3; the *Address* was reprinted in *ibid.*, October 5, 1844, p. 2. All quotations are from those two sources.

those issues, and that the outcome of the election would determine the prosperity of the country and the purity of its institutions. Belying Democratic charges that restoration of a national bank was one of their three "principal measures," the Whigs paid relatively little attention to the currency question. To them, "whether the Labor of America shall be protected by its own Government, or be subject to the arbitrary will and policy of other Governments," was by far the most important domestic question.

Long attacked by Democrats on the ground that their "fondness for excessive legislation" derived from unconstitutional, antirepublican, antiegalitarian, Federalist principles, the Whigs insisted passionately that protective tariffs were inherently constitutional and sublimely patriotic. Acting upon their reading of history, they resolved that the Constitution was ". . . established for the express purpose of protecting our own industry by discriminating duties— that the condition of our country always has required, and still requires such protection . . . [and] that this protection was a primary motive to the Revolution, in its glorious result establishing these colonies as "Free and Independent States."

We need not recapitulate the Whig "proofs" that the Revolution was fought and the Articles of Confederation and Constitution ratified to secure equal rights and protection for American industry. Asserting that those objectives were inseparably connected, they claimed that the Founding Fathers envisioned "the Encouragement of Arts and Manufactures" as "the great lever of Liberty—the great instrument of Independence—the mainspring of their new social power. . . ." And they claimed that they simply followed the Fathers' footsteps when they pushed the tariff argument to the point where it arrived at the positive liberal state and the egalitarian Good Society.

Since experience had demonstrated that American economic progress could not be achieved in "the absence of a common power to establish [uniform] duties and uniform currency, the People of these United States instituted our present Constitution." But, according to the Whig interpretation of the social contract, men did not give up their right to protect their labor when they entered society and formed a government. "What is free government but the united will and the united power of the individuals composing the nation governed? Did any individual entering into society ever part with this power to protect his industry, *except that it might be more bene-*

ficially exerted by the Government as the common trustee and common agent [italics added]? Did the intelligent people of this Union, its Sovereign, intend to divest themselves of this essential of their sovereignty? Wherefore did they establish this Constitution, if not by its legislative functions to enable the sovereignty of the people, then divided, and impaired by division, to act in a joint and vigorous concert, for the common good, as they declare 'the general welfare'?"

Unlike the Democrats, who hailed agriculture as the country's "great interest," denigrated the "few favored manufacturers" as seeking special privileges," and attacked protective tariffs as a violation of equal rights, the Whigs argued that government "encouragement and protection of manufacturers" would help to achieve a democratic, egalitarian American society. "Which of the States have always been the most zealous advocates of Protection? Are they not those most democratic in their institutions, in the feelings, opinions, habits of their people where the suffrage is most widely diffused, the tenure of office most dependent and brief—those States where the laboring population has always exercised the most direct and powerful influence, where property is most equally divided, and most frequently changes owners? Is not this the natural effect of a natural cause? The tendency of the constant exercise of duty protected labor to equalize the condition of men?"

It is immaterial whether the Whig logic was faulty and whether the situation they described actually represented "the natural effect of a natural cause." What does matter is that the Whig version of the positive state made promises that were anathema to men who subscribed to Hamiltonian elitism and paternalism.

Refuting Democratic charges that the positive state necessarily derived from an elitist, antiegalitarian, antidemocratic political theory, the Whigs claimed that they advocated a free government whose power derived exclusively from "the united will . . . of the individuals composing the nation," and whose function was to create the conditions necessary to "equalize the condition of men." By a nice irony of history, the tariff argument invoking that egalitarian ideology was reported to the 1844 Whig convention by John C. Hamilton, a son of Alexander Hamilton. To use understatement, equalizing the condition of men was not an objective his father had proclaimed when he argued for protective tariffs.

The radical differences between the ideologies invoked by the Federalists in their day and the Whigs in theirs constitute an excellent measure of the intellectual revolution that had taken place since 1791 when the elder Hamilton brought forth his famous "Report on Manufactures." As the quotations from the 1844 *Addresses* of the New York Whigs and Democrats demonstrate, it was not over egalitarian ends that they differed, but over the institutional means toward them.

Further analysis of the Whigs' tariff argument underscores another important difference between the Whigs on one side and contemporary Democrats and Federalists on the other. Unlike Democrats and Federalists, the Whigs did not take a Hobbesian view of society and did not conceive of government as the adjudicator of conflicting claims arising from the inherently conflicting interests of different classes and sections; they depicted the state as the promoter of harmony that could lessen or even eliminate, the bases of discord. Their professed beliefs concerning the wonder-working qualities of "protection" may have been unrealistic, or even hypocritical, but they led to an optimistic view of American society, raised the level of individual aspiration, and contributed to a sense of national purpose. The "American System," the Whigs claimed, ". . . secures a better and nearer market and higher prices, both to the North and South, to the East and to the West, of what we have to sell—a better, nearer, and cheaper market to all our States of what we have to buy, while it makes labor more valuable by cheapening its wants, and raising its rewards; which renders that labor more constant, and healthful, and independent; which extends widely the most genial influences, while it approaches more closely, and binds more strongly, and kindly together, the interests and affections of a whole people; which renders them more capable of self-government and more able to resist aggression; increasing our individual and National Independence. . . ."

Again it is immaterial whether the protective tariff actually could or would have achieved all those objectives. What is material is that, *unlike the Democrats, the Whigs treated those objectives as legitimate claims that men might make upon government*. If the tariff failed to render labor more valuable, constant, healthful, and independent, it followed logically from Whig premises that other actions should be taken to secure those results. The roseate expectations held out by the New York Whigs in their *Address* strongly supports the view that, unlike the Democrats, their temperament was not only activistic but optimistic. Living in a democratic republic, they did not fear the state; they regarded it as a powerful, creative instrument for the advancement of "the general welfare."

Aside from the tariff, the New York Whigs placed relatively little emphasis upon domestic issues. They insisted upon distribution of public land proceeds among the states "as a matter of *right* and of *expediency*," and they excoriated the Sub-Treasury as primarily responsible for the "repudiation" of public debts—a doctrine "which palsies credit to its very heart—that mighty modern power in the world, its moral power stimulating, directing and controlling its physical power." Among other evils they ascribed to the Sub-Treasury, it had engrossed the "precious metals" and thereby hindered recovery from the 1837 depression.

Somewhat vague about their own proposals to regulate the nation's money supply, the Whigs claimed that "the great avowed aim of Henry Clay will be to establish a control over the paper issues, such as in this State has rescued us from one of the greatest social evils—an excessive, because unrestricted paper circulation. . . ." (The reference is to currency legislation sponsored by the New York Whigs after the Panic of 1837.) They called for "a *hard money* basis of a currency, not for an oppressive, anti-labor, exclusive hard money circulation. You [the people] know this last can be obtained only in exchange for your prosperity; and when obtained, must soon necessarily disappear. . . ." Failing to press for restoration of a national bank, the Whigs insisted, nonetheless, that the state must play a positive role in monetary affairs and thereby promote rapid economic development.

Although we can disregard some minor issues, the Whig comments on immigration deserve attention. They did not propose restrictive legislation or changes in the naturalization laws, but they did make a covert bid for American Republican support. They accused the Democrats of having permitted ". . . the admission of a State into this Union, Michigan, without a previous enumeration of its inhabitants under the guards interposed by Congress; and after the ascertained fact, that recently arrived aliens, not naturalized, not having renounced their allegiance to their foreign rulers, had exercised the elective franchise—usurping the most sacred privilege of the American citizens in violation of the Constitution and of the laws."

Like the American Republicans, the New York Whigs asked the question: Who should have the right to influence government decisions? And, like the American Republicans, although more covertly, they answered—not recently-arrived immigrants.

2. Locus of Power

Except for a grudging admission that it could not interfere with slavery—"When framing their political systems, the people of the United States were obliged to leave the condition of its population to the policy of each State"—the Whigs failed to indicate any limitations upon the federal government's power. Arguing that the Constitution was established to remedy the difficulties caused by divided sovereignty, they in effect gave the federal government carte blanche to do anything calculated to advance the "general welfare." Henry Clay assumed that the federal and state governments could and would work together harmoniously, and the New York Whigs enthusiastically hailed the American System and its "great advocate [whom] we love and honor and venerate, and will elevate to cover it with the mantle of his wisdom, his genius and his virtues. . . ." They contemptuously dismissed Democratic claims that the state rights doctrine was necessary to the Union's preservation and proclaimed their devotion to the Union on "high, broad, national grounds."

3. Role and Power of Three Branches of Government

Smarting under the Democratic accusation that they had once favored a "monarchical system of government," the New York Whigs updated the charge and turned it against their accusers. As the Whigs saw it, division of power among "the respective departments of our Government," rather than state rights, was *the* constitutional question of enduring interest. "We assert for all the departments their due balance and granted powers; looking to the general good, and as a means of promoting that good, while we yield all the power the Constitution gives to the President, we deny him more, for the reasons that that more, such excess, takes from some other department its due share, and instead of leaving it an equal, renders it a subordinate—practically converting our government, a Representative Democracy, into an elective monarchy. The leaders of our opponents assuming the name of Democracy, war on its principles by giving to the Executive the power of the sword, of the purse, of patronage, of the veto, according to the largest, most extended construction. For the benefits to be derived from the Constitution, *we* look chiefly to the law-making power as the source of those benefits, and to the Judicial power as the guardian of those laws. *They* look to ONE MAN, as the Representative of the Nation, to his opinion as the exponent of its policy, to his WILL as the Government."

The Whigs favored a very broad construction of the Constitution in respect to the powers of the federal government and a very narrow one in respect to the power of the president; the Democrats reversed the order of latitude.

4. Foreign Policy

"Would to God we were spared the duty of bringing before you one more topic, which the late Democratic Convention at Syracuse have passed by in silence, thus admitting that they are seeking to elevate to the Chief Magistracy of this country, men pledged to a measure they cannot defend, and dare not avow. We would speak in a few words of the lately rejected Treaty for what is deceptively called the *Re*annexation of Texas."

A few thousand words later, the New York Whigs stopped denouncing the proposal of the Democratic Party to acquire Texas and Oregon—only to renew the attack later in the form of lengthy resolutions.

Conceding that no constitutional barrier existed, the Whigs argued that Texas should be acquired only "with the acquiescence of the whole Nation." To emphasize the antiannexation position of their presidential candidate, they quoted Clay's statement that the treaty had been made "in decided opposition to the wishes of a considerable and respectable portion of the Confederacy." Moreover, they insisted that the 1844 election be treated as a referendum on foreign policy. They asked: "Are you not, People of New York, in common with those of New-England, New Jersey, Delaware, Pennsylvania, Ohio, Kentucky, Indiana, North Carolina, Georgia, Louisiana, utterly opposed to this Treaty?"

With impassioned rhetoric, the Whigs ascribed "most unworthy and sordid" motives to the men who promoted the treaty. Did not its promoters appeal to an "insatiable avarice of more territory and more sectional power"? Would not acquisition of Texas seriously injure northern, western, and even southern farmers and inevitably bring about war with Mexico—as Clay had warned in opposing annexation? Clearly attempting to rally all "antislavery men" under their banners of freedom and the "rights of man," the Whigs asked rhetorically: "Are you willing People of New York! to increase by assenting to this acquisition, a political power not founded on the numbers of free thinking beings whose will is the only legitimate source of government; but to extend the influence of a compromise of necessity, always sacredly to be observed, but never to be extended beyond the regions which this compromise was understood to embrace?"

Before the Tyler-Calhoun ascendancy, said the Whigs, the federal government had never descended from the platform of Freedom to "exert all its powers for the establishment, extension, perpetuation of Slavery." That the Whig politicians regarded New York public opinion as widely, intensely anti-Texas is evident from the way they posed the issue: ". . . You are now asked, at this time, to vote for Polk and Dallas, to silence conscience, to stifle sympathy —rashly to brave the strong opinion of all Christendom, and to declare yourselves in the most solemn, authoritative, effective manner, in favor of—nay, each of you, personally to authorize the exercise of all the energies of this nation, to make permanent this unhappy relation [that is, annexation]."

The Whigs gave less attention to Oregon than to Texas, but they warned that Polk's election would lead also to immediate occupation of the Pacific territory and would precipitate a war with England. War with England would be not only disastrous: it would be unnecessary because the influx of Americans would eventually persuade England to let it "fall quietly into our hands." But if Polk were elected, the Whigs argued, a civil as well as a foreign war might follow: "Do we not at this very moment, hear urged by leading men of South Carolina, and with approval, severance, and a new confederacy of the South—leagued, banded together to war upon the industry and interests of the North, and of the West? Are not these traitorous counsellors the partisans of James K. Polk? Is it to him you would entrust the integrity of this Republic? . . . Nor were the South quiet, would the people of the North and West, longer submit in silence. Of a Foreign war, forced on us for Texas and Oregon, a civil war may be the immediate and fearful consequence."

Departing from strict observance of categories, we may note that the New York Whigs tried to make the 1844 election turn on the

"Two Great Issues—The Tariff and Texas."[23] The point can best be illustrated by quoting from a long resolution which charged, among other things, that the "Texas scheme" was designed to "divide the people and divert public attention from the great questions of public policy now pending. . . ." The New Yorkers hailed the southern Whigs who had resisted Locofoco appeals to sectional prejudices. They pledged that they would ". . . stand while we live firm under the banner of PROTECTION AND UNION, against all temptations and all assaults against the lust of foreign conquest and the treason of disunion, for 'OUR COUNTRY, OUR WHOLE COUNTRY AND NOTHING BUT OUR COUNTRY.'"

5. Official Self-Image

Because the Whigs' legislative *Address* of May 1844 succinctly delineated the self-image that they projected at length in their convention *Address* and *Resolutions*, it seems more economical to quote from the earlier document: "The Whig party derives its principles from the Revolution. It is deeply imbued with the spirit of the age. It promotes public wealth and happiness by protecting personal industry and by developing those resources with which God has blessed the American States. It seeks improvement, but dreads innovation. It works out reforms, but adheres to existing institutions and submits to existing laws, until they can be peacefully and constitutionally changed. It is devoted to progress, but it does not destroy. It seeks to establish perfect equality of political rights; but it levels upwards not downwards, by education and benignant legislation, not by subverting established laws or institutions.—It is the party of Law,

[23] Unfortunately, the literature gives the impression that "the battle in the Empire State was conducted basically on the old lines of bank and tariff, an arrangement satisfactory to both parties." Garraty, *Silas Wright*, 309-310; "Tariff and the Bank were the most prominent issues argued by the Whigs. . . ." (Muller, "Preston King," 296-297.) At best, this description is applicable only to the Democrats. The Whigs paid little attention to the "Money question" in general, and certainly did not call for a National Bank. For the editorial, "The Two Great Issues—The Tariff and Texas," which accurately summed up the Whig campaign on all levels of officiality, see the *Albany Evening Journal* (d.), October 7, 1844, p. 2. In central and western New York, the Whigs gave even more attention to Texas than to the tariff. Fillmore, for example, made numerous speeches on the "two great subjects," tariff and Texas. He emphasized that the latter was more important than the former, for if Texas was annexed, farewell to all hope for tariff. "With five or six more Slave States, Northern industry and Northern wealth may look in vain in the Councils of the Nation for any legislation for their protection." *New York Tribune* (w.), June 29, p. 3; July 13, p. 2; July 10, p. 3; September 14, p. 3; October 12, p. 1 (all 1844). See also Seward's letters reporting on his speeches during the campaign, Frederick W. Seward, ed., *William H. Seward: An Autobiography*, 1: 715-729.

of Order, of Enterprise, of Improvement, of Beneficence, of Hope and Humanity. Through the action of this great and generous party every attainable national good may be ultimately secured, and through its action we can best promote the more comprehensive interests of freedom and of humanity throughout the World."

Determined to efface the Democrats' portrait of them as anti-democratic Federalists in dishonorable disguise, the Whigs presented their legislative and convention *Addresses* as statements of the "Democratic Whig" party. They struck the same democratic note in the resolutions eulogizing Millard Fillmore, their gubernatorial candidate.

As the Democrats emphasized Wright's rural associations and self-identification with "the great mass of his fellow men," the Whigs emphasized Fillmore's position as "a true and worthy representative of Democratic Republican principles, born in the forest of the noble Western region of our own State, trained among an industrious kindred to hardy toil and manual labor on the farm and in the manu-factory-democratic in all his associations and sympathies . . . *one who never sought to rob the people of the right to choose their own rulers*, but ever distinguished himself in contending for popular rights or constitutional liberty, and in securing to the American laborer his labor's just and high reward." The double-edged resolution referred to Wright's vote in 1823-1824 against popular election of presidential electors and to Fillmore's authorship of the tariff of 1842.

Not only did the New York Whigs portray themselves as democratic, dynamic, and progressive, but they emphasized their devoutness. Frelinghuysen presented "a character beautiful in all the beautiful proportions of religion and virtue, a just man, fearing God. . . ." And in their arguments for the tariff, the Whigs associated protection with "an indispensable duty which we owe to God. . . ." In all, the Whig *Address* managed to work in four separate references to the Deity. This represented a striking difference in the self-images of the parties, for the Democrats avoided any mention of religion.

Finally, we must note that although the Whigs portrayed themselves as antislavery in principle and against its extension in practice, they did not pose as abolitionists. On the contrary, they conceded the legal existence of slavery, failed to call for any government action designed to hasten its demise, and enthusiastically supported a slaveholder for president. Thus, except in relation to Texas, the

[251]

Whig position on slavery did not differ essentially from the Democratic position.[24]

6. Official Image of Opponents

The New York Whigs, like their rivals, believed that attacks upon their opponents' honesty and devotion to principles helped to win elections. They depicted themselves as the democratic party of orderly, dynamic change, the Democrats as "that new party which has risen up among us, which seeks to abridge and limit the Legislative power of the people, while it would enlarge and unlimit the power of the Executive, to set afloat all our national landmarks, to disregard all our soundings, until this nation had become almost a wreck."

Having been criticized by the Democrats for hiding their true sentiments from the people, the Whigs returned the compliment—at length and with heat. In certain parts of the country Polk was pictured as favoring protection, but why then "is he, while turning as it were on a pivot before this nation, presenting to every opinion an approving countenance?" Praising themselves as standing foursquare behind the tariff of 1842 enacted by their party, they held up "to the scorn and condemnation of all intelligent and honorable men the pitiful evasions, the shuffling equivocations and deceitful double-dealing of those who claim to be in any sense the friends of protection, while they are pledged by their public acts and by their nomination, to the destruction of this, the most perfect, judicious and popular measure ever devised for the protection of American labor. . . ."

As with the tariff, so with Texas. The New York Democrats had deliberately avoided comment on the issue because their presidential candidate stood pledged to a measure "they cannot defend, and dare not avow." Polk *openly* associated with disunionists, pro-slavery partisans, and reckless speculators who would not hesitate to touch off a world war to gain their sordid ends. But, according to the Whigs,

[24] It deserves note, however, that where antislavery sentiment was strong, Whig orators tried to lure Liberty voters back into the fold by voicing abolitionist sentiments. For example, emphasizing that he was not a candidate and was speaking *unofficially*, Seward denounced annexation and slavery in the strongest terms, and wound up on this note: "I shall stand on the same ground I now occupy, always demanding the abolition of slavery in America by political argument and suffrage, and by the Constitutional action of all the public authorities. I trust in the instincts of the Whig party, that it will prove faithful to that cause; and when it shall prove false in any hour of trial, it will be time enough to look elsewhere for more effective agency." George E. Baker, ed., *Works of William H. Seward*, 3: 260-274.

Wright's stand on the issue showed that he lacked integrity: "Are you willing to support a man whose acts and whose judgment ever seem at variance—who argues against a Union with Texas, yet support [*sic*] James K. Polk pledged to immediate Annexation? Are you content with such cozenage? The conflict of resisting forces is said to produce the equilibrium of the atmosphere. Perhaps it is by reasoning against his vote, and by voting against his reason, Silas Wright has reached the temperate zone of politics."

Now that we have examined the official images projected in 1844 by the Democratic and Whig national and state parties, we can examine their impact upon the New York voters. To begin with, we will examine the impact of the issues that dominated the 1844 campaign. And, for reasons that will become apparent, we can do so most economically by concentrating upon the Texas issue.

CHAPTER XII

TEXAS ANNEXATION AND NEW YORK PUBLIC OPINION

THE images that national and state parties attempted to project in 1844 undoubtedly differed from the images perceived by the electorate. For one thing, voters probably received more direct exposure to the images projected by local agents and agencies of the parties, and these varied throughout the state and among different groups. Similarly, semiofficial and unofficial agents and agencies more or less subtly altered the portraits, depending upon their own predilections, the social and political environment in which they operated, the groups they were attempting to influence, and day-to-day campaign developments.[1] Finally, the empirical findings of a classic twentieth century study support the assumption that in 1844 the voters' frames of reference distorted their perceptions of parties.[2]

A. Conditions and Conduct of the
1844 Campaign

To the extent to which men identified themselves strongly with one party, they tended to block out displeasing aspects of its image and regard the party as favoring their own principles, policies, values, and attitudes. Another assumption seems equally reasonable: that when voters looked at parties they opposed, the process worked in reverse.

No doubt for most people the process of seeing what one wants to see has more or less definite limits. The actual conduct of an election campaign, as well as the conditions under which it is held, must influence the extent of distortion; if they did not, marked fluctuations in voting behavior would never occur and logical relationships would never exist between the claims of a party and the kinds of men who vote for it. One example makes the point: thousands of abolitionists must have been able to perceive the differences between the Liberty and Whig positions on slavery or they would not have switched parties between 1840 and 1844.

Unless one party secured a near monopoly on all communication media, it would seem highly unlikely—in a long-functioning demo-

---

[1] For example, see Chapter XI, n.24.

[2] Bernard R. Berelson, et al., *Voting: A Study of Opinion Formation in a Presidential Campaign* (Chicago, Ill., 1954), 77-87, 215-233.

cratic system which is characterized by intense, widespread interest in politics—for voters to get seriously out of touch with reality. In 1844, ten years after formal consolidation of the major parties, the New York parties differed so distinctly and conducted such lengthy, well-organized campaigns, that distortion was probably relatively low. Put another way, there were such excellent opportunities to learn what the parties claimed to stand for and represent that New Yorkers who did not have *reasonably* accurate knowledge must not have cared to obtain it. If under those conditions men grossly misperceived party positions, we could infer that they attached great importance to identifying themselves with a given party and blocked out information that hindered their doing so.

Among the conditions under which the campaign was held, these deserve emphasis: both parties projected distinctly different images; both were well organized and did not suffer from open factional splits; both canvassed the state intensively. Several other conditions are also worth noting. 1) In 1844 the Liberty Party put up national and state tickets and, at least in certain rural counties, it had been perfecting its electioneering machinery and tactics for several years. 2) None of the parties held the advantage of having a "native son" on its national ticket; the Democrats and the Whigs both nominated southern slaveholders for president and northerners from other Middle Atlantic states for vice-president. 3) Neither major party ran on the record of the incumbent national administration; the Whigs had repudiated Tyler and the Democrats had failed to claim him. 4) By the summer of 1844 the country had definitely recovered from the severe depression of 1837 to 1843 and was generally prosperous, although agriculture lagged behind other segments of the economy.[3] In short, the voters had a positive, clear-cut alternative to the major parties and neither of the major parties could appeal to state pride or to the sense of resentment against an incumbent administration engendered by economic depression.

B. Was the 1844 Election a Referendum on Texas?

The election of 1844, one of Tyler's biographers has written, "might properly be considered a plebiscite in favor of the Annexation of Texas. The 're-annexation of Texas and the re-occupation of Oregon' was the main plank in the Democratic platform, and the

[3] Willard L. Thorp, *Business Annals* (New York, 1926), 122-123; *New York Tribune* (w.), August 31, 1844, pp. 1, 4.

victory won by this party at the polls would indicate that a majority of the American people were in favor of the acquisition of both of these regions."[4] The claim that the election of 1844 served as a national referendum on Texas has been widely accepted. But is it really credible? A minor caveat to the version quoted above is that the Democrats did not actually receive a majority. They won only because they received pluralities in New York and Michigan. But more fundamental than whether the Democrats received a majority is whether the election can "properly be considered a plebiscite in favor of the annexation of Texas." If systematic procedures could be developed to appraise that claim, it seems reasonable to assume that they could be applied to similar claims about other issues and other elections. Thus the impact of the Texas issue can serve as a case study in the appraisal of claims about the state of public opinion on a given issue.

1. Appraising Contemporary Estimates

As usually happens, the 1844 election outcome led contemporary observers to arrive at contradictory interpretations of public opinion. Men who favored the immediate annexation policy hailed the Democratic presidential victory as proof that the American people endorsed it. David Dudley Field, a prominent New York "anti-slavery Democrat" who had fought against the policy before the election, wrote a lengthy article designed to demolish that claim.[5] "If the election had any such significance, three things must have concurred —first, the question must have been put to the people in a practicable shape, so as to make it understood what they were voting for, and they must have voted upon it; second, it must have received a majority of the votes cast; third, that majority must be so strong and decided as to justify so extreme a measure."

Field set out to "controvert" all three positions. He denied that any connection existed between voting for a president who wanted to see Texas annexed and voting for annexation. "Voting for Mr. Polk did not imply that the elector would have voted also for the annexation. An election signifies nothing as an expression of opinion, unless the opinion alone determines the vote. Does anybody imagine that the voter's opinion upon the annexation question alone de-

[4] Oliver P. Chitwood, *John Tyler* (New York, 1939), 357.

[5] *New York Evening Post For The Country*, November 30, 1844, p. 2. The article was signed "D. D. F." and I have assumed those initials to stand for David Dudley Field. For his opposition to immediate annexation, see *ibid.*, July 27, 1844, p. 1.

termined his vote for or against Mr. Polk? If it were so, what became of the questions of the Bank, Distribution, Tariff? Had they no influence on determining the choice of the elector? If they had, who shall measure the degree of influence on each? Is it not possible, that the vote was given to Mr. Polk, not for, but in spite of his Texas inclination? And if so in one case, why not in many or in most of them? What reason is there then to think that the vote is an index of opinion on this question? There is none. The error arises from a confusion of ideas. Unless an election turns upon a single question, in which personal preferences and party attachments have no part, it cannot be a test of opinion, in respect to it."

Moreover, Field continued, the Democratic plank on Texas was worded so vaguely that men had construed it very differently; support for such an ambiguous resolution, therefore, could furnish no guide to public sentiment. Besides, the Democrats had won by a plurality, not a majority, of the popular vote. "What then, it may be asked, has the election decided? It has decided that the administration should be in democratic hands, and it has decided nothing else. This is much, undoubtedly, because in the present state of parties, the President may prevent the accomplishment of schemes which we look upon as dangerous; but as an expression of the will of the whole people, or as a guide to those who are always watching the currents of public opinion, it amounts to nothing."

In his 1844 analysis, Field anticipated many arguments advanced later by James Bryce, A. Lawrence Lowell, Walter Lippmann, and others on the dangers inherent in using party victories or defeats as opinion indicators. As Bryce put it, "The *result* [italics added] of an election may be determined by the action of an insignificant knot of voters specially interested in a question of slight importance."[6] True. There is a fundamental difference, however, between using election results as the basis of inferences about public opinion, and using the entire range of voting behavior displayed in a number of successive elections for that purpose; in other words, there is a difference between using net turnover and gross turnover.[7] Field correctly claimed that in itself the 1844 Democratic victory

---

[6] James Bryce, *Modern Democracies* (New York, 1921), 1: 159, and 151-162. See also A. Lawrence Lowell, *Public Opinion and Popular Government* (New York, 1914), 24-25, 70-128; Walter Lippmann, *Public Opinion*, 193-197.

[7] The tendency of historians to focus attention upon election results rather than upon voting behavior patterns is discussed in Robert T. Bowers, "Opinion Research and Historical Interpretation of Elections," *Public Opinion Quarterly*, 12: 457-458 (Fall 1948).

could not be taken as an "index of public opinion" on Texas annexation, but he underestimated the amount of information that systematic analysis of voting behavior in 1844 can yield.

Except in limited areas of New York and among certain relatively small groups of voters, Calhoun's proposal to annex Texas was the only *new* issue to receive major attention during the 1844 campaign. True, the Whigs harped upon the tariff of 1842. They credited it with having ended the depression, while the Democrats chanted the praises of the Stop and Tax Law of 1842. Such electioneering simply added new glosses to old arguments over long-established and well-defined party principles and policies, which had long enabled voters to choose between the parties. But the annexation of Texas had never been an issue before. Therefore, if we systematically compare the 1844 state, county, town, and ward statistics with those for previous years, we have a basis for estimating the impact of the new issue on voting behavior. That the issue was new is clear from the line taken by Weed in the *Albany Evening Journal* in July, 1844: "This is the first time since the formation of our Union that the free people of the North have been called upon to approve at the polls, the 'peculiar institution' of the South. We are now asked, by the supporters of James K. Polk, to vote directly for the extension of Slavery."[8]

Like the experts who drafted the Whigs's convention *Address*, Weed, believing that New York public opinion intensely opposed annexation, expected his party to benefit considerably from the issue. Some Democratic observers shared the same belief and feared the same result. Thus in a private letter to Van Buren before the latter publicly came out against annexation, Jabez Hammond wrote: "I cannot in conscience consent to the further extension of it [slavery]. . . . I owe it to candor to say that I could not vote for a candidate . . . who would . . . favor annexation. . . . I may be mistaken, but I I [*sic*] believe there are thousands of Democrats in this State who on the subject think & feel as I do."[9]

Were Weed and Hammond correct? More specifically, to show that public opinion in New York was widely and intensely anti-Texas, what data would we need? The estimate would seem credible if: 1) in 1844 the Democrats suffered severe losses and the Whig or Liberty parties enjoyed corresponding gains for national and

[8] *Albany Evening Journal* (d.), July 27, 1844, p. 2.
[9] Hammond to Van Buren, April 7, 1844, as quoted in Ernest P. Muller, "Preston King," 289.

state offices in areas where the tariff, nativist, anti-Catholic, and anti-rent issues were *not* salient, that is, where no issue other than Texas might reasonably have been expected to produce such results; anti-Texas Democrats could have also indicated their opinions by: 2) voting the Whig or Liberty national tickets and abstaining on state offices; 3) voting the Whig or Liberty national ticket and the Democratic state ticket; 4) not voting at all; or 5) abstaining on national offices and voting the Democratic state ticket. Though these alternatives are arranged to suggest declining degrees of intensity, if a significant proportion of Democrats had selected any one of them, the inference would seem credible that public opinion in New York was widely and intensely anti-Texas. In short, for reasons given later, the extent to which Democrats chose any of the five alternatives is the best single indicator of public opinion on the Texas issue.

2. Constructing an Anti-Texas Party Scale

Of the three parties appealing to New Yorkers for their votes in 1844, the Liberty Party most unequivocally and single-mindedly opposed annexation.[10] The New York Whigs took an equally anti-Texas stand, but their national convention had maintained discreet silence. Moreover, Henry Clay's first public statement of strong opposition (in April) became somewhat blurred by a subsequent series of "clarifying" letters.[11] Actually, those letters failed to alter his basic position of hostility to annexation along the lines that Calhoun, Tyler, Polk, and other immediate annexationists proposed— and the issue in dispute was whether the government should act favorably on their proposal. Nonetheless, the abolitionists and to a lesser extent the New York Democrats seized upon Clay's letters to attack Whig sincerity on the issue. Seeking to counterbalance these developments, the New York Whigs stepped up their anti-Texas activities. For example, Fillmore, Seward, and other leading Whig orators made fiery speeches in areas where anti-Texas sentiment was likely to be strongest and emphasized that southern as well as northern Whig senators had solidly opposed Calhoun's treaty.[12] Thus any

10 My own analysis supports the following conclusion by the most recent student of the Liberty Party campaign: "The main issue of the campaign of 1844 as far as the Liberty party was concerned was the annexation of Texas; and it was on this question that the rivalry between the Whig and Liberty parties centered." Betty Fladeland, *James Gillespie Birney: Slaveholder to Abolitionist*, 233-234.

11 Clement Eaton, *Henry Clay And The Art Of American Politics*, 173-175.

12 Greeley conceded that "shameful perversions" of Clay's letters by Liberty and Democratic presses had destroyed the possibility that most Abolitionists would re-

New Yorker who wanted to express opposition to annexation without appearing to support abolitionism could have voted Whig and felt that he was clearly registering his opinion.

As noted above, the New York Democratic resolutions did not mention Texas by name, but they endorsed the entire national platform that hailed reannexation at the "earliest practicable period" as a great American measure. They also lauded the nomination of Polk who, unlike Clay, favored immediate annexation, without qualification and with enthusiasm. Moreover, after the state conventions, as the campaign excitement mounted, the strain for consistency which strongly affects political parties began to make itself felt. The tendency was not universal, qualifications and reservations were expressed, but the New York Democrats increasingly conformed to the position of their national party on Texas. Many county conventions officially applauded annexation, and the *Argus* took on a more pronounced pro-Texas coloration. As a result, campaign rallies were treated to rousing renditions of songs that must have sounded cacophonous to Martin Van Buren who a few months earlier had acted on advice to come out publicly against annexation:

> The Mechanic and the Farmer
> Both have buckled on their armor
> And have gathered here together
>   Like freemen for a fight;
>
> Against Bank machination
> And high-tariff taxation—
> They will go for Annexation,
>   And Dallas, Polk, and Wright.[13]

---

turn to the Whig fold in order to prevent annexation. It is important to recognize that the Whigs' public and private laments over Clay's letters stemmed from their alleged effects upon the abolitionists, not upon the electorate at large. Whether Clay's penchant for letter writing cost him abolitionist votes and the election, as Weed maintained, is the kind of question that historians will always have great difficulty in answering. Yet, in my opinion, the voting data do not support the speculative conclusions of Weed and other contemporary experts about the impact of Clay's letters. In March 1844, after the Texas issue had arisen, and before Clay published any letters on Texas, Seward estimated the 1844 Liberty vote would be about 16,000, the figure it had reached in 1843. At the November elections, the Liberty presidential ticket received almost exactly the vote predicted by Seward. This strongly suggests that the overwhelming majority of Liberty voters responded to Birney's argument that desertion to the Whigs would mean the end of their party. As noted above (p. 135), the Liberty vote stabilized in 1843 and remained relatively unchanged through 1847. See the discussion in *New York Tribune* (w.), September 28, p. 5; October 5, p. 5; October 8, p. 8 (1844); Frederick Bancroft, *Life of William H. Seward*, 1: 149-150.

[13] During the campaign, the *Argus* carried reports of official conventions and ral-

To paraphrase slightly, New Yorkers who wanted to "go for Annexation" *had* to go for "Dallas, Polk, and Wright"; at the very least, if the opponents of annexation wanted to register their opinion, they could not go for Polk and Dallas.

3. The Liberty Vote as an Opinion Indicator

That Liberty voters in 1844 were anti-Texas needs no demonstration. To infer that New York public opinion was anti-Texas, however, we would have to discover that the party's 1844 vote increased sharply, compared to previous years. If it did score such gains, we might then reasonably infer that anti-Texas opinion was so intense and widespread that it had either converted many men to abolitionism or had driven many nonabolitionists to vote for the party most unequivocally opposed to annexation. But it did not score such gains.

On the state level, the Liberty vote actually declined, from 4.5 per cent in 1843 to 3.1 per cent in 1844. In raw numbers, it declined from 16,097 to 15,136. This last figure, however, represents the 1844 vote for governor; the party's presidential vote declined less and stood at 15,812, or 3.3 per cent of the larger total vote for that office. But the state totals may not have accurately reflected the effectiveness of the party's anti-Texas appeal, for in many areas it did not have the machinery to exploit its position. Thus its vote in the five counties where it was strongest, best organized, and long-established constitutes the best indicator. In those five counties, political interest ran unusually high, and the 1844 turnout of eligible voters ranged from 90.4 per cent to 93.1 per cent.

Despite the all-out campaign that the Liberty Party waged against Texas, Table 1 will show that the party barely managed to hold on to its old adherents, much less gain new ones as a result of the new issue.

---

lies in almost every county in the state and in literally hundreds of towns and wards. In addition to speeches, resolutions, addresses, and the like, it reprinted many editorials from Democratic papers throughout the state. Careful study of the *Argus* warrants the conclusion that the *Post*'s position on Texas did not accurately reflect the position taken by New York Democrats in general. For example, see Albany *Argus* (w.), June 15, p. 193; July 13, pp. 228, 230; August 3, p. 254; August 10, pp. 259, 261, 262; August 17, p. 269; August 31, p. 281; October 5, p. 324; October 19, pp. 338, 340; October 26, p. 350; November 2, 356 (1844). As Wright's biographer perceptively notes, the Democrats exploited the "spirit of expansion" that Texas represented. "Despite the fact that Wright had come out and stayed out against immediate annexation, the party found nothing inconsistent in associating his popular name with the general idea of adding the Lone Star Republic to the Union." (John A. Garraty, *Silas Wright*, 322-323.)

TABLE 1

NEW YORK LIBERTY VOTE, FIVE STRONGEST COUNTIES, 1840-1844

| | Madison | | Clinton | | Cortland | | Oswego | | Cattaraugus | |
	%	No.	%	No.	%	No.	%	No.	%	No.
1840	2.9	254	0.7	29	0.6	31	1.8	151	1.0	58
1841	5.6	430	1.1	41	3.5	161	3.8	283	3.6	174
1842	7.5	574	3.4	121	4.9	232	5.0	383	3.2	167
1843	26.1	1751	22.2	766	10.6	477	14.3	731	9.6	457
1844a	15.4	1371	10.4	481	10.2	542	9.4	846	7.7	454

a Vote is for governor. In these counties it did not vary much from the party's presidential vote and was higher in Madison and Clinton, lower in Cattaraugus, and almost identical in Cortland and Oswego.

4. The Whig Vote as an Opinion Indicator

The failure of the Liberty Party to benefit from the Texas issue does not necessarily indicate much about public opinion. Conceivably, many New Yorkers who strongly opposed annexation were unwilling to vote for abolitionism; they could have voted Whig, but we cannot assume that any or every Whig vote *necessarily* reflected an anti-Texas opinion. Men indifferent to the issue or even men who favored annexation may well have continued to vote for "their party."

We can assert this general proposition: because men developed a loyalty to party that committed them emotionally as well as intellectually, it cannot be automatically assumed that in continuing to vote for the party they necessarily favored its stand on a specific issue—particularly, a new issue. On the other hand, we can reasonably infer that they did not *intensely* oppose its stand. More precisely, we can infer that men who voted Whig in 1844 either did not feel intensely pro-Texas or did not regard the issue as important—compared to other considerations influencing their behavior and opinions. In other words, the problem is to ascertain what men thought or felt about Texas not as an abstract issue, but as one strand of an interrelated web of opinion. Having acquired historical perspective, analysts can, with detachment, abstract an issue from the total situation and try to examine it in isolation. In real life, men cannot and do not. They must always choose among a variety of alternatives, and their choices reflect the relative importance they attach to the available alternatives. That is, consciously or unconsciously they weigh the values they attach to different influences operating upon them. In effect, their vote answers the question, *"Given the existing situation,* how shall I act to maximize my satisfaction?"

5. The Democratic Vote as an Opinion Indicator

If the argument thus far is accepted as reasonable, it follows that, to appraise estimates that anti-Texas opinion in New York was intense as well as widespread, we must look for changes among normally Democratic voters. Of course, such estimates do not require us to find that a majority of Democrats chose any one or all of the five alternatives listed above. Revolutions in voting patterns on that scale have never occurred in New York, and it would be unreasonable to expect that any issue could, in less than a year, produce a change of such magnitude. But if intense anti-Texas sentiment existed among the electorate as a whole, some significant proportion of rank and file Democrats must have registered their protests on election day. Emphasis is placed on rank and file Democrats because party leaders, by the very nature of their roles, frequently have to act in ways that do not reflect their own opinions. As a result, their behavior is usually not a good indicator of public opinion and is frequently an extremely poor one.[14]

The figure is somewhat arbitrary, but let us assume that a decline of 15 per cent (from 48.2 to 41.0 per cent) in the Democratic presidential vote in New York from 1840 to 1844 would unmistakably indicate that something other than the normal oscillation between elections had occurred. For the moment, let us also assume that Texas was the only issue (or factor) that could have caused that decline. Given those conditions, if such a decline occurred, we might then credibly infer that a "large proportion" of the Democratic rank and file were strongly anti-Texas. My reasoning is based on these assumptions:

When men hold opinions contrary to the position officially adopted by the party to which they "belong," a much smaller proportion of them act in accord with their opinions than actually hold them— particularly in an era when "turncoat" was the epithet for the present-day honorific, "independent voter." (It seems premature to try to translate the vague term "much smaller proportion" into a nu-

---

14 If Hammond's account is accurate, all the signers of the "secret circular," except for himself, and all the leaders to whom it was addressed "supported with zeal and energy the election of Mr. Polk. . . ." (Jabez Hammond, *Life and Times of Silas Wright*, 501.) This is an excellent illustration of the point that party leaders are not free agents and are moved to act by considerations other than their opinions on issues. The contention here is that, if one wants to ascertain the state of public opinion on an issue, one must study the public. Of course, under certain circumstances, party leaders' behavior can be a good indicator of public opinion. But in my judgment, it must always be used as one item in an index.

merical ratio.) The underlying assumption here is that, apart from all other considerations, men who change their voting behavior patterns must overcome strong self-generated and socially-generated pressures upon them to remain "faithful to their party" and not "desert to the enemy."

Support for this line of reasoning does not depend solely upon logical assumptions or upon impressions gained from close study of source materials. The available empirical evidence suggests that voters have a strong psychological need to bring their personal opinions into harmony with the position of their party. Thus the following quotation summarizes the findings of a recent series of voting behavior and opinion formation studies, based upon repeated personal interviews: "*Under the increased pressures of a campaign, people have an increased tendency toward consistency, in all relevant aspects.* As time goes on, as we compare material collected early in the campaign with those obtained at later stages [from repeated interviews], we find that people abandon deviant opinions on specific issues to agree with the position taken by their party (or at least to perceive such agreement); in consequence, inconsistencies on various issues reduce in favor of two major opinion patterns characteristic for each of the two parties. In 1948, focusing on primary groups, we found that disagreements between friends and families disappear and make way for a homogeneity of attitude within various social groups."[15]

If we take into account the potency of the forces which reduce the psychological strain experienced by voters who disagree with "their" parties, this inference seems reasonable: to produce voting changes of the magnitude hypothesized above, a party's position on an issue must be both intensely and widely unpopular among its rank and file, and the issue must be regarded as relatively important.

This line of reasoning can be pushed further. If the Texas issue had led a significant proportion of Democrats to desert their party in 1844, then it would also seem reasonable to infer that a large majority of Whigs were strongly anti-Texas. For, if the Whig official position *reflected the opinions of many Democrats*, in all likelihood it also reflected the opinions of a much larger proportion of its own rank and file. Or, to state a general proposition: if significant voting shifts occur from one party to another, we can make inferences about the opinions of members of *both* parties.

15 Berelson, et al., *Voting*, 284-285, and 277-304.

6. What Proportion of Democrats Actually Voted Against Texas Annexation?

Applying this line of reasoning to the empirical data, we can go on to appraise the estimates made by Hammond, Weed, and other well-informed contemporary observers. Contrary to their estimates, systematic analysis of the voting statistics over time and space indicates that public opinion in New York was either not *intensely and widely* anti-Texas, or that the issue was not generally regarded as *important relative to other factors influencing voting behavior.* The state totals accurately reflect what happened on all levels: they demonstrate that all but a minuscule fraction of the normally Democratic voters either must have agreed with or accommodated themselves to their party's stand on Texas.

TABLE 2

NEW YORK DEMOCRATIC VOTE, PRESIDENT AND GOVERNOR, 1840, 1844

| | 1840 | | 1844 | |
	No.	%	No.	%
Pres.	212,527	48.2	237,588	48.9
Gov.	216,726	49.0	241,090	49.4

Table 2 again illustrates the advantages gained from viewing election returns in historical perspective. Contrary to the traditional interpretation of the discrepancy between the vote for Polk and Wright in New York, the table shows that in 1844 the Democratic state ticket ran ahead of the national ticket by *less* than its 1840 margin. It is not reasonable, therefore, to assume automatically that Wright's stand against the Texas treaty or his personal popularity considerably benefited his party—particularly when all the Democratic state candidates received almost identical votes. Even if the assumption were correct, at best, little more than one per cent of the men who voted for Wright exercised the various options available to them to express disapproval of the Democratic position on Texas.

Table 3 shows that on balance (that is, net difference), about 1,400 of the men who voted the Democratic state ticket voted the Whig presidential ticket, about 1,400 failed to vote for president, and about 700 voted Liberty. In all likelihood, the latter were erstwhile Democrats who had gone over to Liberty before the Texas issue arose and who split their ballots in 1844 to influence the election for state offices. For in 1843 the Liberty Party had received 16,097 votes,

[265]

and the table shows that its presidential ticket approximated that figure, although it declined slightly. That the party's vote declined rather than increased in 1844 suggests that the Texas issue caused few if any normally Democratic voters to switch to Liberty.[16] Of the 2,800 voters who on balance split their tickets between the Whigs and Democrats on national and state levels, presumably half of them felt intensely enough about Texas to vote for Clay, the others "declined voting at all for presidential electors," as Jabez Hammond later described his own course of action.

TABLE 3

NEW YORK PARTY VOTE, PRESIDENT AND GOVERNOR, 1844

| | President | | Governor | |
	No.	%	No.	%
Dem.	237,588	48.9	241,090	49.4
Whig	232,482	47.8	231,057	47.4
Lib.	15,812	3.3	15,136	3.1
Total	485,882	100.0	487,283	99.9

Though the state totals indicate the magnitude and direction of ticket-splitting in 1844, additional data are needed to support the inference that New York Democrats were relatively unaffected by the Texas issue. Since it was not the sole determinant of voting behavior, losses on Texas may have been counterbalanced by gains on other issues particularly salient to certain voting groups. For example, as noted in earlier chapters, we know that the Democrats benefited from changes in the composition of the electorate as well as from increased support among New non-British immigrants and Catholics generally. Thus particular attention was given to areas where Democratic gains and losses were likely to have stemmed from the Texas issue.

Analysis of the statistics in selected areas yielded results almost identical with the state totals. Between 1840 and 1844 oscillation considerably below the norm for presidential elections could be accounted for almost entirely by factors other than Texas, namely, changes in the composition of the electorate, growth of the Liberty

---

[16] Historians may have been led astray by Hammond's assertion that "those democrats who thought it wrong to vote for Mr. Polk, on account of the Texas question, either declined voting for presidential electors, or voted the abolition ticket." (*Silas Wright*, 502-503.) The voting statistics indicate that in all likelihood the Democrats who voted Liberty in 1844 had gone over to that party before the issue arose.

Party *between 1840 and 1843*, nativist anti-Catholic issues, anti-rent, backlash of the Patriot War and border excitement, the tariff. In fact, it was impossible to find any county where either the Democrats or the Whigs may have significantly gained or lost because of the Texas issue, and almost impossible even to find a town or ward where the Democrats or Whigs may have significantly gained because of it. Thus systematic analysis of the data discredits estimates which hold that in 1844 New York public opinion was intensely and widely for or against Texas annexation. Based upon the equivocal resolution adopted by the Democratic state convention and upon other indicators, however, I have the impression that annexation was mildly unpopular among the electorate as a whole, and highly unpopular *in certain limited areas where antislavery sentiment was intense.*

C. The Hidden-Persuaders Syndrome

In an election post-mortem, Horace Greeley in effect conceded the accuracy of the estimate of New York public opinion on Texas presented here. His concession is particularly convincing because Greeley was trying to support a directly contradictory estimate: ". . . All the losses sustained by the Whigs through Fraudulent Voting with the diversions from their ranks by Abolition and repugnance to Nativism, would have been unavailing, had the People been permitted to know what were the main questions [Texas and Tariff] in difference between the two great parties and so to decide intelligently upon them. But this Loco-Focoism resisted and prevented. It could not do otherwise and not be beaten. Therefore, while its public meetings, its speakers, its journals, in the *South*, were open, bold and ardent in their advocacy of the Immediate Annexation of Texas to this Country, regardless of consequences, this question was widely declared at the *North* to be by no means distinctively or decisively in issue. The Evening Post, the most respectable and influential Polk paper in this City, repudiated the issue and opposed Annexation. Silas Wright, who had powerfully opposed the Texas Treaty in the Senate, was made the Polk Candidate for Governor of New-York, by which nomination the Van Buren anti-Texas men were drawn into the support of Polk, New-York carried for him, and his election secured. Thus while Texas gained for Polk the votes of Georgia and Louisiana, the game was so played as not to lose him a single Northern vote."[17]

Greeley's admissions are revealing and convincing, his interpretations are factually and logically untenable. The statement that the Democrats did not lose a "single Northern vote" on Texas was, of course, pure hyperbole. Nonetheless, it admitted that the issue had little impact on New York voting behavior.

Trying to reconcile his admission with his interpretation, Greeley grossly exaggerated the role and influence of the *Evening Post* and ignored this crucial fact: as the campaign progressed, the differences between the two parties widened increasingly and obviously. Actually, the "secret" proposals made by the small group clustered around the *Post* were so poorly received that they dropped the idea of organizing an anti-Texas movement among Democratic leaders. And Greeley would have been hard pressed to find more than a handful of Democratic papers in the state that took an anti-Texas line. Contrary to his above assertions, during the course of the campaign the national Democratic Party's unequivocal stand on annexation received official and semiofficial endorsement at many county conventions and public meetings, as well as editorial support from many Democratic journals in New York. Thus, had Greeley's estimate of public opinion been accurate, in counties where annexation was officially endorsed and publicly hailed, significant Democratic losses would have occurred. But they did not.

Greeley's logical errors, however, are more important than his factual ones. Like many American commentators in the mid-twentieth century, he suffered from what can be called the hidden-persuaders syndrome. He claimed in effect that although "the People" were strongly anti-Texas, they had completely succumbed to the propaganda of unscrupulous Locofoco manipulators and had been rendered incapable of perceiving the differences between the Whigs and Democrats on Texas.

[17] *The Whig Almanac And United States Register For 1845* (New York, 1845), 4. Actually, Greeley conceded that the Whigs had "misgauged" the party loyalty of New York Democrats; which is only another way of saying that they did not consider the issue important compared to other factors operating upon them. *New York Tribune* (d.), December 23, 1844, p. 2. It is also worth noting that the quotation in the text asserted that "Texas gained for Polk the votes of Georgia and Louisiana. . . ." Yet as late as September 1844, the New York Whig *Address* had declared that the people of those two states were "utterly opposed to this [Texas] Treaty"—a declaration not borne out by the election. This again illustrates the point that contemporary estimates must be subjected to sharp scrutiny and are not necessarily good opinion indicators.

Even if Greeley's description of Democratic tactics were accurate, he ignored the crucial consideration that the Whigs conducted a very well-organized, long, enthusiastic campaign, and in many places held much greater control of communication media than did their opponents. Given the dominant patterns of small-town life in New York during the 1840's, it was fallacious to assume that Democrats had been hermetically sealed-off from all opportunities "to know what were the main questions in difference between the two great parties and so to decide intelligently upon them."

If the Democratic rank and file were strongly anti-Texas in 1844, except with voters in limited areas or among highly specialized groups, the most skillful manipulators could not have prevented them from perceiving the issues and voting to express their convictions. In fact, Greeley unwittingly undermined his argument on Texas by conceding that the Whigs had suffered losses because of "repugnance to Nativism." Although the Whig position on "nativism" was more ambiguous than the Democratic position on Texas, the non-British immigrants and Catholics had perceived the distinction between the parties and acted accordingly.

To state the proposition in more general terms: when effective party competition exists in a democratically-organized society characterized by intense political interest, "hidden persuaders" achieve their objectives only if "the People" are relatively unconcerned with the issues about which they are being persuaded or manipulated.

In 1844 New York voting patterns were little affected by current issues such as Texas, the Whig tariff of 1842, the Democratic Stop-and-Tax Law of 1842. What, then, did determine New York voting patterns in 1844? More precisely and significantly, how can we interpret the mass support received by the major parties from 1834 to 1844?

To answer that specific question, we need to be guided by some general theory of voting. The one that has guided the present study is described in the next chapter and applied to the 1844 election in Chapter XIV.

CHAPTER XIII

OUTLINE FOR A THEORY OF AMERICAN VOTING BEHAVIOR

"THERE is occasions and causes why and wherefore in all things," Shakespeare assures us. Historians find it easier to accept that proposition in general than to apply it in particular. Human motives are so complex that even when we are able to reconstruct human behavior, we are not necessarily able to reconstruct the "why and wherefore." Specifically, to identify who in New York in 1844 voted for whom does not necessarily enable us to explain why they did. But it does give us valuable clues. Put another way, systematic classification of voters on the basis of attributes such as membership in socioeconomic, ethnocultural, or religious groups stimulates *questions* that may lead to credible explanations. The working assumption of this study is that the question comes first, the "word" comes later.

The study's research design has thus far been based on elementary logic. Once historians know what happened and where and when it happened, it seems reasonable to believe they are in a better position to detect who caused it to happen. Going on to take another leaf from Sherlock Holmes's book, we can say that once historians know *who* did something, they are in a better position to reconstruct motives.

For example, it is highly improbable that we must invoke Chance to explain these phenomena: 1) In New York, in 1844, "immigrants" voted overwhelmingly for one party, whereas "natives" tended to divide much more evenly. 2) The New British and New non-British displayed almost completely opposite voting patterns. 3) Catholics voted overwhelmingly Democratic, Protestants tended to divide evenly. 4) "Puritans" and "non-puritans" voted in significantly different ways. 5) Urban and rural voters tended to vote alike. 6) With certain exceptions, no significant relationships between voting behavior and economic class (or occupation) can be detected. But if Chance did not produce these phenomena, what did?

Transforming factual descriptions of who voted for whom into a series of questions constitutes, I believe, a crucial stage in research design and practice. It forces us to think concretely about why Protestant Irish and Catholic Irish citizens, for example, ranged themselves on opposite sides of the political barricades. Concrete questions of that order are more conducive to fruitful research than inherently vague speculations concerning the partisan behavior of otherwise undifferentiated men.

A well-grounded and well-developed theory of voting behavior, combined with concrete questions about group affiliations over time and place, would make it easier to interpret the 1844 New York results. Unfortunately, no such theory exists at present. True, from Plato's time to the present, we can find "sporadic disquisitions on the meaning, method and motivation of voting." And empirical studies have advanced almost countless hypotheses about the determinants of voting behavior. But as Samuel J. Eldersveld puts it, to date all such efforts "fall far short of integrated theory construction"[1]—a conclusion peculiarly applicable to American political historiography.

One response to the lack of a credible theory of American voting behavior might be to ignore it. Dispensing with attempts to develop a general orientation to voting, we might concentrate exclusively upon digging up empirical data relevant to the particular problems that attract us. Or we might concentrate exclusively upon theory construction before proceeding to empirical research.

In the present study I have rejected the notion that historians must choose between "integrated theory construction" and no theory. I have, instead, attempted both to develop some crude theoretical generalizations and to exploit clues provided by empirical identification of who in New York voted for whom.

A. Some Crude Generalizations About American Voting Behavior

Other than Frederick J. Turner's frontier-section version and Charles A. Beard's class version of economic determinism,[2] the historical literature provides no set of interrelated principles to guide

[1] Samuel J. Eldersveld, "Theory and Method In Voting Behavior Research," in Heinz Eulau, et al., *Political Behavior*, 268, and 267-274, *passim*.

[2] The Turner and Beard theses usually are treated as fundamentally opposed; in my opinion, they stem from the same source and, closely examined, make the same economic determinist assumptions. In his *Economic Interpretation of the Constitution of the United States* (Macmillan Co., 1954 printing) XIX, and 239-241, Beard explicitly acknowledged his heavy dependence upon Turner and the work of the latter's students. The European origin of Turner's and Beard's versions of economic determinism is discussed in Lee Benson, *Turner and Beard*.

researchers attempting to organize the data of American voting behavior. One major reason for the popularity of the Turner and Beard theses is, I believe, that they give a semblance of order to what otherwise seems a bewildering multiplicity of unrelated "facts." No doubt the two theses have serious logical and empirical defects. But at least both men attempted to rescue American historians from metaphysical notions about the country's "divine democratic mission," or the "peculiar political genius of the Teutonic race," as well as from the intellectually sterile position of seeing the past as "merely chaos floating into chaos."[3]

It now seems clear, however, that credible interpretations of American voting behavior cannot rely upon either the Turnerian or the Beardian versions of economic determinism—a conclusion that in no way denies that their *search* for an overall theory entitles them to a high place in the American historical pantheon.

It also seems accurate to observe that American historians are now adrift on the sea of intellectual uncertainty from which Turner and Beard once seemed to rescue them. Fortunately, two books have recently appeared that may help us to attack the difficult problems of integrated theory construction. In a sense, what I attempt to do in this chapter is to consolidate and extend the complementary theses presented by Richard Hofstadter in *The American Political Tradition* (1948) and Louis Hartz in *The Liberal Tradition in America* (1955).

1. Identifying Areas of American Political Agreement

As is true of most significant innovations, after Hofstadter showed the way, we can discover earlier statements that resembled his thesis. But to stress precursors misses the point. Unlike earlier, vague statements, his book explicitly called for and gave strong impetus to a fundamental reorientation of American historiography. Breaking free from the Turnerian and Beardian frames of reference that focused upon political conflict, Hofstadter focused upon the "common climate of American opinion." "It is generally recognized that American politics has involved, among other things, a series of conflicts

---

[3] Beard was quoted to this effect in Howard K. Beale, "What Historians Have Said About the Causes of The Civil War," *Bulletin 54, Theory and Practice In Historical Study: A Report of the Committee On Historiography* (Social Science Research Council, New York, 1946), 55.

between special interests ... and that it has not shown, at least until recently, many signs of a struggle between the propertied and unpropertied classes. What has not been sufficiently recognized is the consequence for political thought. The fierceness of the political struggles has often been misleading; for the range of vision embraced by the primary contestants in the major parties has always been bounded by the horizons of property and enterprise. However much at odds on specific issues, the major political traditions have shared a belief in the rights of property, the philosophy of economic individualism, the value of competition; they have accepted the economic virtues of capitalist culture as necessary qualities of man. ... The sanctity of private property, the right of the individual to dispose of and invest it, the value of opportunity, and the natural evolution of self-interest and self-assertion, within broad legal limits, into a beneficent social order have been staple tenets of the central faith in American political ideologies. . . ."[4]

Hofstadter's thesis is consonant with ideological clashes deriving from different conceptions of the proper balance of agriculture, commerce, and industry in a liberal capitalist society. Also consonant with it are clashes over the division of profits, or over the best way to develop and preserve a liberal capitalist society. That the slave segment played an important role in the American economy until the Civil War does not affect the essential validity of the thesis. Southerners were sometimes carried away by flights of rhetorical fancy when they discussed their "peculiar institution," but racist doctrines enabled most southerners to accept the shared beliefs of liberal capitalism. The rubric "peculiar institution" testifies to the exceptional nature of slavery and the extent to which it was regarded as outside the mainstream of American society.

Hofstadter simultaneously enlarged and sharpened our vision by giving new, substantive meaning to the old concept of American uniqueness. He saw that one of its major components was that throughout most of our national history, no significant group has challenged the *legitimacy* of a capitalist system of *political economy*. And Louis Hartz in effect extended the concept by focusing attention upon another major component of American uniqueness: wide agreement on the fundamentals of *political theory*.

The title of Hartz's book summarizes his thesis—the liberal tradi-

---

[4] Richard Hofstadter, *The American Political Tradition* (New York, 1948), VII-VIII, and *passim*.

tion is *the* American political tradition.[5] In his reading, liberalism means the classic theories of John Locke unencumbered by "all sorts of modern social reform connotations." In that sense, "Locke dominates American political thought, as no thinker anywhere dominates the thought of a nation. He is a massive national cliché." And although Hartz nowhere explicitly defined liberalism in the "classic Lockian sense," he would presumably agree with George Sabine that "instead of a law enjoining the common good of a society, Locke set up a body of innate, indefeasible, individual rights which limit the competence of the community and prevent interference with the liberty and property of private persons."[6]

As the critical determinants of American history and politics, Hartz emphasized two closely related factors: "the absence of feudalism and the presence of the liberal idea." He organized his book around a famous Tocqueville dictum: "The great advantage of the Americans is, that they have arrived at a state of democracy without having to endure a democratic revolution; and that they are born equal, instead of becoming so." Repeated frequently throughout the Hartz book, the phrase, "born equal," expressed the idea that Americans never experienced subjection to the "canon and feudal law."

Statements of an innovating, broad-ranging thesis almost inevitably sacrifice precision for impact. Thus, in my opinion, Hartz followed Tocqueville too closely and exaggerated the extent to which feudalism and the canon law have been absent, the liberal idea present, men born equal, and democracy has prevailed in American history. By the 1840's, however, as I tried to suggest earlier, the nation had essentially completed the transformation from a liberal aristocratic republic to a populistic democracy. And long before, America could accurately be described as a politically liberal society, in the "classic Lockian sense." After 1789, men differed strenuously on whether government should represent property or people; but restoration of a political system based on monarchy or hereditary nobility was unthinkable—and practically unthought of.

Although Hartz and Hofstadter concentrated upon different aspects of American political theory and experience, both have forcefully directed the attention of historians to the broad and deep areas

[5] Louis Hartz, *The Liberal Tradition In America* (New York, 1955), *passim.* Another book, "The American Civil War: A War Against National Unification," will try to show how that hypothesis facilitates a more credible explanation of the Civil War.
[6] George Sabine, *A History of Political Theory* (New York, 1956, rev. ed.) 529.

of fundamental agreement that make the country relatively unique. In effect, they have viewed American history as the record of a liberal capitalist society, relatively unscarred by "feudal tenures, centralized and arbitrary government, a national church, a privilege-ridden economy, and hereditary stratification."[7] As I reformulate it, the combined Hofstadter-Hartz thesis holds that in the United States, broad and deep agreement has existed upon the very issues which elsewhere have provided the fundamental bases of political conflict, namely, form of government, relations between church and state, and system of political economy. Of course, there has always been some disagreement on fundamentals, particularly on church and state relations. But compared to elsewhere, disagreement in this country has been relatively narrow in scope and limited in intensity.

This does not mean that there have been no significant, profoundly experienced American political conflicts. Quite the contrary. Reversing Von Clausewitz, I am saying that politics essentially is war carried on by other means—even if men fight over nothing more fundamental than the expression of different ideas about how to achieve the same objectives. And, apart from short-lived insurrections such as the Shay's and Whiskey rebellions, the Civil War demonstrates that on at least one occasion American political conflicts grew so intense as to require resolution by armed force. (In a subsequent book, I hope to show that the Civil War can be accounted for within the framework of the theory sketched in the present book.)

Given the specific conditions of American historical development and the existence of a federal system of government,[8] rather than deduce that agreement on fundamentals will necessarily produce harmony, it seems more logical to deduce that agreement on fundamentals will permit almost every kind of social conflict, tension, and difference to find political expression. An almost endless list of such conflicts, tensions, and differences virtually compiles itself when we

---

[7] Clinton Rossiter, *Conservatism In America* (New York, 1955), 67. The fact that this quotation is from a self-styled conservative's view of "the American Political Tradition" suggests the fundamental agreement which exists between "liberals" and "conservatives" in the United States. For an analysis of the wide areas of agreement on political fundamentals in the United States, in contrast to the deep disagreement on "great principles" in Europe, see *New York Tribune* (w.), July 26, 1851, p. 4.

[8] My thinking concerning the relationships between the American governmental and party systems has benefited considerably from reading a draft of a forthcoming book, Morton Grodzins, *American Political Parties and the American System*.

consider that the United States is relatively unique in the following *combination* of characteristics:

A country of continental proportions, it contains vast amounts and varieties of natural resources; it has been settled at considerably different times and in considerably different ways by an unequalled number of intermingled religious and ethnic groups from an unequalled number of different cultures; most of its inhabitants have been physically and socially mobile to an unparalleled degree; with certain exceptions at times and places, most of its inhabitants have had equal legal rights and opportunities to become "successful," and have been stimulated to do so by the strongest cultural imperatives.

In an extremely heterogeneous society whose members tend to have high personal levels of aspiration, with a federal government system and agreement on political fundamentals, it seems logical to predict that a wide variety of factors will significantly determine voting behavior and that political parties will function essentially as decentralized aggregates of state and locally based organizations. The prediction assumes that deep, sustained cleavages over political fundamentals would lessen the possibility that many factors operate to influence voting behavior; the absence of such cleavages would increase the possibility.

The theory may be summarized in propositional form: the wider the area of agreement on political fundamentals, the more heterogeneous the society (or community), the larger the proportion of its members who have high levels of personal aspirations, and the less centralized the constitutional system, then the greater the number and variety of factors that operate as determinants of voting behavior.

Applied specifically to the United States, this proposition leads us to claim that all American history is reflected in past and present voting behavior. As a result, because it requires us to enlarge the range of data that we consider, I regard the theory derived from the Hofstadter-Hartz thesis as better designed than its predecessors to orient research in American political historiography. The theory does not focus attention exclusively or primarily upon disagreements arising from the simultaneous existence of different "stages of society" or clashing economic interests. Rather, it assumes that in the United States, unlike other countries, almost every social conflict, tension, and disagreement may function potentially as a significant determinant of voting behavior.

If the assumption is granted, we can then deduce that a comprehensive theory of American voting behavior must satisfy the following requirements: 1) It should be consonant with the agreement on political fundamentals stressed by Hofstadter and Hartz. 2) It should not only identify but classify the kinds of determinants that have influenced American voting behavior. 3) It should specify the conditions under which certain determinants are likely to exert more rather than less influence upon voting behavior. 4) It should identify the kinds of voters most likely to be influenced by certain determinants under specified conditions.

I cannot even pretend to offer such a theory. In this book I try to do little more than make a start upon the problem, by trying to develop a compressed, crude, and incomplete classification system in which voting determinants can be more or less systematically ordered. Such a guide to research can, I hope, help to generate empirical propositions and thereby contribute to a general theory of American voting behavior.

2. Why Bother With Classification Systems?

Historians who are skeptical of the value of scientific procedures when applied to refractory human beings in nonlaboratory or nonexperimental situations, may ask: Why bother with devising an abstract classification system? Why not concentrate upon finding out the actual determinants of voting behavior in specific situations?

In my opinion, a clear, logical system of categories helps to alert historians to the *possible* determinants of human behavior in specific situations. It is axiomatic that before decisions are made about the relative importance of any determinant, the range of determinants that may have operated in a given election should be considered. The record demonstrates that the axiom has not always been recognized. For example, I believe that lack of a comprehensive classification system has significantly contributed to the long dominance of economic determinism in American political historiography.

If we look only for "economic factors," we are likely either to find *only* economic factors or *no* economic factors at work. Collecting only certain limited types of economic data, we ignore the possibility that other determinants may have modified or counterbalanced the impact of economic factors. It seems reasonable to assume, therefore, that a comprehensive classification system can serve to guide us, and help to guard us, against such errors of omission.[9]

A set of comprehensive, clearly-defined categories serves as more than a check list. By providing a framework for ordering data in some systematic and logical fashion, it brings into focus relationships among empirical data that are not readily apparent.[10] Thus insights derived from seeing how one determinant influences voting behavior can illumine other determinants that have much the same effect. Conversely, recognizing the uniformities that link a number of determinants points up sharper distinctions among them and leads to fuller understanding of how they individually influence behavior.

No doubt a "gift" for historical research, a sense of the "human condition," and saturation in source materials enable some scholars who ignore "scientific procedures" to detect causal relationships hidden from others who faithfully use them. Genius makes its own rules, however, and I do not maintain that *all* historians need the aid of a formal classification system. But, particularly during the early stages of research, when assailed by impressions of multitudinous economic, political, intellectual, cultural, and social "forces" at work, it is likely that most historians see the world of human motivation as William James imagined that external sensory impressions seem to a baby: "one great, blooming, buzzing confusion. . . ."[11] In seeking to find order and value among "minute particulars," all historians, whether they are aware of it or not, use some general principles of classification. Henry James says that the artist, searching for "hard latent *value*," should sniff "round the mass as instinctively and unerringly as a dog suspicious of some buried bone."[12] Perhaps. But the argument here is that most historians would find it helpful to combine the intuitive and the directed approaches.

B. A Tentative Classification System for American Voting Behavior

At this early stage of development, the main function of the theory

[9] I have developed this argument at greater length in an essay called "A Critique of Beard and His Critics." See *Turner and Beard.*

[10] For the advantages of qualitative classification systems, see Paul F. Lazarsfeld and Allen H. Barton, "Qualitative Measurement in the Social Sciences: Classification, Typologies, and Indices," in Daniel Lerner and Harold Lasswell, eds., *The Policy Sciences* (Stanford, Cal., 1951), 155-182.

[11] William James, *The Principles of Psychology* (Dover Publications, Inc.: United States, 1950 ed.), 1: 488.

[12] Henry James, *The Spoils of Poynton*, New York, 1922 printing, V-VI.

sketched above may well be to widen the frames of reference of American historians. Two quotations from editorials by Horace Greeley transform the vagueness of "a wide range of factors" into a more concrete, vivid image of Americans behaving politically. The first quotation calls attention to a subtle process by which group voting patterns, originally shaped by a "political" issue (defined later), tend to be perpetuated after the resolution, or disappearance, of the conflict: "In Connecticut a good deal of sectarian bitterness exists and thousands of Episcopalians, Methodists, Universalists, etc., who would be Whigs almost anywhere else, usually vote Loco-Foco [Democratic] in Connecticut, primarily from hostility to the 'Standing Order of Orthodox Congregationalists,' who formerly were favored by law in Connecticut [disestablishment took place in 1818], who are still by far the most numerous denomination there, and who are somehow mixed up in the popular sentiments of the other sects with the Whig party; so that while an 'Orthodox' citizen votes as *Political considerations* [italics added] impel him to do, a citizen of another church or no church is strongly drawn toward the support of the opposite party by considerations which have properly nothing to do with Politics. This side-current may not always be perceptible even to those drawn by it, but it is none the less potent for that; and we believe that not less than an eighth of the votes cast against the Whig party are influenced by variance of religious creed from the church with which the Whig party is in that State popularly identified."[13]

Systematically analyzed, the process described by Greeley falls into three stages. During the first stage, an issue (here church-state relations) generates intense conflicts until it is resolved by some government action, or until the issue ceases to command attention and disappears from the political arena. In the second stage, antagonisms aroused by the original conflict remain acute and influence voting behavior through the formation of what sociologists call "negative reference groups." That is, certain voters continue to range themselves against each other, even though the original political conflict is no longer an active issue (for example, Connecticut Episcopalians "vote against" Congregationalists after as well as before disestablishment). In the final stage, sufficient time elapses so

13 *New York Tribune* (w.), March 22, 1851, p. 5. Although unsigned, the editorials quoted here have all the hallmarks of Greeley's style and I am reasonably certain that he wrote them. But the points made in the text do not depend upon correct identification of the editorial's author.

that neither the original conflict nor the subsequent political antagonisms stemming from it are perceptible to contemporaries. Nevertheless, both factors continue to influence voting behavior in the
form of *political roles* traditionally played by members of certain
groups (for example, Connecticut Episcopalians vote Democratic
because members of that group "always have").

A consideration not mentioned by Greeley deserves emphasis. During any one of the three stages described above, the emergence of
another political issue that is related to the original conflict, or that
pits the same antagonists against each other, reinforces established
group voting patterns and makes them more visible to contemporaries. And, though not as directly, much the same results are produced by antagonisms originating outside the political sphere (for
example, Episcopalian and Congregational denominational rivalries).

The next quotation is from an editorial by Greeley which also
observed that voting behavior was determined by factors other than
views on politicoeconomic issues. If a "real" political issue, such as
the tariff, were forcefully presented to the workers in any machine
shop or shoe factory in the Union, Greeley insisted, three fourths
would vote Whig: "But the very shop wherein fifteen out of twenty
workmen would be with us on the Tariff issue fairly made and fully
considered, will often give a majority *against* us in the absence of
such discussion. Jones hates the Whigs, because Esq. Simpson is a
leading Whig, and feels too big to speak to common people. Marks
has been trained to believe that the Whigs were Tories in the Revolution and starved his father in the Jersey prisonship; so he is bound
to hit them again at each election. Smithers is for a Tariff himself,
but his father before him was a Democrat, and he isn't going to turn
his coat. Smolker don't object to anything his Whig shop mates
propose; but he is a Foreigner and thinks the Whigs hate foreigners,
so he feels bound to go against them. Pitkin is a heretic in religion
and most of the leading Whigs he knows are Orthodox; and he can't
stand Orthodoxy anyhow you can fix it. And so, for one or another
of a hundred reasons, *equally frivolous or irrelevant* [italics added]
voters are piled up against us not for anything we as a party affirm
or propose, but because of considerations as foreign from the real
issues of the canvass as is the subjugation of *Japan*."[14]

14 *Ibid.*, September 11, 1852, p. 2.

I. Three Categories of Voting Determinants

In the quotation above, Greeley emphasized men's conscious motives. But, as the earlier quotation shows, he recognized that voting determinants operating on less conscious levels are no less potent. For our present purposes, the accuracy of Greeley's specific observation is immaterial. But his editorials illustrate how we can classify the determinants of American voting behavior under three main headings or categories. In time, I believe they can be developed to form an inclusive classification system; and dependent upon the specific elections and groups analyzed, we can devise subcategories for each of these three main categories:

1) *Pursuit of political goals by individuals or groups.* For example, the disestablishment of the "Standing Order of Orthodox Congregationalists" in Connecticut; the establishment of a protective tariff.

2) *Individual or group fulfillment of political roles.* For example, "Smithers is for a Tariff himself, but his father before him was a Democrat, and he isn't going to turn his coat"; Connecticut Episcopalians continuing long after 1818 to vote against the "Congregational Party."

3) *Negative or positive orientation to reference individuals or groups.* For example, "Jones hates the Whigs because Esq. Simpson is a leading Whig, and feels too big to speak to common people"; "Marks has been trained to believe that the Whigs were Tories in the Revolution and starved his father in the Jersey prisonship; so he is bound to hit them again at each Election." (The quotation would have exemplified positive orientation had it read: "Jones *likes* the Whigs because Esq. Simpson is an admirable man and he is a leading Whig.")

As is true of any classification system, these categories are doubtless easier to distinguish analytically than empirically. But surely significant differences exist and can be recognized among these three types of alleged behavior: a) Connecticut Episcopalians voting before 1818 to abolish a State Congregational Church; b) men voting Democratic because their fathers voted Democratic and they weren't going to "turn their coats"; c) men voting Democratic because they substituted the Whigs for the Tories who had maltreated their fathers.

A. PURSUIT OF POLITICAL GOALS. If, for our present purposes, we assume that Greeley accurately observed voting patterns, then a clear-cut political issue originally determined the voting behavior of Connecticut Episcopalians. They used political means to get the state to take "political action" which they regarded as beneficial to them, or to the community at large, or to both. Political actions are broadly defined here to include actions taken by any state agency in respect to laws, policies, rulings, government personnel, and government structure. Sometimes voters' choices (including no choices) are determined by their opinions of party positions on specified political actions, or a general, more vaguely-defined program of action; at other times, they are determined by the belief that the candidates of one party will carry out desired political actions either more effectively or more faithfully than will the candidates of another party. Whether the desired political actions represent grand "disinterested" measures, petty "selfish favors," or appointment of members of a particular group to a particular office, all behavior determined by such considerations is assigned to the category, "pursuit of political goals." Concrete examples may clarify the discussion and indicate how subdivisions can help differentiate voting behavior within the same main category.

According to this classification system, passage of a high tariff law and appointment or election of an Irish Catholic to high office are both defined as political goals. Desire for a high tariff exemplifies an economic goal, desire for appointment of an Irish Catholic exemplifies a status goal (that is, attainment of a political objective that would give members of certain groups greater power to command respect or deference from other members of the community or society). Though their motives differ significantly, men who pursue either one of those goals are seeking to get the state to take some action, or are approving some action the state has taken. In other words, their common desire for state action determines and links the behavior of men who pursue the different kinds of economic and status goals described above. (Of course, men can also pursue "nonpolitical" economic and status goals, that is, goals that do not require state action.)

For our present purposes, it is irrelevant whether voters are consciously aware that they are seeking political goals or whether historians can empirically distinguish among degrees of conscious awareness. The point is that, logically at least, a category can be

created to encompass all voting behavior designed to produce specified state actions. By definition, therefore, voting behavior determined by other considerations is assigned to one of our remaining
two categories.

B. FULFILLMENT OF POLITICAL ROLES. As the Greeley quotations
pungently suggest, men knew and used the concept of social role long
before social scientists invented the term. In this context, brief definition and exposition convey its central premise and indicate its usefulness to a theory of American voting behavior: "The ways of behaving which are expected of any individual who occupies a certain
position constitute the [social] *role* . . . associated with that position."[15]

Individuals occupy many positions, however, and the great majority of them do not usually carry expectations of prescribed *partisan*
political behavior (for example, males, husbands, adults). Moreover, role definitions vary, at least in the United States, and positions expected to produce certain ways of behaving politically at one
time and place do not necessarily carry the same expectations at
other times and places. In short, occupancy of a certain position
constitutes a "political role" only when it is associated with clearly
defined and recognized ways of behavior. Such roles, I contend, are
unlikely to be deduced theoretically by analysts and must be discovered empirically.

In Greeley's description, Smithers' father was a Democrat in an
era when sons were expected to vote for their fathers' parties. Thus,
despite his agreement with the Whigs on a "real" political issue
(tariff), he voted Democratic. Otherwise he would have regarded
himself and have been regarded by others as "turn[ing] his coat,"
that is, not fulfilling his political role. It is worth noting that Smithers could conceivably have favored a protective tariff strongly
enough to disregard the pressures exerted upon him by his political
role. That he did not do so indicates, therefore, the relative importance he attached to his political role and to his political goal.

Establishing the category "fulfillment of political roles" makes
it easier to discover in voting behavior essential similarities which
might otherwise appear disparate. Men may vote in a particular
fashion because they are their fathers' sons, because they are mem-

---

15 Theodore M. Newcomb, *Social Psychology* (New York, 1956 printing), 280. In
discussing and using the social role concept, I have considerably benefited from
reading the relevant chapters in this text on social psychology.

bers of certain ethnic, religious or socioeconomic groups, because they reside in certain areas or political units, because they belong to and are loyal to a certain political party. Whatever the surface differences, at least two significant uniformities characterize the voting behavior that fulfills political roles. It is determined primarily by membership in a certain group or occupancy of a certain position and by adherence to tradition or habit rather than by a desire to have the state take certain actions or follow a less precisely defined general course of action.

Inconveniently for a fool-proof classification of voting behavior, men's motives in real life are less neatly compartmented and less easily distinguished than we should like. But lines of demarcation are universal problems for analysts. Whatever phenomena or objects are classified, whatever kind of system is used, borderline cases always cause trouble and blurring always occurs as one moves away from the extremes. Though historians can never dispense with judgment in classifying determinants of voting behavior, the argument here is that agreement is not always impossible. For example, significant differences clearly distinguish these phenomena: 1) Connecticut Episcopalians using political means to rid themselves of politically-established disabilities; 2) the same men voting for one party because their group has traditionally done so.

In both of these hypothetical cases, membership in a religious group determined how men voted. But in the first case, to attain their objective some specific state action was necessary. In the second it was not; they may well have voted for the traditional party of their group even though they preferred the program of the opposing party and thought its candidates were better qualified. Thus it seems reasonable and possible to differentiate between the pursuit of political goals and the fulfillment of political roles.

C. ORIENTATION TO REFERENCE GROUPS AND INDIVIDUALS. Like the type of voting behavior assigned to the category "fulfillment of political roles," the type assigned to our third category is not primarily determined by a desire for specific state action. But it differs from the second type of behavior in a crucial respect: it designates men who behave according to patterns set by *groups to which they do not belong, or by certain individuals whose patterns influence them in determining their own.* The difference between those two categories is perhaps best suggested by quoting Robert K. Merton on the difference between "social role" and "reference group" theories: "That men act in a social frame of reference yielded by the groups of which they are a part is a notion undoubtedly ancient and probably sound. Were this alone the concern of reference group theory, it would merely be a new term for an old focus in sociology, which has always been centered on the group determination of behavior. There is, however, the further fact that men frequently orient themselves to groups *other than their own* in shaping their behavior and evaluations. . . .

"In general, then, reference group theory aims to systematize the determinants and consequences of those processes of evaluation and self-appraisal in which the individual takes the values or standards of other individuals and groups as a comparative frame of reference."[16]

Unlike Smithers, whose vote was determined by his political role, Marks voted Democratic because he identified the Whigs with the Tories and wanted "to hit them [Tories] again at each Election." In Merton's terms, the Tories represented for Marks a negative reference group. Thus his behavior fundamentally resembles that of Jones who voted against the Whigs because he identified them with the arrogant Esquire Simpson whom *he* wanted "to hit again at each Election." But we surely are justified in saying that the behavior of Smithers, Marks, and Jones differed from that of Connecticut Episcopalians who voted to achieve disestablishment, or from that of iron manufacturers in Essex County, New York, who, we have seen, voted to secure a high protective tariff.

In an attempt to distinguish between such varied types of voting behavior, some political analysts have classified men as acting rationally and irrationally. In my opinion, such categories have value connotations that make them necessarily subjective and drastically limit their usefulness. That contemporaries and later historians have sometimes stigmatized men's behavior as irrational because it was designed to achieve objectives that *they* regarded as undesirable is not news. And that historians with different frames of reference frequently disagree about the rationality of exactly the same behavior is not news either. Why then employ categories more likely to compound than to reduce confusion?

16 Robert K. Merton, *Social Theory and Social Structure*, 234. American historians in particular, I believe, would benefit heavily from the two chapters dealing with reference group theory. *Ibid.*, 225-386.

The system suggested here makes two assumptions that may help us to overcome subjective influences: 1) Men try to act so as to maximize their satisfactions. 2) Different men achieve maximum satisfaction in different ways. These assumptions, of course, tell us nothing about the kinds of men who find maximum satisfaction in specified types of behavior, nor why they do and other men do not. That is not the point. The point is that from these assumptions it logically follows that equally rational men may find maximum satisfaction in widely different or directly contradictory behaviors.

Judged by the criterion of maximum satisfaction, for example, it may have been as rational for Marks to hit the Whig-Tories and Jones to lash out at the arrogant Esquire Simpson as for iron manufacturers to vote Whig in order to secure a high tariff. *The different objectives to be achieved, rather than the degree of rationality displayed*, is what intrinsically differentiates those two types of behavior. And, I maintain, historians are more likely to agree about the different objectives men want to achieve than they are about the "rationality" of men's different objectives.

To act either in agreement with or in opposition to the pattern established by some other individual or some group other than their own is the objective of men whose voting behavior is assigned to this third category. By definition, therefore, the question of what determines the behavior of the reference groups or individuals is irrelevant; the relevant point is that they help to determine the voting behavior either of men who belong to other groups or of other individuals.

D. COMBINATIONS OF DETERMINANTS. It is worth repeating that the three main categories sketched above are more easily established analytically than demonstrated empirically. It is also worth noting that I do not regard monistic explanations of voting behavior as credible, whether the "single factor" is ascribed to all men or to specific individuals and groups. "No man," Coleridge observed, "does anything from a single motive." Thus the problem of interpreting voting behavior at a given time and place is always to decide which *combination of determinants* influenced voters identified by some attribute, or set of attributes. Under certain conditions, and in certain cases, it may be possible to give particularly heavy weight to one determinant or factor. But such assessments are not monistic. They recognize that other determinants contribute to the same result, although to a lesser degree.

Having sketched a crude, partial theory of American voting behavior and a classification system consonant with it, we can now apply them to New York voting patterns in 1844.

CHAPTER XIV

INTERPRETING NEW YORK VOTING BEHAVIOR

IN RECENT DECADES, a "great debate" has raged, to an unprecedented extent, over historiographic theory. Oversimplifying, we can identify the two main schools of American contestants as "subjective relativists" and "objective reconstructionists." They have engaged in sustained theoretical battles, but have been unable to reach even partial agreement. The former argue that assessing the significance and relevance of data must inevitably be left largely to subjective, personal judgment; the latter argue that if relevant source materials are available, historians can develop concepts and procedures that help them to minimize the role of subjective factors while they try to reconstruct past reality, independently of personal frames of reference, ethical values, and visions of the good and the beautiful.[1]

Since the debate centers around the most fundamental issues in historiography, it is likely, at best, to remain unresolved for a long time. But the area of disagreement has, I believe, been exaggerated. Unnecessary confusion has resulted from failure to distinguish among substantive questions according to their intrinsic difficulty. Put another way, even when relevant data are available, some types of questions are necessarily more difficult to answer than others. It is more difficult, for example, to find out why New Yorkers voted as they did in 1844 than to find out what happened in that election compared to other elections, or find out who voted for whom. These questions are radically different. Their solutions require radically different kinds of data and procedures. It seems useful, therefore, to distinguish between "factual questions" and "interpretative questions."

Answers to factual questions tell the historian in effect what he has to explain; by definition they do not require him to engage in inter-

[1] Those ideas were developed at length in a paper I gave at a session of the 1954 meeting of the American Historical Association, "An Operational Approach to Historiography" (Bureau of Applied Social Research, Columbia University, 1954, dittoed). Subjective relativist views predominate in Social Science Research Council, *Bulletin 54, Theory and Practice in Historical Study* (New York, 1946); objective reconstructionist views predominate in SSRC, *Bulletin 64, The Social Sciences in Historical Study* (New York, 1954).

pretation. Though they present technical difficulties, call for systematic, painstaking research, require intellectual clarity and good judgment in drawing logical inferences, objective answers to them can be obtained without resort to subjective values and personal frames of reference. For example, historians who differ over the good and the beautiful are not likely *on that account* to differ over the credibility of answers to who voted for whom in New York in the 1844 election. Differences may arise, of course, but it is less likely that they would stem from conflicting subjective values, or that they could not be resolved by collection and ordering of the relevant "factual data"—provided that the source materials were available and that procedures had been developed that were capable of extracting those data from the sources. The argument, in short, is that the relativist-reconstructionist debate concerns primarily one type of question, and that a great deal of historical research deals with phenomena which are intrinsically capable of objective reconstruction.

Further, once factual questions are credibly answered, historians stand in a far better position to pose interpretative questions in meaningful and reasonably precise form. Questions can then be derived from reasonably well-documented facts or inferences, not from metaphysical, or vague, or erroneous impressions. And systematically establishing the "facts" not only suggests the relevant interpretative questions to raise, but simultaneously narrows the range of possible answers and gives researchers the psychological security of knowing they are erecting soundly-based structures of explanation.[2]

A. Patterns in New York
Voting Behavior

To get down to cases: Before we can regard any interpretation of 1844 New York voting behavior as "potentially verifiable," we must show that it conforms to all known facts and credible inferences about what happened and who voted for whom.[3] Once we recognize that the Jacksonians won either by narrow majorities before 1837 or by narrow pluralities after that date, or frequently failed to win by any margin, it will surely become apparent that there is no basis

[2] Discussions with Paul F. Lazarsfeld impressed me with the utility of distinguishing between questions that are essentially factual and essentially interpretative.
[3] The "potentially verifiable" concept is discussed in Lee Benson, "Research Problems in American Political Historiography," in Komarovsky, ed., *Common Frontiers of the Social Sciences*, pp. 118-119.

for explanations that tell why they were the "popular party." Similarly, explanations of why the Jacksonians won strong support from low-status socioeconomic groups or classes become incredible once we recognize that, in fact, they did not win such support. This book's interpretation of New York voting behavior, therefore, has been developed from the group patterns that have been established with *reasonable* credibility and *reasonable* accuracy. Further research may modify or discredit those patterns, but at the moment they appear to possess substantial credibility.[4]

1. Polarity in Voting

New York voters did not divide along class lines. Other nonpolarized voting patterns are also evident. Major party strength varied considerably in the rural counties and, to a lesser extent, in the cities, but an urban-rural cleavage had not yet materialized; that is, neither the Democrats nor the Whigs drew disproportionately from urban or rural voters. Though political cleavages had developed between free thinkers and orthodox believers and between puritans and non-puritans, and though we can say that a "Catholic vote" apparently existed by 1844, a "Protestant vote" had not yet manifested itself. There are some indications of sectarian political divisions, but none that members of that broad group generally showed any preferences *as Protestants* for either major party. Similarly, native groups, with the exception of Negroes and Huguenots, had not yet developed polarized voting patterns, although perceptible differences existed among them. As earlier chapters have attempted to demonstrate, with the exception of free thinkers, puritans, Negroes and Huguenots, post-1790 immigrants were the only groups who displayed sharply polarized voting patterns in New York. All the New British groups overwhelmingly voted Whig; all the New non-British groups overwhelmingly voted Democratic.

Viewed superficially, these nonpolarized voting patterns might seem to support the argument that voting behavior cannot be interpreted objectively. It might be argued that the historian, confronted

---

[4] To an extraordinary extent, some historians have tended to treat Martin Van Buren's partisan rhetoric as gospel truth. For example, they have accepted his thesis that American political struggles have invariably pitted "the business community" against other sections of society. See his *Inquiry into the Origin and Course of Political Parties in the United States* (New York, 1867), 175-232, particularly 226-227. It is worth repeating that I do not maintain that my claims have been "proven," only that they appear to me more credible than any other claims yet made about the social bases of New York voting behavior.

with an apparently random distribution of behavior, must either eschew interpretation or stress some motive (or variable) that derives from his subjective frame of reference. And that argument might seem to be strengthened when we recall that content analyses revealed distinct differences in the principles and policies of the major parties in New York. If the party differences were distinctly different, and yet the great bulk of the electorate distributed their ballots at random, how then can we expect to reconstruct objectively men's motives for voting?

But the operative words in the above paragraph are "viewed superficially." Even if we exclude areas where immigrants tended to live in significant numbers, when we get down to the *town and ward level*, it becomes evident that voting patterns actually were sharply polarized rather than evenly divided. That is, many rural towns and urban wards cast very heavy Democratic or Whig votes. In different counties, and frequently within the same county, members of the same native group did vote strongly Democratic in some towns and strongly Whig in others. But since *polarized local* voting patterns did exist, *the absence of political polarization among native groups identified by widely inclusive group attributes* (ethnocultural, religious, class, residence) is highly significant; this is in effect the same kind of observation that Sherlock Holmes made when he recognized the significance of the finding, "the dog *didn't* bark."

For example, recognition that revived nativist, anti-Catholic movements scored impressive political successes during the 1850's tells us much about the failure of the American Republicans to receive support in 1844 (except in areas with relatively large percentages of Catholic and New non-British immigrants).[5] Seen in that perspective, the failure of the American Republicans shows that the conditions which would lead the native Protestant electorate to respond politically to nativist, anti-Catholic issues had not yet developed during the 1840's. It is not surprising, therefore, that perceptible Democratic-Whig differences over those issues should have had relatively little impact upon voting behavior patterns firmly fixed before 1844. Similarly, the failure of the Liberty Party to re-

[5] My 1954 paper, "An Operational Approach to Historiography," advanced the hypothesis that the nativist, anti-Catholic movements of the 1850's not only derived their force from the rapid increase in immigration after 1844, but were largely responsible for the political "revolution" that began in 1854. That hypothesis will be developed in a subsequent book, tentatively entitled, "New York Public Opinion and the American Civil War: An Essay in the Logic and Practice of Historical Inquiry."

ceive support except from a small number of "ultraist" Whigs testifies to the limited political impact of issues connected with slavery.
Under those conditions, our theory would predict that a "wide
variety of factors" influenced native Protestant voters throughout
the state—a prediction consonant with the marked variations in
major party strength evident on the level of rural towns and urban
wards.

It is true that the major New York parties differed distinctly over
principles and policies, but seen in perspective, their differences were
relatively narrow in scope. That is, the differences manifested themselves within the framework of deep agreement on political fundamentals. Despite their clashes over the positive state, locus of government power, role of different government branches, and foreign policy,
both the Democrats and Whigs stood firmly committed to political
democracy (for white men) and to liberal capitalism. And both were
committed at least officially to separation of church and state—
although, as the content analyses in Chapter X were designed to
show, the Whigs projected an image calculated to win support from
pious Protestants. Significantly, the only really sharp cleavages
evident among native voters in 1844—the orthodox-free thinker and
puritan-nonpuritan splits—related to fundamental church-state
issues.

The above "facts" seem to warrant the inference that party differences over *socioeconomic* issues did not have sufficient impact to
alter voting patterns already fixed by 1832; some localized, minor
shifts and some temporary fluctuations occurred, but the patterns
remained essentially unchanged. Irreconcilable with the Jacksonian
Democracy assumption that socioeconomic principles and policies
primarily determined political cleavages, this finding "fits" the theory of voting behavior derived from the Hofstadter-Hartz thesis.
In the absence of intense, widespread ethnocultural and religious
conflicts, the theory predicts that American voting patterns will
vary widely among members of native groups identified by any of
the broad attributes noted above. Instead of dividing into solid blocs,
voters are likely to be more or less influenced by: 1) long-established
political associations and loyalties (going back decades and, in some
places, generations) ; 2) local leadership and local antagonisms having nothing properly to do with politics, according to the Horace
Greeley definition of political propriety (p. 280) ; 3) local historical
traditions, conflicts, needs, and issues; 4) differences in party or-

ganization and control over communication media, as well as differences in control over ostensibly nonpolitical institutions.

In short, the theory leads to this prediction: unless very intense ethnocultural and religious antagonisms fuse members of the dominant native Protestant group into solid blocs, a multiplicity of "localistic" factors will produce wide variations in their voting patterns.

Far from conceding that marked variations on the town and ward level prevent objective interpretations of American voting behavior, I believe that the theory advanced here, together with sufficiently detailed research, can produce credible explanations of why certain native Protestant communities in New York voted strongly Democratic and others strongly Whig. To support that contention, without in any sense claiming to "prove" it, I offer an analysis of voting behavior in Rockland and Chautauqua counties, the highest and second lowest-ranking Democratic counties in 1844. (Chautauqua, instead of Genesee, the lowest-ranking county, is used because several unusually good local histories can be drawn upon; the available Genesee histories are comparatively less useful.)

B. Voting Behavior in Rockland and Chautauqua Counties

If we take into account the state's remarkably heterogeneous electorate, no two counties in New York can serve as an adequate sample for interpretative analyses. If we wanted to provide a detailed interpretation of local variations in voting behavior, we would have to analyze almost microscopically at least ten or twelve counties. But since the purpose is to illustrate concretely the general conclusion that "localistic" factors significantly influenced native Protestant voting patterns from 1826 to 1844, examination of two extreme counties enables us economically to isolate and identify some of the major factors that produced variations in party support among members of the dominant group in New York State.

1. Rockland County

From the first Jackson campaign under the Albany Regency's colors in 1828, Rockland County led all the rest in devotion to the party rallying around "Old Hero." Earning that distinction in 1828 by the narrowest of margins (71.5 per cent compared to Putnam's 71.4 per cent), it widened the gap over time. The marked general tendency toward less dispersion of county percentages after 1832 has already been noted (Chapter VII), but in 1844 Rockland still cast a very high Democratic vote, 68.0 per cent, compared to 64.0 per cent in second-ranking Putnam. What kind of a county was Rockland and how can we explain its voting behavior patterns? (The observations offered below are not *equally* applicable to all communities belonging to the same ethnocultural category as Rockland. That Rockland cast a much heavier Democratic vote than the overall estimate of 60 per cent for Yorkers demonstrates that it was not typical. But precisely because it was not typical, analysis of that county deepens our understanding of the Jackson Party's mass support and helps us to identify some factors that led certain kinds of men to rally around Jacksonian symbols, creeds, and programs.)

A. THE PAST AS PROLOGUE TO THE PRESENT. Rockland, located on the west bank of the Hudson opposite Westchester County, was first settled in the seventeenth century by Dutch farmers. Originally part of Orange County, it achieved independent status in 1798. By 1844 it contained some small-scale manufacturing and commercial establishments. Its population included considerable numbers of transplanted Yankees in Ramapo and Irish Catholics in Haverstraw, but it can still be regarded as the prototype of the prosperous old Dutch farming communities that dotted the Hudson, Mohawk, and Schoharie valleys.[6]

Even before Antimasonry erupted in 1827, when election time came around, Rockland already counted heavy Van Buren Republican majorities. In 1820, for example, 87.7 per cent of the county's voters cast ballots for "Little Van's" faction. That figure, however, was unusually high and in 1826, just before the new fluctuation phase began, the Van Burenites received only 59.6 per cent of Rockland's vote. Written in the late nineteenth century by a "native son," a local history provides valuable insights into the county's political allegiance after 1787. The disastrous aftermath of the Revolution ". . . touched lightly on Orange [which then included Rockland]. She was a producer that supplied for her own consumption and had surplusage. Liberty to her residents meant as little interference from outside sources as possible. It was with an unpleasant feeling that

---

[6] J. H. Mather and L. P. Brockett, *A Geographical History of the State of New York* (Utica, N. Y., 1848), 273-276; David Cole, ed., *History of Rockland County, passim*; Frank B. Green, *History of Rockland County* (New York, 1886), *passim*; Arthur S. Tompkins, ed., *Historical Record . . . of Rockland County* (Nyack, N. Y., 1902), *passim*.

they submitted to a majority rule in the State government, when that rule did not benefit them, and they paid their ever increasing taxes for the benefit of sister counties, which were not yet self-supporting, with many a murmur. But those sections they thus aided indirectly were of their own State.

"When now therefore, the proposition to form a central government was heard, it was greeted by the residents of this County with vehement protest . . . the people of Orange felt that the proposed federation was only a name for another form of tyranny, and that under the simple title of President lurked the authority of King."[7]

Perhaps an even stronger reason for the county's political course, suggested the same historian, derived from Governor George Clinton's unchallenged leadership of the agrarian up-country. Together with other "representative men of Orange and Ulster," Clinton resisted the adoption of the Federal Constitution and carried those River counties along with him. (Ulster registered 95 per cent against the Constitution and Orange apparently failed to cast a single Federalist vote.)[8] "I have dwelt at length on the topic of the feeling in this section toward the National Constitution because it explains Rockland's stand in politics. Two creeds are transmitted from parents to children through generations, that of their religion and that of their political faith, and it is seldom that either is changed. The question of Federation or not found our County Anti-Federal. Incensed by defeat, the opposition to centralization grew, became stronger as the years passed, and at last found its party affiliation and name in the rise of Democracy. The spirit of County love, the intermarriage between members of long-resident families, have kept an unusually large proportion of natives in the County, and those old families retain their reverence for the political faith of their fathers."[9]

Before we reformulate this perceptive analysis of political stability in Rockland, let us look closely at the county's prototype community.

B. THE BANNER TOWN OF THE NEW YORK DEMOCRACY. Clarkstown, a very prosperous agricultural town fronting on the river, gave the Democrats 89.9 per cent of its vote in 1844 and became the banner unit of the New York Jackson Party and the most homogeneous

[7] Green, *Rockland County*, 149.
[8] *Ibid.*, 150-151. For the popular votes on the Constitution, see the table in E. Wilder Spaulding, *New York In The Critical Period* (New York, 1932), 203.
[9] Green, *op.cit.*, 152, 293.

political community by a considerable margin. That astonishing figure was no fluke; in 1820 the town recorded 230 of its 242 votes for "Little Van's" faction.

Socially as well as politically, Clarkstown constituted a remarkably homogeneous community. In fact, if we accept some propositions recently advanced by social psychologists, the sentence is best reformulated: because Clarkstown constituted such a socially homogenous community, it functioned as such a politically homogeneous one. Though expressed in terms perhaps unfamiliar and uncongenial, these propositions advanced by social psychologists have considerable potential usefulness for American historiography:

"With respect to uniformity of group opinion, we can specify two major mechanisms affecting uniformity. Communication among the members of the group will tend to result in shared opinions. The more interaction within the group, the greater the uniformity of any given amount of opinion within the group. At the same time, the effectiveness of any given amount of communication within the group is a function of the extent to which members of the group feel needs to stay within the group. Thus, the greater the *cohesiveness of the group*, the greater the uniformity of group opinion. . . . We can specify two major additional propositions within this subsystem [of variables affecting opinion uniformity]. First, the interaction in the group increases as group cohesiveness increases. Second, increases in the uniformity of group opinion result in increases in group cohesiveness. That is, not only does group identification affect the goals of individuals who identify with the group, but also the identification of others with groups affects the strength of group pressures on the individual. . . . Group cohesiveness also is positively related to the range of control exercised by the group. The more cohesive the group, the more willing are its members to enforce group demands on the individual. Group cohesiveness restricts intragroup competition that would otherwise weaken the group's control over the individual member."

And the final proposition is: "The stronger the individual's identification with a group, the more likely that his goals will conform to his perception of group norms."[10]

During the period covered by this study, probably no community in New York provided a better test for and illustration of these propositions than did Clarkstown.

[10] James G. March and Herbert A. Simon, *Organizations* (New York, 1958), 60-61, 65.

The first Dutch settlers began cultivating its fertile soil in 1686, and it remained "emphatically an agricultural town" as late as the 1880's. It then possessed more tillable land than any other township in the county, was still devoted almost entirely to agriculture, and contained no large villages. To a remarkable extent its inhabitants were "connected by ties of blood or marriage." Further strengthening and tightening social bonds, the Dutch Reformed Church, formally organized in 1749, remained the only one in town until 1824. An offshoot took root in that year, but the mother church continued to flourish, boasted the "handsomest, costliest" building and was "considered the pride of the village." As one local historian put it, with the early inhabitants, particularly the leading families, the Dutch Reformed Church functioned as the major community institution and served both "as a religious and social centre."[11]

One substantive example dramatically illustrates the stolidly conservative spirit, set of beliefs, style of life, and mode of action of that Dutch farming community. Particularly in the close-knit village of Clarksville, more than a century and a quarter after settlement began, many inhabitants had retained their ancestors' belief in witchcraft "and many hair-raising tales were told by them on cold winter nights beside the blazing wood fire and the light of 'tallow dips.' " As a result, "This neighborhood has the doubtful honor of having been the scene of the last trial for witchcraft held in New York State, possibly the last among a so-called civilized people."[12]

During the early nineteenth century, butter production had not yet progressed to where Dutch farm wives invariably succeeded in "making their churnings." But one year, failures were unusually frequent and many other strange portents and signs appeared to suggest that a supernatural agency was bewitching the community. In time, suspicion came to fasten on an "outsider," the widow of a Scotch physician who lived isolated and alone. Excitement mounted so rapidly that an extra-legal jury of neighborhood farmers convened to subject her to trial by time-tested methods. "The place selected for the trial was an old mill, which stood on the site of the present mill. The mode of trial was by balance. The suspected woman was brought to the mill, was seated in one dish of the big mill scale, and held till a board-covered, brass-bound Bible was placed in the opposite dish. If, in the test which was to follow, the Bible out-

<hr />

11 Cole, ed., *Rockland County*, 112-127; Green, 414-426; Tompkins, ed., *Historical Record of Rockland*, 1: 415-432.
12 *Ibid.*, 446; Green, 418-419.

weighed the woman, it would be conclusive evidence that she was in league with the evil one. If to the contrary, she raised the Bible, it was equally conclusive she was innocent."

Fortunately for the widow, she raised the board-covered, brass-bound Bible.[13]

C. FULFILLMENT OF POLITICAL ROLES. Though this fragment of Rockland folklore has undoubtedly been colored in the telling over time, it vividly illustrates the propositions cited above and points up a fundamental culture characteristic of many Dutch (and Palatine and Old British) farming communities in eastern New York. In my opinion, we need not force the material to see underlying uniformities in Clarkstown's witchcraft trial, the Rip Van Winkle legend of the long sleep, and the retention by the old families in Rockland and other eastern counties of "their reverence for the political faith of their fathers." Among other things, these phenomena all reveal ingrained resistance to change, stubborn preservation of old modes of thought and old ways of doing things, and the operation of powerful sanctions to maintain group solidarity and adherence to group norms.[14]

In several senses, time marched on during the era of Transportation Revolution and passed by Clarkstown's inhabitants. Taking little heed of sweeping changes in many other communities, they tilled their ancestral fields much as their ancestors had tilled them and they abided by their fathers' faith in state rights and negative government. More precisely, in accounting for the extraordinarily high Democratic percentage in Clarkstown (and many other Yorker communities), I give heavy weight to their fulfillment of political roles.

But it is not enough to invoke the concept of fulfillment of political roles and write that men voted as their fathers did or had. Inertia may be the first law of history; change surely runs it a close second. Under what conditions one or the other predominates is, in major respects, *the* historical question. Obviously in 1844 not all men everywhere in New York trod political paths marked out by their

[13] Green, 419.

[14] For example, see the description of Coeyman's Landing in Albany County, which, in the late nineteenth century "retains in a marked degree much of its ancient conservative Dutch sentiment, and the spirit of modern progress has been dormant these two hundred years. . . ." Its early settlers were "largely of the Dutch," and they "held with tenacity to the traditions of their fathers." George R. Howell, ed., *History of the County of Albany, N. Y.* (New York, 1886), 824-837.

fathers, or by themselves, in previous elections. As the 1827 to 1832 and 1854 to 1860 fluctuation phases demonstrate, traditional party loyalties do not always form immovable barriers to change.

It is true, of course, that the Dutch and general Yorker cultural pattern placed a relatively high premium upon stability and actively distrusted innovation, particularly when compared with cultural patterns common among the "restless Yankees" in some sections of the state. "The Dutch," begins a barbed, revealing anecdote, "are hard to be moved. . . ."[15] Although that hard-to-be-moved pattern accounts largely for the decisive impact of political roles in Rockland, I believe it was reinforced by determinants best assigned to the other two categories, "pursuit of political goals" and "orientation to reference groups and individuals."

D. PURSUIT OF POLITICAL GOALS. Whatever their long-range impact, the Erie Canal and similar "internal improvements" tended in the short run to injure rather than benefit farming communities in eastern New York. Unquestionably, improved transportation facilities in the state's central, western, and northern sections seriously diminished Rockland's prized location advantages.[16] Thus, as the quotation on pages 294-295 suggests, neither William Seward's "magnificent" plans for internal improvement nor Henry Clay's vision of an "American System" was calculated to fire enthusiasm among Rockland farmers who by "instinct" and by tradition abhorred state expenditures and taxation for any purpose, let alone to aid "competitors."

Unless gifted with unusual foresight and capable of visualizing the indirect, long-range benefits that positive government action designed to foster the "general welfare" might eventually bring them, Rockland's tradition-minded and tradition-bound farmers were, like their post-Revolutionary sires, likely to respond to the party that preached the doctrines of the negative liberal state and state rights. Part of their tradition, it is crucial to note, was resistance to social order imposed by political government, as distinct from social order imposed by community mores and customs. Emphasis upon the almost instinctive differences between Dutch individualism and Yankee propensity for official community action must

15 Dixon Ryan Fox, *Yankees and Yorkers*, 199.

16 For an excellent analysis, see David M. Ellis, *Landlords and Farmers in the Hudson-Mohawk Region: 1790-1850*, 159-183. As late as 1882, the Erie Canal was being denounced as ruinous to agriculture in eastern New York. See my *Merchants, Farmers, and Railroads*, p. 170.

be ranked high among Dixon Ryan Fox's most perceptive insights.[17] Translated into our terms, areas influenced by the Dutch tradition were more likely to respond to political doctrines logically and psychologically consonant with egoistic and localistic outlooks, attitudes, and habits than to "collectivistic," universalistic, political doctrines.

Viewed superficially, Rockland's resistance to an ambitious state program of internal improvement and its devotion to the Jackson Party might lend support to the Jacksonian Democracy concept and contradict the argument presented in this study. Again the operative phrase is "viewed superficially." In the first place, appeals to "economic interest" *reinforced* behavior patterns that long antedated Jackson's leadership. Second, and more significantly, Rockland attitudes and opinions on internal improvements must be seen as only one expression of a pervasive, deep-rooted cultural antipathy to state action of any kind, whether to improve transportation facilities (especially other areas' facilities), to "regulate the consciences of men," or to raise educational levels and intellectual capacities. A concrete illustration may clarify and support the generalization.

As noted previously, pious Yankees tended to respond to Antimasonic-Whig appeals for state-guided and state-enforced "moral reformation." In contrast, though the Dutch did not lack piety or respect for ecclesiastical authority, their conception of the church "was by no means as vivid and embracing as that held in New England. Along the Hudson or on the islands about the harbor [of New Amsterdam] it would have seemed absurd to adopt church membership as the touchstone of political capacity." That Fox was referring to seventeenth century Yankee-Dutch antagonisms only points up the deep-rooted nature of their cultural differences. Actually, he went back even further: "The United Netherlands, to be sure, were as Protestant as England, and more so, but there was little or no ecclesiastical tyranny. The church, dominated by the Calvinist tradition, took little direction from the state. James the First across the channel, justified the English system with an epigram, 'no bishop, no king'; the Dutch wanted neither."[18]

Fox's observations, translated into our terms and period, help to explain Rockland's strong Jacksonian proclivity. The inference seems reasonable that the classically liberal Dutch tradition influenced the county's voters to pursue political goals which called for

[17] Fox, *Yankees and Yorkers*, 65-71.   [18] *Ibid.*, 34-35, 66-67.

minimal state action. But surely it is significant that in 1826, after the Erie Canal had gone into full operation, Rockland gave only 59.6 per cent of its votes to the Van Buren faction; after the Antimasonic crusade began, however, it cast 71.5 per cent of its votes for the *anti*-"Church and State" party in 1828, and 72.4 per cent in 1832. This pronounced shift between the two equilibrium years underlines and sharpens observations made in earlier chapters: although issues touching upon church and state relationships had explosive political potential, it was not religious piety in general but puritanism in particular that conditioned men to respond to the Antimasonic-Whig positive state doctrines. As the *Albany Argus* angrily asserted,[19] the anti-Jacksonians had no basis for claiming that they were "the party of all the 'religion' and all the 'decency.' " Among other things, the vote in Clarkstown and many other "God-fearing," "respectable" Yorker communities strikingly demonstrated that the anti-Jacksonians were at best the party of men dedicated to a *particular* conception of "religion" and "decency."

E. NEGATIVE REFERENCE GROUPS. In addition to fulfillment of political roles and pursuit of political goals, negative orientation to reference groups was among the cluster of determinants responsible for Rockland's leading the Democratic list. Specifically, the Dutch and other Yorkers in Rockland appear to have ranged themselves politically against the Yankees and Negroes—and voted accordingly.

The estimate in Chapter VIII had Yankees voting 55 per cent Whig, 45 per cent Democratic, but that estimate applies to the state as a whole. In areas where the Dutch and Yankees came into more or less direct contact, we can reasonably infer from the voting statistics that social and cultural antagonisms found political expression. As noted in the same chapter, Rockland's lowest-ranking Democratic unit was Ramapo, an interior agricultural town originally settled by twice-transplanted Yankees from Hempstead, Long Island. But the Ramapo electorate was by no means exclusively Yankee, for over time many Dutch from neighboring towns had drifted into it and diluted its Yankee character. This seems to account for its 56.5 per cent Democratic vote and Clarkstown's 89.9 per cent Democratic vote. Additional support for this inference derives from the patterns of high-Yorker, high-Democratic town and low-Yorker, low-Democratic town that tend to show up in almost all counties where the Yorkers and Yankees competed for dominance.

19 See pp. 195-196 above.

No systematic study of Yankee-Yorker antagonisms has yet been made, but impressionistic evidence concerning their existence and intensity is abundant and convincing. One of Rockland's local histories, for example, freely commented upon the antagonism between Dutch and English settlers, and the chronicler of Ramapo offered this revealing account of early Rockland church history: ". . . About the year 1750 (possibly in the case of the English Church a trifle earlier) two churches were organized in the neighborhood, the one in what was afterward Ramapo; the one for the Dutch and so designated; the one a Reformed church; the other a Presbyterian; the natural result of the denominational preferences which the different founders had brought with them from their native lands."[20]

To illustrate the generalization made in Chapter VI that essential uniformities exist among ethnocultural antagonisms, whether those antagonisms express themselves within the "native Protestant" group or between its members and "foreign Catholics": an 1807 newspaper advertisement for men to work on turnpikes in Greene County, not far up the Hudson from Rockland, succinctly informed readers: "No Dutchman need apply unless he is pretty well Yankeyfied."[21]

A century later, in hailing the better relations that eventually developed between the two groups, the descendant of a leading Dutch family in New York State bore witness to the intensity of their erstwhile antagonisms. His introduction to a Schenectady County history observed: "We Dutchmen of old, from old Peter Stuyvesant down, abhorred the Yankee and the prejudice of the Mohawk [Valley] Dutchmen was the most stolid of them all. The repulsion was natural, not entirely unreasonable. The New Englander was smart, the burgher was only honest. . . . The restless eagerness of the Down Easter disturbed the taciturn Hollander who, secure in the conviction of his own honesty and that of his old neighbors distrusted that glibness to which his race fell easy victims. In olden time the interloper was received because he could not be kept away, but his probation was long before he met a warm welcome by the Dutchman's fireside."[22]

Though we must concede the absence of any systematic study bearing on the point, the inference seems logical that the Antimasonic excitement intensified the Dutch tendency to regard Yankees as a

20 Cole, op.cit., 285.
21 J. B. Beers & Co., History of Greene County, New York, 53.
22 Austin A. Yates, Schenectady County, New York (New York, 1902), VII.

negative reference group and to shape their voting behavior accordingly. As repeatedly emphasized above, it is true that many Yankee communities, particularly in eastern and northern New York, remained steadfastly Van Buren Republican-Jackson Democrat. But the overwhelmingly Yankee counties in western New York "notoriously" formed the enthusiastic core of the anti-Van Buren-Jackson forces. If the argument is sound, those Antimasonic-Whig voters tended to be precisely the kind of puritanical, activist Yankees most offensive to "Dutchmen of old." Moreover, they demanded precisely the kind of activist, collectivist state most repugnant to those "Dutchmen." It seems reasonable, therefore, to infer that hostility to puritanical Yankees significantly reinforced and increased Rockland's traditional devotion to the party championing state rights and opposing positive state action.

The available evidence also suggests that hostility to Negroes influenced Rockland voting behavior. During the eighteenth century many slaves were owned in Rockland (and eastern New York generally), and the state did not abolish the institution until 1827. In the rural areas, the Dutch probably used slave labor to a greater extent than any other Yorker group. Several different kinds of data suggest that the Rockland electorate resented the movement for emancipation before 1827, and the movements for free Negro unrestricted suffrage in New York and nation-wide abolition thereafter.

In 1792 Governor George Clinton, the leader of the Orange and Ulster "yeomanry," was up for reelection. Among other things, his supporters denounced his opponent, John Jay, as the president of the Manumission Society who desired "to rob every Dutchman of the property he possesses most dear to his heart, his slaves. . . ."[23]

By the 1830's and 1840's New York State's abolition of slavery was no longer a live issue. But issues relating to free Negroes and slavery increasingly came to the fore. Thus the Weed-Seward-Greeley wing of the Whig Party strenuously urged passage of a constitutional amendment providing equal suffrage for Negroes. Eventually, a referendum on the amendment was held in 1846 and Rockland County voted 96.4 per cent against equal suffrage, narrowly trailing two other eastern New York counties in this clear-cut test of anti-Negro sentiment.[24]

An observation in a local history provides another excellent indi-

---

23 E. Wilder Spaulding, *His Excellency George Clinton* (New York) 1938, 202.
24 Computed from statistics in *The Whig Almanac For 1847* (New York, 1847), 44.

cator of the county's deep and abiding hostility to Negroes. "In Rockland County were many, who, for one reason or another, defended slavery. The passage of the 'Fugitive Slave Law' [in 1850] found these citizens willing and anxious to execute its mandates."[25] Nothing similar can be found in histories of strong Whig counties.

As will be noted in greater detail below, virulent hostility to free Negroes was part of the political stock in trade of the New York Jackson Party. Thus the data in this section suggest that the party's attitudes toward free Negroes and its position on the equal suffrage and slavery issues perceptibly strengthened its attraction for Rockland County voters.

2. Chautauqua County

During the 1827 to 1853 cycle, New York voting behavior most closely approached equilibrium in 1844. In that year, if we compare Chautauqua and Rockland counties, we find that within the general framework of American and New York life they resembled each other in only one basic characteristic. Although Chautauqua was more agrarian,[26] agriculture dominated the social and cultural structures of both counties.

A. THE PAST AS DIFFERENT FROM THE PRESENT. Rockland, located on the Hudson River, had excellent transportation facilities to the largest city and seaport in the country; Chautauqua, located on the southwestern border of the state, had relatively poor transportation facilities to any city. Completion of the Erie Canal in 1825 ended Chautauqua's isolation, but not until May 14, 1851, when the Erie Railroad finally reached the village of Dunkirk on Lake Erie, did the county begin to enjoy good transportation facilities: "The consummation of the great enterprise, which had been anxiously awaited through long years of doubt and despondency, was appropriately followed by a CELEBRATION AT DUNKIRK.

"This was a joyous occasion, not only to the citizens of this county, but to thousands in every county in the 'southern tier.' These 'sequestered counties,' as they had long been called, having participated but slightly in the benefits of the 'grand canal,' were at length favored with a 'road to market.' "[27]

---

25 Green, 283.

26 In 1840, agricultural pursuits occupied 80.9 per cent of the labor force in Chautauqua, 63.1 per cent in Rockland. Computed from the 1840 census statistics in J. Disturnell, *A Gazetteer of the State of New York*, 449-472.

27 Andrew W. Young, *History of Chautauqua County, New York* . . . (Buffalo,

Rockland was settled in the seventeenth century; Chautauqua was inhabited only by Indians until 1802 when the first white man "fully consummate[d] a settlement by acquiring an ownership to the soil and making real, substantial and permanent improvements."[28] But large numbers of migrants did not come to Chautauqua until the 1820's, when the "prospect of the early completion of the Erie Canal stimulated emigration."[29] Unlike the previous settlers who were "mostly frontiersmen from the western borders of settlements in New York and Pennsylvania," the new migrants were from settled communities in New England and eastern New York.[30] Thus, although Scotch-Irish and Germans from Pennsylvania predominated among the early settlers, by 1845 the people of Chautauqua were "mainly of New England extraction," and "nearly all of American birth, and almost entirely of British descent . . . never have the people of the county been so purely of British extraction since then."[31] As Rockland was the prototype of the old Dutch communities in eastern New York, Chautauqua was the prototype of the new Yankee communities in western New York.

The Rockland Dutch, who settled at an earlier date and enjoyed better transportation facilities than the Chautauqua Yankees, also enjoyed greater prosperity. As we have seen in Chapter VII, even after completion of the Erie Canal the Chautauqua settlers tended to find the going so hard that they organized violent "agrarian movements." To quote a local historian on conditions in 1835, "The inhabitants were still poor, their lands in most instances were unpaid for, and all that they had was represented by the labor that they had expended in clearing and improving their lands." Between 1835 and 1845, conditions failed to improve, and toward the decade's close the county "was actually decreasing in population. This remarkable falling off in the increase of population, from 1835 to 1845 is believed to have been due to the fact that there was during that period a large emigration from Chautauqua County to the west, caused by the hard times that followed the great financial crash in 1837, and the discouraging delay in building the Erie Railroad."[32]

N.Y., 1875), 150-151. See also Emory F. Warren, *Sketches of the History of Chautauque County* (Jamestown, N.Y., 1846), 85; Chautauqua History Company, *Centennial History of Chautauqua County* (Jamestown, N.Y., 1904), 1: 596.

28 *Centennial History*, 1: 70.

29 Georgia D. Merrill, ed., *History of Chautauqua County, New York* (Boston, 1894), 277.

30 Chautauqua History Co., *op.cit.*, 1: 119.

31 *Ibid.*, 1: 305-310.   32 *Ibid.*, 1: 137-146.

Clearly, the Rockland Dutch were much more prosperous than the Chautauqua Yankees, not because they had greater talent or more enterprising spirit and ability to cope with changed conditions, but because they had a considerable headstart and great advantages of location. Living in long-settled, tightly-knit, homogeneous communities, the Dutch stolidly followed the ways of their fathers and their fathers' fathers; they can be called traditionalists. Unlike them, the Yankees who lived in Chautauqua in 1844 had migrated from many communities in New England and eastern New York, had barely emerged from the "frontier period," and had forcefully displayed that "restless eagerness" and passion for "improvement" that disturbed the Dutchmen in eastern New York. At a time when puritanism had not yet become desiccated and essentially negative and ritualistic, the Chautauqua Yankees as a group might be called both puritans and innovators; that is, they believed in self-improvement in all respects, in man's responsibility to make the world virtuous and moral, and in social progress. In these beliefs they differed radically from the Dutch and from those Yankees whose credo Preston King summarized when he observed that "the world . . . was good enough for him as it stood . . ." (p. 108).

The devotion of the Chautauqua Yankees to self-improvement and social progress formed the theme of a county historian's eulogy to their educational ideals: "In 1824, during the pioneer period, two years before the Erie Canal was built, while the stumps were still standing on the village green, and the fires still burning in sight in the fallows, the Old Fredonia Academy was incorporated. . . . In the academy founded by these pioneers, Latin, Greek and the higher branches were thoroughly taught. . . . For a while no seminary west of Hamilton College gave better instruction than Fredonia Academy."

Since Chautauqua established at least six academies between 1824 and 1839, we can believe that "Chautauqua in an early day gained a reputation for its educational ideas. . . ."[33]

Their educational ideas, however, expressed only one aspect of the Chautauquans' passion for improvement and responsiveness to crusades. Though we must discount the hyperbole inevitable in a centennial history, the following quotation helps us to understand why in 1844 the Yankees in Chautauqua differed politically from the Dutch in Rockland:

[33] *Ibid.*, 1: 9, 108, 147.

"The regard that a citizen has for the county in which he lives is usually strong indeed. The Chautauquan has good reason for pride in his. From being the most obscure of backwoods regions it is now the foremost rural county in the state. . . . More than ordinary energy has characterized its people. It has been a center whence new ideas and vigorous policies have emanated. Anti-Masonry which once revolutionized the politics of the nation, had its chief beginning here. In Chautauqua the Republican Party displayed its earliest and most aggressive action. And here is a center of spiritualistic thought. While we may dissent from these opinions, we must recognize the vigor and independence of thought they imply.

"From germs planted in Chautauqua have sprung movements of undisputed usefulness. It was in the backwoods of Chautauqua that its citizens originated the idea of building the New York and Erie Railroad, and in this county the first public meeting was held to promote it. The first subordinate grange was organized in Fredonia. Chautauqua was also the birthplace of the Women's Christian Temperance Union, the benign influence of which extends to every part of our land, even beyond the seas. Here on the shore of our beautiful lake, the Chautauqua Assembly was founded, has long flourished, and, like the banyan tree, rooted new trunks in other states and lands."[34]

Geneseeans would dispute the claim that "Anti-Masonry . . . had its chief beginning" in Chautauqua, and "revolutionized" overstates the movement's direct impact. But Antimasonry did profoundly change American politics and its after-effects largely determined voting behavior in Chautauqua in 1844.

Prior to the outbreak of political Antimasonry in 1827, Chautauqua, unlike Rockland, had no fixed political creed and no fixed political patterns. Like most frontier areas, its population was in a constant state of flux, a condition unconducive to political stability. The following quotation probably best summarizes Chautauqua politics before 1827: "During the early part of the Pioneer Period [1802-1825], when the people of the county were divided between Republicans and Federalists, Chautauqua County gave a small Republican majority. Later in the Pioneer period, when the Federalist party had become extinct, and the people of the county were divided between Bucktails and Clintonians, the Bucktails or Tammany wing,

<hr />

34 *Ibid.*, 1: 346-347.

or the Democratic Party proper, were in a decided majority, except when DeWitt Clinton himself was a candidate."[35]

The election statistics for 1826 support the conclusion that before Antimasonry broke out, Chautauqua voters tended to divide evenly. In that equilibrium year, even with Clinton running for re-election, the Van Buren "Bucktails" received 46.7 per cent of Chautauqua's vote.

But the "storm and fury of anti-Masonry" ended the period of near equilibrium. In 1844, with 37.0 per cent, Chautauqua ranked as the second lowest Democratic county in the state (Genesee was the lowest) ; Rockland, it will be recalled, ranked highest with 68.0 per cent. Antimasonic intensity is best conveyed, perhaps, by quoting from the chronicler of Freemasonry in Chautauqua County. (His father, ironically enough, had contributed largely to the "rapid growth of the Anti-Masonic Party in Chautauqua County. . . ."[36])

"From the organization of Forest Lodge, in July, 1816, to 1826 —a period of ten years—Freemasonry rapidly increased in numbers and lodges in this county, and many of the best and foremost men among those who came hither to establish homes, became enthusiastic Masons, and encouraged its growth and influence. Clergymen, teachers, physicians, lawyers, merchants, bankers, recognized its value and worth, joined themselves to its numbers and became a part of it. . . ."

Then, unfortunately, came the mysterious disappearance of William Morgan and the investigation of his possible abduction and murder: "The people believed that he was murdered by Masons and were aroused to a high degree of fury and hatred. A storm of resentment burst, that carried everything before it. Neighbors were arrayed against neighbors; friendships, that had commenced in the new land by people who had come into a new county and needed a bond of union to enable them to stand together under distress and privation, were ruthlessly broken; families were estranged; even churches were divided. The present generation can form no adequate conception of the bitterness and hatred that prevailed. Politicians seeing their opportunity seized the occasion and built upon it a political party that intensified and kept alive the burning passions for nearly a generation. . . .

"The conviction and punishment of all who were proved to have

[35] *Ibid.*, 1: 118.
[36] *Ibid.*, 1: 160, 606-608. The quotations below are from *ibid.*, 1: 606-607.

engaged in unlawful acts, did not satisfy the unreasonable fury of the people. The resentment and hatred were turned with irresistible force upon the institution of Freemasonry. Its members were pursued with hatred; denied social privileges; scorned and scoffed at as accomplices in a murder that was never proved. Freemasonry itself was charged with being an unholy agency created and sustained of Satan. Nothing since the persecution in New England of those charged with witchcraft, equalled the bitter hatred that was visited upon the men who were known to be Freemasons."

The Antimasons in Chautauqua may also have been spiritual kin to their forebears in New England who hunted witches and hanged women; but we can better appreciate the ideology of the age when we recognize that they expressed their "fanaticism" in a movement dedicated to achieving equality and the "supremacy of the law." And we can better appreciate the differences between anti-Jacksonians and Jacksonians when we recognize that the energetic, innovating Chautauqua Yankees hunted Masons and helped to "revolutionize" American politics while "freeing" their community from "aristocracy," whereas, shortly before then, the Rockland Dutch had followed their ancestral ways and tried a woman for witchcraft while freeing their community from evil spirits.

Of course, I am not suggesting that belief in witchcraft formed *the* dividing line in New York politics between native Protestants; I am suggesting that attitudes toward change, rather than differences in economic status and occupation, formed *a* dividing line between men who were puritanical and responsive to innovation and other men who may have been pious but who clung to tradition and wanted Old Hero to restore the past. The point can be illustrated by comparing Portland, the highest-ranking Whig town in Chautauqua, with Clarkstown, the highest-ranking Democratic town in Rockland.

B. THE "INLAND FARMING TOWN" OF PORTLAND. Portland lies on the east shore of Lake Erie but it has no harbor. As late as 1902 its chronicler described it as "little else than an inland farming town."[37] In 1840, with 83.8 per cent of its labor force engaged in agriculture, it was slightly more agrarian than Clarkstown on the Hudson, which had 76.4 per cent of its labor force in agriculture.[38] Though its chronicler later boasted that the "soil of the whole town

[37] *Ibid.*, 2: 933-934.
[38] Computed from the 1840 Census statistics in Disturnell, *Gazetteer of New York*, 449-472.

is well adapted for agriculture" and "no town in the county stands in advance of it in the average valuation of the land, considering its adaptability for these purposes,"[39] we can be reasonably certain that before the coming of the Erie Railroad, Portland was not as prosperous as Clarkstown—certainly not in 1827 when Antimasonry burst into politics.

In that year Portland had been settled for less than two decades. Its first town meeting was held in 1818. In the same year, through the efforts of a missionary sponsored by a New England society, a Congregational church was formed and organized religion began (the first informal public religious meeting was held in 1810). "This church is a land mark in the religious life of Portland." But in short order, Methodists, Baptists, and Universalists also testified to the piety of the Portland people. Although precise estimates are impossible, it seems clear that Yankees formed the dominant element in the town.

According to the local chronicler, informal schooling began in the same year as informal religion, 1810. "No schools were established by law until 1814," he begins almost apologetically, "but the people have always been proud of their schools. They have ever been of a high order and it would be difficult to find another town of like population that has furnished so many first-class teachers." And in 1824 the *"Portland Library Association* was incorporated . . . with forty-seven corporators." By 1832 the new town boasted an Academy.[40] Again we have had to rely upon the impressionistic evidence provided by local historians, but it seems reasonably certain that although the Yankee farmers in Portland prospered less than their Dutch counterparts in Clarkstown, they placed a higher premium on educational and intellectual improvement.

That the Portland pioneers constituted a less tightly-knit society than the Clarkstown "old Dutch" is indicated by the voting statistics for 1820, the year when the Federalist Party formally disbanded and the Clintonian and Van Buren factions competed for power. In Portland the Van Buren ticket received 43.5 per cent of the total vote, in Clarkstown, 95.0 per cent.[41]

A decade later, after Antimasonry had set in motion the 1827 to 1853 cycle, and during the fluctuation phase, the Jackson Party

39 Merrill, ed., *Chautauqua County*, 549.

40 *Ibid.*, 553, 558-561.

41 Computed from the Official Canvass of the 1820 election, in the files of the New York Secretary of State, Albany, New York.

received 32.3 per cent of the total vote in Portland; in Clarkstown, it received 67.3 per cent. By 1834, however, when the Whig Party organized formally, Clarkstown had settled into political stability. In that year it gave the Jackson Party 92.8 per cent of its total vote; in 1840, 91.2 per cent, and in 1844, 89.9 per cent.

As we might expect, Portland's voting history differed considerably from that of Clarkstown. Although the basic pattern was firmly set by 1834, it was not until 1840 that voting behavior approached equilibrium in Portland; this is probably because of the shifting composition of the electorate during the town's early decades. In 1834 the Jackson Party received 32.5 per cent of the total vote; in 1840, 24.9 per cent; and for the duration of the cycle's stable phase it oscillated from that figure—24.8 per cent in 1844, 26.3 per cent in 1852. (I have been unable to locate the 1852 voting statistics for Clarkstown, but since the county vote remained stable, it seems reasonable to assume that the town vote also remained stable.)[42]

The analysis of voting patterns has been extended to 1852 in order to emphasize this point: the Yankee farmers in Portland were more prosperous in 1852 than they (or their counterparts) had been during the late 1820's and early 1830's, and they more nearly approximated the economic status of the Dutch farmers in Clarkstown; nevertheless, their voting behavior remained relatively unchanged and continued to differ radically from that of the Clarkstown Dutch.

C. FULFILLMENT OF POLITICAL ROLES. From the material presented thus far, the inference seems reasonable that in 1844, in Chautauqua as in Rockland, voting behavior largely reflected the fulfillment of political roles. As we have seen, after the Antimasonry fury abated and the major parties in New York adopted clear-cut conflicting principles and policies of political economy and theory, new issues arose (for example, Texas annexation) and were agitated, and old ones (the tariff) taxed the ingenuity of politicians to express in new ways the same "immutable truths." And yet, despite what now seems to be the incredible mass interest in politics, voting behavior remained relatively unchanged in Chautauqua and Rockland counties, *and in the state generally.*

Having identified themselves so emotionally with one political party during the 1827 to 1832 fluctuation phase, New York voters thereafter continued to maintain partisan allegiances until *new noneco-*

42 For the sources of the town voting statistics, see Appendix I.

nomic conflicts developed that were intense enough to dissolve the bonds of old loyalties and old associations. Whether or not that is a credible interpretation of the fluctuation phase that began in 1854, a local historian in effect invoked our concept, fulfillment of political roles, to account for voting stability in Chautauqua County. Discussing the election of 1828, he observed: "The year 1828 was one of the most important in the history of political parties in the county and state, and we may say also in the nation. The Anti-Masons, since the election of 1827, had greatly increased in numbers. They were not generally favorable to General Jackson for president, because he was a Mason. They preferred Adams, because he was not. . . . The result of this election in Chautauqua is very interesting, as it shows how the Whig, the great rival of the Democratic Party, began to exist in the county. John Quincy Adams when he was elected president in 1824, was as truly a Democrat [*sic*] as was Jackson, or as were his other competitors. Events had now made Adams the leader of that wing of the old Republican Party which was destined a few years later to join with the Anti-Masons and form the Whig Party. We give the vote in each of the towns of the county, to illustrate this fact, and also to show the then existing sentiment of the county upon the exciting subject of anti-Masonry, as it appeared in the principal election in which its separate strength was exhibited. . . .

"The Democratic vote for President was but thirty-six more than the Democratic vote for Governor; and the sum of the votes for the Adams Party and the Anti-Masonic candidates for Governor was but twenty-five more than the votes polled in the county for Adams for President. This proved that the same voters that voted for Jackson voted also for Van Buren and that the electors who cast their votes for Thompson and Southwick for Governor voted also for Adams for President.

"One familiar with the history of the politics of the county during successive years of struggle between Democrats and Whigs, and the still later contests between Democrats and Republicans can trace to the present time in the vote of the county and in each of the towns of the county the strong impress that Anti-Masonic sentiment made upon the minds of the people and we may realize to what extent an isolated and comparatively trifling circumstance will fix men's opinions and determine their actions for generations."

He then gave the election statistics for 1830 and observed: "This vote is interesting as it indicated what the political complexion of the county and its different towns was destined to be for many years thereafter."[43]

The Morgan affair can be described as a "comparatively trifling circumstance" only in the sense that it precipitated the Antimasonic storm; but the local historian's description of voting stability after 1830 was essentially correct—as we can see from Table 1 below:

TABLE 1

VAN BUREN—"DEMOCRATIC PARTY" PERCENTAGES, 1826-1852

	Chautauqua	Rockland	New York State
1826	46.7	59.6	49.1
1832	36.0	72.4	51.5
1834	39.4	73.4	51.8
1840	37.6	72.7	49.0
1844	37.0	68.0a	49.4
1852	35.0	70.4	50.3

a The American Republican-Whig coalition was probably responsible for the temporary Democratic decline.

As was true of Rockland County, it is not enough to say that by 1832 Chautauqua voting patterns had become fixed and that thereafter men continued to fulfill their political roles; we must also find out what reinforced the political roles of the proverbially "restless" Yankees.

D. PURSUIT OF POLITICAL GOALS. In contrast to the Dutch farmers in Rockland, the Yankee farmers in Chautauqua were members of an ethnocultural group with a strong propensity for official community action to promote material and moral progress. In both cases their group interests reinforced their group propensities.

The location advantages of the Rockland Dutch help to explain their continued allegiance to the Democratic Party which preached the doctrine of the negative liberal state; the location disadvantages of the Chautauqua Yankees help to explain their continued allegiance to the Whig Party which preached the doctrine of the positive liberal state. In other words, it is not surprising that Chautauqua's poor transportation facilities should lead its voters to respond to the party which sought "to project and carry out a magnificent scheme of internal improvements by the exercise of powers doubtful and dangerous"—the Whig image projected by the 1844 New York

43 Chautauqua History Co., op.cit., 1: 159-160, 161.

Democratic *Address*. Not only with internal improvements but with economic issues generally (for example, "land questions"), an activist state was more likely to benefit the struggling farmers in Chautauqua than the established farmers in Rockland.

We have already noted that the Dutch and the Yankees tended to differ in their attitudes toward state-guided and state-enforced "moral reformation." We need not assume that all Chautauquans were puritans and all Rocklanders nonpuritans to deduce that significantly different proportions of them wanted the state to operate as "a great regulator of . . . [the] consciences of men"—to quote the Democratic leader, Preston King, on the kind of state that "should not be tolerated" (see pp. 105-109). That Chautauquans in 1844 were more likely than Rocklanders to respond to a party identified with state-imposed "moral reformation" is suggested by the impressionistic evidence found in their county histories. For example, although Rockland local historians pay stock tributes to the piety of their county's inhabitants, they do not represent them as holding the attitudes suggested in the following quotation from the first *History of Chautauque County*, published in 1846:

"The Chautauque County Temperance Society was organized in 1829. Its origin can hardly be said to have indicated its future strength, and wide spread usefulness and success. At its first organization, it was composed of only fifteen members. So general was the use of intoxicating drinks, so firmly had man become wedded to the habit, and so harmless was the indulgence then regarded, that but few men possessed the moral courage to stand up in the face of the world, and proclaim their determination to put away the evil from among them. But such has been the success of the enterprise, that the great mass of the people are not only in the practice of total abstinence, but have publicly arrayed themselves on the side of temperance and virtue, in aid of one of the most extensive and efficient reformations of modern times.

"Other benevolent societies have since been organized, and are still diffusing their benefits among the people. Among these may be named the Bible Missionary, and Sabbath School Societies, the anniversaries of which, with that of the County Temperance Society, are regularly held by appointment at the same time and place."[44]

The argument can be summarized briefly: by 1844 the pursuit of different political goals (material *and* moral) reinforced the dif-

[44] Warren, *Chautauque County*, 98-99.

ferent voting patterns of Chautauquans and Rocklanders which had essentially been fixed by 1832.

E. NEGATIVE REFERENCE GROUPS. Unlike the Dutch in Rockland County, the Yankees in Chautauqua by 1844 did not yet tend to range themselves politically against any ethnocultural group. No other native white group disputed their dominant position in their section of New York and few Negro slaves had ever lived there. Again we must rely on impressionistic evidence, but the inference seems reasonable that the Chautauqua Yankees, in contrast to the Rockland Dutch, did not regard free Negroes as a negative reference group—at least not so that they influenced their voting behavior.

As we have seen (p. 304), a Rockland local historian observed that many of its citizens "defended slavery." A radically different tone pervades the Chautauqua local histories. According to the first history, published in 1846: "When that benign law, so consonant to the spirit of philanthropy, was enacted in 1817, providing for the gradual emancipation of all persons held in slavery in this State; and for the entire freedom of all born thereafter within its limits, it found eight persons in bondage in this county, whose masters resided here. Under its remedial influence, that stain upon the escutcheon of this State, has long since been entirely obliterated, and it is believed that not a vestige remains of its accumulated evils, within our territories."[45]

Opposition to slavery did not necessarily mean support for Negro equality. In the 1846 referendum on Negro suffrage 59.9 per cent of the Chautauquans who participated voted against the elimination of property qualifications.[46] Nevertheless, since the comparable figure in Rockland was 96.4 per cent, we can infer that anti-Negro sentiment was less intense in the western county where slavery had never taken root than in the eastern county where it had been relatively important. That inference is also supported by their different attitudes toward the Fugitive Slave Law of 1850.

In Rockland, we have seen, many citizens wanted to defend the mandates of the Fugitive Slave Law; in Chautauqua: "Prior to the enactment of the Fugitive Slave Law, masters could take and carry back their slaves under the Constitution, but there were no effective penalties for aiding or secreting them. Until that law was passed comparatively few runaway slaves crossed into Canada, and

[45] Ibid., 67.
[46] Computed from The Whig Almanac For 1847, 44.

many were residing securely in Chautauqua County, as in other parts of the North. The severe penalties imposed by the Fugitive Slave Law for feeding, employing and aiding them in their flight, rendered it dangerous for the slave not only to attempt his escape from bondage, but to remain in the free states; accordingly many who had been quietly residing in the free states sought safety in other places. The passage of the Fugitive Slave Law immediately caused a spontaneous secret combination of men and women apposed [*sic*] to slavery, to assist the slaves to escape, resulting in what is known as the 'Underground Railroad.' It extended from the slave states to Canada. Four main lines are said to have extended through the State of New York, with many laterals, at least two of which passed through Chautauqua County."[47]

We can now see that a common set of values and attitudes inspired the various "crusades" that gave western New York its name, "the Burned-over District," and influenced voting behavior in that section. In 1844 the Democratic Party received 26.6 per cent of the total vote in Harmony, Chautauqua County; in 1834 it had received 25.6 per cent. A town chronicler described its *"First Baptist Church"* as follows: "The church very early commenced sabbath school work, and has received great strength from it. It ever took strong grounds against all secret, oath-bound societies. When slavery divided churches and brotherhoods, this old church of Harmony ever lifted its voice and recorded its vote in favor of freedom; in the civil war it offered its sons as warriors, and gave its solemn vows to stand by the 'stars and stripes.' "[48]

The impressionistic evidence cited here suggests that in Chautauqua County, Southern slaveowners, not free Negroes, served as a negative reference group. Officially, the New York Whigs described themselves as members of a broad national party. But on nonofficial levels they described themselves as the party of "Northern Freemen" and their opponents as "Northern Dough-Faces" who "ignobly cowered under the vaporings and gasconade of Southern 'Chivalry.' "

During the campaign of 1844 Thurlow Weed's paper charged

[47] Chautauqua History Co., 1: 196-197. A "station" of the underground railroad existed in Rockland County, but "because of the existence of . . . slave-hunting feeling [in the county], the almost absolute secrecy of the 'Underground railroad' system became imperative. It was realized among the pro-slavery residents, that escaping negroes were being passed through this section, and dire were the threats made against Abolitionists if they were detected, but those engaged in the enterprise took good care not to be discovered." Green, *Rockland County*, 283.

[48] Merrill, *op.cit.*, 841.

that "Texas or Disunion" was "the cry now set up by the Loco Focos of the South in the expectation that they will again succeed in bullying the North into compliance with their arrogant demand." Until recently, "Mr. VAN BUREN, the Chief of 'Dough-Faces,' has been holding the North in abeyance to the South." But he wavered on "the scheme of Texas Annexation" and was "thrown overboard by a Convention instructed and pledged to nominate him! And the reason for abandoning him was openly and insultingly avowed. No man not in favor of the 'Immediate Annexation of Texas' with its Debt and its Slaves, and with the certainty of provoking a War with Mexico, could receive the votes of the South."[49]

As we have seen, the new issue of Texas annexation had little effect upon established voting patterns in Chautauqua or New York generally. The deduction here, however, is that the New York Whigs encouraged voters to regard the arrogant "Southern 'Chivalry' " as a negative reference group, and that the tactic had greater success in reinforcing their hold upon the electorate in Chautauqua than in Rockland.[50]

C. Negroes, Irish Catholics, "New British"

Chautauqua Yankees and Rockland Dutch tended to polarize politically, but in general members of white native Protestant ethnocultural groups tended to divide evenly (that is, not more than 60-40). In contrast, Negroes, Huguenots, and immigrant groups voted as solid blocs. We can infer that ethnocultural groups who voted as solid blocs were influenced by special factors which aroused intense emotions and tended not to influence other groups. It also seems reasonable to infer that those factors did not relate to socioeconomic issues. Why, for example, should party differences over the tariff have led Negroes in 1844 to vote 95 per cent Whig and Irish Catholics 95 per cent Democratic? Their opposite patterns become logical, however, when we view them as having been influenced primarily by

[49] *Albany Evening Journal*, June 19, 1844, p. 2; June 27, 1844, p. 1.

[50] To illustrate that western New York Whigs responded to this tactic, we can quote from an account of the speech made at a huge rally in 1844. "The infamous and treacherous scheme of South Carolina Nullifiers to dissolve the Union, or else Annex Texas as a Slave Territory—as a new and unlimited market for the sale of human flesh and blood, to be raised in the thirteen Slave States now in the Union, never received a more withering exposure and rebuke. . . . Hundreds unconsciously shed tears of sympathy as the eloquent speaker described the wrongs and the cruelties of that accursed system of human bondage which the Nullifiers at the South, and their aiders and abettors at the North, are now moving heaven and earth to extend in this Republic." *New York Tribune* (w.), August 17, 1844, p. 8.

their positive and negative orientations to reference groups and their subsequent fulfillment of political roles. To support this interpretation, we focus attention upon three ethnocultural groups who voted as blocs.

1. The Negroes

As we have seen, the Van Buren faction wrote into the 1821 Constitution the provision requiring property qualifications for Negro voters. The provision did more than limit the number of Negroes who could vote: it simultaneously increased their isolation within New York society and their dependence upon those whites who accepted them at least as members of the political community. An appeal later made by "colored men" conveys the symbolic importance of their political segregation: "Think not that we are over anxious or that we set too high a value on the ballot-box. You can imagine its worth to yourselves—can you not faintly conceive of its worth to us? True, we are colored men; but have not colored men eyes, hands, organs, dimensions, senses, affections, passions? Are we not fed with the same food, hurt with the same weapons, subject to the same diseases, healed by the same means, warmed and cooled by the same Winter and Summer as yourselves? If then, we are like you in those things, remember the golden rule, and vote for us, that we may become like you in others."[51]

The colored men made their appeal during the campaign to elect delegates to the New York Constitutional Convention of 1846, which would decide whether political equality applied to Negroes. On that question the major parties differed radically. To quote the *Morning News*, a leading organ of the Radical Democracy opposed to equality for "Blacks," "The principal object of the Whigs who have participated in the movement for a Convention to revise the Constitution of this State, has been to procure the right of suffrage for the Negroes to the same extent that it is enjoyed by white citizens."[52] The *New York Tribune*, engaged in a running debate with the *Morning News*, stated the Whig position as follows: "This question of Suffrage is in truth fundamental to all others. On the one side stand Equality, Reason, Justice, Democracy, Humanity; on the

[51] Letter signed Charles S. Morton and others, reprinted from the *Northern Star*, in *New York Tribune* (w.), March 25, 1846, p. 4.
[52] *New York Morning News*, March 21, 1846, p. 2.

other are a base, slavery-engendered prejudice and a blackguard clamor against 'Niggers.' "[53]

In essence, the *Tribune* accurately stated the different party positions on Negro equality—positions which stemmed from the different attitudes Whigs and Democrats had long held and expressed toward Negroes.[54] Because of the Constitutional Convention, the differences were expressed particularly sharply in 1846 and indicate clearly why Negroes voted so solidly against the New York Jacksonians' version of democracy.

The *Morning News* did not adopt the anti-Negro vocabulary of abuse employed by less "high toned" Democratic papers, but it expressed the same underlying attitudes.[55] Urging support for Democratic candidates to the Constitutional Convention, it observed that the equal suffrage issue formed only part of a larger subject: "The subject resolves into the question, not merely whether we shall give negroes the right of suffrage, but whether we shall endeavour to overcome the great laws of nature, which do not permit two distinct and uncongenial races of men to mingle together in harmony or in mutual self-government. Holding the opinion that such a result is impossible, and undesirable if it were otherwise, we can see no useful object to be attained by trying to effect it; and we are confident that any attempt to do so by allowing Negro suffrage, would be attended with evils and disasters which would be deplored when too late."[56]

When he was attacked by the *Tribune* for advocating views antithetical to his professed belief in democracy, the editor of the *News* replied by noting that though he had not written the articles, their general doctrines "met our entire approval." "It is a pity they [the 'superior' and the 'inferior' race] are united together in the same community at all. It is no good policy to attract more and more of the Black Race by such political bounties on their entrance and

[53] *New York Tribune* (d.), April 21, 1846, p. 2.

[54] See the pioneering article on the subject, Dixon Ryan Fox, "The Negro Vote In Old New York," *Political Science Quarterly*, 32: 263-275 (No. 2, 1917). We badly need an intensive study of how and why American political parties have operated over time to foster or dispel prejudice. But no reason exists to doubt that in New York, during the Age of Egalitarianism, the Jacksonians used anti-Negro prejudice as a weapon against their Whig opponents.

[55] Engaged in a factional fight with *The Globe* over delegates to the convention, it defended Samuel J. Tilden from the "base charge advanced against him by the *Globe* of being in favor of *Negro Suffrage*. . . ." *New York Morning News*, April 29, 1846, p. 2.

[56] *Ibid.*, March 21, 1846, p. 2.

residence among us. Their augmentation in number ought to be rather discouraged than favored."[57]

Two quotations from *Tribune* editorials represent Whig views and further point up the difference between Whig and Democratic attitudes toward Negroes. ". . . The pandering of the Loco-Foco Party, in utter contempt of their own avowed principles, to this vulgar and hateful Prejudice [against 'Blacks'], cherished mainly by the weakest or worst of our own Race, *will* be remembered, because it ought to be, by the Blacks, when it will not be so fashionable and Democratic to insult or kick a Black man at the Polls as it now is."[58]

In effect, the *Tribune* claimed that the Democrats used Negroes as a negative reference group: "Wherever in our State there is no pervading Anti-Slavery sentiment, there the Loco-Focos are red-mouthed and vociferous against Black Suffrage at all hazards. Hostility to 'Niggers' is their great card, by which they hope to carry their Delegates [to the Convention] in this City and all the close [Hudson] River Counties."[59]

Since the Whigs had favored equal suffrage before 1846, the Negroes' solid vote can partly be attributed to their pursuing a political goal.[60] But, as the quotations above show, the different party positions on the suffrage issue stemmed from their fundamentally different attitudes toward Negroes as members of society. Thus it seems reasonable to say that Negro voting behavior in New York was primarily determined by this factor: men most hostile to them tended to be Democrats, men most favorable to them tended to be Whigs. Put another way, once we find that Democrats were considerably more likely to be "Nigger-Haters," we can deduce from our theory of American voting behavior that Negroes would range themselves solidly against the Democratic Party. And, as we shall see, because essentially the same kind of factors influenced their behavior, the theory also helps to account for the bloc votes cast by Irish Catholics and New British.

[57] *Ibid.*, March 31, 1846, p. 2.
[58] *New York Tribune* (w.), April 4, 1846, p. 3.
[59] *Ibid.*, April 11, 1846, p. 5.
[60] Thus the 1844 *Address* "Of The Democratic Whig Members of the Legislature of New York," in listing a number of amendments to the Constitution that were of great importance, observed: "The spirit of the age condemns the narrow policy which, by a property qualification, disfranchises a small portion of the people." *New York Tribune* (w.), May 18, 1844, p. 4. I do not mean to imply that the New York Whigs *officially* adopted the principle of equal suffrage; as was generally true of "moral issues," the Whigs made their stand known through nonofficial agents and agencies.

2. Irish Catholics

Unlike Negroes, Irish Catholics had white skins and had never been slaves; thus no political party or faction stigmatized them as being inherently incapable of becoming members of the community. But as early as 1827, their capacity and right to become *full-fledged* members of the community were denied by leading organs of the Adams faction—and affirmed by leading organs of the Van Buren-Jackson faction.

Supporters of Adams were disheartened by the 1827 election returns which added up to victory for their Republican opponents. Regarding the returns as ominous for the 1828 presidential contest, the *New York American* argued, "It appears as a general proposition, both plain and just, that political privileges should belong exclusively to the natives of the country." The *New York National Advocate* stated the same proposition in these words: "It is time to cease to make citizens of the subjects of European governments." In the *Advocate*'s view, the half-million Irishmen in the United States particularly threatened the nation's well-being, for their voting behavior showed they lacked the qualities necessary to participate intelligently in American politics. In the recent New York election, "Everything in the shape of an Irishman, was drummed to the polls and their votes made to pass. . . . It was emphatically an *Irish triumph*." As might be expected from the election returns, the Regency's *Albany Argus* took a different view of the voting of naturalized citizens and strongly defended their "rights of Citizenship."[61]

By 1832 the Antimasons had created a militant, *Protestant* "Church and State Party." And Irish Catholic voting patterns had crystallized along the lines feared by the Adamsites and anticipated by the Jacksonians. After the election returns were in, the leading Antimasonic paper, Thurlow Weed's *Evening Journal*, denounced and ridiculed the "multitude of Foreigners . . . chiefly Irishmen" who had been fraudulently naturalized. "The Foreigners who have voted away our rights, and assaulted and maimed our citizens, will soon be calling for Charity to support themselves and their families." According to the *Journal*: "Jacksonism, in its most ferocious and appalling aspects, was displayed at our Polls yesterday! Axes, Knives, Paving Stones, and Bricks were the *arguments* used by the FOREIGN Mercenaries who were under pay by the Albany Regency. . . . Such

---

61 See the long editorial, "The rights of Citizenship," in the *Albany Argus* (s.w.), November 27, 1827, p. 3.

[321]

are the legitimate fruits of Jacksonism! Our rights and liberties are not only gone, but our LIVES are at the mercy of abandoned FOR-EIGNERS, instigated by the still more abandoned officeholders."[62]

Before the election the *Argus* had appealed to Irishmen to vote for the democratic Jacksonians who welcomed them into the community and defended them from the autocratic hypocrites who were their enemies: "Remember, that four years ago, the aristocrats, who now cajole you, accounted your support a disgrace, and reproached the Jackson Democratic Party as being composed of 'homebred villains and renegade Irishmen.' "[63]

After the election the *Argus* pointed to unrestrained attacks against the Irish by anti-Jacksonians. It triumphantly observed: "Nothing can exceed the virulence and malignity of the Coalition [Antimasons-National Republicans] journals towards our Irish population, except the assiduous and disreputable but vain efforts of the same factions to win them over to the support of the Aristocracy."[64]

In later years Thurlow Weed experienced a change of heart—or at least advocated a change of tactics. And, as we have seen, his wing of the Whig Party continued to court Irish Catholics, even when they persisted in voting Democratic. To no avail. The Irish Catholic pattern set by 1832 prevailed in 1844. No doubt the pattern prevailed partly because New York Democrats bestowed petty favors upon Irish Catholics, continued to oppose changes in the naturalization laws, and continued to preach "Jeffersonian principles" in relation to immigration and matters of conscience. But that does not satisfactorily explain why Democrats and Whigs tended to take opposite positions on issues of deep concern to Irish Catholics (and other New non-British).

A more satisfactory and comprehensive explanation emerges when we recognize that immigrant Irish Catholics and native puritanical Protestants viewed each other as negative reference groups whose values, beliefs, attitudes, and ways of life clashed fiercely.[65] Since our theory assumes that antagonisms in nonpolitical spheres of American life find expression in American politics, we can say that

[62] *Albany Evening Journal* (s.w.), November 9, 1832, p. 2.

[63] *Albany Argus* (s.w.), November 9, 1832, p. 2.

[64] *Ibid.*, November 13, 1832, p. 2.

[65] For example, see the long editorial attacking the *New York Observer* for its attacks upon the "Romish Party," in the *Freeman's Journal*, August 31, 1844, pp. 68-69. See also Ray A. Billington, *The Protestant Crusade* (New York, 1952 printing), *passim*.

Irish Catholic voting behavior in New York was primarily determined by their reactions to the men generally most hostile to them (puritanical Protestants), who tended to be Whigs, and to the men generally most favorable to them ("Jeffersonian liberals"), who tended to be Democrats.

Of course, as we have seen, hostility to Irish Catholics cut across party lines. But two deductions seem reasonable: 1) More than any other sizeable groups, militant puritanical Protestants were likely to express hostility to immigrants whose religious beliefs differed so sharply from their own. 2) In turn, the Irish Catholics reciprocated their hostility and aligned themselves with men opposed to the Protestant "Church and State Party." In politics, as in other spheres of life, "The enemy of my enemy is my friend."

Our interpretation of bloc voting receives further support when we observe that Irish Catholic-Negro conflicts shaped and reinforced the political patterns of both low-status groups. We need not discuss those conflicts in detail, for historians have documented them.[66] And we need not rely solely upon twentieth century theory to deduce the political consequences of Irish Catholics and Negroes regarding each other as negative reference groups. In 1846 the *Tribune* in effect invoked that theory to explain the defeat in New York City of Whig candidates to the state Constitutional Convention: "The polls were given up almost wholly to the Adopted citizens of German or Irish birth, who are always on hand (to their praise be it spoken and the shame of our born Freemen!) but who on this occasion were called out by skillful appeals to their hatred of the unfortunate African Race. It was mournful to see hundreds who have not been six years in the Country earnestly and abusively clamorous for the disfranchisement of men whose fathers' fathers were born here, and many of them shed their blood for the defense of our liberties in the war of the Revolution."[67]

The *Tribune*'s analysis is particularly convincing, and illuminat-

---

[66] Fox, in *Political Science Quarterly*, 32: 274-275; Robert Ernst, *Immigrant Life in New York City: 1825-1863*, 71, 104, 107. Discussing the "Irish hatred of abolitionism," Ernst quotes Irish Catholic newspapers: "During the Abolition Riot of 1834 [in New York City] the Negroes, under the protection of *'gloomy and giddy-brained puritans* [italics added], behaved themselves with 'a swagger of artificial consequence, and an assumption of equality.' 'Why,' wrote a Catholic editor, 'should the sable race of Africa, to whom the inscrutable wisdom of providence has denied the power of intellect, the amenity of the moral affections, and the grace and whiteness of form, presume to enter the lists of human perfection with . . . superior grades of society . . . which they never can attain?' " *Ibid.*, 153.

[67] *New York Tribune* (d.), April 29, 1846, p. 2.

ing, because it rejected the argument of Whig nativists that the "adopted citizens"—the New non-British—had shown themselves to be unfit for full membership in the community. "That the Adopted Citizens generally manifested a most discreditable, unjust disposition to deprive the Colored Race of Equal Rights is most true. . . . Yet Truth compels us to add this base, aristocratic clamor against 'Niggers' originated not with Adopted but with Native Citizens, and was potent in influencing the votes of one class as well as the other [in various parts of the state]."[68]

3. New British

Although the statement drastically oversimplifies complex phenomena and processes, we can say that in essence the New British voted Whig because the Irish Catholics voted Democratic. And our interpretation gains comprehensiveness when we say that the positive as well as the negative reference groups of the New British influenced their political behavior.

To a greater or lesser extent, all immigrants belonged to "outgroups" and faced difficult social and psychological problems upon arrival in the United States as strangers and aliens. The dictionary defines an alien not only as "one born in or belonging to another country who has not acquired citizenship by naturalization and is not entitled to the privileges of a citizen," but as "one who has been estranged or excluded." To overcome their estrangement, and their exclusion, and become members of the American community, in spirit as in law, aliens had to do more than receive naturalization papers. They had to win acceptance by the native "in-group."[69] But their eventual success in becoming "assimilated" depended largely upon their initial desire and capacity to become acculturated.

Acculturation, a relatively recent term, is generally credited to American anthropologists. A satisfactory definition of the concept has not yet been developed, but we quote the one most widely used: "Acculturation comprehends those phenomena which result when groups of individuals having different cultures come into continuous first-hand contact, with subsequent changes in the original cultural patterns of either or both groups."[70]

---

[68] *Ibid.*, May 4, 1846, p. 2.

[69] On "in-groups" and "out-groups," see Robert K. Merton, *Social Theory and Social Structure*, 284-299.

[70] Ralph Beals, "Acculturation," in A. L. Kroeber, et al., *Anthropology Today* (Chicago, 1953), 621-639. To my knowledge, Oscar Handlin was the first American

Surveying the literature on the acculturation of American ethnic groups, one anthropologist suggests a crucial difference between acculturation and assimilation: "The acculturation of an ethnic group in the United States—its acquisition of the culture of the dominant group—is an exclusive function of the group's desire and capacity for acculturation; but assimilation—the disappearance of group identity through nondifferential association and exogamy [marriage 'outside the tribe or blood group']—is a function of both dominant and ethnic group behavior. And in some instances, even when the ethnic group desires assimilation, *the dominant group prevents it* [italics added]."[71]

Compared to the Irish Catholics (and other immigrants), the New British possessed greater desire and capacity for acculturation. Moreover, their aspirations for assimilation received warmer, more positive response from the dominant group. Essentially, the American cultural pattern was British in origin and Protestant in faith; as a result, although the cultural patterns of English, Scottish, Welsh, and Protestant Irish immigrants differed significantly from the American, they differed in degree, not kind. This relative lack of differentiation from native white Protestants simultaneously encouraged and permitted the New British to acquire the culture of the dominant group; in other words, the New British could become Americanized more easily than could the Irish Catholics.[72]

Two closely related processes hastened the Americanization of the New British and their conversion into staunch Whigs: 1) They distinguished themselves from low-status immigrants, in part by expressing hostility to them—especially to the Irish Catholics. 2) They identified themselves with natives whom they regarded as exemplifying *the* American cultural pattern, in part by expressing hostility to low-status immigrants—especially Irish Catholics.[73]

---

historian to use the concept of acculturation. My thinking on the subject has been considerably influenced by his pioneering study, *Boston's Immigrants: A Study in Acculturation* (Cambridge, Mass., 1941).

[71] Melford E. Spiro, "The Acculturation of American Ethnic Groups," *American Anthropologist*, 57: 1244 (1955).

[72] See Ernst, *Immigrant Life in New York City*, 37-47, 122-184.

[73] The behavior of the New British supports and is supported by the hypothesis that "the selection of reference groups is largely governed by the capacity of certain groups to confer some prestige in terms of the institutional structure of the society." Merton, *Social Theory and Social Structure*, 305-306. We can extend that hypothesis by observing that hostility to low-status groups also serves to confer prestige upon members of other groups who are not securely located in the society. Like northerners who emigrate to the South in the twentieth century and become

To a considerable extent, of course, conflicts between New British and Irish Catholics simply represented the transplantation to the New World of conflicts long fought in the Old World. In 1844, for example, the *Freeman's Journal*, "read chiefly by the Irish or Americans of Irish parentage,"[74] described nativism as follows: "The truth is, there are too many reasons to believe that the present movement is but a British attempt to engraft insidiously on the hated stock of American Republicanism, the principles of the Irish Orangeman —[Protestant Irish]. . . . The most active, though not the most prominent of the *Native* Americans in New York, and probably in Philadelphia also, have been Irish Orangemen."[75]

Similarly, early in 1845 the *New York Evening Post* emphasized that the "so-called American Party" had more ancient and deep-rooted sources than the desire to "put civil disabilities on the population of foreign birth": "There is also connected with the present controversy, a religious persecution, far more to be deprecated than any attempt at political disfranchisement, and which proposes to re-enact among us the bloody contests that disgraced the sixteenth century, between the Catholics and Protestants, or at least to introduce into this country the Orange processions, so long the scourge of Ireland.—Why was it that so many foreigners enrolled themselves among the *professed* [italics added] nativists and were among the most clamorous of their party? It was not that they desired their own proscription, but that they were willing to jeopard [*sic*] their own political rights to gratify their religious hate."[76]

We can go beyond the *Post* to suggest that, for the New British, hostility to Irish Catholics did more than gratify ancient religious and ethnic hates; it identified them with and earned them the approval of contemporaries who belonged to the dominant group and who claimed the right to define Americanism. Thus another Democratic paper, the *Brooklyn Eagle*, charged that when Whig "natives" decried "foreign influence in American politics," their real target was not foreigners in general, but those "born in Ireland." In fact, according to the *Eagle*, any immigrants who voted Democratic were subjected to attack by men whose sympathy was with

publicly anti-Negro, New British who came to the United States in the nineteenth century found it useful to become publicly anti-Irish Catholic—a pattern of behavior that simultaneously satisfied interest and inclination.

[74] Ernst, *op.cit.*, 158-159.
[75] *Freeman's Journal*, May 11, 1844, p. 364.
[76] *Evening Post For The Country*, March 27, 1845, p. 3.

the few, not the many. "No exception" was taken to the English and the Scotch, for example, because they "make good Whigs."[77]

The *American Republican,* the leading organ of the nativist, anti-Catholic movement, provides even more convincing evidence that the New British acted politically in order to differentiate themselves from Irish Catholics (and other low-status immigrants) and to identify themselves with the dominant group. Its editor reported that an "Englishman told us that he had concluded not to take out his naturalization papers as he did not want to have his name published in a list of newly naturalized Irishmen." Moreover, he observed, "It is well known that a large portion of the intelligent English naturalized citizens will vote the American Republican ticket, and we trust, that other enlightened and patriotic adopted citizens will do the same."[78]

It is not important whether the *American Republican* and the *Post* exaggerated the number of New British who voted for the nativist-Whig coalition in 1844; what is important is this: if adopted citizens—could there be a more revealing term?—voted Democratic, they ranged themselves with Irish Catholics and exposed themselves to charges that they were unenlightened, unpatriotic "foreigners"; if they voted Whig, they ranged themselves against Irish Catholics and, at worst, exposed themselves to Democratic charges that they supported "the aristocratic party"—charges not likely to diminish seriously their self-esteem or lessen their chances of winning acceptance by the dominant group and thereby accelerating their upward social mobility. In fact, identification with "aristocrats" might well have pleased immigrants striving to climb the American social ladder.

Having examined the political behavior of the New British, the Irish Catholics, and the Negroes, we can reasonably conclude that the stand of the major parties on socioeconomic issues had *relatively* little effect upon bloc voting in New York; we must attribute that phenomenon more to factors initially associated with positive and negative reference groups and subsequently with fulfillment of political roles. Party differences on certain political issues of deep

[77] *Brooklyn Eagle,* November 9, 1844, p. 2. All during 1844, the *Eagle* engaged in a running battle with the *Brooklyn Advertiser,* a Whig paper strongly nativist in tone. The *Eagle* repeatedly derided its rival's "British editor"—using "British" as a derisive adjective.

[78] *American Republican,* November 4, 1844, p. 2.

interest to nonmembers of the dominant group did exist; but these differences, I suggest, stemmed from differences originating outside the political sphere. They were less a cause than a consequence of voting behavior. (For example, largely because Irish Catholics had long voted Democratic, in 1844 the major parties took different positions on naturalization laws.)

CHAPTER XV

JACKSONIAN DEMOCRACY—CONCEPT OR FICTION?

ISTORY never repeats itself, historians do. Commenting upon this phenomenon, Thomas C. Cochran estimates that "history probably suffers more than any other discipline from the tyranny of persuasive rhetoric." To illustrate his point, he observes that "A. M. Schlesinger, Jr. and Joseph Dorfman . . . may argue about the interpretation of 'Jacksonian Democracy,' but they both accept the traditional concept as central to the synthesis of the period."[1] Following his lead, I have focused upon two questions: What empirical phenomena can logically be designated by the concept Jacksonian Democracy? Does the traditional concept help us to understand the course of American history after 1815?

A. The Concept of Jacksonian Democracy

Although all concepts are logical abstractions, they refer to some empirical phenomena. By definition, they refer "either to a class of phenomena or to certain aspects or characteristics that a range of phenomena have in common. . . . [Concepts] are abstractions from reality, designating types of movements, persons, behavior, or other classes of phenomena."[2]

Analysis of the concept of Jacksonian Democracy reveals that every version contains these elements: 1) Andrew Jackson and his successors led (really or symbolically) a particular political party; 2) the party drew its leaders from certain socioeconomic classes or groups; 3) the party received strong mass support from certain socioeconomic classes or groups; 4) the party formulated and fought for an egalitarian ideology that envisioned not only political but social and economic democracy; 5) the party implemented a program derived from or consonant with its egalitarian ideology; 6) the opposing party drew its leaders and mass support from different socioeconomic classes and social groups, and opposed egalitarian ideas and policies.

[1] Thomas C. Cochran, "The Social Sciences and The Problem of Historical Synthesis," *Bulletin 64, The Social Sciences in Historical Study* (Social Science Research Council, New York, 1954), 158-160.

[2] *Ibid.,* 91-93. See also Robert K. Merton, *Social Theory and Social Structure,* 89-93, 114-117.

Having identified the kinds of phenomena and relationships that are designated by the concept, we can go on to ask: did those phenomena and relationships exist in reality during the "middle period" of American history? For example, did the Jackson Party advocate and implement a program of economic democracy and social reform? Or is it more accurate to say that, in general, the Jackson Party denounced and fought against such programs?

1. Changing Definitions of the Concept

To my knowledge, no one has shown that contemporaries used the term Jacksonian Democracy to designate the ideology, values, attitudes, principles, and policies of Jackson Men, the contemporary term for men who supported the Republican Party. At present, we cannot be sure who *invented* the Jacksonian Democracy concept or when historians generally began to accept it. But the concept seems to derive from the frontier thesis associated with Frederick Jackson Turner and to have won general acceptance soon after 1900. We can be sure, however, that it has meant and now means very different things to different historians, and that attempts to clarify its meaning constitute a major field of work in American historiography.[3] If at this late date the concept remains unclarified, it seems reasonable to doubt that it is solidly based in reality.

When we examine the literature over time, we find that historians, in trying to abstract from reality a set of phenomena and relationships that could be subsumed under the Jacksonian Democracy concept, had to make assumptions that later proved untenable. In other words, when they systematically collected data that discredited earlier assumptions, they retained the concept by redefining it on the basis of still other erroneous assumptions.

No matter how the concept has been defined, it has assumed that a strong causal relationship existed between Andrew Jackson's real or symbolic role in politics and the progress of movements dedicated to egalitarian and humanitarian ideals or objectives. It has also assumed that during the period from 1825 to 1850, both on leadership and mass levels, party battles represented reasonably clear-cut ideo-

---

[3] See Frederick Jackson Turner, "Contributions of the West to American Democracy," in *The Frontier in American History* (New York, 1950 printing), 243-268, and *passim*. For an illuminating review of the literature on Jacksonian Democracy, see Charles G. Sellers, Jr., "Andrew Jackson Versus the Historians," *MVHR*, 44: 615-634 (March 1958). A less comprehensive, but provocative, analysis is presented in Marvin Meyers, *The Jacksonian Persuasion: Politics and Belief*, 1-10.

logical and political conflicts between two types of men. In different versions of the concept, the types of men are identified by different criteria, for example, "frontier democrats" and supporters of "the old established order," "liberals and conservatives," "the business community and the other sections of society," "enterprisers and capitalists." No matter how the concept is defined, as I read the source materials and analyze the data, its underlying assumptions are, at least for New York, untenable.

2. Concept versus Reality

Taking New York as a test case, this book has tried to show the existence of an unbridgeable gap between historical reality and the concept's assumptions about the leadership, mass support, ideology, and program of the Jackson Party. "Old Hero," it is true, served as the party's rallying symbol. But the other assumptions of the concept conflict with the available evidence.

The leadership of the New York Democratic Party does not appear to have been recruited from "the other sections of society" that allegedly struggled "to restrain the power of the business community"—to cite Arthur M. Schlesinger, Jr.'s, version of the concept.[4] Neither Schlesinger's version, nor any other version that assumes there were significant differences in the class nature of party leadership, appears credible. Instead, the evidence indicates that the same socioeconomic groups provided leadership for both parties.

We have also seen that in New York the concept makes erroneous assumptions about the class nature of mass support for the major parties. In one form or another historians have tended to accept Martin Van Buren's analysis, but the evidence discredits his claims that the Jackson Party championed the "producers" against the "special interests." According to his persuasive rhetoric, the Jacksonians took the side of the producers in the conflict between "those who live by the sweat of their brow and those who live by their wits." When we penetrated the rhetorical surface and struck hard data, however, we found that farmers, mechanics, and "working classes" did not form the "main-stay of the Democratic party."[5] Instead of low-status socioeconomic groups, the Jacksonians' strongest support came from relatively high-status socioeconomic groups in the eastern

[4] Arthur M. Schlesinger, Jr., *The Age of Jackson*, 505-523.
[5] Martin Van Buren, *Inquiry into the Origin and Course of Political Parties in the United States*, 175-232. The "sweats" and "wits" division is found on pp. 226-227.

counties, and relatively low-status *ethnocultural and religious groups* in all sections of New York.

Politically hard-pressed by the People's Party, the Antimasonic Party, the Working Men's Party, and finally the Whig Party, the Van Buren faction and then the Jackson Party eventually capitulated and adopted the egalitarian ideology advocated by their opponents. But, contrary to the assumptions of the concept, the Jackson Party attacked rather than sponsored the Whig idea of the positive liberal state functioning to "equalize the condition of men" by enabling "the people to act in a joint and vigorous concert for the common good . . . [or, as the Founding Fathers phrased it] the general welfare."[6]

Moreover, if action is the real test of doctrine, the Jackson Party in New York stood firmly by its ideology. Instead of vigorously implementing, it uncompromisingly opposed political programs that required the state to act positively to foster democratic egalitarianism, economic democracy, social and humanitarian reform. How then can we reconcile the actual ideology and program with any version of the concept?

The evidence suggests that in New York Jacksonian Democracy can designate men who shared only one general characteristic: after 1828 they voted for candidates nominated by the Republican Party. That party expressed a particular ideology and implemented a program consonant with it, but its ideology and program derived from the old doctrines of state rights, strong executive, freedom of conscience, and the new doctrine of negative government. But why equate those doctrines with *democracy*? Why make the party that advocated them either the champion or the instrument of the democratic, egalitarian, humanitarian movements that emerged during the second quarter of the nineteenth century? Both on logical and empirical grounds, it seems a more credible hypothesis that in New York those movements progressed in spite of rather than because of the "Jackson Men" and the "Jackson Party."

3. Is the Concept Useful?

In addition to asking what empirical phenomena can logically be designated by the Jacksonian Democracy concept, I have raised the question whether the concept helps us to understand the course of American history after 1815. Since the present book has focused

---

6 See pp. 243-244 above.

upon a single state, I cannot pretend to have answered that question convincingly. But two conclusions do appear to be warranted: 1) The concept of Jacksonian Democracy has obscured rather than illuminated the course of *New York* history after 1815, has distracted historians from the significance of their own work, and has led them to offer interpretations that are contradicted by their own findings. 2) Since events in New York are invariably cited by historians who accept some version of the concept, systematic research may find that in other states the concept also does not conform to reality. These two conclusions receive additional support when we examine one of the most recent, and in many respects most penetrating, studies of the period.

In what may well come to be regarded as a classic study of banking in America, Bray Hammond argues that the Jacksonian "cause was a sophisticated one of enterpriser against capitalist, of banker against regulation, and of Wall Street against Chestnut." The last phrase refers to the New York City bankers who, Hammond claims, played leading roles in the campaign to defeat recharter of the Bank of the United States, operating out of Philadelphia headquarters. Writing in a characteristically ironic vein, he asserts that the "Jacksonian revolution" democratized business "under a great show of agrarian idealism" by humbly-born, rugged individualists who "made the age of Jackson a festival of *laissez faire* prelusive to the Age of Grant and the robber barons." And he stresses heavily the idea that Jacksonians came up from the farm to do battle with "the established urban capitalists, mercantile and financial": "In their attack on the Bank of the United States, the Jacksonians still employed the vocabulary of their agrarian backgrounds. The phraseology of idealism was adapted to money-making, the creed of an earlier generation becoming the cant of its successor. Their terms of abuse were 'oppression,' 'tyranny,' 'monied power,' 'aristocracy,' 'wealth,' 'privilege,' 'monopoly,' their terms of praise were 'the humble,' 'the poor,' 'the simple,' 'the honest and the industrious.' . . . Neither the President, nor his advisers, nor their followers saw any discrepancy between the concept of freedom in an age of agrarianism and the concept of freedom in one of enterprise. . . . Notwithstanding their language, therefore, the Jacksonians' destruction of the Bank of the United States was in no sense a blow at capitalism or property or the 'money power.' It was a blow at an older set of capitalists by a newer, more numerous set. It was incident to the democratization of business, the diffusion of enterprise among the mass of people, and the transfer of economic primacy from an old and conservative merchant class to a newer, more aggressive, and more numerous body of business men and speculators of all sorts."[7]

In my opinion, Hammond's treatment of the democratization of business after 1825 represents a major contribution to American historiography and lights the way to further progress. But, as I have tried to show while tracing the movement for free banking, his own researches help to refute the assumption that business democratization in New York must primarily be attributed to farm-born Jacksonians of humble background, *or to any other kind of Jacksonians*. Attention is directed here toward showing how, in the passages quoted above, the Jacksonian Democracy concept imposes severe strains upon logical consistency.

Were not many of the Wall Street and other New York bankers who worked to destroy the Bank of the United States the very archetypes of the "established urban capitalists" against whom the alleged Jacksonian revolution was allegedly directed? Did not many of those bankers hold high rank in the Republican Party of Andrew Jackson? In New York State, did they not hold either high rank or considerable influence in Tammany Hall and the Albany Regency, which contributed so much to Jackson's election? Indeed, didn't many of those bankers owe their position as "established urban capitalists" to the "monopoly charters" granted them for long and loyal service to the Republican Party? Didn't the great majority of the Jackson Party in the New York legislature oppose the movement led and supported by the Whigs to "democratize" banking? But if those and similar questions require affirmative answers— Hammond, I believe, would agree that they do[8]—it becomes logically impossible to attribute the democratization of business in New York State to farm-born Jacksonians revolting against established urban capitalists.

Another logical inconsistency fostered by the Jacksonian Democracy concept is illustrated by Hammond's emphasis upon the "agrarian" vocabulary Jacksonians employed to attack the Bank. Were abusive terms, such as oppression, tyranny, monied power, and

---

[7] Bray Hammond, *Banks and Politics in America*, 326-329.

[8] Most of these points are implicit, at least, in the political history of New York that Bray Hammond relied upon heavily. See Jabez D. Hammond, *History of Political Parties in the State of New York*, 2: 297-302, 327-333, 349-352, 419-420, 447-449, 478-479, 484, 489-499.

aristocracy, exclusively or primarily agrarian? Had they not been used by nonagrarians, too, long before Andrew Jackson became a national political figure and long before business began to be democratized? *Didn't the men who passionately opposed "King Andrew" and his party use essentially the same terms of praise and abuse as the men who passionately supported him?* Had not the Antimasons adapted to politics the vocabulary of sectarian abuse, referred to Van Buren's Safety-Fund "scheme" as a "monster" institution, and denounced the "moneyed aristocracy, existing in the city of Albany, which owns the Mechanics' and Farmers' bank"? Why assign Jacksonians a monopoly on terms commonly used during the Age of Egalitarianism by large numbers of men in all parties? Similarly, if most Jacksonians were farm-born, were not most anti-Jacksonians also farm-born? If some established urban capitalists opposed the party of Jackson, were not others counted among his most ardent supporters? In short, before we draw conclusions about the class composition of the Democratic and Whig parties, we must systematically analyze the opponents of the "Jackson Party," as well as its adherents.

Since Hammond accepts the traditional concept as central to the synthesis of the period, he, like other commentators beginning with Tocqueville, attributes characteristics and ideas and policies to Jacksonians that, at least in New York, are either more accurately associated with their opponents or best described as common to members of both major parties. Thus he emphasizes the importance of the New York Free Banking Act; but instead of attributing its passage to the long campaign waged by the opponents of the Jackson Party (Working Men, Antimasons, Whigs), he attributes it to the groups that actually fought against the Act, the urban Locofocos and the rural Radical Democrats.[9] Perhaps we could find no better illustration to support the conclusion that the Jackson Democracy concept has distracted historians from the significance of their own work and has forced them to operate within an inadequate framework of ideas.

B. An Alternative Concept and Hypothesis

Since I do not believe that the concept helps us to understand New York history after 1815, the question arises of whether we can replace it with a more adequate and realistic concept. In a sense,

9 B. Hammond, *op.cit.*, 572-604.

of course, that question is premature; systematic studies of other states may show that the traditional concept is well-founded and that New York is, at most, a special case. But suppose it turns out that New York is a representative state and that the findings reported in this book are credible. What then?

Let us go far beyond the evidence now available and assume that we must reject the concept of Jacksonian Democracy. Since its rejection forces us to break out of the traditional framework of ideas, we undoubtedly will stumble and fumble around for some time to come. We can tentatively begin, however, by discarding the old caption for the period and substitute the Age of Egalitarianism for the Age of Jackson. Marvin Meyers has recently observed that historians agree "that the second quarter of the nineteenth century is properly remembered as the age of Jackson."[10] I, for one, disagree. If my assumptions are sound, that caption drastically distorts reality by exaggerating the significance and role of Andrew Jackson, the Age of Egalitarianism expresses the central tendency of the period and does not associate that tendency with a particular party. In Karl Mannheim's phrase, the caption expresses "the ideology of an age."[11]

No doubt any caption for a period distorts reality; for example, an increasingly sophisticated defense of slavery developed simultaneously with the victory of egalitarian ideas. But when we substitute the Age of Egalitarianism for the Age of Jackson, we substitute a general phenomenon for a particular individual, and can go on to substitute the concept of egalitarian revolution for that of Jacksonian revolution (or Jacksonian Democracy). Tocqueville's celebrated dictum to the contrary, Americans were not "born equal" and did have "to endure a democratic revolution." After 1815, not only in politics but in all spheres of American life, egalitarianism challenged elitism and, in most spheres and places, egalitarianism won. Thus, if we accept the egalitarian revolution concept, we are in a better position to see that during the 1830's and 1840's political battles were less over ends than means. The major parties in New York developed the conflicting doctrines of the negative liberal state and the positive liberal state, but in time, both parties accepted egalitarianism as the ideology of the Good Society.

We can push this reasoning further: once we develop the concept

[10] Meyers, *The Jacksonian Persuasion*, p. 2.

[11] Karl Mannheim, *Ideology and Utopia* (New York, n.d., Harvest Books ed.), 55-56.

of the "egalitarian revolution," we may be in a better position to account for the transformation from the aristocratic liberal republic of the early nineteenth century to the populistic egalitarian democracy of the mid-nineteenth century. One possible answer, or hypothesis, is that the egalitarian revolution after 1815 was largely, although by no means exclusively, the product of the Transportation Revolution which occurred after 1815 and fostered, stimulated, and accelerated tendencies already present in American society and culture.[12] I do not pretend that the present study has "proved" that hypothesis; at the moment, the hypothesis is impressionistic and crude, and it cannot even be stated precisely, let alone verified.

Before we can test the hypothesis that the Transportation Revolution was the "main cause" of the egalitarian revolution, we must state it differently. As stated, the hypothesis probably does suggest some relationships between the two revolutions. But it is too ambiguous to be tested, and it seems to assume that "impersonal forces" determine human behavior—a metaphysical assumption that retards historiographic progress by obscuring the fact that history is made by men.

When we focus upon men or groups of men, rather than upon "forces" or "factors"—terms mechanically borrowed from physical scientists who deal with different kinds of causal problems—we are in a better position to assess the relative importance of determinants. In explaining a sequence of events, we can then claim that certain men played more important roles than other men. Such claims are more precise, more meaningful, more consonant with every-day "common sense" explanations of every-day experience and behavior than are those that purport to assess the relative importance of "economic forces," "cultural forces," and the like. Moreover, when we focus upon human beings, we can support our judgments of relative importance by using criteria such as the number of men, their different power to control the apparatus of opinion-making and decision-making, their persistence over time in translating ideas into action and objectives into reality. In contrast, it is extraordinarily difficult to find and use criteria to measure the relative importance of "impersonal forces."[13] Thus I believe that causal explanations of

12 Support for this hypothesis is found in George R. Taylor's illuminating new preface to John R. Commons *et al.*, eds., *A Documentary History of American Industrial Society* (Russell & Russell: New York, 1958), Vols. v and vi.

13 See my discussion of the problem in "Causation And The American Civil War," *History and Theory*, Vol. i, No. 2 (1961).

human behavior might better take the form, "Who Caused the Egalitarian Revolution?", than "What Were the Causes of the Egalitarian Revolution?" (Civil War, American Revolution, English Revolution, French Revolution).

If this line of reasoning is valid, my hypothesis should specify who (members of what groups) played greater and lesser roles in the egalitarian revolution after 1815. It also should specify why the Transportation Revolution both impelled and permitted them to speed the transition from an aristocratic to an egalitarian society. At present, I cannot state the hypothesis in those terms. Nevertheless, it does identify some causal relationships that seem consistent with the relevant data for New York, and the relevant data now available for American history between 1815 and 1860. It seems reasonable to assert, therefore, that if further research and analysis shows that we must reject the Jacksonian Democracy concept and hypotheses derived from it, the concept and hypothesis sketched here warrant consideration as alternatives toward a more satisfactory synthesis of the period.

APPENDIX I

Sources for Election Statistics

ALTHOUGH any useful study of New York political history must depend upon an analysis of voting behavior, election statistics have never been systematically collected and are not readily available. To piece together the historical record, therefore, it has been necessary to use a variety of sources.

Compiled under the direction of the Secretary of State of New York State, the official canvass for state offices from 1822 to 1868 is available in manuscript form at the New York State Library. Unfortunately, this source does not give the vote for president or for state officers by urban ward and rural towns; actually, it does not even give the vote by counties for all elections in the series. The Secretary of State, however, does have in his possession the official canvass for the 1820 gubernatorial election, by wards, towns, and counties. For the 1826 and 1827 returns by counties, see the *Albany Argus* (s.w.), December 8, 1826, p. 2; December 7, 1827, p. 2. The only source located for the 1828 presidential returns by counties is *ibid.*, November 23, 1832, p. 3.

For other sources of election returns from 1828 to 1844 inclusive, see Edwin Williams, ed., *New York Annual Register* (New York, 1830-1845), 10 vols., published irregularly; O. L. Holley, ed., *New York State Register*, 1843, 1845-1846 (Albany, N.Y., 1843, 1845-1846). These volumes give the vote for president and governor by wards and towns for 1830, 1834, 1838, 1840, 1842, 1844.

For elections from 1834 to 1900, the most convenient source is the annual *Tribune Almanac* (from 1838 to 1854, *The Whig Almanac*). Unfortunately, although it gives the returns for federal and state offices, it gives the town and ward returns for 1858, 1860, 1864 only. In some cases its figures vary from those of the official state canvass. Because the official canvass had to be filed by a certain date, I regard the *Tribune Almanac* as more reliable since it corrected errors in the official canvass.

APPENDIX II

Economic Classification of Political Units

Based upon the average value of dwelling per family in 1855 and 1865, rural towns were assigned to five categories: 1) unusually prosperous ($800 and over); 2) very prosperous ($600-799); 3) prosperous ($400-599); 4) marginal ($300-399); 5) poor ($100-299). As noted in the text, these data are not available before 1855, but impressionistic evidence supports the conclusion that the *relative* economic status of towns changed little between 1844 and 1855.

No town was classified unless the Census reported the value for at least 80 per cent of the total number of houses. To compute the average value of dwelling per family, the number of dwellings for which values were given was first compared to the total number of dwellings and the percentages calculated. That is, if a town contained a total of 807 dwellings and the value was reported for all 807, its percentage was 100 per cent. Then the total value of all dwellings was divided by the total number of families. But if the value of only 90 per cent of the dwellings was reported, then their total value was divided by only 90 per cent of the number of families (for example, if a town contained 100 families and the value of only 90 per cent of the dwellings was reported, their total value was divided by 90). The raw data are found in *Census of the State of New York, for 1855* (New York, 1857), 1-15, 229-247; *Census of the State of New York for 1865* (Albany, 1867), 1-17, 254-273.

Independent criteria confirmed the reliability of the main criterion. Although it can be assumed that county histories exaggerate the prosperity of the communities they describe, I found that descriptions of the *relative* prosperity of towns within a county generally corresponded to the results obtained by computing the average value of dwelling per family; that is, the "unusually prosperous" towns of a county were described in much more roseate terms than were its "poor" towns.

In addition to county histories, gazetteers provided impressionistic descriptions of the relative prosperity of towns. Several of the gazetteers were particularly useful because they were published during the 1830's and 1840's, others because they contained reasonably comprehensive descriptions. See Horatio G. Spafford, *A Gazetteer of the State of New-York* (Albany, 1824, rev. ed.); Thomas F. Gordon, *Gazetteer of the State of New York* (Philadelphia, 1836); J. Disturnell, *A Gazetteer of the State of New York* (New York, 1842); J. H. Mather and L. P. Brockett, *A Geographical History of the State of New York ...* (Utica, N.Y., 1848); J. H. French, *Gazetteer of the State of New York*

(Syracuse, 1860); Franklin B. Hough, *Gazetteer of the State of New York* (Albany, 1872).

Another criterion of the relative prosperity of towns within a county is provided by twentieth century studies of New York land values. A number of these studies have been published by the Cornell University Agricultural Experiment Station under this general title, "An Economic Study of Land Utilization in —— County, New York." Their statistical findings correspond to those I derived from the New York State censuses of 1855 and 1865.

Ethnocultural Groups in New York,
Estimated Percentages, 1845

The estimates presented here are designed only to suggest the *relative* proportions of certain ethnocultural groups in the population of New York. For, when we attempt to reconstruct the composition of the population in 1845, we have reasonably firm figures for two categories only, Negroes and foreign-born. (I assume that foreign-born inhabitants constituted the overwhelming majority of the 1.9 per cent of the population whose nativity was unknown.) But if we begin with these figures, we can go on to make calculations that result in the following estimates:

A.	Negroes	1.7 per cent
B.	Foreign-born	
	(post-1790 immigrants)	15.0
	Descendants	3.5
C.	Yankees	63.5*
D.	Penn-Jerseyites	2.0
	Descendants	2.0
E.	Others	0.5
F.	Yorkers	11.8

* I estimate, however, that Yankees comprised 65 per cent of the *electorate*, since the foreign-born included aliens who were not entitled to vote, and since only a tiny percentage of Negro adult males satisfied the property qualification for voting.

Since the Negroes and foreign-born totaled 16.7 per cent, other groups in the population must add up to 83.3 per cent. A learned contemporary traveller and observer, Timothy Dwight, estimated that by 1820 Yankees comprised from 60 to 67 per cent of the New York population—an estimate accepted as reasonably accurate by David M. Ellis, the historian of New York who has studied the problem most carefully. The proportion of Yankees was probably increasing by 1820 and probably continued to increase for some years after completion of the Erie Canal. But by 1845 the proportion of Yankees was probably declining as a result of emigration to the West by "natives" and settlement in the state by "immigrants." Thus it seems reasonable to strike a balance between Dwight's minimum and maximum figures and set our estimate at 63.5 per cent.

Totalling the Negroes, foreign-born, and Yankees, we find that all other groups could not have exceeded 19.8 per cent. Since the big wave of immigration did not come until the late 1830's and early 1840's, it seems reasonable to estimate that American-born descendants of immigrants comprised only 3.5 per cent of the total population in 1845 (that is, about one quarter of the foreign-born total). And from the United States census we find that, in 1850, 2 per cent of New York inhabitants had been born in Pennsylvania and New Jersey. We cannot be far off the mark, therefore, if we assume that the same proportion lived in the state in 1845, and if we assume that 2 per cent of the inhabitants had been born in the state and were of Penn-Jersey descent.

Since the statistics for 1850 show almost no migration to New York from states other than New England, Pennsylvania, and New Jersey, we can estimate the "others" as 0.5 per cent. When we total all the estimates thus far, we are left with a residual figure of 11.8 per cent for the Yorkers.

I do not pretend that the estimates presented here are more than roughly accurate, but they are consistent with impressions gained from saturation in the source materials of New York history. At any rate, they seem to be of the right order of magnitude.

The census returns are found in the *Census of the State of New York for 1845* and in the *Seventh Census of the United States, 1850*. Dwight's estimate is found in his *Travels in New-England and New York* (New Haven, 1821-1822), 3: 266-267. See also David M. Ellis, "The Yankee Invasion of New York, 1783-1850," *New York History,* 32: 3-17 (January 1951).

INDEX